Personal Financial Literacy

Jeff
Madura

Mike
Casey

Sherry J.
Roberts

PEARSON

Boston   Columbus   Indianapolis   New York   San Francisco   Upper Saddle River
Amsterdam   Cape Town   Dubai   London   Madrid   Milan   Munich   Paris   Montréal   Toronto
Delhi   Mexico City   São Paulo   Sydney   Hong Kong   Seoul   Singapore   Taipei   Tokyo

To my wife Diane for all of her encouragement during this project.
—Mike Casey

To my parents, John and Jean Roberts, for teaching me how to be a lifelong learner.
To Terris, Abigail, Ariadne, and Meghan, this textbook is for your future.
—Sherry J. Roberts

Editor in Chief: Donna Battista
Acquisitions Editor: Katie Rowland
Editorial Project Manager: Emily Biberger
Editorial Assistant: Elissa Senra-Sargent
Managing Editor: Jeff Holcomb
Associate Production Project Manager:
   Alison Eusden
Senior Manufacturing Buyer: Carol Melville
Senior Media Buyer: Ginny Michaud
Cover Designer: Jonathan Boylan

Manager, Rights and Permissions: Jill C. Dougan
Manager, Image Research: Rachel Youdelman
Image Researcher: Melody English
Director of Media: Susan Schoenberg
MyFinanceLab Content Lead: Miguel Leonarte
Senior Media Producer: Melissa Honig
Project Management: Gillian Hall
Composition and Artwork: Laserwords
Printer/Binder: Courier Kendallville
Cover Printer: Lehigh-Phoenix/Hagerstown

The Career Clusters icons in Chapter 5 are being used with the permission of the States' Career Clusters Initiative, 2009, www.careerclusters.org.

Credits and acknowledgments borrowed from other sources and reproduced, with permission, in this textbook appear on the appropriate page within text or on page xii.

Library of Congress Cataloging-in-Publication Data

Madura, Jeff.
   Personal financial literacy / Jeff Madura, K. Michael Casey, Sherry J. Roberts.
      pages cm.
   Revised edition of author's Personal financial literacy, copyrighted 2010.
   Includes index.
   ISBN 978-0-13-211660-2—ISBN 978-0-13-211922-1 (annotated instructor's edition)
   1. Finance, Personal—United States. I. Casey, K. Michael. II. Roberts, Sherry J. III. Title.
   HG179.M2522 2014
   332.02400973—dc23   2012051221

1 2 3 4 5 6 7 8 9 10

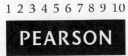

PearsonSchool.com/Advanced

ISBN-13: 978-0-13-211922-1
ISBN-10: 0-13-211922-6

TO THE TEACHER,

From the sub-prime mortgage crisis to the stock market's roller coaster ride, financial literacy—or more importantly, lack thereof—is all over today's news. As your students scan the headlines, it's clear that mastery of personal finance is increasingly vital at an earlier age than ever before.

With many schools offering personal finance as a core curriculum course, and in many cases mandating it as a requirement for graduation, we saw an opportunity to create a program specifically for high school students—one that gives them the basic tools and knowledge to make informed financial decisions.

Personal Financial Literacy offers a practical, highly accessible focus, demonstrated by features like its unique end-of-chapter problems. This edition added Essential Questions at the beginning of each chapter with a related activity in the end-of-chapter activities. This feature will emphasize the importance of learning about *Personal Financial Literacy*. In addition to addressing key No Child Left Behind (NCLB) requirements, *Personal Financial Literacy* meets financial literacy education standards as defined by JumpStart and the National Business Education Association Standards. The skills addressed in *Personal Financial Literacy* cross a variety of curriculum areas, including math, social studies/economics, career and technology, and consumer science.

Personal financial literacy has become one of the graduation requirements for many states. This text has been developed and revised to help simplify the task of bringing students up to speed on financial responsibility. We believe the features within the text will have a great appeal for you and your students, including its real-world applications, hands-on practice, and multiple assessment opportunities.

We look forward to helping you open up a world of financial literacy possibility for your students!

All the best,

Jeff Madura
Mike Casey
Sherry J. Roberts

Real-World Applications

From start to finish, *Personal Financial Literacy* is filled with examples, stories, and applications designed to grab the attention of today's high schooler.

Essential Question

An Essential Question, posed at the beginning of each chapter, is designed to engage students and guide inquiry-based instruction that fosters critical-thinking and deepens content understanding. An activity at the end of the chapter helps students answer the Essential Question.

ESSENTIAL QUESTION

Why is a budget such a key component of the financial plan?

Chapter-Opening Scenarios

These engaging introductory stories set the stage and are revisited throughout the chapter to illustrate the issue being addressed and its relevance to students.

Terris walked into his new apartment and sat down. After completing a prestigious music program in New York, the day he had been working toward for years was finally here. In his hands was his first paycheck from his first real job! At long last, he could begin to live the life of his dreams.

Immediately he began to think about the purchases he had been putting off for so long—a new car, a laptop, some nice clothes. Maybe he could buy season tickets for baseball or a new stereo system. Or perhaps he could finally make good on his promise to his friend Martin to take that road trip to Chicago. Now he had the income to afford these things—or, at least, to pay off his credit card bills.

Just as he was getting excited, Terris seemed to hear a small voice in his head. It was his grandfather. "Use your head, Terris," he could almost hear him say. "Be sure to put something away for a rainy day!"

Terris sighed. He realized he probably could not afford to get all the things he wanted right away. He also knew he had to think about more than just spending his new paycheck. At the same time, he was ready to treat himself. He had worked hard to get to this point, and he felt he deserved to enjoy the rewards.

Learning Objectives

Correlated to the main chapter heading, these clearly stated goals help students connect classroom learning to their own lives.

LEARNING OBJECTIVES

- Explain the steps involved in creating a budget
- Describe the steps involved in creating a personal balance sheet
- Understand the importance of budgeting in your financial plan

Professor FIN

This cartoon representation of an instructor relates funny and interesting facts about the world of personal finance.

Prof. FIN

Facts about the "graying of America":

- Because of healthier lifestyles, Americans have added 25 years to their life spans over the last several decades. In 2005, there were 36 million Americans over the age of 65. By 2020, this number is expected to be closer to 55 million.
- One million Americans turn age 60 every month!

Finance ONLINE

Finance Online now features an activity that can be Web-based using the tools and resources mentioned.

Finance ONLINE

Web sites such as **www.insure.com** provide life insurance quotes and links to specific companies depending on the need. Go to one of these sites and get a quote for $50,000 of life insurance.

Personal Financial Literacy provides extensive, immediate opportunities to reinforce concepts, assess mastery, and demonstrate relevance to both real life and other curriculum areas.

Key Terms

Taken from each chapter's learning objectives, these terms are prominently listed right at the start of the chapter and identified in the margins for clarity and emphasis. To bring learning full circle, questions that involve these key terms and additional concepts are also included in the end-of-chapter sections.

KEY TERMS

bond
budget
investment
market value
mutual fund
personal balance sheet
real estate
stock

MATH for Personal Finance

Reinforces the basic math skills students need to navigate the real world of personal finance. This feature meets Phase 1 of NCLB requirements.

MATH for Personal Finance

Lakisha's car is worth about $6,000 and she still owes $1,200 on it. She has an outstanding credit card balance of $450.

What is her net worth?

Solution: Lakisha's net worth is $6,000 − $1,200 − $450 = $4,350.

CHECKPOINT

"How am I doing?" Lets students self-assess their mastery of key concepts and each chapter's Learning Objectives.

☑ **CHECKPOINT**

What are the steps involved in creating a budget?

Teamwork

Ideas for group activities, related to the concepts and content, allow students to practice topics just covered.

Teamwork

In a team, use the Internet to research health care insurance fraud. Develop a newsletter providing information about insurance fraud. Your newsletter might include information on the costs of insurance fraud to others, how insurance fraud makes health care costs rise, tips on reporting insurance fraud, and the consequences of being suspected of insurance fraud. Your newsletter could also be a Web page, multimedia presentation, or other form of getting the word out about this important subject.

Student Workbook

In addition to practice features found within the text, look here for additional practice and assessment opportunities, including vocabulary checks, math checks, and open-response questions. Sample pages from the *Student Workbook* appear at the end of this Preface. The workbook is available for purchase. See page vii for details.

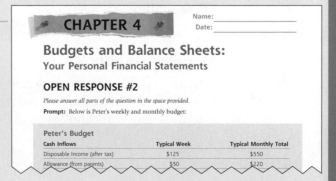

CHAPTER 4

Name: _____
Date: _____

Budgets and Balance Sheets:
Your Personal Financial Statements

OPEN RESPONSE #2

Please answer all parts of the question in the space provided.

Prompt: Below is Peter's weekly and monthly budget:

Peter's Budget

Cash Inflows	Typical Week	Typical Monthly Total
Disposable Income (after tax)	$125	$550
Allowance (from parents)	$50	$220

"You Do It" icons in the text indicate that students can apply the concept being discussed using the workbook activity indicated.

YOU DO IT

Assessment

Personal Financial Literacy combines a rich array of end-of-chapter questions and problems with a robust *Student Workbook* for multiple opportunities to assess subject knowledge. These tools also give students multiple opportunities to put their critical thinking, math, cross-disciplinary, ethical reasoning, and team-building skills to the test.

What Are the Connections?

End-of-chapter activities illustrate links between personal finance concepts and other curriculum areas, including math, technology, science, and language arts. Weekly writing prompts meet Phase 1 of the NCLB language arts requirement.

Teamwork

Provides ideas for group activities to assess comprehension and application.

What Are Your Finance Math Skills?

Students gauge their knowledge through real-life scenarios that allow for assessment of both chapter content mastery and math skills.

What Do You Know?

End-of-chapter activities focus on the essential question to develop students' critical-thinking skills while they learn the fundamentals of personal finance.

Essential Question Activity

These end-of-chapter activities focus on the essential question posted at the beginning of the chapter to further develop students' critical-thinking skills while they learn the fundamentals of personal finance.

Test Prep Questions

These multiple-choice, end-of-chapter problems may be used for quizzes or student review.

Student Workbook

Provides additional assessment opportunities, including vocabulary checks, math checks, open-response questions, and personal finance activities. The workbook is available for purchase. See page vii.

The Program

The *Personal Financial Literacy* program combines critical content and student-friendly delivery with the flexibility and support tools you need.

Student Supplements

The following resources are available for purchase:

Student Workbook (0132167565)

This workbook features open-response questions, additional vocabulary review exercises, and personal finance activity worksheets.

Math Workbook (0132167573)

This workbook provides additional math-focused practice and assessment opportunities, from basic math drills to more complex math for personal finance.

Teacher Supplements

Most of the teacher supplements and resources for this text are available electronically at no charge to qualified adopters from the Instructor Resource Center (IRC). Upon adoption or to preview, please go to www.PearsonSchool.com/Access_Request and select Instructor Resource Center. You will be required to complete a brief one-time registration subject to verification of educator status. Upon verification, access information and instructions will be sent to you via email. Once logged into the IRC enter your text ISBN 0-13-211660-X in the **Search our Catalog** box to locate your resources.

The following items are available to qualified adopters:

Annotated Teacher Edition (0132119226)

The *Annotated Teacher Edition* of the single-volume text includes answers and solutions to all "Checkpoint" questions and end-of-chapter questions and problems.

Instructor's Resource CD-ROM (0132182637)

The *Instructor's Resource CD-ROM* includes the following items:

- **Test Item File** with multiple choice, matching, true/false, and short answer questions. The Test Item File is also available in easy-to-use TestGen®. TestGen® enables instructors to view, edit, and add questions; transfer questions to tests; and print different forms of tests.
- **Teacher Guide** with lesson plans, tips on teaching the chapter, Internet resources, information on differentiated learning, and additional activities.
- **Annotated Editions** of the *Student Workbook* and *Math Workbook* with solutions to all questions and problems.

MyFinLitLab™ (www.MyFinLitLab.com)

MyFinLitLab™ is a powerful online homework, tutorial, and assessment system.

Assignments

With MyFinLitLab™, teachers can create, edit, and assign online homework and tests using content developed from end-of-chapter and Math Workbook material that is marked with the MyFinLitLab™ logo. Teachers can also import Test Bank questions for added flexibility. All student work is tracked in the MyFinLitLab™ gradebook.

Study Plan

Students can take preloaded sample tests and receive personalized study plans based on the test results. Study plans diagnose weaknesses and link students directly to tutorial exercises covering topics they need to practice.

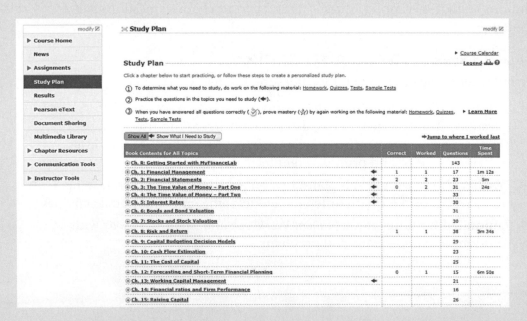

Pearson eText

The Pearson eText within MyFinLitLab provides students access to the text whenever and wherever they can access the Internet. The eText pages look exactly like the printed text, and include powerful interactive features.

Chapter Resources

MyFinLitLab also offers a wealth of additional resources, which include:

- Web links broken down by chapter.
- Web Exercises broken down by chapter.
- Glossary Flashcards that will help you review key terms from the book.
- Spreadsheets for all the *You Do It!* Student Activities.
- The complete Glossary in PDF form.

Access to MyFinLitLab with Pearson eText is provided with textbook purchase.

Upon textbook purchase, students and teachers are granted access to MyFinLitLab with Pearson eText. High school teachers can obtain preview or adoption access for MyFinLitLab in one of the following ways:

Preview Access

- Teachers can request preview access online by visiting www.PearsonSchool. com/Access_Request, using Option 2. Preview Access information will be sent to the teacher via email.

Adoption Access

- With the purchase of this program, a Pearson Adoption Access Card, with codes and complete instructions, will be delivered with your textbook purchase. (ISBN: 0-13-034391-9)
- Ask your sales representative for an Adoption Access Code Card (ISBN: 0-13-034391-9) or
- Visit PearsonSchool.com/Access_Request, Option 3. Adoption access information will be sent to the teacher via email.

About the Authors

Jeff Madura

Jeff Madura is the SunTrust Bank Professor of Finance at Florida Atlantic University. He has written several textbooks, including *Financial Markets and Institutions*. His research on finance has been published in numerous journals, including *Journal of Financial and Quantitative Analysis; Journal of Money; Credit and Banking; Financial Management; Journal of Financial Research; and Financial Review*. He has received awards for excellence in teaching and research and has served as a consultant for financial institutions. He has served as a director for the Southern Finance Association and Eastern Finance Association, and also served as president of the Southern Finance Association.

K. Michael Casey

Mike Casey is the McCastlain Professor of Finance and Interim Dean of the College of Business at the University of Central Arkansas. He has a doctorate in finance from Louisiana Tech University and has served as a media consultant for Active Learning Technologies, Inc. He has published over 80 refereed journal publications in such journals as *The Financial Review, The Journal of Computer Information Systems, The Review of Business Information Systems, Real Estate Review, The Journal of Property Investment and Finance, The Journal of Real Estate Finance and Economics, The Quarterly Review of Economics and Finance*, and *The Journal of Lending and Credit Risk Management*. Dr. Casey has also worked as a Registered Investment Advisor Representative for Mustard Seed Financial, LLC, a fee-only financial planning firm.

Sherry J. Roberts

Sherry J. Roberts has been teaching for over 27 years. She taught 14 of those years as a business education teacher at the secondary level. Dr. Roberts currently teaches at Middle Tennessee State University in the Jennings A. Jones College of Business. Her presentations include international, national, regional, and state levels on the subjects of instructional technology and business education. As a consultant for Roberts Educational Consultants, Dr. Roberts provided professional development in instructional technology, writing portfolios, open response, and business education. She also has been an instructor with the University of Central Arkansas Insurance Education Institute and Personal Finance Institute. Her doctorate is from the University of Louisville in Curriculum and Instruction.

Acknowledgments

The authors extend their thanks to the many people who have offered their support and guidance throughout this project.

Thanks to Donna Battista, Katie Rowland, Emily Biberger, Alison Eusden and Gillian Hall for all your hard work during the revision of the book. You've been a wonderful team to work with. Mike Casey would like to thank Sherry Roberts for having such a great idea and pushing him to collaborate, and Sherry Roberts would like to thank Mike Casey for listening to her idea and helping to transform that idea into a book.

We would like to thank the following educators who have generously shared their constructive criticism on every chapter and feature during the development of the book:

Tim Ballas, *Marion Technical Institute, Florida*

Gary Benson, *Seward High School, Alaska*

Matt Bergman, *Cocalico High School, Pennsylvania*

Jennifer Birkmeier, *Blaine High School, Minnesota*

Sandi Bullington, *Neosho High School, Missouri*

Nettie Carson, *Mullins, Alabama State Department of Education, Alabama*

Amy Collette, *David Crockett High School, Tennessee*

Mary Davis, *Marian Catholic High School, Pennsylvania*

Renee Dickson, *Mcguffey High School, Pennsylvania*

Shok Dylan, *Bronx School of Law and Finance, New York*

Monica Edwards, *Greene County High School, Mississippi*

Marilyn Erwin, *Pickens County High School, Alabama*

Lori Fordyce, *St. Joseph Central, Missouri*

Marlene Grabbe, *Marion Technical Institute, Florida*

Jon Greenwalt, *New York State Education Department, New York*

Linda Hayes, *Northampton High School, Pennsylvania*

Melanie D. Herring, *Fike High School, North Carolina*

Joel Hilbrink, *Ninilchik High School, Alaska*

Todd Howsare, *Dunedin High School, Florida*

Elaine Hutson, *Union High School, Missouri*

Chakita Jackson, *Hazelwood West High School, Missouri*

Brenda A. Jenkins, *Fredericktown High School, Missouri*

Frank Lane, *Salisbury High School, Pennsylvania*

Linda Leeking, *Warwick School District, Pennsylvania*

Linda Love, *Villa Maria Academy, Pennsylvania*

Lana Main, *Brandon Valley High School, South Dakota*

Audrey Marshall, *Auburn High School, Alabama*

Larry Mark McGee, *West Johnston High School, North Carolina*

Barbara McQueen & P.D. Jackson, *Olin High School, Alabama*

Kenneth Mengani, *Franklin K. Lane High School, New York*

Judy Mitchell, *Thomas More Prep, Marian, Kansas*

Michele Moore, *Monrovia High School, Indiana*

Trey Ondrus, *Siegel High School, Tennessee*

Linda Ralston, *Nikiski Middle/High School, Alaska*

Barbara Ramsdell, *Elk River High School, Minnesota*

Kay Roberts, *Red Spring High School, North Carolina*

Amy Rosenkrans, *MD Council on Economic Education, Maryland*

Bonnie Sibert, *Nebraska Department of Education, Nebraska*

Heidi Stirm, *Melba High School, Idaho*

Carl Sundell, *Hunter High School, Utah*

Thomas Svehla, *Oak Park High School, Missouri*

Deb Tettenborn, *Abraham Lincoln High School, Iowa*

Marla Thompson, *North Platte High School, Nebraska*

James Timmons, *Heide Trask High School, North Carolina*

Eileen Tims, *Memorial Senior High School, Texas*

Margaret A. Wanger, *Interboro High School, Pennsylvania*

Patricia Wheatley, *Turkeyfoot Valley Area High School, Pennsylvania*

The following people provided reviews for this second edition:

Marci Boland, *Clayton High School, Missouri*

Antonio Carrico, *Coeur d'Alene High School, Idaho*

Tony D'Apice, *Greece Odyssey, New York*

Doug Dietrich, *Eureka High School, Missouri*

Diane H. Eades, *Brocton High School, New York*

Cynthia Gordon, *Monroe High School, New York*

Cynthia Knight, *Springfield High School, Vermont*

David Lamberti, *Burlington High School, Vermont*

Willie Roberts, *Cheyenne Mountain High School, Colorado*

Kathleen Kelly Rogers, *Charles Finney School, New York*

Ellen Schulman, *Uniondale UFSD, New York*

Megan M. Sovie, *Gouverneur Central School, New York*

Brittany Young, *Union High School, Oklahoma*

—Jeff Madura, Mike Casey, and Sherry J. Roberts

Credits

Contents in Brief

Detailed Contents

Unit 2 Income & Careers 69

Personal Financial Literacy

CHAPTER 1

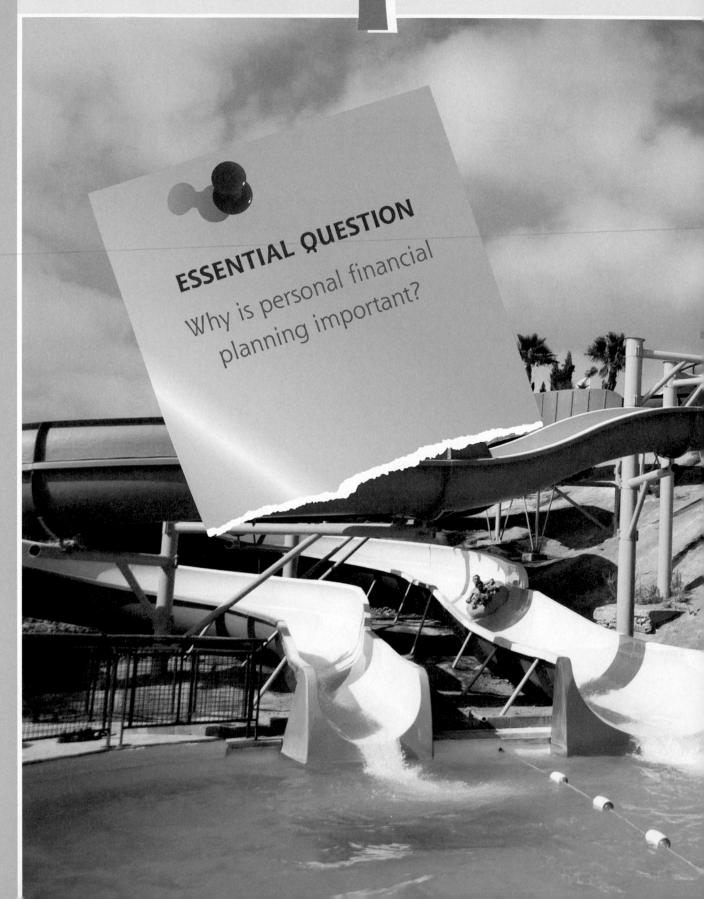

ESSENTIAL QUESTION

Why is personal financial planning important?

OVERVIEW OF PERSONAL FINANCE

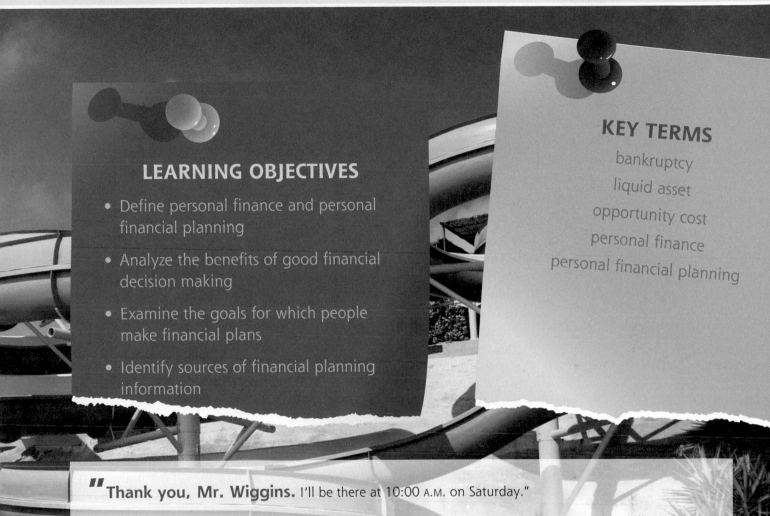

LEARNING OBJECTIVES

- Define personal finance and personal financial planning

- Analyze the benefits of good financial decision making

- Examine the goals for which people make financial plans

- Identify sources of financial planning information

KEY TERMS

bankruptcy

liquid asset

opportunity cost

personal finance

personal financial planning

> **"Thank you, Mr. Wiggins.** I'll be there at 10:00 A.M. on Saturday."

Lindsey put down her cell phone and smiled. She had landed her first job, and it was at the mall. A thousand questions popped into her head. How much money would she make every week? Should she loan Alicia that $20 to help her buy those new jeans? How much of her earnings would her mom expect her to save for college? How long would it take her to save enough money to buy that sleek new phone? Now that she had a job, could she apply for and get a credit card? Then she wondered about how much money she'd need for her planned trip to the water park this Saturday with Alicia and Deanna—before realizing that she'd have to cancel that date in order to go to work.

In an instant, Lindsey's excitement about her new job had faded. She and her friends had been planning the water park outing for weeks. They were going to be very irritated with her. But she knew she couldn't miss her first day of work.

She also knew that having a job and a little more money was going to make her life easier—and more fun—in a lot of ways. It would just take a little more planning and adjusting to fit everything in.

personal finance: Financial issues that can affect an individual.

Lindsey's financial decisions—decisions about money—are just beginning. Yet even the decisions she makes today can affect her future. For that reason, Lindsey needs to learn how to make better financial decisions. So do you. Becoming knowledgeable about the many financial issues that can affect an individual—that is, about **personal finance**—should be a goal for everyone. All people can improve every aspect of their lives, including their personal lives, by learning about personal finance and making good financial decisions.

The thought process used in financial decision making will vary from person to person and situation to situation. However, all good decision makers will use the same basic tools. The purpose of this text is to help you understand how the decisions you make are actually financial decisions and to provide the knowledge, skills, and tools necessary to make good choices.

The choice is yours. Do you want to live paycheck to paycheck like some of the people you know? Do you want bill collectors hounding you? Or do you want to have the peace of mind that comes with financial security? Manage your cash wisely and you can have the latter. Good planning and money management not only gives you peace of mind, but it also allows you to have all those things you think you want—in due time. Along with a little self-discipline, the techniques and tools you will learn about in this book can change your life.

WHAT IS PERSONAL FINANCIAL PLANNING?

personal financial planning: Process of planning every aspect of your personal finances.

Personal financial planning is the process of planning every aspect of your personal finances. This process includes planning your spending, your borrowing or financing, and your saving and investing in order to achieve the highest quality of life possible. Who doesn't want that? Everyone does!

The Vocabulary of Personal Finance

Keep in mind that any time you learn a new subject such as personal finance you also will be learning a new language or vocabulary. Mechanics, plumbers, and businesspeople all have vocabularies that are unique to their skills or trades. Personal finance is no different. Your ability to understand these concepts and tools hinges on your studying the terms and phrases that have unique meanings in the context of personal finance.

Steps to Personal Financial Planning

Every one of you needs to create your own personal financial plan. This plan will be a detailed road map that outlines your financial goals and the spending, financing, and saving and investing steps that will allow you to achieve those goals. The more detailed you get, the better the plan will be. A good plan will include creating a budget as well as plans for managing your liquid assets. Your **liquid assets** are those things you might have that can be very rapidly converted to cash without a risk of significant loss. An example of a liquid asset is a savings account at a bank. A good financial plan will also include plans for managing your borrowing and a plan to make sure you have enough insurance to protect your assets (houses, cars, and other assets). Additionally, a personal financial plan includes developing a plan for investing and your ultimate retirement.

Perhaps one of the most critical decisions you will face in your life is the decision regarding the type of career you want to pursue. After all, much of your life will be spent on the job, so shouldn't you spend some time thinking about finding the right job fit for your personality? Equally as important as finding a job suited to your personality is finding one that has a pay and employee benefit package that allows you to afford the things you need.

What are some of the fastest growing jobs and the salaries you can expect to receive? Figure 1.1 lists expected salaries for a number of the fastest growing jobs. In general, as you will see in Figure 1.2, the more education you have, the higher your salary. Lindsey's mom understands that, which is why she's going to require Lindsey to save some of her income from her new job for education. Lindsey might not appreciate that now, but she probably will when she gets to enjoy the higher income her education will help make possible.

Don't forget that the United States and perhaps your state and local governments will take a cut of your paycheck in taxes. So, we need to spend some time focusing on paying taxes and how tax planning contributes to your overall financial health. The overall health of the economy also factors in when discussing employment prospects and taxation.

In today's financial world, people face many opportunities to make purchases and investments with borrowed money. Understanding the concepts of credit and borrowing are central to maintaining both short-term and long-term financial health. Credit and borrowing are powerful tools. Used wisely, they have the potential to make increased wealth possible. Used improperly, they can lead to financial disaster. The danger is not remote. Sadly, many hardworking people suffer serious problems with credit—simply because they do not plan. Many of you may know someone who has had a vehicle repossessed or even lost a house because he or she failed to make payments on time. Once something like this happens it makes it extremely difficult to buy anything on credit again for several years. Your credit is something that should be built and protected so that when you need it for a major purchase you can get the best financing deal.

liquid assets: Something owned that can be rapidly converted to cash without a risk of significant loss.

Cash is a liquid asset.

FIGURE 1.1 Fastest-Growing Occupations, 2010–2020

Among the factors you should consider when choosing a career are the employment outlook and the expected wages you will receive.

2010 National Employment Matrix title	Employment 2010	Employment 2020	Change, 2010–20 Number	Change, 2010–20 Percent	Median annual wage, 2010
Total, All Occupations	143,068.2	163,537.1	20,468.9	14.3	$33,840
Registered Nurses	2,737.4	3,449.3	711.9	26.0	64,690
Retail Salespersons	4,261.6	4,968.4	706.8	16.6	20,670
Home Health Aides	1,017.7	1,723.9	706.3	69.4	20,560
Personal Care Aides	861.0	1,468.0	607.0	70.5	19,640
Office Clerks, General	2,950.7	3,440.2	489.5	16.6	26,610
Combined Food Preparation and Serving Workers, Including Fast Food	2,682.1	3,080.1	398.0	14.8	17,950
Customer Service Representatives	2,187.3	2,525.6	338.4	15.5	30,460
Heavy and Tractor-Trailer Truck Drivers	1,604.8	1,934.9	330.1	20.6	37,770
Laborers and Freight, Stock, and Material Movers, Hand	2,068.2	2,387.3	319.1	15.4	23,460
Postsecondary Teachers	1,756.0	2,061.7	305.7	17.4	45,690
Nursing Aides, Orderlies, and Attendants	1,505.3	1,807.2	302.0	20.1	24,010
Childcare Workers	1,282.3	1,544.3	262.0	20.4	19,300
Bookkeeping, Accounting, and Auditing Clerks	1,898.3	2,157.4	259.0	13.6	34,030
Cashiers	3,362.6	3,612.8	250.2	7.4	18,500
Elementary School Teachers, Except Special Education	1,476.5	1,725.3	248.8	16.8	51,660
Receptionists and Information Clerks	1,048.5	1,297.0	248.5	23.7	25,240
Janitors and Cleaners, Except Maids and Housekeeping Cleaners	2,310.4	2,556.8	246.4	10.7	22,210
Landscaping and Groundskeeping Workers	1,151.5	1,392.3	240.8	20.9	23,400
Sales Representatives, Wholesale and Manufacturing, Except Technical and Scientific Products	1,430.0	1,653.4	223.4	15.6	52,440
Construction Laborers	998.8	1,211.2	212.4	21.3	29,280
Medical Secretaries	508.7	718.9	210.2	41.3	30,530
First-Line Supervisors of Office and Administrative Support Workers	1,424.4	1,627.8	203.4	14.3	47,460
Carpenters	1,001.7	1,197.6	196.0	19.6	39,530
Waiters and Waitresses	2,260.3	2,456.2	195.9	8.7	18,330
Security Guards	1,035.7	1,230.7	195.0	18.8	23,920
Teacher Assistants	1,288.3	1,479.3	191.1	14.8	23,220
Accountants and Auditors	1,216.9	1,407.6	190.7	15.7	61,690
Licensed Practical and Licensed Vocational Nurses	752.3	920.8	168.5	22.4	40,380
Physicians and Surgeons	691.0	859.3	168.3	24.4	111,570
Medical Assistants	527.6	690.4	162.9	30.9	28,860

Source: Employment Projections program, U.S. Department of Labor, U.S. Bureau of Labor Statistics.

If you are like most people, you will have some financial goals that are far in the future. Reaching them will involve saving money. Learning how to invest that money wisely can speed your progress toward that goal. Indeed, at this point in your life, time is on your side. Considering the number of years you have to work with, even small monthly contributions to your savings can result in the buildup of vast sums of money. In fact, if you begin now and have some discipline, most of you should be able to amass more than $1 million by the time you retire. This is possible with a monthly commitment that is lower than what many ordinary people pay each month on their car loan.

FIGURE 1.2 Comparison of Income among Education Levels

Education can be quite costly, but in general it will pay for itself in a relatively short time.

Education	Median Level of Annual Income
Master's degree	$66,144
Bachelor's degree	53,976
Associate's degree	39,844
Some college	37,024
High School diploma	32,552
Less than high school diploma	23,088

Source: Bureau of Labor Statistics, 2011.

The Need for Personal Financial Planning

While people in the United States are on average among the wealthiest people in the world, many Americans pay little or no attention to their personal finances. They rely on credit cards and other forms of debt to the point where the debt and financial problems begin to control their existence. Consider these facts:

- More than 30% of high school students use a credit card and more than 80% of undergraduate college students have at least one credit card.

- According to the American Bankruptcy Institute, 1.3 million people will file for personal bankruptcy in 2012. While still significant, this number is down slightly from the record number of filings that occurred in 2005. Approximately 2 million filings occurred in 2005 in advance of Congress making changes to personal bankruptcy laws. **Bankruptcy** is a legal process in which a court takes over some of the finances of a person who is unable to pay his or her bills.

- Twenty-five percent of consumers indicated that they have more credit card debt than emergency savings.

- About half of all people surveyed who are working full-time in the United States report that they live paycheck to paycheck. That is, they have no money available for paying bills or meeting their needs aside from what they receive in their paychecks. About 40% of people who work full-time do not save money for retirement. Those people who do save money for retirement tend to save very little.

- Many employers now check your credit history before offering employment. Bad credit can cost you a job.

MATH for Personal Finance

Lindsey got her first paycheck and noticed that she only took home $62.45 this week. She worked 10 hours and made $8 an hour.

How much did her employer withhold from her paycheck?

Solution: Lindsey's gross pay was $8 an hour × 10 hours = $80. However, taxes withheld by her employer reduced her take-home pay to $62.45. The total amount withheld from her check was $80 − $62.45 = $17.55.

Activity #1

bankruptcy: A legal process in which a court takes over some of the finances of a person who is unable to pay his or her bills.

In other words, people just do not prepare well for the future. With health care costs going up, anticipated problems with Social Security, and other uncertainties about the future that will impact everyone, it makes sense to learn everything you can about personal finance. This knowledge will mean you are in control of your destiny. Why let someone else dictate what you can afford to do in the future?

✓ CHECKPOINT

It is the process of planning all aspects of your personal finances.

What is personal financial planning?

BENEFITS OF GOOD FINANCIAL DECISION MAKING

Poor financial planning can prevent you from achieving your dreams. It can even put you at risk for serious financial problems.

opportunity cost: Cost of pursuing one option instead of another expressed as the value of the activity you gave up.

Activity #2

You will be better able to accomplish your goals in life.

An early knowledge of personal finance can help you accomplish your goals. In fact, it can help you define your goals. What type of career are you interested in pursuing? Just like Lindsey, you may wonder how much money certain jobs pay. Should you go to college? Should you buy a car? Should you work part-time or focus all of your efforts on school and try to get a scholarship? Should you really apply for that credit card? What are the pros and cons of that decision?

An understanding of personal finance helps you make informed decisions about your personal situation. For example, every time you decide to buy a DVD (or anything else) you incur an **opportunity cost**. In other words, you give up the opportunity to do something else with that money. Rather than buying the DVD, you could have used the money to go to the movies, buy a pizza, or put gas in your car. You could have also put the money in savings. When you begin to view every purchase in terms of its opportunity cost, you may begin to change your spending habits.

Consider the money you spend on sodas every year. If every day you buy one soda that costs $1.25, you end up spending $456.25[1] on sodas during the year. You could have spent that money on something else. Or you could have saved and invested some of that money. Think about the fact that you could begin to save $100 a month at age 16 and accumulate over $1 million by the time you turn age 56 if you were able to earn a 12% annual return.

Learning about financial decision making may help you to begin thinking in these terms. Money does not buy happiness, but financial security certainly makes life easier. Good financial decisions lead to flexibility and allow you to achieve your true desires in due time without fear of not being able to make the payments.

✓ CHECKPOINT

What do you stand to gain from your knowledge of personal finance?

[1] $1.25 × 365 days = $456.25 per year in total cost.

WHAT ARE YOU PLANNING FOR?

Every person is different. Everyone has his or her own personal goals. These can range from starting a business to taking a dream vacation. The possibilities are endless. Brainstorm a bit here and see what personal goals you have that might require saving some money. Remember Lindsey? She wants a new phone. What do you want? You will see that some of your goals will be short-term in nature, and others may require years to accomplish. A phone should be a short-term goal. Saving enough money to buy a house is obviously a much longer-term goal. With good planning, you can identify and begin working toward short-term, intermediate-term, and long-term goals—all at the same time.

Education

One of the major decisions that you will be required to make very soon is whether to pursue a college degree or some other type of post-high school education. Refer to Figure 1.2 and note that there is a significant relationship between the number of years of education and your earnings potential. At this point in your life, you should begin to explore various career options and determine the education required to pursue each option. While you should always focus on a career that holds your interest, it is also important to investigate the expected payoffs. Education is costly both in time and money. You should spend some time planning your career choice and then engaging in financial planning to determine how to pay for that education.

Emergencies/Rainy Day Fund

Most people will have an emergency need for funds at some time in their lives. Unexpected events, such as car breakdowns, occur often. Good financial planning will help you establish an emergency fund that will help you weather any future financial crisis. Financial planning forces you to think about and plan for those unexpected expenses or the possibility of an

MATH for Personal Finance

Jacob earns $8 an hour at the pizza place and he is scheduled to work four hours this afternoon. However, Tara called and wanted to know if he could go to a movie.

Assuming the movie will cost Jacob $10, what is his opportunity cost of going to the movie?

Solution: Jacob will forego earning $8 an hour × 4 hours = $32. He will also spend $10 that he would not spend if he were working. Therefore, his opportunity cost of going to the movie is equal to $32 or the lost income he could have earned. His total cost of attending the movie is $42, the opportunity cost of $32 + the $10 out-of-pocket cost.

Did you know that Google began as a research project? And that Famous Amos cookies were originally home-baked cookies presented to clients to entice them to sign with the William Morris Agency, a company that represents entertainers and writers?

Larry Page and his fellow Stanford University student, Sergey Brin, formally incorporated Google Inc. in a friend's garage on September 7, 1998. What began as a school research project by Page is now a multibillion dollar company.

Famous Amos was started by Wally Amos when he worked for the William Morris Agency. After encouragement, he opened his first store in Los Angeles. Now his cookies are sold all around the country.

While these entrepreneurs began careers that may not have been planned, both needed some savings, investments, loans, and education to be successful. Research another entrepreneur who began a company on a "shoe string" budget. What education or training did he or she have before beginning a business? What makes an entrepreneur successful?

Prof. FIN

Michael is thinking about buying a car and is comparing two vehicles. One gets 14 miles per gallon (mpg) and the other gets 28 mpg.

Assuming he drives 4,000 miles per year and gas is $3 a gallon, how much money would he save by buying the more fuel-efficient car?

Solution: Since he expects to drive 4,000 miles per year, we can calculate that he will use 4,000 / 28 mpg = 143 gallons of gas at $3 per gallon = $429 spent per year on fuel. The other vehicle will cost twice as much to drive since he would use 4,000 / 14 mpg = 286 gallons × $3 a gallon = $858 spent on gas for the year. Therefore, his savings for buying the more fuel-efficient vehicle would be the difference, or $858 − $429 = $429.

interruption in wages as the result of illness or job loss. If you begin to plan for the unexpected now, you can be sure that there is enough money set aside to cover those expenses.

Buying a Car

Do you want to own a car someday? Will your parents provide it? Or will you have to pay for it with your own money? When do you want to buy it? At age 16? At age 18? While a Maserati might be out of reach financially, a good used $5,000 vehicle is probably possible if you take the right steps. If you can set a specific goal, good financial planning can help you determine whether you can eventually afford the car. It can also help you identify the steps you need to take to achieve ownership.

Buying a Home

Some of you may already be thinking about your dream home. Some of you may want to travel the world and just rent a place to live for a time in an exotic location. Regardless of your desire, you can begin planning financially to achieve your goals. You can actually begin saving now for the down payment on your first home. What better time to accumulate wealth than when you are young?

Why worry about something today that may be years down the road? The earlier you begin, the less money you have to set aside on a regular basis. If you plan carefully, you can set aside money for long-term goals while still having money left over for more short-term desires. The key is planning.

And remember: It gets increasingly more difficult to save money when you have to pay rent and buy groceries. Take advantage of your freedom and your youth now.

Having a Family

Families are expensive. To have a child and put that child through college is estimated to cost more than $250,000 over the child's life from birth to age 22. That is quite a bit of money. Should you begin planning for some of those expenses now? What about a car at age 16 for the children you might have? Are your children going to public school or private school? These are all decisions that may be impacted by your wealth. A good financial plan can allow you to have the financial flexibility to make these choices instead of having them made for you.

Retirement

At this stage of your life it is difficult to think about retirement. However, do you know someone who retired at age 40 or 45 and now does exactly what he or she wants to do? Contrast that with someone you know who hates his or her job and is still working at age 70. While many people may choose to work well into their 60s or 70s because they enjoy working, many people do it because they have no other options. Financial planning can give you those options. You can begin to build your wealth at an early age. This may allow you to retire at age 40 or 45. While you may decide to continue working, it is nice to have the option to retire.

Charitable Giving

A number of people have a strong desire to donate some of their money to worthy causes, and charitable giving is an important component of many financial plans. Some people may prefer to accumulate wealth and provide a large sum to a specific charity. Others may give smaller amounts on a regular basis. Knowledge of financial planning can help you achieve whatever goals you may have in this area.

Many of you are beginning to think about college. The number one concern is how to pay for it. That is one area of financial planning you will be dealing with as you plan for graduation and the future. Whether you plan to attend a two-year or four-year college or attend a technical school, finances are a critical component of your financial plan.

Where can you go to find sources online that will help with funding your education in the future? Make a list of these sources.

Prof. FIN

✓ CHECKPOINT

What three categories of goals should you plan for?

You should plan for short-term goals, intermediate-term goals, and long-term goals.

SOURCES OF INFORMATION

It may seem difficult or even frightening to think about some aspects of financial planning right now. Goals may seem too numerous or out of reach. The stakes of good and bad decisions may seem high. Fortunately, there are many resources available to help you make good choices. And remember—time is on your side.

The Internet

The Internet can be a wonderful source of information about a number of financial aspects of your life. You can use the Internet to research prices of major purchases or look up investment performance data. There are a number of Web sites that provide payment calculators or information on wealth building. However, the Internet also poses some dangers. You need skill and care to evaluate the quality of information you find there. And you must always be cautious about advice from sources that are selling a service. The Internet has its share of unethical people trying to defraud you and increase their wealth at your expense.

Judging the Advice of Financial Planners/Advisors and Financial Information

Understanding personal financial planning will help you make good decisions about how to spend money, finance purchases such as cars and houses, and save and invest your money. However, many of you may want

Finance ONLINE

When putting together your personal financial plan, it is good to have a variety of resources available to you. On many financial Web sites, you can find calculators to help you do many things, including determine a mortgage payment and calculate investments and savings. Go online and find three Web sites that provide financial calculators. Make a list of each of these sites and note the different types of calculators they offer.

Each person is responsible for judging the quality of the advice he or she receives.

to turn some of these decisions over to professionals who understand all the tax laws and can monitor your investments more closely.

Lindsey's Uncle Joe may want to manage her money for her, but is he competent? He acts goofy at every family function and Lindsey's mom told her that Uncle Joe filed for bankruptcy 10 years ago. Should she trust him with her money? Oddly enough, many people select financial advisors and entrust their future to people whom they know even less about than their Uncle Joe. Many people spend more time picking out music to download than they spend choosing a financial advisor. Understanding financial planning will help you determine whether an advisor is giving you advice that is in your best interest. Figure 1.3 contains a list of things to consider when selecting a good financial advisor.

Again, the Internet is a good source of information about financial planners. Stick with planners who have reputable credentials such as a Certified Financial Planner (CFP) or Certified Public Accountant (CPA), since credentials indicate a certain level of knowledge about financial planning. Remember that no matter who you hire to help you with your finances, you are responsible for monitoring your own investments. Be cautious. Never rush into a financial decision. If someone tries to rush a decision, it is rarely good for you.

✓ CHECKPOINT

Who is responsible for judging the quality of financial advice you receive?

FIGURE 1.3   Questions to Ask When Selecting a Financial Advisor

It is vital to use great care when evaluating a personal financial advisor.

1. **Do they have a certification such as the CFP or CPA?**
   These are important credentials that indicate a certain level of training and expertise.

2. **Does their area of expertise match your needs?**
   Obviously you want an advisor who can help you meet your own goals.

3. **Can they provide you with references from current clients?**
   A good advisor should have many satisfied clients.

4. **Are they able to recommend independent products or do they only sell financial products that generate commissions or referral fees?**
   Some advisors only sell products that bring financial benefits to *them*.

5. **Do they make you feel comfortable?**
   The relationship between you and your advisor should not be uneasy or tense.

CHAPTER REVIEW

SUMMARY

- Personal financial planning is the process of planning your spending, financing, and saving and investing to create your best possible financial future. Your financial planning decisions allow you to develop a financial plan, which involves a set of decisions on how you plan to manage your spending, financing, and investing.

- You will find that an early knowledge of personal finance can help you avoid common financial pitfalls and accomplish your goals, whatever they are. You will see that most goals have a financial component.

- There are many good reasons to plan for your financial future, but some common goals include getting an education, preparing for emergencies, buying a car or home, having a family, retiring, and donating to charity.

- There are many resources available to help you make your financial decisions. One resource is the Internet. Other resources include financial planners or advisors. Financial planners or advisors can help you with all aspects of your financial decisions including monitoring your investments and keeping you posted on tax law.

Key Terms and Concepts

1. What does the high rate of **bankruptcy** suggest about the average person's understanding of personal finance?

2. What is an example of a **liquid asset**?

3. Why is it important to become knowledgeable about financial issues that can affect your **personal finances**?

What Do You Know?   MyFinLitLab

1. (a) Define personal financial planning.

   (b) Why is learning about personal financial planning important?

2. (a) Define opportunity cost.

   (b) Give an example of opportunity cost.

3. (a) Name some factors that might affect your choice of career and eventually your finances.

   (b) How would you expect the earning of a college degree to affect your financial plans?

Answers:
Key Terms and Concepts

1. The high rate of bankruptcy suggests that many people do not engage in adequate personal financial planning. While bankruptcy is not always avoidable, there are many situations where good financial planning would have kept filing bankruptcy from being necessary.

2. A good example is a savings account at a local bank.

3. Financial issues can impact every aspect of your life. Understanding financial issues and financial planning can eliminate many of the common financial problems people face.

Answers:
What Do You Know?

1. (a) **Knowledge** Personal financial planning is the planning of all financial aspects of your life. (b) **Analysis** It is a key to identifying and reaching many life goals.

2. (a) **Knowledge** An opportunity cost is the cost of the opportunity passed up by any decision. (b) **Application** An example would include going to a movie with money that was going to go into a college fund. There are other examples students could provide for this answer.

3. (a) **Comprehension** Your career should be determined based on your interests and abilities, the amount of education required, and also potential for employment in your chosen field. Different careers have different salary expectations and therefore impact your lifetime earnings ability and your finances. (b) **Analysis** More education tends to lead to more earnings, which can create new opportunities and options in a financial plan, but it also requires an investment.

4. (a) Why is it important to begin saving for retirement while you are young?

   (b) What is the significance of the generally low rate at which people save for retirement?

5. (a) How do your goals affect decision making for your financial plan?

   (b) Explain how you might be able to work toward short-term, intermediate-term, and long-term goals at the same time.

6. (a) Why plan for the future?

   (b) Why might you need to revise your financial plan?

7. (a) How can financial planning help you plan for your future education?

   (b) Why is it worth investing significantly in education?

8. (a) List some information available on the Internet that might be useful for financial planning.

   (b) Describe one way you might use some of this information for financial planning purposes.

9. (a) What does certification tell you about a financial planner?

   (b) Why do you think you must be responsible for your own financial plan, no matter who you get to help you?

10. (a) What type of person needs to engage in personal financial planning?

    (b) Does having wealth reduce a person's need for financial planning? Explain.

What Are Your Finance Math Skills?   MyFinLitLab

The first three questions correlate to *Math for Personal Finance* features located throughout the chapter.

1. Ryan worked 40 hours during the first week of his summer job and made $9 an hour. His paycheck was for $332.46. How much did his employer withhold from his paycheck?

2. Justin's boss said work was optional this afternoon, so Justin decided to skip work and go swimming with his friends. Normally he would have worked three hours. Assuming he makes $11 an hour and the swimming trip will cost him $8 in gas, what is the total cost of Justin's decision to go swimming?

3. Mary Beth would like to buy a more fuel-efficient vehicle instead of driving her mom's gas guzzler. Assuming she can find a car that gets 32 miles per gallon (mpg) and her mom's car only gets 16 mpg, how much will she save if she usually drives about 3,000 miles a year and the average price of gasoline is $3.75 a gallon?

4. Assume you drink eight sodas per week and they cost $1.59 each. How much money can you accumulate over the course of the year if you opt to save the money instead?

4. $8 \times \$1.59 \times 52 = \$661.44$

5. If you worked an extra two hours a week during your junior year in high school and you average bringing home $9 an hour, how much money could you accumulate over that 52-week period?

5. $2 \times \$9 \times 52 = \$936$

6. What is the opportunity cost of going to the football game on Friday night instead of working at the mall when you make $7.50 an hour and usually work six hours?

6. $\$7.50 \times 6 = \$45$

7. Assume you wanted to save $2,000 to buy a used car 18 months from now. How much money do you need to save every week to accomplish your goal?

7. $\$2,000 / 78 = \$25.64$

8. If you decide to study 4 hours more a week during your junior year (32 weeks) with the expectation of getting a $2,000 scholarship to college, how much is your study time worth per hour?

8. $\$2,000 / (4 \times 32) = \$15.63$

What Would You Do?

Read the comic strip. Is what Pierce (the red-headed character) did by calling in sick right or wrong (ethical or unethical)? Many employers pay their employees even when they are sick, but sometimes if you call in sick, you will not receive pay for that day. What happens at work when Pierce calls in sick? Does someone else have to do his work? Since he called in sick, is it right for him to go out to the mall to visit friends?

1. If you were Pierce's employer, what would you do if you found out that he had called in sick but was not really sick?

2. If you were Pierce's coworker, what would you think about Pierce's decision?

3. How might Pierce's action affect the business where he works?

What Are the Connections? Math, Language Arts, and Technology

1. Prepare a list of financial decisions you are likely to make over the next 5 years and then the next 10 years. For example, think of what you hope to purchase over that time, or how much progress you hope to make toward specific goals. Be specific about anticipated dollar costs for each decision. If spreadsheet software is available, develop a chart that shows what you can do to begin preparing for these decisions. If you do not have access to a computer, use paper and pencil to prepare the chart.

2. Prepare a personal goal statement that explains how you plan to carry out the steps of your financial plan for the next 5–15 years.

Teamwork

In a team, develop a presentation explaining to teens why it is important for them to begin personal financial planning. You may create a brochure, write a newsletter, produce a skit, or present a video presentation. Be creative, but make sure you stress information discussed in this chapter and the importance of personal financial planning. You might include information you have researched in the library or on the Internet.

ESSENTIAL QUESTION ACTIVITIES

Complete these activities to answer this chapter's Essential Question: *Why is personal financial planning important?*

1. *On your own*: You have learned that planning for the future includes more than making a decision to further your education or to become wealthy. An important part of all these decisions involves planning your personal finances. Using the journal in MyFinLitLab or on paper, fill in the following information: (column A) brainstorm what you want to plan for in the next five years; (column B) what financial decisions need to be made for what you plan; (column C) how can financial planning help you achieve these plans?

2. *As a class*: (a) Brainstorm what financial plans need to be made over the next five years. (b) Develop a financial plan to achieve three of these items on the list. Provide information on how planning can help with each of these.

TEST PREP QUESTIONS

1. The *best* definition of personal financial planning is
   a. a process of mapping decisions for spending, borrowing, and saving and investing in order to achieve financial goals.
   b. an investment schedule established by a financial advisor to help a person pay a debt.
   c. the process of determining how much a person can afford to pay for a house based on the person's income.
   d. the comparison between the cost of education and a person's projected income.

2. Which is a true statement about Americans saving for retirement?
   a. Most Americans save more money than they need for retirement.
   b. Americans do not need to save for retirement since Social Security will cover expenses during retirement years.
   c. Fewer than half of Americans have a retirement account.
   d. The average American saves 9% of annual income for retirement.

   2. c

3. Which is a true statement about the relationship between education and a person's earning power?
   a. The age a person starts to work determines earning power more than the person's education.
   b. The average person with an associate's degree can expect to earn 20% more than a high school graduate earns each year.
   c. A person with a master's degree can expect an annual income that is double that of a person with a bachelor's degree.
   d. A college education does not influence a person's earning power during the first five years of employment.

   3. b

4. Which person's goal is correctly matched with a sound financial plan to achieve the goal?
   a. Buying a new computer for college in the fall: depositing 25% or more of weekly take-home pay in a bank savings account.
   b. Having a down payment for a house in 10 years: saving 1% of take-home pay in a checking account each month.
   c. Having enough money to retire in 25 years: buying all of the things needed now and beginning to invest in 15 years.
   d. Buying a new cell phone in two months: making the purchase on credit and paying the minimum balance each month.

   4. a

5. Money in an emergency fund should be used to pay for
   a. items that suddenly go on sale.
   b. necessary expenses when a person loses a job or is unable to work because of illness or injury.
   c. large expenses such as a house or college education.
   d. long-term investments such as stocks.

   5. b

6. The following statement about financial advice on the Internet is true.
   a. If the information has been posted to the Internet, it is reliable information.

   6. c

Chapter Review **17**

b. If the information comes from a company that is selling financial products, it is sound, objective information.

c. There are a number of valuable sources of information on the Internet that can be used for financial planning.

d. The Internet protects individuals against the loss of money by not allowing unethical financial advisors to post their information.

7. d **7.** When a person decides to use the services of a certified financial planner, the person will

a. no longer need to check on how her money is invested.

b. make a steady profit on the money invested by the planner.

c. need to make all investments with the same planner.

d. check in regularly with the planner to review investment decisions.

8. c **8.** A person decides to bike to school rather than drive his car. The opportunity cost related to this decision is

a. the money that is saved by not buying as much gas for the car.

b. the exercise that riding the bike provides.

c. the time that might be saved by driving the car.

d. the shorter route from home to school that the bike can take.

UNIT

1

Financial Responsibility & Decision Making

CHAPTER 2

ESSENTIAL QUESTION

What are the components of a financial plan?

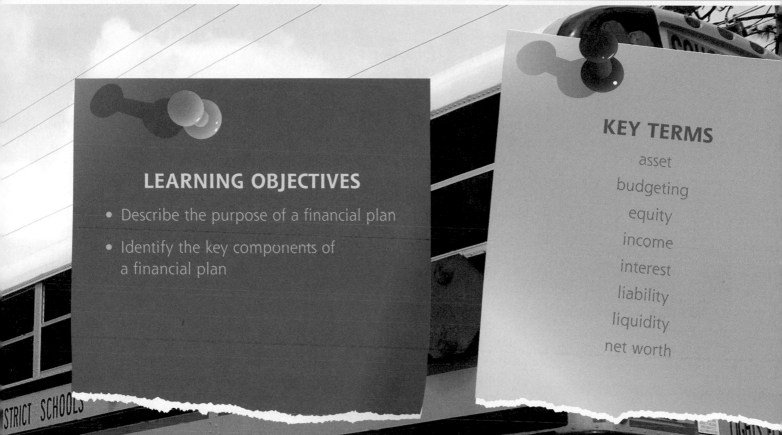

THE FINANCIAL PLAN

LEARNING OBJECTIVES

- Describe the purpose of a financial plan
- Identify the key components of a financial plan

KEY TERMS

asset

budgeting

equity

income

interest

liability

liquidity

net worth

Rafael could hear his mom and dad having a heated discussion again about money. Would it ever end? Every week it seemed his family was short on money and long on bills. Most of his friends said it was the same at their house—except for one. Juana said her mom and dad never fought about money. They lived in a nice house but they did not drive new cars like his mom and dad. Oddly, Juana's dad worked at the same job as his dad. Juana's mom did babysitting while his own mom worked at a grocery store. They all had similar jobs, but Juana's parents did not appear to have money problems. What were Juana's parents doing that his parents were not doing? Whatever it was, Rafael wanted to learn about it. He wanted to be in the place where he did not have to worry about money.

Rafael got sadder and sadder as he listened to his parents argue. He was supposed to tell his mom and dad that he needed $20 for a field trip the next day. But after this latest fight, he decided to forget about it. He would stay at school instead.

Rafael was dreaming about something that his friend Juana's parents apparently had: financial stability. For most people, however, financial stability does not happen by accident or through good fortune. It requires careful planning and effort. In this chapter, you will study the steps to making a personal financial plan, which can serve as the basis for financial success in your life.

WHAT IS A FINANCIAL PLAN?

As Rafael thought more about why Juana's family seemed to have more money than his family, he became more and more curious. What were they doing that his family was not doing? One big difference was that Juana's family had a financial plan in place and stuck to it. They didn't have to argue over every financial decision. They just followed their plan.

Making a budget is a basic part of personal financial planning.

A **personal financial plan** involves specifying financial goals and describing in detail the spending, financing, and investing plans needed to reach those goals. A good financial plan is like a builder's blueprint: It spells out every aspect of how to accumulate and grow wealth and provide for emergencies. It helps ensure that as you move forward in your life, you are making steady progress toward your financial goals.

As shown in Figure 2.1, a solid financial plan addresses seven key components. Each of these areas is a critical piece of your personal financial plan, and each component requires you to make a set of personal decisions. When you are finished, you will have a comprehensive road map to help you achieve your dreams. You are now going to spend some time understanding each area. Later, you will have the chance to apply what you have learned when you create your own personal financial plan.

A financial plan is like a builder's blueprint; it spells out every aspect of your financial life and helps you accumulate wealth and plan for emergencies.

☑ CHECKPOINT

What is the purpose and function of a financial plan?

FIGURE 2.1 Components of Your Financial Plan

The components of your financial plan work together to help you build a solid financial future.

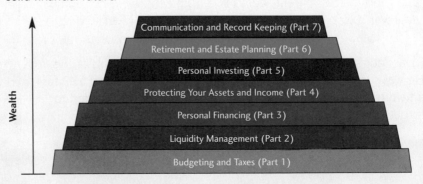

Wealth

- Communication and Record Keeping (Part 7)
- Retirement and Estate Planning (Part 6)
- Personal Investing (Part 5)
- Protecting Your Assets and Income (Part 4)
- Personal Financing (Part 3)
- Liquidity Management (Part 2)
- Budgeting and Taxes (Part 1)

The first step in building a financial plan is to develop an understanding of its different parts. You will now explore the seven components and how they can help you achieve financial security.

Prof. FIN

As the U.S. economy strengthens after emerging from the recent recession, spending by teenagers is beginning to slowly increase. Retailers report a rise in sales in junior clothing lines, electronics, and sports equipment. This increase in spending has occurred despite a decline in the teen population. In fact, during the period of the recession, the United States saw a decline in the number of young people in the age group of 12–17 year olds. Those who were teenagers at the beginning of the recession are now older, and while their spending habits may have changed during the recession, they appear to be spending again. In addition, those entering their teenage years during or after the recession are beginning to spend.

Research online information about the spending trends of teens. What are the most popular items teens purchase? Do you agree with your findings? Do your findings appear consistent with the purchasing patterns of you and your friends?

Source: www.marketingcharts.com/interactive/teen-market-to-surpass-200-billion-by-2011-despite-poplation-decline

COMPONENT ONE: A Plan for Your Budgeting and Taxes

Budget planning, or **budgeting**, is the process of forecasting future expenses and income. In other words, it involves asking how much you plan to spend next week or next month, and what is the expected source of that money. The purpose of a budget is to plan your spending and saving, given your income level, so that you can meet your needs and wants.

Creating a budget involves four steps:

1. Determining your net worth
2. Establishing your income
3. Identifying your expenses
4. Considering the impact of taxes

Step 1: Determining Your Net Worth. The first step in budget planning is to determine where you are right now financially. Do you have money in the bank? Do you owe people money? Do you have a job? What are your expenses? Answering these questions can help you to get an accurate picture of your current financial position. This, in turn, will help you recognize how far—or near—you are from your goals and help you set budget priorities.

The formula for determining your net worth is as follows:

Net Worth = Assets − Liabilities

budgeting: The process of forecasting future expenses and income.

MATH for Personal Finance

Emily's car is worth approximately $5,300 according to the Kelley Blue Book Web site (**www.kbb.com**), but she still owes $1,600 on her loan. She also has $800 in a savings account.

What is Emily's net worth?

Solution: Emily's assets are a car worth $5,300 and $800 in savings for a total of $6,100. Her liabilities are the $1,600 loan. Therefore, her net worth is $6,100 − $1,600 = $4,500.

FIGURE 2.2 Calculating Net Worth

The formula for net worth is asset − liability = net worth. What would happen if the owner of the car were to sell it for its actual market value? (The owner would wind up with $3,000.)

You own $3,000 (net worth)

The bank owns $2,000 (liability)

Asset = $5,000

assets: Anything owned, such as cars, motorcycles, and homes.

liabilities: What we owe, or our debt.

net worth: The difference between assets and liability.

equity: The amount of a specific asset that we own after subtracting any liabilities.

Think about it like this. What if Rafael's dad owned a car worth $5,000? That car is called an asset. **Assets** are anything we own, such as cars and motorcycles. Your parents might own their house or a farm. Those are all assets. Your baseball card collection is also an asset.

For now, let's look at Rafael's dad's car that is valued at $5,000. He still owes the bank $2,000 on the car loan. That remaining debt is called a liability. **Liabilities** are what we owe, or our debt. If this car were the only asset and the only liability that Rafael's dad had, his **net worth** would equal $3,000, or the difference between the value of the asset (car) and his liability of how much he still owes on the car.

Asset	=	Car worth	$5,000
Liability	=	Amount owed on the car	− $2,000
Net Worth	=	Car value minus amount owed	$3,000

Sometimes you will hear people refer to a person's equity in a car or a home or other asset. **Equity** means ownership. In the example above, Rafael's dad has $3,000 equity in the car. If he paid off the remaining $2,000, his equity would be $5,000.

As you save money, you will accumulate more assets (including cash) and increase your net worth. You will also have the chance to reduce your liabilities, which will also increase your net worth. In other words, you can increase your net worth by increasing your assets or decreasing your liabilities. Check out Figure 2.2. What color will the car be when Rafael's dad pays off the loan? How much will his net worth be at that time assuming the car is still worth $5,000?

Prof. FIN

Did you know that the Millennial Generation averages $158 billion per year in disposable income? This group is a prime target for marketers! It is estimated that 40% of teens have a checking or savings account in their own name. Marketers look at "spaces" that teens occupy more than others when marketing plans are made. This includes advertising in skateboard parks, concert venues, and sporting events. More marketers are moving to the Internet to attract the Millennial Generation buyer.

Make a list of all the ads you have seen or heard today. Where were these ads? Based on the ad content and location, who were they targeting?

Source: www.business.com/guides/marketing-to-teens-1135

income: Money coming in through wages earned, allowance, or other sources.

Step 2: Establishing Your Income. A key factor in shaping a budget is understanding your income. **Income** is the money coming in through wages earned, allowance, or other sources. Having an income is the major means by which a person saves money, builds wealth, acquires assets, and fulfills wants and needs. How much income you have will determine many of the details in your budget.

A person's income often depends on decisions he or she makes about education and career choice. In general, more education or specialized training translates into more income. Think about the people you know. Who makes a good income? What jobs do they do? You will probably list a number of professions, some that require a college degree, such as medical professionals and teachers. Others, such as electricians, mechanics, and plumbers, received very specialized training. In almost every case, you will find that higher income comes with higher levels of education and/or training.

Step 3: Identifying Your Expenses. Your expenses are also important in your budget. When you create your budget, you will estimate how much money you are spending every month. Typical expenses might be clothing and entertainment. Some of you might even have a car payment and related expenses. Refer to the chart in Figure 2.3 for household expenditures for two different age groups. Note that your consumption patterns will change over time and are highly dependent on your stage of life.

You will need to have accurate estimates of your expenses to determine how much you can save. Remember that saving for the future requires sacrificing spending today. If you spend $20 on a DVD today, that is money you can't save. Think about the fact that if you manage to save $20 a week for 52 weeks a year, you would accumulate over $1,000.

$20 × 52 weeks = $1,040 total savings.

Step 4: Considering the Impacts of Taxes. Income taxes—money owed to government on earned income—may also impact your budget. In general, the more money you make, the higher the share of your income

MATH for Personal Finance

Jamal makes $9 an hour and works about 15 hours a week. He also gets a $25 per week allowance.

What is his total annual income?

Solution: $9 an hour × 15 hours per week = $135 per week × 52 weeks per year = $7,020 per year income from his job. He also gets $25 per week × 52 weeks per year = $1,300 per year income from his allowance. His total annual income is equal to $7,020 + $1,300 = $8,320.

FIGURE 2.3 How We Spend Our Money

Average annual expenditures can vary significantly depending on your stage of life.

Shares of average annual expenditures spent on major components for selected ages, 2010

Item	Under 25 years	65 years and older
Food	14.8	12.4
Housing	34.8	35.4
Apparel and services	5.7	2.6
Transportation	17.1	14.2
Health care	2.8	13.2
Entertainment	4.4	5.1
Cash contributions	1.1	6.2
Personal insurance and pensions	7.4	5.1
All other	11.9	5.8

Source: www.bls.gov/opub/focus/volume2_number12/cex_2_12_chart2_data.htm

you will pay in income taxes. As your income level increases, you will want to begin to include tax planning in your financial plan. For example, you may want to save some of your income in ways that help you put off or avoid taxes. Examples include certain retirement or college savings plans. Tax laws change constantly, and many of your financial decisions will have tax impacts that you will want to consider.

COMPONENT TWO: A Plan for Managing Your Liquidity

Did you ever go to the store to buy something only to realize that you didn't have enough money? You had a liquidity problem. In other words, you did not have enough liquid assets to cover that purchase. Liquid assets include cash and assets that can be quickly and easily turned into cash. Your level of **liquidity**, then, refers to how much readily available cash you have on hand for meeting immediate wants and needs. Note that your liquidity is very different from your net worth. You may have a number of valuable assets, but if they are not liquid, they will be of little use to you when facing a short-term financial need.

For example, what if your car breaks down or you need new tires? Or, what if, like Rafael, you need $20 to pay for a field trip? The fact that you own a car worth $5,000 will do little to help you solve such problems. These types of expenses require liquid assets. A good financial plan will help you manage your liquidity so that you don't get caught off guard by an unexpected expense.

Money management and credit management decisions are both involved in liquidity management. **Money management** involves making decisions about how much cash or liquid assets to keep in reserve and how much to invest in less liquid assets, such as **real estate** (buildings and land). If you find out you don't have enough money to cover your immediate needs, then you need more liquidity. You may have the money invested but not easily and quickly accessible. Money management helps you determine how much money to keep liquid to avoid cash shortfalls.

One way to determine how much money Rafael might need for the year is to keep track of last year's needs and set aside enough cash to cover that amount, plus some additional money. For example, if Rafael needed $500 last year to cover field trips, school supplies, and the cost of playing a sport or traveling with the band, then that amount is a good starting point. After planning for some additional, unforeseen expenses, Rafael may determine

liquidity: How much readily available cash you have on hand for meeting immediate wants and needs.

YOU DO IT

Activity #1

FIGURE 2.4 Managing Your Liquidity

Making sure you have enough cash on hand—managing your liquidity—involves managing your money and managing your use of credit.

he needs approximately $1,000 readily available to satisfy his liquidity needs. Money management would involve putting that money in a short-term investment that would allow easy access and not penalize him for withdrawal.

Credit management involves making decisions about getting credit and using credit. Credit is commonly used to cover immediate cash shortfalls, so it increases liquidity. But credit, and particularly credit cards, can be very costly. When you use credit (borrow money), the lender charges interest on the money you borrow. Think about **interest** as rent on the money. Some lenders charge higher rent (interest) on money than others. In general, it is not wise to rely on credit cards if you will not be able to pay back the borrowed money quickly. A financial plan should contain a credit management plan. This might involve details such as limiting the number of credit cards you have and the amount of credit you can use at any one time. Figure 2.4 shows an illustration of liquidity management.

interest: "Rent" on money you borrow.

COMPONENT THREE: A Plan for Your Financing

Major purchases such as cars, houses, and paying for college typically require borrowing money for long periods of time. Most of the time you do not have time to accumulate enough wealth to pay cash for a house. However, it is common to pay a portion of the cost of a house or car and to take a loan for—or **finance**—the remaining amount. For example, you may save $1,000 for a down payment on a $4,000 car and finance the remaining $3,000. Figure 2.5 illustrates the financing process you might go through to buy this car.

FIGURE 2.5 Financing Process

Making a major purchase often involves using some of your own money and financing the rest.

Ruston plans on buying a car that is priced at $3,500. He has saved $1,000 for a down payment and his grandparents have agreed to contribute another $500 toward the purchase.

How much of the vehicle will Ruston need to finance?

Solution: Ruston can put a total of $1,500 down on the car and finance the remainder, which is $3,500 − $1,500 = $2,000.

Managing your risk and preventing loss through insurance is key to your long-term financial security.

This type of borrowing differs from the temporary, short-term borrowing that credit cards are often used for. Longer-term financing is usually available at a lower cost to the borrower than can be found with credit cards. Still, use of long-term financing requires great caution. For example, if you cannot pay back the $3,000 you borrowed for that car, the lender may take the car back from you. You lose the car—and the $1,000 you already paid toward it.

There are a number of factors that will determine how much you can borrow and the payment terms. **Payment terms** include the specific information about the interest rate the lender will charge you and the time period for paying back the loan. Remember, lenders make their money by charging you rent (interest) on the money they loan. Prior to making a loan lenders will determine your overall creditworthiness which is an assessment of how likely you are to pay back the loan.

However, some lenders will loan you more money than you should borrow. Remember that every time you borrow money, you have a payment schedule that requires you to make timely payments. Most of the time these payments are monthly. If Rafael's parents are having liquidity problems, what does that indicate about their monthly payment obligations? It's very possible that Rafael's parents have borrowed too much money and do not have enough flexibility in their budget to provide for emergencies. A comprehensive financing plan would prevent that from happening.

COMPONENT FOUR: A Plan for Managing Your Risk

As you accumulate assets, you need to devise a plan to protect those assets. For example, if you buy a car, what happens if that car is stolen or rammed in a parking lot by another car? Unless you have insurance on that car you will suffer the loss of that asset yourself. You are assuming all the **risk**—the possibility of a financial loss. Risk is related to the likelihood of loss. If there is a greater chance of your suffering a financial loss, then the risk is higher. For that reason many people purchase insurance.

Insurance planning is a component of your financial plan that determines the types and amounts of insurance you need. What other assets should you have insured? People typically insure houses, boats, cars, and other major assets. However, you also need insurance to cover you in case of other unexpected events, such as an illness or injury. Many of your parents also have life insurance that will provide a cash amount in the event of their death. Life insurance protects the loved ones left behind.

COMPONENT FIVE: A Plan for Your Investing

You know you need to accumulate some funds for liquidity to meet day-to-day expenses and to pay for sudden unexpected events. Any other funds that you do not spend should be invested with the expectation of earning even more money. Common types of investments include stocks, bonds, mutual funds, and real estate.

Who do you think is more likely to be investing: Rafael's parents or Juana's parents? Since money for investment tends to be money remaining after paying necessary bills, you might suspect Juana's parents are more likely to be investing. As a result, they are likely to have even more money available to meet their wants and needs.

People invest money so they can make more money. But you should always remember that different types of investments have different levels of risk. Riskier investments can produce great returns—but they may also experience significant losses. That is, a risky $1,000 investment may earn $200, $300, or more in a good year. But it may also lose money—or even lose all of its value.

COMPONENT SIX: A Plan for Your Retirement

How many of you know people who are retired? Have you noticed that some people retire earlier than others? People who retire early are often people who began planning for retirement while they were young. Retirement planning involves determining how much to save for retirement every year and how to invest that money. The government provides several ways to save for retirement that allow you to accumulate wealth without paying taxes until you retire. By putting off paying taxes until later, you increase the amount invested. This, in turn, may increase the amount of money the investment earns.

COMPONENT SEVEN: A Plan for Communicating and Keeping Records

Communicating your financial plan to your family is critical. Sometimes you may hear someone quarreling over money and you will learn that the dispute could have been avoided with clear communication.

Equally as important as making personal financial decisions and communicating those decisions is keeping good records. You will need these records when you file your taxes and when you calculate your net worth. Your heirs may also need them at some point. Good financial records can be a motivational tool. You will find that if you actually write your goals down and periodically refer to them, you will be much more likely to achieve them.

Rafael doesn't want his financial situation to end up like that of his parents. He can start by identifying his goals and writing them down. Then he can begin to identify steps he can take to achieve those goals.

CHECKPOINT

What are the components of a financial plan?

Finance **ONLINE**

There are many sources on the Internet for researching investing. One such site is **moneycentral.msn.com/ home.asp**. What information on this site can help consumers? Make a list of information found on this site that could help you, the consumer, as you make financial decisions.

YOU DO IT

Activity #2

1. Budgeting and taxes; 2. Managing liquidity, or ready access to cash; 3. Financing large purchases; 4. Managing risk; 5. Investing; 6. Planning for retirement and transferring wealth; 7. Communicating and keeping records.

CHAPTER REVIEW

SUMMARY

- Financial planning involves specifying financial goals and describing in detail the spending, financing, and investing plans needed to reach those goals. Your plan will be like a blueprint for your financial future.

- A good financial plan contains seven key components: (1) budgeting, which requires an understanding of concepts such as net worth, income, expenses, and taxes; (2) managing liquidity, including management of money and credit; (3) financing large purchases; (4) managing your risk, through the use of insurance; (5) investing your money; (6) planning for retirement and transferring wealth; and (7) communicating and keeping records.

Key Terms and Concepts

1. Why is it important to have a personal financial plan?

2. What is the difference in money management and credit management?

3. What is meant by managing your risk?

What Do You Know?   MyFinLitLab

1. (a) What are the components of a financial plan?

2. (a) Define budget planning.

   (b) What elements must be assessed in budget planning?

3. (a) How is your net worth calculated?

   (b) Why is knowing your net worth important?

4. (a) What factors influence income?

   (b) Why is an accurate estimate of expenses important in budget planning?

   (c) How do tax laws affect the budgeting process?

5. (a) What is liquidity?

   (b) What two factors are considered in managing liquidity?

   (c) How are they used?

6. (a) What factors determine how much you can borrow?

   (b) Can you rely on a lender to lend you the appropriate amount of money? Explain.

7. (a) What is the purpose of insurance?

   (b) Explain how owning a car or house exposes you to financial risk.

8. (a) What is the primary objective of investing?

   (b) Why would you not invest all the money you have available?

9. (a) How do your financial goals fit into your financial plan?

   (b) Why should goals be described in detail?

10. (a) Why is it important to communicate your financial plans?

6. (a) **Comprehension** Factors include your creditworthiness, the interest rate, and time period for paying back loans. (b) **Analysis** No. Lenders might loan you more than you are really able to pay back.

7. (a) **Comprehension** Insurance helps manage your exposure to risk. (b) **Analysis** When you own a home or car, you stand to lose wealth if something happens to the car or house and you lack proper insurance coverage.

8. (a) **Comprehension** To increase the value of your assets. (b) **Application** Some investments are risky and may not be liquid.

9. (a) **Comprehension** Your goals are the basis for the specifics of your financial plan. (b) **Evaluation** If you list very detailed goals it makes it easier to identify the steps needed to achieve that goal.

10. (a) **Evaluation** By communicating your goals and plans to your family you can avoid some conflicts over the decisions you make.

What Are Your Finance Math Skills?   MyFinLitLab

The first three questions correlate to *Math for Personal Finance* features located throughout the chapter.

1. Maria has a car that she could sell for about $7,000 according to her uncle who is a used car dealer. However, she still owes $2,200 on her car loan. She has $1,100 in her checking account and $300 in cash. What is Maria's net worth?

2. Assume you make $10 an hour and work 20 hours a week. In addition, you receive $1,200 a year in income from a trust fund. What is your total annual income?

3. Kedra would like to buy a vehicle that is priced at $4,100. Assume she has saved 20% of the purchase price for a down payment. How much money does she need to finance?

4. Assume you work 12 hours per week and make $7.50 per hour. How much is your annual income?

5. You have a car worth $3,200. You owe $1,400 on the loan. You also owe $320 on a credit card. How much are your total liabilities?

6. Assume you took $2,500 in cash out of your savings account and bought a car worth $2,500. How much did your net worth change?

7. If you intend to begin saving 25% of your income and you bring home $50 a week, how much will you save in one year?

8. What is the value of your total assets if you have a car worth $4,000, you owe $1,500 on the car loan, and you have a baseball card collection valued at $750?

Answers:
What Are Your Finance Math Skills?

1. $7,000 − $2,200 + $1,100 + $300 = $6,200

2. ($10 × 20 × 52) + $1,200 = $11,600

3. .80 × $4,100 = $3,280

4. Assuming you work 52 weeks, you would earn $4,680 or (12 × $7.50 × 52)

5. $1,400 + $320 = $1,720

6. Your net worth did not change since your assets and liabilities remained the same.

7. $50 × .25 × 52 = $650

8. $4,000 + $750 = $4,750.
Note: Total assets do not equal net worth.

What Would You Do?

Danielle has been invited to her friend's house for an afternoon pool party. It is going to be a great time, and all her friends are planning to go—if they can get a ride. Danielle is the only one who has access to a car at the moment. The trouble is, the car she has access to is owned by her parents. Danielle just got her driver's license, and her parents have not yet changed insurance coverage on their SUV so that she is covered in the event she has an accident while she's behind the wheel.

Danielle's friends have been pushing her to take the SUV. After all, they point out, she has a key to the vehicle. And her parents aren't supposed to be home until after the pool party is over, so they will never know. It's only a couple of miles across town. What, they say, could go wrong?

1. What risk would Danielle be taking to drive the SUV without the proper insurance coverage?

2. What are the possible costs to Danielle if she makes the wrong choice?

3. What would you do in this situation?

What Are the Connections? Language Arts, Math, and Technology

Many of you will continue your education after high school graduation. Research three post-secondary (college/university, technical college, vocational school) or training programs that you might want to attend following high school. Collect data for each of these that include the following information:

- Tuition for one year (dollars per hour or per semester) or training costs

- Other expected fees, such as housing and cafeteria costs

- Estimated costs of getting to and from each facility (home to campus/training site)

If you have access to spreadsheet software, design a spreadsheet of the information showing the comparisons of the costs for each. If not, use paper and pencil to design the spreadsheet.

Then write a paper about your findings. This paper should include any graphs, charts, or tables that will help you show comparisons between education/training programs. When you make the comparisons, keep in mind the possible benefits of one type of education/training program over another. Explain why additional education/training after high school is necessary or important. As part of your paper, answer the following questions:

1. Why is it important to research colleges/universities or training programs of your choice at an early age?

2. What does planning for these expenses have to do with financial planning?

3. How can you communicate with your parents or high school counselor your plans for further education upon high school graduation?

Teamwork Service-Learning Activity

Prepare a group presentation about the steps of a financial plan. Create a brochure or newsletter that shows the steps of making a financial plan. Imagine that this brochure or newsletter might be used for a PTO meeting at your school, placed in the guidance counselor's office, or sent home with school announcements for students to share with their parents. Work together in a team to find information from the text and on the Internet that you might use to help explain the need for and steps of making a financial plan. Remember that it is important not only to explain or describe the steps but also to explain why it is important for young people to have a financial plan in place.

In your brochure or newsletter, be sure to give examples of information that are needed for each step. For example, what does a budget look like or what taxes should be included? Include any graphics that might be helpful in the explanation of the steps. These might include pictures, graphs/charts, or tables.

ESSENTIAL QUESTION ACTIVITIES

Complete these activities to answer this chapter's Essential Question: *What are the components of a financial plan?*

1. *On your own:* You have learned the seven components of financial planning. Using word processing or presentation software, or paper, develop a diagram of each step. Be sure to include an example for each step.

2. *As a class:* With the class divided into seven groups, each group will pick one of the components of a financial plan and develop a presentation to explain that component. This presentation may be a demonstration, report, PowerPoint presentation, or skit.

1. b **1.** A financial plan is created like a
   a. map of the world.
   b. blueprint for building a house.
   c. bank account statement.
   d. receipt for an item purchased with a credit card.

2. c **2.** A person increases his net worth by
   a. buying a new car with a 10% down payment from savings and a 90% loan.
   b. making purchases with a credit or debit card.
   c. increasing assets and decreasing liabilities.
   d. transferring money from a savings account to a checking account.

3. c **3.** A person has a house worth $100,000, a mortgage of $90,000, savings of $5,000, a car valued at $10,000, a $7,000 car loan, and $3,000 in credit card debt. This person's net worth is
   a. $115,000.
   b. $100,000.
   c. $15,000.
   d. $5,000.

4. c **4.** A financial plan does not include
   a. managing risk.
   b. retirement planning.
   c. bankruptcy.
   d. investing.

5. d **5.** A person increases liquidity when he
   a. buys more items on credit and fewer items with cash.
   b. uses money saved to buy an asset like a car.
   c. uses cash to pay off credit card debt.
   d. makes weekly deposits in a bank savings account.

6. c **6.** "Good credit management" means
   a. making purchases with credit or debit cards.
   b. using credit to make purchases that cost more than $1,000 and paying the minimum required each month.
   c. using credit to make purchases when the buyer knows she can quickly pay the amount owed.
   d. making most purchases on credit in order to track money spent.

7. b **7.** Why is insurance a method of managing risk?
   a. Insurance protects assets from being lost or damaged.
   b. Insurance limits a person's financial loss if an asset is lost, stolen, or damaged.
   c. A person's liabilities are reduced when insured assets are lost or stolen.
   d. A person's budgeted monthly expenses are covered by insurance.

8. A 21-year-old college graduate starting her first full-time job wants to buy a home by age 30. Why should she include this goal in her financial plan?

8. b

   a. She can apply for a mortgage now while she is young and rates are low.

   b. She is more likely to achieve her goal if she starts saving and investing now in order to have the down payment needed to buy the house.

   c. She can start buying things for her house while she is living with her parents and has limited expenses.

   d. She can buy the house as soon as she finds the one she likes.

CHAPTER 3

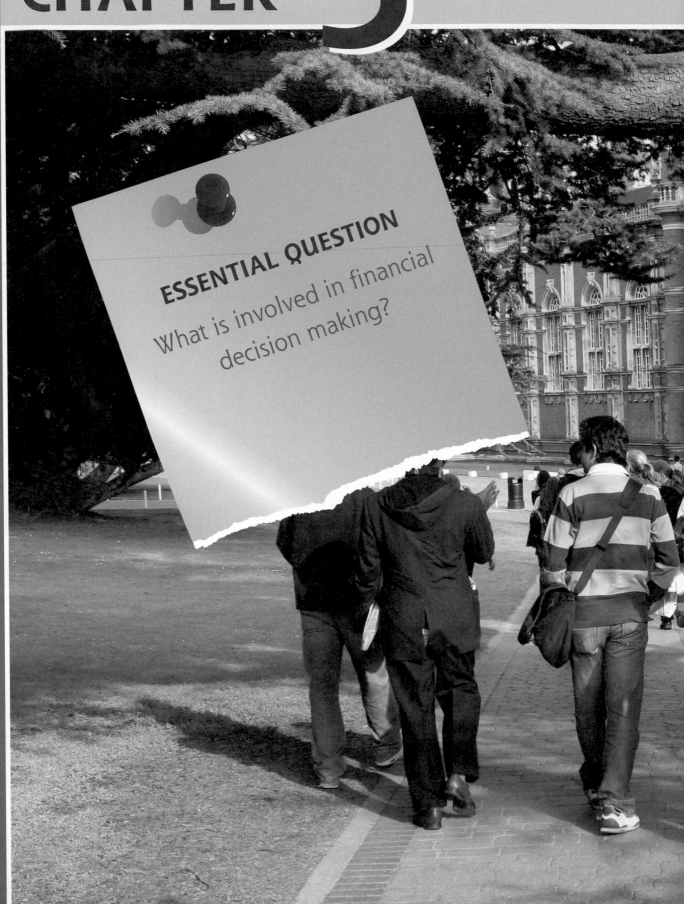

ESSENTIAL QUESTION

What is involved in financial decision making?

FINANCIAL DECISION MAKING

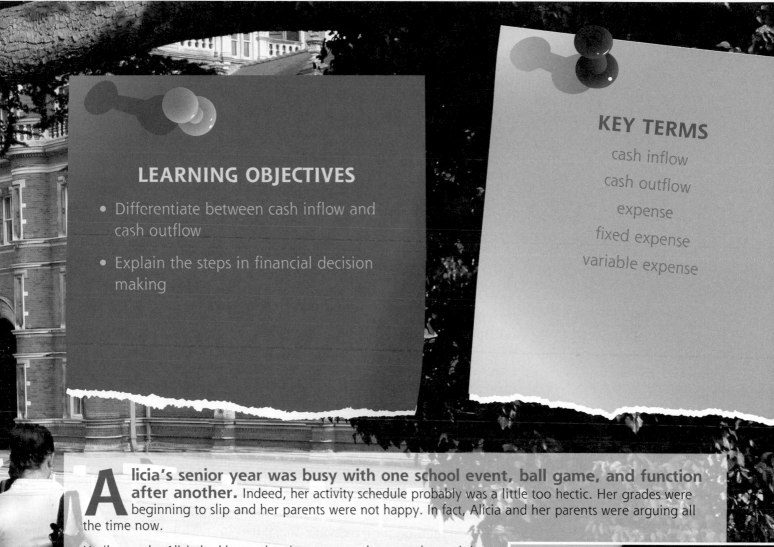

LEARNING OBJECTIVES

- Differentiate between cash inflow and cash outflow

- Explain the steps in financial decision making

KEY TERMS

cash inflow

cash outflow

expense

fixed expense

variable expense

Alicia's senior year was busy with one school event, ball game, and function after another. Indeed, her activity schedule probably was a little too hectic. Her grades were beginning to slip and her parents were not happy. In fact, Alicia and her parents were arguing all the time now.

Until recently, Alicia had been planning to stay at home and attend the local university in the fall. But now, she was rethinking those plans. After a recent, especially bad argument with her mother, Alicia promised herself that as soon as she graduated from high school, she would get an apartment of her own. Then, she could do whatever she wanted to do, whenever she wanted to do it. Excited by this idea, Alicia began to gather some information.

First, she considered her income. She earned about $300 a month waiting tables—not enough to live on, but if she were willing to work Friday and Saturday nights, she could make another $80 per weekend night. Of course, this would mean giving up many social activities.

Alicia then thought about getting loans to help with college expenses. If she borrowed money, she could work a little less *and* still go out on the weekends. Sure, it would be a pain to have to pay back the loans in a few years. But by that time she would have a good job, and anyway it was a long time in the future.

The next day Alicia shared her thoughts with her friend Tiffany. Tiffany's face lit up. "Let's move in together and split the costs!" Tiffany said. "I can't wait to get away from my parents, too." Tiffany said her uncle could give them full-time jobs at his hardware store. "I was sort of thinking about going to college," said Tiffany. "But my uncle said he'd pay me $10 an hour—that's $350 a week! If I can make that kind of money, college can wait!"

Prof. FIN

With the economic crisis, parents' attitudes toward saving for their children's college education began to change. Since a survey done in 2007:

- Sixty-seven percent of parents are saving for tuition. This is up from the 58% in 2007.

- Seventy-five percent say they don't want their child to graduate from college

with a huge debt. More are asking their children to work part-time to help pay for college.

- Sixteen percent of the college tuition will be covered based on current and expected savings. This is down from 24% in 2007.

Source: lifeinc.today.msnbc.msn.com/_news/2011/08/23/7450317-parents-falling-behind-on-saving-for-kids-college?lite

At first, Alicia thought Tiffany's ideas sounded great. But the more she thought about it, the more doubts she had. First, Tiffany was not the most reliable person Alicia knew. She was not sure about sharing an apartment with her. While $350 a week sounded great, Alicia knew that taxes would reduce that amount by a bit. A nice apartment might cost $800 a month or more. Then there was telephone, cable, electricity, gas, food, a car . . . and putting off college—was that a good decision?

Alicia has a lot to think about. Should she move out? If so, how should she pay for it? Should she work more? Take out a loan? Get a roommate? Put off college so she can earn more money today?

This dilemma facing Alicia is not unusual. In some form or another, we all face these kinds of questions, and the questions do not end. For the rest of our lives, we will face choices about our cash inflow and outflow. Having a solid method for making financial decisions and answering these questions can have a big impact on our lives.

CASH FLOW AND YOUR FINANCIAL FUTURE

At the heart of Alicia's dilemma are questions about cash flow. She faces choices about **cash inflow**—money that she receives from different sources—and **cash outflow**—money that she may spend.

Think about the key components of a financial plan. Each component of your plan also reflects decisions about how you get or use cash. For example, budgeting decisions determine how much of your income you spend on products and services—and how much you have left over. How much you have left over is related to your plans to manage liquidity: how much cash you have available, and how much you rely on credit to meet your wants and needs. Your available cash is also related to what and how much you finance, how much you invest, and so on. The central role of cash in your financial plan is illustrated in Figure 3.1.

Like Alicia, you will face many questions as you build your financial plan and make other financial decisions in life. Some of these questions are outlined in Figure 3.2.

These questions can be difficult to answer and they can have effects that you might not anticipate or recognize for a long time. For example, Alicia's decision about moving out may affect her education, which could in turn affect her ability to save, invest, and plan for retirement. You can see that the effects of that decision could send ripples throughout the rest of her life.

cash inflow: Money received from various sources.

cash outflow: Money paid out or spent.

☑ CHECKPOINT

What is cash inflow and cash outflow?

Cash inflow is money that you receive from all sources. Cash outflow is money that you spend.

FIGURE 3.1 How Financial Planning Affects Your Cash Flows

At the heart of your financial planning is the cash you have available and what you decide to do with it.

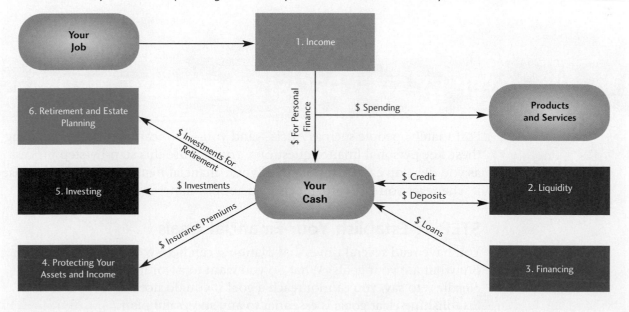

FIGURE 3.2 Examples of Decisions Made in Each Component
of a Financial Plan

At each stage of creating your financial plan, you will face a number of challenging decisions.

A Plan for:	Types of Decisions
1. Managing your income	What expenses should you anticipate?
	How much money should you attempt to save each month?
	How much money must you save each month toward a specific purchase?
	What debt payments must you make each month?
2. Managing your liquidity	How much money should you maintain in your checking account?
	How much money should you maintain in your savings account?
	Should you use credit cards as a means of borrowing money?
3. Financing	How much money can you borrow to purchase a car?
	Should you borrow money to purchase a car or should you lease a car?
	How much money can you borrow to purchase a home?
	What type of mortgage loan should you obtain to finance the purchase of a house?
4. Protecting your assets and income	What type of insurance do you need?
	How much insurance do you need?
5. Investing	How much money should you allocate toward investments?
	What types of investments should you consider?
	How much risk can you tolerate when investing your money?
6. Your retirement and estate	How much money will you need for retirement?
	How much money must you save each year so that you can retire in a specific year?
	How will you allocate your estate among your heirs?
7. Communicating and keeping records	Where will you store your records?
	Where do you intend to keep your backup files?
	Who needs to be made aware of this information?

STEP-BY-STEP DECISION MAKING PROCESS

Fortunately, people such as Alicia—and you—can learn a process for facing these key personal finance questions. You can use this step-by-step process as you develop each component of your financial plan. Indeed, you can use it whenever you face difficult choices about finances.

STEP 1: Establish Your Financial Goals

You have read several times that planning can help you achieve your goals. But what are your goals? What do you want to accomplish in the future? Needless to say, you cannot reach a goal if you do not know what it is. Establishing clear goals is essential to any successful plan.

Understand that there are many different types of goals. People may have more than one of them. For example, you may have a goal of making a particular purchase and of getting out of debt. Like Alicia, you may want to move into your own apartment or get a college education. How about a car? Maybe you would like to pay off debt or finish college debt free. Some of you may want to start your own plumbing business or catering company. Maybe you would like to have $200,000 in total wealth by age 40 or you might be interested in helping a charity buy a new facility.

You can categorize your financial goals in terms of when you hope to accomplish them as follows:

- **Short-term goals** are those you plan to accomplish within the next year.
- **Intermediate-term goals** are those you aim to meet within the next one to five years.
- **Long-term goals** will take more than five years to accomplish.

A short-term goal might be to save enough money to buy an MP3 player in a few weeks. An intermediate-term goal may be to save enough to buy a nice used car next year. A long-term goal might be to save enough money for the down payment on a house in the next 10 years. As your goals become more involved, you will need a more specific and ambitious financial plan. Refer to Figure 3.3 to look at a sample of Alicia's goals.

It is essential that you set realistic goals. Goals must be achievable. It does not do any good to set a goal that you can never reach. If you focus on unrealistic goals, you will likely become discouraged when you do not achieve them. On the other hand, establishing an achievable goal encourages you when you accomplish it or as you see that you are making progress toward it. For example, what if Alicia wanted to save $1,200 a year for her college education? If she is successful in the first three months and has accumulated $300, she will feel encouraged to continue saving. If she said she wanted to save $12,000 a year for her college education, she would likely be very disappointed at the end of three months and probably abandon her goal.

Remember—you will set a number of goals for your financial life. In particular, you will want to set goals for each of the components of your financial plan.

FIGURE 3.3 Alicia's Goals

Setting goals—and discriminating between short-term, intermediate-term, and long-term goals—is the first step in achieving them.

Short-term	Intermediate-term	Long-term
Buy MP3 Player	Graduate from college	Accumulate $20,000 for a down payment on a house in 10 years
Increase income by $80 a week	Buy a better vehicle next year	Earn a graduate degree
Save money for a deposit on rent and utilities	Accumulate $5,000 in savings in the next five years	Accumulate $100,000 in savings by age 40
Save $1,200 this year for college		
Complete senior year with a 3.0 GPA		

Dewanna needs to save $1,500 by August to pay for her tuition. She only has 12 weeks remaining before school starts, and her boss is letting her work 20 hours per week. She brings home about $9 an hour after taxes are withdrawn from her check.

Is it possible for her to save the $1,500?

Solution: Yes, it is possible. She makes $9 an hour × 20 hours per week = $180 per week × 12 weeks = $2,160 she will make prior to school starting.

expense: Anything on which we spend money.

fixed expense: Those expenses that remain the same from period to period.

variable expense: Those expenses that may change from one period to the next.

You may not know when your next variable expense will occur, but you can plan to be ready when misfortune strikes.

STEP 2: Evaluate Your Current Financial Position

Imagine you are traveling in an unfamiliar city. You know you want to get to the museum. You have located it on a map. But how do you get there? In which direction should you travel? Before you can chart your course on a map, you must identify your starting point.

The same principle is true for your personal finances. You need an accurate picture of your current personal and financial situation. Only then can you plan effectively. For example, your decisions about how much money to spend next month, how much to save, and how often to use your credit card depend to a large extent on your current situation. A person with low debt and a lot of assets will make different decisions about spending and saving than a person with a lot of debt and no assets. Single people with no dependents make different decisions than married people with children. People make different decisions at age 18 than at age 50.

Since financial goals are tied to your income, you can see that they are also tied to your level of education and your choice of career. Simply put, having a good, solid income allows you to set more and loftier goals.

For this reason, Alicia is right to be concerned about Tiffany's plans to delay college. This decision may be right for some people at some times. It may even allow these two young women to reach their short-term goals (and even some intermediate-term goals) more quickly. But Alicia is correct to consider the impact of this decision on her long-term financial well-being.

Now let's take a look at the next leg of the journey. You may know where you are and where you want to be, but you also need to know what roads to take to get there. In Alicia's case, she can map out her current financial condition and what she hopes to achieve. Then, she can begin to figure out how she might reach her goal by making accurate forecasts. A **forecast** is a projection about what will happen in the future. For business and personal finance, forecasts typically involve making projections about cash flows—money you have coming in (inflow) and going out (outflow). Obviously, when we are evaluating our financial position, it is helpful to make projections about the future.

For individuals, cash inflow is referred to as **income**. You can get income from some external source, such as a job, allowance from your parents, or a scholarship. You may also get income from savings or investments—for example, interest earned on a savings account.

Most people also have cash outflows to consider. We refer to these as expenses. An **expense** is anything on which we spend money. Examples include the phone bill and car payments. Some expenses we are obligated to pay every month and may be fixed. For example, rent of $600 a month would be a **fixed expense**. Fixed expenses, by definition, remain the same from period to period. Other expenses may be variable, or change from one period to the next. Your phone bill is an example of a **variable expense**. Each bill differs depending on how many minutes you use in the billing period.

Think about Alicia. She already makes $300 a month waiting tables. That is, she makes $3,600 per year. She wants to forecast the impact of an increase in the number of Friday and Saturday nights she works. Assuming $80 in tips for each night worked, Alicia should make an extra $8,320 next year (104 Friday and Saturday nights per year × $80 each = $8,320). This forecast can help Alicia determine how much spending money she will have for the year. She can forecast an $11,920 cash inflow from waiting tables and tips.

However, waiting tables is not cost free to Alicia. In order to do her job, occasionally she has to make some cash outflows. These outflows are her expenses. Alicia's expenses include the purchase of her uniforms for work and the cost of getting them dry-cleaned. The difference between her cash inflow (money from waiting tables) and her cash outflow (job expenses) is her profit. Refer to Figure 3.4 to look at Alicia's forecast if she moves out.

STEP 3: Identify and Evaluate Options for Accomplishing Your Goals

There may be multiple roads that reach the same destination. The same is true for financial goals. Often there are several ways to achieve a goal.

Alicia realizes this. Her goal is to move out of her house while attending college. That is, she wants to create a budget in which she can afford the rent and additional expenses. Toward this end, she is considering adding hours to her work schedule. She is also thinking about taking a loan to help pay for college expenses. She has discussed the idea of having a roommate so that renting an apartment would be less costly. She has even considered the possibility of postponing college in order to pursue full-time work.

There are probably other options Alicia could consider. For example, she might seek some financial aid to help lower the costs to her parents. She might consider getting education at a less costly school—perhaps a community college. Refer to Figure 3.5 to look at Alicia's options.

MATH for Personal Finance

Jared anticipates working 10 hours a week during the 34-week school year. He will work 40 hours per week for the remaining 18 weeks when school is out.

Assuming he makes $8 an hour, what is his forecast for income next year?

Solution: 34 weeks × 10 hours per week = 340 hours worked during the school year. Forty hours per week × 18 weeks while not in school = 720 hours. His total hours worked = 340 + 720 = 1,060 hours × $8 an hour = $8,480 in forecasted income.

FIGURE 3.4 Alicia's Cash Flow Forecast (Income-Expense) Assuming She Moves Out

Look at Alicia's forecast. As you can see, Alicia's expected expenses if she moves out exceed her expected income.

Annual expected cash inflow (income)

Current Job	$300 per month × 12 months	$3,600
Work additional weekends	$80 night × 104 nights	$8,320
	Total cash inflow (income)	**$11,920**

Annual expected cash outflow (expenses)

Rent	½ of $800 per month	$4,800
Utilities	½ of expected $300 per month	$1,800
Food	$300 per month × 12 months	$3,600
Auto expenses (insurance, gas, etc.)		$3,600
Additional expenses, including uniforms and dry-cleaning	$50 per month × 12	$600
Entertainment	$100 per month × 12	$1,200
	Total cash outflow (expenses)	

FIGURE 3.5 Alicia's Options

Alicia has identified several options, all of which might enable her to achieve certain goals.

Option 1	Move into an apartment. Alicia realizes this will only be possible if she has at least two roommates and works more than just weekends or takes out college loans.
Option 2	Continue to live at home with her parents while going to college.
Option 3	Work full time and postpone college.

Activity #2

There is an element of risk in all financial decisions. Knowing your tolerance for risk can help you make the choices that are right for you.

Two of these plans have the potential to help Alicia reach her goal of moving out of the house after graduation. Of course, each option probably has its drawbacks and shortcomings. Refer to Figure 3.6 for a look at the pros and cons.

You need to take a similar approach to all aspects of your financial plan. This can be tricky: Sometimes one decision has a major impact on your financial plan. For example, if Alicia takes out student loans in order to get through college, it will have an impact on the financing component of her financial plan and affect her for many years.

STEP 4: Pick the Best Plan

After you develop multiple ways to achieve a goal, you need to decide which option is most realistic and works for you. Two people who seem to be in identical situations may still opt for two different plans. Your tolerance for risk and your self-discipline often determine which particular plan offers the best option for achieving a specific goal. **Risk** is often defined as the likelihood of loss. Think about different tolerances for risk in terms of a football game. Your school may be playing last year's state champs in the opening game. Some of your team members are dreading the game because they realize the risk that they will lose is very high. These players have a low risk tolerance. However, some other team members welcome the risk. They are excited about the game because even

FIGURE 3.6 Pros and Cons of Alicia's Options

In general, each option will offer certain benefits—"pros"—and drawbacks—"cons." You must identify and evaluate both in order to make good decisions.

	Pros	Cons
Option 1	More freedom to make her own decisions	Very expensive
Option 2	Cheapest alternative while in college	Less freedom to make her own decisions
Option 3	More freedom to make her own decisions	Postpones education that could lead to higher income—has a high opportunity cost (lost future income) and may harm progress toward long-term goals

FIGURE 3.7 Different Paths to Same Goal

Different people may find different ways to accomplish the same goal.

Alicia	Raphael
Step 1: Establish Goal	
• Get a four-year college degree from University X	• Get a four-year college degree from University X
Step 2: Evaluate Your Current Financial Position	
• Has a job and savings she can use for spending money	• Has no job or resources
• Is likely to receive scholarships	• Is unlikely to earn scholarships, but is eligible for government grants and loans
• Is eligible for loans	• Must pay for dorm room or apartment to attend University X
• Has option of living at home rent-free	
Step 3: Identify and Evaluate Different Ways to Accomplish Your Goals	
• Could get apartment—with roommates and increased work schedule	• Could get job
• Could borrow money and work less	• Could live at home and attend lower-cost, nearby community college for first two years, then transfer to University X
• Could live at home and work less	• Could attend four-year school *if* he gets a roommate and takes out loans
Step 4: Pick the Best Plan	
• Live at home and cut back work schedule	• Get a part-time job and save money
• Use combination of savings, earnings, and scholarship money to graduate debt-free	• Use grants to begin education at community college while living at home
	• Use savings and perhaps loans for final two years at University X

though the risk is high, the potential reward is huge. They realize that if they are able to beat the state champs, they will achieve much recognition. Neither of these two attitudes is right or wrong. Each indicates different tolerances for risk.

You can apply the same thought process to your financial decision making and financial plan. Some of you will choose plans that have a higher level of risk of loss but also have a higher potential payoff. Others will pick plans with lower risk that are more certain to accomplish the ultimate goal. Alicia may choose a different plan than Tiffany would choose to achieve the same goal. Both options may be good for each individual.

What if two people want to get a college degree? Refer to Figure 3.7 for a summary of how Alicia and one of her other friends, Raphael, might choose different paths or plans to achieve their goal.

STEP 5: Periodically Evaluate Your Plan

After you pick a plan, you need to monitor your progress because sometimes your plans may falter or get off track. Unless you are monitoring your progress toward your goals, it is likely that you will not notice a problem and make any needed adjustments.

YOU DO IT

Activity #3

MATH for Personal Finance

Lesia's original financial plan required that she save $100 a month for two years in order to have $2,400 for the down payment on a car. However, after one year she has only managed to save $1,000.

What will Lesia need to do in order to accomplish her original goal?

Solution: Lesia needs to save another $1,400 to reach her original goal ($2,400 – $1,000 she has saved = $1,400). To accomplish that goal in 12 months she will need to save $1,400 / 12 = $116.67 per month. She will have to increase her savings to $116.67 per month to accumulate $2,400 by the end of next year.

1. Establish your goals; 2. Evaluate your current financial position; 3. Identify and evaluate the options for reaching your goals; 4. Pick the best plan; 5. Evaluate your plan periodically; 6. Revise your plan as necessary.

Let's say Alicia has opted to work six Friday and Saturday nights each month to earn enough money to fund her budget and pay rent on an apartment. After several weeks of doing this, she notices that she does not make $80 every night. In fact, the average amount she makes for weekend shifts is really closer to $60. Alicia needs to reconsider her forecasts—and reconsider whether her goals are feasible. She may have to make some adjustments in her plan in order to make it work.

Step 6: Revise Your Financial Plan as Necessary

What happens when you determine your plan is unachievable or too restrictive? You need to revise it. But remember: Any revision to one part of your financial plan may impact other aspects of your plan.

✓ CHECKPOINT

What are the steps of financial decision making?

CHAPTER REVIEW

SUMMARY

- Financial decisions—and financial planning—begin with questions about cash flows. Each component of your financial plan reflects or is affected by your decisions about cash inflow and cash outflow.

- There are six steps that are critical for making financial decisions and creating your personal financial plan. (1) establish your financial goals; (2) evaluate your current financial position; (3) identify and evaluate different ways to accomplish your goals; (4) pick the best plan; (5) evaluate your plan periodically; and (6) revise your financial plan as necessary.

Key Terms and Concepts

1. What is the difference between **cash inflow** and **cash outflow**?

2. What is the difference between a **fixed expense** and a **variable expense**?

3. What is the difference between a short-term goal and a long-term goal?

What Do You Know?   MyFinLitLab

1. (a) Explain how cash inflow and outflow affects the components of your financial plan.

2. (a) What are the three different types of financial goals?

   (b) What key quality must all financial goals have?

3. (a) What is the role of forecasting in financial planning?

   (b) How does forecasting relate to one's decision about education?

4. (a) Why is it necessary to identify your current financial position before making further financial plans?

   (b) Explain why a person's current financial position might affect his or her financial plans.

5. (a) Explain how speeding progress toward a short-term goal might slow progress toward a long-term goal.

6. (a) Identify at least three different possible sources of income.

7. (a) **Comprehension** Different options are the equivalent of different roads one might follow on a map to reach the same destination. (b) **Analysis** Multiple options increase the chances that you will find one with the best combination of benefits and drawbacks for your individual situation.

8. (a) **Comprehension** Individuals with a high tolerance for risk tend to take more risks such as borrowing more money than low risk tolerance individuals. (b) **Analysis** One's willingness to accept risk or not may eliminate certain choices and options from consideration or make others seem more attractive.

9. (a) **Comprehension** When you revise one part of your plan, you must check to see how other parts of the plan have been affected. (b) **Synthesis** You might revise your plan when your goals or your circumstances change.

7. (a) Using the metaphor of a roadmap, to what feature do different options for reaching financial goals compare?

(b) What are the benefits of picking multiple options for achieving financial goals?

8. (a) What is the difference between a high and a low tolerance for risk?

(b) Explain how risk and an individual's tolerance for it can affect planning.

9. (a) What must you do when you revise one part of your financial plan?

(b) Why might you need to revise your financial plan?

Answers:
What Are Your Finance Math Skills?

1. $8 × 10 × 10 = $800. Even if she saved her entire paycheck for the 10-week period, she would not be able to save the $1,000.

2. Kage's forecast income is $9.50 × 12 × 17 = $1,938.

3. Connor needed $150 × 18 = $2,700. He has only saved $1,200, so he still needs $2,700 − $1,200 = $1,500. He has eight months to save that amount, so he will need to save $1,500 / 8 = $187.50 per month.

4. Monthly expenses will be approximately $260 to $280 per month, given that phone is $45, car payment is $140, and food (20 × 52) / 12 = $86.67. So $45 + $140 + $86.87 = $271.67.

5. It is not feasible because your income is just barely enough to make payments, with nothing left for insurance, gas, and other unforeseen expenses.

6. You can afford the video game if you cut back on food and gas spending or if you increase your income.

7. Kaden's cash inflow is roughly $288 a month (assuming a 4.5 week month): $80 × .8 × 4.5 = $288.

8. You will need to work about 12 hours—assuming no additional expenses related to working more ($1,000 / $7 = 142.86 hours / 12 = 11.9).

What Are Your Finance Math Skills?   MyFinLitLab

The first three questions correlate to *Math for Personal Finance* features located throughout the chapter.

1. Echo wants to put a $1,000 down payment on a car 10 weeks from now. She works about 10 hours per week at her current job. She brings home about $8 an hour after taxes are withdrawn from her check. Is it possible for her to save the $1,000?

2. Kage expects to work an average of 12 hours a week next semester. Assuming he makes $9.50 an hour and works the entire 17-week semester, what is his forecast for income next semester?

3. Connor intended to save $150 a month for the next 18 months to purchase a fishing boat. However, after 10 months he has only managed to save $1,200. What will Connor need to do in order to accomplish his original goal?

4. Assume your phone bill averages $45 a month and you have a car payment that is $140 per month. You also spend about $20 a week on food. How much are your monthly expenses?

5. You make $50 a week and you want to buy a car with an expected payment of $200 a month. Is that a feasible goal?

6. Can you afford to buy a $50 video game every month if you make $40 a week and spend an average of $150 a month on food and gasoline?

7. How much is Kaden's monthly cash inflow if he earns $80 a week but about 20% is withdrawn from his check for taxes?

8. If you want to increase your income next year by $1,000, how many additional hours will you need to work per month if you make $7 an hour?

What Would You Do?

Dennis has decided on a car to purchase. He has a financial plan that he put together in his economics class. During that class, Dennis decided that a car purchase would need to wait until he had enough in his savings account for a good down payment.

Gregory, Dennis' friend, is going to sell his car so that he can go to trade school after high school. Dennis has always liked Gregory's car. He knows it is in good condition because Gregory is planning to become a mechanic after trade school and always works on his car.

Dennis is faced with a problem. He does not have the money in his savings to pay what Gregory is asking. He is also thinking of his financial plan. Is this really the time to purchase a car, even a great car like Gregory's? If he purchases the car, he will have to ask his parents for a loan to help him pay for it.

1. If you were in Dennis' place, what would you do?

2. Where could Dennis go to get a loan? What considerations should he make when thinking about a loan?

3. Should Dennis follow his financial plan or revise it? What should he do to help him make this decision?

What Are the Connections? Science and Technology

Think about a purchase you want to make, or an event you want to attend in the next few months. This might be an MP3 player, a new audio system for your car, or a day at a spa that includes a new hair style, nails (manicure and pedicure), and a massage. It might be tickets to see your favorite group or team. How will you make a decision about what to purchase? How will you pay for it? What steps do you need to take to help you make this decision?

Develop a flowchart that shows what steps you will take in your decision-making process. You could use poster board to display your flowchart or you could use a software program to help you design your flowchart. Be sure to think about all the decisions and events that will be needed to get to the "finish line"—that final purchase or event you want to attend. Include steps for evaluating progress along the way—with options for responding depending on your progress toward your goal.

Teamwork Service-Learning Activity

As a team, develop a public service announcement (PSA) about the steps involved in good financial decision making. A PSA is an audio or video presentation that brings awareness to the public. This one should tell the importance of financial planning for teens. Think about what you have learned in this chapter.

For your PSA, you should work together to write and perform a simple skit or presentation that helps others understand the process you have read about in this chapter 3. You can present your PSA live or in audio or video format.

ESSENTIAL QUESTION ACTIVITIES

Complete these activities to answer this chapter's Essential Question: *What is involved in financial decision making?*

1. *On your own:* This chapter has outlined the steps for making financial decisions. Using the example in Figure 3.2, develop a chart that is similar to help you begin planning for your future after graduation. This may include saving for college, buying a car, or getting a job. Using paper, spreadsheet software, or a poster, make two columns and label each accordingly: "A Plan for:" and "Types of Decisions." Think about the six steps that were discussed in this chapter as you begin developing your financial plan.

2. *As a class:* Brainstorm each step in financial planning. Some questions you might want to ask: What decisions do you need to make at each step? What might happen to change your financial plans along the way?

MyFinLitLab TEST PREP QUESTIONS

1. a
1. The best description of cash inflow is money
   a. received from different sources, such as salary and interest earned on bank accounts.
   b. spent for items that must be included in a budget, such as rent and utilities.
   c. invested in financial products, such as stocks and bonds.
   d. left after paying for items included in a financial plan.

2. c
2. A person's cash outflow includes
   a. liquid assets a person has accumulated.
   b. money spent by a company to pay a person's salary.
   c. payments by a person to a retirement account.
   d. the difference between the asking price of two houses for sale in the same neighborhood.

3. c
3. Which is the correct order for making financial decisions?
   a. Put goals in writing, rethink goals if necessary, have a plan of action, set specific goals.
   b. Be realistic about goals, put goals in writing, implement goals, have specific goals.
   c. Set specific goals, put goals in writing, have a plan of action, rethink goals if necessary.
   d. Have a plan of action, set specific goals, implement goals, put goals in writing.

4. Which is a true statement about goals? 4. b
   a. A person should only work on one goal at a time.
   b. Intermediate-term goals are those that can be accomplished in one to five years.
   c. A person should accomplish short-term goals before starting on any other goals.
   d. A short-term goal should be tied to a long-term goal.

5. Which one of the following does *not* show a correct match? 5. b
   a. Cash inflow: scholarship award
   b. Cash inflow: interest paid on a loan
   c. Cash outflow: insurance premiums
   d. Cash outflow: tuition

6. A high school student starts a lawn mowing business. His riding lawn mower cost $1,000; gas for the season is $2,000. He spends $500 for gas driving to and from jobs, $300 for supplies and repairs, and $200 for a trimmer. Each of his 20 customers pays $40 a week for a 20-week season. What is the outcome of this business venture? 6. a
   a. He makes a $12,000 profit.
   b. He makes a $4,000 profit.
   c. He has an $8,000 total cash inflow.
   d. He has a $4,000 total cash inflow.

7. A financial plan should 7. b
   a. be followed as it is written until the goals set in the plan are achieved.
   b. be evaluated periodically and revised as needed.
   c. only be revised when a person's job changes.
   d. remain the same unless a person changes financial goals.

8. Which of the following is a correct statement? 8. a
   a. If cash inflow exceeds cash outflow, a person has a surplus to save or invest.
   b. An expense is considered a cash inflow.
   c. Fixed expenses should be paid before variable expenses.
   d. Cash outflow can be reduced by buying everything on credit.

CHAPTER 4

ESSENTIAL QUESTION

Why is a budget such a key component of the financial plan?

BUDGETS AND BALANCE SHEETS
YOUR PERSONAL FINANCIAL STATEMENTS

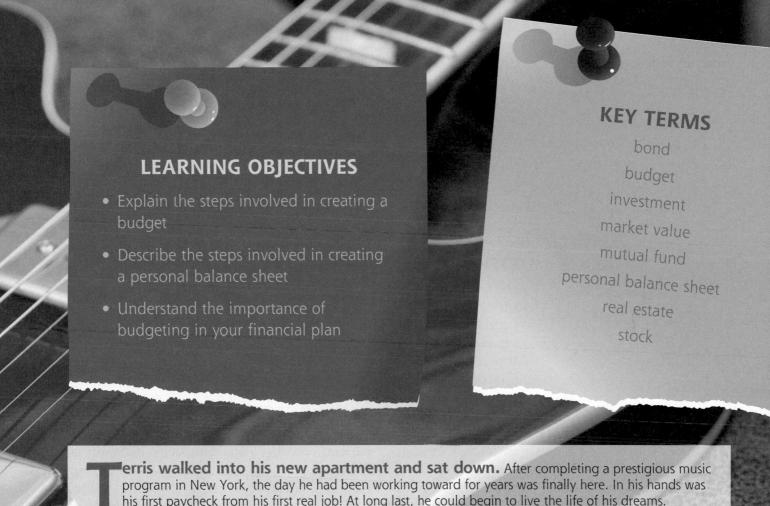

LEARNING OBJECTIVES

- Explain the steps involved in creating a budget

- Describe the steps involved in creating a personal balance sheet

- Understand the importance of budgeting in your financial plan

KEY TERMS

bond

budget

investment

market value

mutual fund

personal balance sheet

real estate

stock

Terris walked into his new apartment and sat down. After completing a prestigious music program in New York, the day he had been working toward for years was finally here. In his hands was his first paycheck from his first real job! At long last, he could begin to live the life of his dreams.

Immediately he began to think about the purchases he had been putting off for so long—a new car, a laptop, some nice clothes. Maybe he could buy season tickets for baseball or a new stereo system. Or perhaps he could finally make good on his promise to his friend Martin to take that road trip to Chicago. Now he had the income to afford these things—or, at least, to pay off his credit card bills.

Just as he was getting excited, Terris seemed to hear a small voice in his head. It was his grandfather. "Use your head, Terris," he could almost hear him say. "Be sure to put something away for a rainy day!"

Terris sighed. He realized he probably could not afford to get all the things he wanted right away. He also knew he had to think about more than just spending his new paycheck. At the same time, he was ready to treat himself. He had worked hard to get to this point, and he felt he deserved to enjoy the rewards.

Terris's situation is one in which you may find yourself one day. He is anxious to begin living his life as a working adult. But what he needs to do, he realizes, is to sit down and look at where he is financially—and where he wants to go. In other words, Terris needs to make a budget and a personal balance sheet.

CREATING A BUDGET

budget: A forecast of future cash inflows and outflows.

Creating a budget is a key part of your financial plan. A **budget** is a forecast of future cash inflows and outflows. Once you have identified your personal goals, you need some specific plans about how to reach those goals. Your household budget provides that guidance. It gives you a detailed roadmap to your financial future.

Think about Terris's goals. He wants to pay off his credit cards, save some money for a rainy day, and treat himself to a few things he wants. Can he accomplish all those goals? If he plans well and doesn't attempt to do all of them at once, he can achieve his goals. A budget will be his detailed plan of action for the next several years.

Activity #1

STEP 1: Create a Personal Cash Flow Statement

The first step in the budgeting process is to identify your current cash inflows and outflows. The primary cash inflow for most people is their salary, hourly wages, or any money they earn. However, some people may have income from savings accounts or other similar sources. Others may receive an allowance of some type. In addition, if you receive money from a scholarship, that is income, too. Any money that you have coming in is a cash inflow.

Your cash outflows are any money that you have going out. Expenses such as car payments or insurance premiums are cash outflows. At some point you may begin paying rent and utilities or your cell phone bill. These are all cash outflows. Cash outflows are typically impacted by family size, age, and your personal spending habits.

Activity #2

Your personal cash flow statement records cash inflows and outflows. This allows you to easily track where your money comes from and where it goes. Check out Figure 4.1 to see where Terris's money has gone in the past two months.

FIGURE 4.1 Terris's Personal Cash Flow Statement

A personal cash flow statement compares cash inflows to cash outflows and is the first step in creating a budget.

Cash Inflows	January	February
Disposable (after-tax) income	$2,500	$2,500
Interest on deposits	0	0
Income from investments	0	0
Total Cash Inflows	**$2,500**	**$2,500**

Cash Outflows	January	February
Rent	$600	$600
Cable TV	50	50
Electricity and water	60	60
Telephone	60	60
Groceries	300	300
Health care insurance and expenses	130	430
Clothing	100	100
Car expenses (insurance, maintenance, and gas)	200	500
Recreation	600	600
Total Cash Outflows	**$2,100**	**$2,700**
Net Cash Flows	**+ $400**	**−$200**

STEP 2: Turn Your Cash Flow Statement into a Budget

The next step is to turn your personal cash flow statement into a budget. To do this, you must forecast your net cash flows for a period of time into the future. A good budget should cover anticipated cash inflows and outflows for several months to a year or more.

As you work on this step, it's important to think about how your cash flows might change from month to month. Will you spend more money at certain times of the year, or are your cash flows similar from month to month? What about the holiday seasons? Be sure that you consider expected but irregular expenses. Examples include activity fees for school functions or money for your spring break activities. A yearly vacation is another example of an expense that will not show up in the typical month.

Indeed, many people find that expenses occur unexpectedly. Car breakdowns or medical emergencies are unpredictable—but, unfortunately, nearly certain to strike at some point. What happens when you are at college and you unexpectedly need to return home for a weekend? Who will pay for the gas? At other times an opportunity may arise for you to take a ski trip or go to a concert with friends. A good budget will force you to set

Who will pay for gas? Good planning can make it possible for you to meet unexpected expenses.

aside money to take care of unexpected expenses and to take advantage of unexpected opportunities.

Taking your personal cash flow statement and turning it into a budget for an entire year involves some guesswork and estimating. Obviously, you cannot plan the precise cost of events or expenses that have not occurred yet. Don't worry. You can always go back and adjust the budget as you get more information. This annual budget can help you identify times when you can save money and times when you will have more outflows than inflows.

Look at Figure 4.2. When should Terris be saving?

Working with and Improving Your Budget

By now you can see that a budget is a great planning tool. A budget can help you save money for major purchases, unexpected expenses, and unexpected opportunities. After all, you don't want to be broke when

FIGURE 4.2 Terris's Annual Budget

An annual budget projects inflows and outflows for an entire year and should help ensure that you have adequate net cash flows.

Cash Inflows	Typical Month	This Year's Cash Flows (equal to the typical monthly cash flows × 12)
Disposable (after-tax) income	$2,500	$30,000
Interest on deposits	0	0
Income from investments	0	0
Total Cash Inflows	**$2,500**	**$30,000**
Cash Outflows	**Typical Month**	**This Year's Cash Flows**
Rent	$600	$7,200
Cable TV	50	600
Electricity and water	60	720
Telephone	60	720
Groceries	300	3,600
Health care insurance and expenses	130	1,560
Clothing	100	1,200
Car expenses (insurance, maintenance, and gas)	200	2,400
Recreation	500	6,000
Charitable giving	100	1,200
Total Cash Outflows	**$2,100**	**$25,200**
Net Cash Flows	**+$400**	**$4,800 (difference between cash inflows and outflows)**

someone offers you a month's stay in Europe if you will just buy the plane ticket.

Indeed, one of the primary benefits of your budget is that it will help you anticipate future cash shortfalls. For example, think about Terris's situation. He is earning a good, steady income now. But he also needs to be thinking about some significant expenses. For example, in Figure 4.1 you can see that Terris spent only $200 on his car in January but he spent $500 on it in February. His car is old and it was due for its annual inspection. He had known there were several things wrong that he'd need to fix—at the cost of several hundred dollars. A budget will help him plan for those expected outflows and save money to cover the unexpected outflows that happen as well.

Sure, it may be tempting for him to satisfy all his desires at once— perhaps by continuing to overuse his credit card. However, this is a risky path that leads many people into financial disaster. With a good budget, Terris can meet his wants and needs without a costly and unwise dependence on credit.

As you gather new information— and perhaps identify new expenses—you should adjust your budget.

Assessing the Accuracy of the Budget

One of the things you need to do is periodically evaluate your forecasts and compare those with the actual cash flows. It's a good idea to look at last month's forecasts or the last three months' forecasts and compare those with actual numbers.

The best way to know exactly how you spend your money is to keep an expense journal. Write down every nickel you spend during the course of a week or a month. It might really surprise you where your money is going. Sometimes you will find that you underestimated your cash outflows or were too optimistic regarding your cash inflows. The difference between what you forecast to happen and what actually happens is known as **forecast error**. After you look at your forecast error, you may find that you need to adjust your spending. If you continue to come up short of money at the end of each month, you need to increase your income or decrease your outflow. Let's look at Terris's summary data for the last three months in Figure 4.3. Should he take any action?

Terris obviously needs to revisit his budget. His forecasts are not matching up with reality. He needs to increase his income or decrease his outflow. Review the details in Figure 4.1. What are some ways Terris could reduce his outflows?

Step 1: Creating a personal cash flow statement. Step 2: Turning a cash flow statement into a budget. Step 3: Working with and improving your budget.

FIGURE 4.3 Terris's Actual Versus Forecast Cash Flows (Three-Month Period)

It is easy to make forecasting errors, and you should be thorough in checking that your actual and forecast cash flows match.

	Forecast	Actual
Cash Inflows	$7,500	$7,500
Cash Outflows	6,300	7,400
Net Cash Flows	1,200	100

 CHECKPOINT

What are the steps involved in creating a budget?

CREATING A PERSONAL BALANCE SHEET

A budget helps ensure that you have a positive net cash flow. But what will you do with the cash you have left over? One of the tools you can use to help you make that decision is a personal balance sheet. While the budget tracks our cash flows over time, the **personal balance sheet** tells us our financial position at a point in time. The personal balance sheet is a summary of our assets (what we own, such as a car or cash in the bank), our liabilities (money we owe, such as a personal loan we need to pay back or a car loan), and our net worth (assets minus liabilities). Your personal balance sheet is what you use to keep track of your overall wealth—your net worth.

> **personal balance sheet:** A financial statement that tells your financial position at a specific point in time.

Having a good picture of your net worth is essential for financial planning. Knowing where you stand will help you decide how to manage your liquidity, your credit and borrowing, your investments, and more.

Assets

Assets are items of value that a person owns, and they can be classified in several ways. Typical asset categories are liquid assets, household assets, and investments. While many of you may not have assets in all of these categories, at some point in the future you will if you apply the tools learned in this text.

Liquid Assets

Liquid assets are financial assets that are either cash or can be quickly and easily converted to cash without significant loss of value. What does this mean? Every asset can be converted to cash, but some may require that you drop the price to sell it quickly. A house, for example, may be worth a lot of money, but it may take months to sell it at its full value. However, liquid assets can be turned into cash in a hurry without dropping the price. Liquid assets include money in checking and savings accounts.

Liquid assets are necessary for covering unexpected emergency expenses. When we talk about money management we are referring to liquid assets.

While the key quality of liquid assets is quick availability, it's also important that liquid assets be making money—that is, earning interest. For this reason, it's common to keep liquid assets in an interest-bearing checking or savings account.

Household Assets

Another type of asset is **household assets**. These include those assets typically owned by a household—for example, cars, houses, and furniture. In general, household assets will make up a larger proportion of a person's balance sheet than liquid assets.

When you create your personal balance sheet you will need to evaluate the true market value of your household assets realistically. The **market value** of something is what it would be worth if you sold it today. While you may have paid $12,000 for a car two years ago, it may only be worth

Finance ONLINE

Each year *Forbes* magazine lists the top 100 billionaires in America. Some who have appeared in this list include

- **Bill Gates** with over $59 billion,
- **Warren Buffett** with over $36 billion,
- **Sheldon Adelson** with over $21.5 billion, and
- **Alice Walton** with over $20.9 billion.

Go to **www.forbes.com** to see the complete list. Research two of these billionaires and see how they got their start toward building their fortunes.

> **market value:** What something would be worth if you sold it today.

$6,000 today. You should list the value of the car as $6,000 in this case. A guide to car market values can be found on a number of Web sites, such as Kelley Blue Book (www.kbb.com). House values may be harder to find, but you can estimate those based on what similar houses have sold for in your neighborhood recently. Various Internet sites, such as eBay, may be the best source of values for your other possessions.

Investments

Investments are the third major category of assets. An **investment** is something you acquire with the ultimate goal of making money. That is, an investment is something you buy that you believe will actually increase in value over time. Some of the more common investment assets are stocks, bonds, and real estate. Some people invest in collectibles, but they are much harder to evaluate and require very specialized knowledge.

Bonds are basically certificates that function like IOUs—promises to repay a certain amount of money at some future time. For example, a company or government decides to issue a series of bonds valued at $1,000 each. An investor agrees to buy one of these bonds by giving $1,000 to the bond issuer. In return, the bond issuer agrees to pay interest to the owner of the bond, and also to repay the original $1,000 at some point in the future. So, when you buy the bond, you are essentially loaning the issuer money. The issuer will pay you interest until the maturity date and at that time they will pay back the $1,000. People buy bonds with the expectation of receiving interest income while they hold the bond and getting their money back when the bond matures. However, bond issuers are not always able to pay interest or even to return the original investment. For this reason, investing in bonds involves some risk.

Perhaps some of you have Series EE savings bonds issued by the U.S. government. This type of bond is somewhat different from the bonds described above. Savings bonds do not pay interest while you hold the bond. Instead, they accrue interest and increase in value.

Prof. FIN

In a survey by Bankrate.com, many people in the United States have more debt than they have savings. Here are some findings from this survey:

- Forty percent of Americans earning less than $30,000 have more credit card debt than savings.

- Forty-six percent of Americans with a high school education or less have more credit card debt than savings.

Compare this to these findings:

- Seventy percent of Americans earning more than $75,000 have more in savings than credit card debt.

- Sixty-four percent of college graduates have more in savings than in credit card debt.

How much savings do you have? Do a simple survey of your classmates. Ask how many have savings accounts. Also, ask how many have credit cards in their name. For those who have credit cards in their name, ask how many are at their credit limit. Conduct this survey properly by not gathering any names or personal information and present your findings in a spreadsheet.

Source: lifeinc.today.msnbc.msn.com/_news/2012/02/21/10468068-one-in-four-americans-has-more-debt-than-savings

stocks: Certificates that represent fractional ownership of a firm.

mutual funds: Professionally managed investments that allow investors to pool their money in order to invest in a larger variety of financial assets such as stocks and bonds from many different companies.

MATH for Personal Finance

Emily owns 50 shares of Company Y's stock that is currently selling for $170 a share. She also owns 65 shares of Company Z's stock worth about $47 a share.

What is the total value of her stock holdings?

Solution:

Company Y
50 × $170 = $8,500

Company Z
65 × $47 = $3,055
Total = $11,555

real estate: Homes, rental property, farms, and other land.

Making purchases with credit cards that you cannot pay off quickly is a bad move.

Stocks are certificates that represent fractional ownership of a firm. For example, you could start a business and sell ownership fractions to 100 different people. Each share of ownership would represent 1% of the business and would be called a share of stock. Most firms have millions of shares outstanding, so one share of stock is usually a very small fraction of ownership in that company. People buy stocks with the expectation that the company will do well and the value of the stock will increase. As with bonds, however, there is some risk. It's possible that the value of the stock will decline or even disappear entirely.

Mutual funds are created so investors can pool their money in order to invest in a larger variety of financial assets, such as stocks and bonds from many different companies. Mutual funds are managed by professional portfolio managers who decide which stocks and/or bonds to purchase. Therefore, individual investors who buy shares in the fund do not have to be experts in stock or bond selection. Most mutual funds require a minimum investment that typically ranges between $500 and $3,000. With mutual funds, the risk of loss is generally spread across many different investments. So, even if one or two of the fund's stock or bond investments collapse, the fund itself may decline only a little. This can help protect an investor from a severe drop in the value of an investment. Still, mutual fund investments can and sometimes do lose their value.

Mutual funds can be used for a variety of purposes. One such use is a Section 529 College Savings Plan. Parents, grandparents, or other relatives can open 529 plans for their children and make contributions designed to be used for education. The plans help investors avoid some taxes on the earnings and withdrawals from the plans. Mutual funds are commonly used as investments for 529s.

Real estate includes homes, rental property, farms, and other land. Rental property includes houses or commercial property that is rented out to others. Some people buy timberland or farms with the expectation that it will generate revenue over time and also increase in value.

Liabilities

Liabilities represent the amount of debt a person owes. These debts can be split into two categories: current liabilities and long-term liabilities.

Current liabilities are debts that must be paid off within one year. Credit card balances are the most common form of a current liability for individuals. When you charge something on your credit card, you will be billed for those charges during the next billing cycle. In other words, when used properly, a credit card acts like a short-term loan that should be paid off every month. When you pay that credit card bill, you are eliminating that current liability.

Long-term liabilities are debts that will take longer than one year to pay off. Student loans, car loans, and home mortgages are common examples of long-term liabilities. Each payment you make contains an interest component and some amount that will reduce the initial liability (the principal). After making all the required payments on time, the long-term liability is eliminated.

Note that many people use credit cards in a way that creates a long-term liability. They make purchases with their cards that they cannot pay off quickly. As a result, they pay interest on their debt and reduce their liability by only a very small portion every month. In general, using credit cards to create a long-term liability is a bad move. The interest rates charged on most credit cards far exceeds the interest rate individuals could get at a bank or credit union for long-term financing. It is much better to pursue other kinds of financing, such as bank loans, for long-term liabilities.

Net Worth

Net worth is the difference between your assets and your liabilities.

Net worth = Value of your total assets – the sum of your total liabilities

To put it another way, if you sold all of your assets today and paid off your debt (liabilities), the remaining amount would be your net worth. Some people find that they have a negative net worth and may be on the verge of bankruptcy.

Figuring your net worth is an easy way to measure your wealth. It makes it easy to track your wealth over time. The way you figure your net worth is with a personal balance sheet. You can see an example in Figure 4.4. How much is Terris worth?

Changes in Your Personal Balance Sheet

Your personal balance sheet changes as you acquire new assets and/or new liabilities. If you spend all your income on living expenses, your balance sheet will remain the same. However, if you run up your credit card debt and do not pay off the balance at the end of the month, your net worth will decline. If you save some money, your net worth will increase. You can increase your net worth in two ways. One way requires that the value of your assets increases by more than the value of your liabilities. For example, you may buy stock that increases in value. As long as you maintain the same level of debt, your net worth will increase. The other way is to pay down debt on your assets that hold their value.

FIGURE 4.4 Terris's Personal Balance Sheet

A personal balance sheet gives you a quick assessment of where you stand financially at a specific point in time.

Assets

Cash	$3,200
Car	4,000
Musical instruments	5,500
Furniture	1,200
Total Assets	**$13,900**

Current Liabilities

Student loan	$2,500	
Credit card balance	3,000	
Total Current Liabilities		**$5,500**
Net Worth ($13,900 – $5,500)		**$8,400**

Analysis of Your Personal Balance Sheet

What do lenders look at before they make a loan? They want to see if you can make the payments. One of the tools they use is your personal balance sheet. Loan officers often use a debt-to-asset ratio to determine whether you have borrowed too much money. For this reason alone, you should pay careful attention to your personal balance sheet. Keeping it in good shape can influence the options you have for making financial decisions and constructing a healthy financial plan. Look again at Figure 4.4. You can see that Terris's debt-to-asset ratio is $5,500/$13,900 = 39.5%. Remember, this particular ratio is often used by lenders to determine whether you have enough wealth to repay debt. According to a lender, lower is always better.

YOU DO IT

Activity #3

You need to identify and then add up all of your assets and all of your liabilities. You then subtract the total of your liabilities from the total of your assets to determine your net worth.

✓ CHECKPOINT

What are the steps in creating a personal balance sheet?

BUDGETING AND YOUR FINANCIAL PLAN

YOU DO IT

Activity #4

Your cash flows obviously feed into your personal balance sheet. If your cash inflows exceed your cash outflows, you will either increase assets or reduce liabilities. This will show up on your balance sheet in the form of increased net worth (see Figure 4.5). The personal balance sheet is basically a scorecard. It tells you how much your level of wealth is changing, and it gives you information you can use when building your financial plan.

Budgeting helps in financial planning because it forces you to evaluate your current financial condition and also helps you answer the following questions:

- How can I improve my net cash flows in the near term?
- How can I improve my net cash flows in the long term?
- What decisions should I make about using credit, borrowing, and investing?

An evaluation of your budget might identify places where you can reduce outflows or places where you can increase cash inflows. Either of these actions will help create wealth.

FIGURE 4.5 Relationship Between Your Cash Flows and Balance Sheet

When your cash inflows are greater than your outflows, you increase your net worth.

Budgeting helps you evaluate your current financial condition and determine how to improve net cash flows and make wise credit, borrowing, and investment decisions.

✓ CHECKPOINT

What is the importance of budgeting to your financial plan?

CHAPTER REVIEW

SUMMARY

- The budgeting process allows you to monitor and control cash inflows and outflows. By examining the difference between your forecast and your actual cash inflows and outflows, you can anticipate future problems and make adjustments in your budget that will help you reach your financial goals.

- Your personal balance sheet tells you your financial position at a point in time. It is a summary of your assets, your liabilities, and your net worth. Assets can be listed as liquid assets, household assets, and investments. Liabilities represent the amount of debt you owe and can be split into two categories: current liabilities and long-term liabilities.

- Budgeting can help you manage your cash flows to increase your net worth, which you can use in building a financial plan.

Key Terms and Concepts

1. What is a forecast error?

2. What is the difference in liquid assets, household assets, and investments?

3. What is the difference between current liabilities and long-term liabilities?

What Do You Know?   MyFinLitLab

1. (a) What is the purpose of a budget?

   (b) How can a budget help when you are anticipating cash shortages or a cash surplus?

2. (a) How do you assess the accuracy of your budget?

   (b) How can finding forecasting errors improve your budget?

3. (a) Describe the process of creating an annual budget.

4. (a) Suppose you want to change your budget to increase your savings. Explain what you could do.

5. (a) What is the purpose of a personal balance sheet?

   (b) How can a personal balance sheet help you when you are making financial decisions?

6. (a) Briefly define and give examples of each category of asset.

   (b) Why do you think stocks are not considered liquid assets?

Answers:
Key Terms and Concepts

1. It is the difference between an actual value and the predicted value for a certain variable.

2. Liquid assets are those assets that can be easily converted to cash without a significant loss in value. Household assets are assets that are typically owned by a household—for example, cars, houses, and furniture. Investments are assets you acquire with the ultimate goal of making money.

3. Current liabilities are debts you owe that are due within the next twelve months; long-term liabilities are debts you owe that will take longer than one year to pay off.

Answers:
What Do You Know?

1. (a) **Comprehension** A budget helps you forecast future inflows and outflows. It provides a plan of action for achieving financial goals. (b) **Application** It helps ensure that there is money available to meet unexpected or unplanned shortfalls.

2. (a) **Application** You check the accuracy of your budget by keeping an expense journal to see if your forecasts match reality. (b) **Analysis** By finding and eliminating forecast errors, you can create a more accurate budget and adjust your cash inflows or outflows as necessary.

3. (a) **Comprehension** First you must create a cash-flow statement. Next, you use that information to forecast inflows and outflows for a full year. Then you assess the accuracy of your budget and revise it as necessary.

4. (a) **Synthesis** Possible answer: You could cut expenses somewhere or find ways to increase your income.

5. (a) **Comprehension** A personal balance sheet helps you identify your financial situation at a given point in time. (b) **Application** By knowing where you are financially, you are better able to make decisions about how to get where you want to be.

6. (a) **Comprehension** An example of a liquid asset is cash in your wallet; an example of a household asset is a car; and an example of an investment is a bond. (b) **Analysis** It is not possible to convert stock into cash quickly without risking a significant loss.

7. (a) **Knowledge** Bonds are like IOUs—promises to repay a debt, with interest, at some point in the future. (b) **Knowledge** Stocks represent partial ownership in a company. (c) **Knowledge** Mutual funds are professionally managed collections of multiple investments, of which investors can own shares. (d) **Evaluation** Bonds return by paying interest on the principle invested. Stocks provide a return if the company performs well and increases in value (and some may pay dividends). Mutual funds can increase or decrease in value depending on the performance of the investments they hold.

8. (a) **Knowledge** A current liability includes a credit card bill and a long-term liability includes a loan that is payable over many years. (b) **Application** Failure to pay a credit card bill can convert a current liability into a long-term liability.

9. (a) **Synthesis** Net worth identifies what your assets are worth after all your liabilities have been satisfied and therefore provides a snapshot of your total wealth.

10. (a) **Comprehension** Net worth increases as you increase your assets or decrease your liabilities. (b) **Evaluation** Purchasing assets will not increase your net worth if you incur liabilities—that is, take loans—to make the purchase.

Answers:
What Are Your Finance Math Skills?

1. Your net worth increases by $1,000, to $3,650.

2. Your net worth increases by $750, to $3,400.

3. You have no money available to save and you are forecasting a cash shortfall.

4. $20 × $112 = $2,240

5. $3,700 + $578 + $2,100 = $6,378

6. $3,100 + $400 = $3,500

7. 100 shares of Apple Inc. × $536 = $53,600
40 shares of Ford Motor Company × $9.85 = $394
$53,600 + $394 = $53,994

8. ($4,000 − $1,500) + $500 + $350 = $3,350

---

7. (a) What are bonds?

   (b) What are stocks?

   (c) What are mutual funds?

   (d) Describe how each of these provides a return on your investment.

8. (a) Give an example of a current liability and a long-term liability.

   (b) What's an example of how a current liability can be converted into a long-term liability?

9. (a) Explain how net worth is a measure of wealth.

10. (a) Describe how your net worth increases.

    (b) Will the purchase of additional assets always increase your net worth? Why or why not?

What Are Your Finance Math Skills? MyFinLitLab

The first three questions correlate to *Math for Personal Finance* features located throughout the chapter.

1. Let's assume your net worth is currently $2,650. What happens to it if you get a $1,000 gift from your grandparents?

2. In the previous problem, what happens to your net worth if you spend $250 of the gift and save the remainder?

3. According to your budget forecast you will have expenses of $1,200 next month and income of $800. How much do you have available to save?

4. What is the value of Stephanie's stock holdings if she owns 20 shares of a company that are worth $112 each?

5. What is the value of your total assets if you own stocks worth $3,700, have $578 in a savings account, and own a motorcycle valued at $2,100?

6. Michael has $3,100 in his savings account, $400 in his checking account, and owns a truck worth $2,300. How much does he have in liquid assets?

7. Kevin's grandfather left him 100 shares of Apple Inc. and 40 shares of Ford Motor Company. How much is his stock worth, assuming Apple sells for $536 a share and Ford sells for $9.85 a share?

8. Jawanda's car is worth about $4,000 and she owes $1,500 on it. She also has a sound system valued at $500 and $350 in her checking account. What is her net worth?

What Would You Do?

Dani is applying for a loan so that she can purchase a new car. On her application, she is asked to write down the value of the assets she owns. She does not have many items of value—except for a custom-made guitar her parents bought for her when she was in high school. She does not know the value of the instrument, but she knows it originally cost $2,000—and that fine instruments often increase in value. She also knows that the greater the value of the instrument, the better her chances are to be approved for a loan. She is tempted to put down the value of the guitar at $5,000.

1. If you were in Dani's place, what would you do?
2. What might happen if Dani gives an inflated value for the guitar?
3. How might Dani solve this problem?

What Are the Connections? Math and Technology

Record your expenses for one month. What did you purchase? How many times did you buy gas? Did you eat out? What extra purchases or expenses did you have this month? Were any of those expenses unexpected?

Make a spreadsheet that lists all the expenses you had for the month. Continue to design the spreadsheet to show expenses that have occurred and plan for those you might have for the next two months. How much money will you need to cover the expenses for the next two months? Have you planned for unexpected expenses? How can you plan for the unexpected?

Teamwork

In a team, develop a budget for a Volunteer Day luncheon and ceremony. Your Volunteer Day will be designed to thank the parents/community who have helped at your school throughout the year. The budget needs to include the following:

- Funds for printing handouts about the Volunteer Day
- Lunch for 25 people
- Certificates or small thank-you gifts for the school volunteers
- Any other items you think might be needed to make the day a success

Write a proposal to the administration of your school requesting that your organization be allowed to have a Volunteer Day. Be sure you include in your proposal the date of the event, how you are going to get the word out about the day, and the importance of having such a day. Include your budget with your proposal.

MyFinLitLab TEST PREP QUESTIONS

1. a **1.** Creating a cash flow statement is a good way for a person to determine how much money the person
   a. receives from various sources over the course of a month.
   b. has left at the end of the year to buy holiday presents.
   c. actually spent on food this year.
   d. needs to pay for medical expenses each month this year.

2. d **2.** Which is a true statement about a budget?
   a. A budget should remain the same from month to month.
   b. A person's budget should be the same as other people with the same income.
   c. When a person spends more than he has budgeted, he should reduce his cash inflow.
   d. A budget should include both fixed and variable expenses.

3. d **3.** A personal balance sheet
   a. shows how much is available each month to pay for necessities.
   b. shows how much money a person has available for savings.
   c. is used to determine if a person's budget is realistic.
   d. is a picture of a person's financial well-being at a point in time.

4. b **4.** Which asset is correctly matched with its description?
   a. House: liquid asset.
   b. Car: household asset.
   c. Mutual fund: liquid asset.
   d. Checking account: investment asset.

5. d **5.** The purpose of investing money is to
   a. increase a person's net worth each month.
   b. qualify for a low interest rate bank mortgage.
   c. pay for car loans, credit card balances and other monthly debt.
   d. have an asset that will increase in value over time.

6. When a person applies for a loan, the lender will review the person's balance sheet in order to find out if he
   6. a
   a. has enough assets to cover both current liabilities as well as the debt created by the new loan.
   b. is following his monthly budget.
   c. has made good investments in stocks and bonds over the time he has been employed.
   d. will be able to pay back the loan within three years.

7. How does a person determine her net worth?
   7. c
   a. Subtract investments from cash inflow.
   b. Add interest earned on investments to salary.
   c. Subtract liabilities from assets.
   d. Add cash outflow to savings.

8. Which of the following shows, in the correct order, the steps a person should take to organize his financial life?
   8. b
   a. Create a financial plan, determine net worth, establish financial goals.
   b. Create a personal cash flow statement, create a budget, develop a personal balance sheet.
   c. Establish financial goals, create a personal balance sheet, create a personal cash flow statement.
   d. Determine net worth, create a personal cash flow statement, create a budget.

UNIT

2

Income & Careers

CHAPTER 5

ESSENTIAL QUESTION

What is involved in choosing a career and applying for a job in that career path?

CAREERS AND EDUCATION

LEARNING OBJECTIVES

- Explain the process for choosing a career path

- Identify different sources of information for researching careers

- Discuss how one can gain the skills needed for a career choice

- Describe the process of applying for a job

KEY TERMS

accreditation

apprenticeship

certification

compensation

internship

résumé

Logan grabbed another heavy box and lifted it onto the conveyer belt. He liked his part-time job unloading trucks because it gave him time to think and he got paid to work out. He also knew that unloading trucks did not fit into his long-term plan. It was all right for now, but he could see that it was not the career he wanted.

Although Logan knew he did not want to unload trucks forever, he was really not sure what he wanted to do with his life. His older brother, Daniel, who was a diesel mechanic, had gone to vocational school. Daniel was paid pretty well and really liked his job, but he came home covered in grease and oil—something that did not appeal to Logan. Their mom and dad were both high school teachers. But the thought of dealing with a roomful of rowdy teenagers did not appeal to Logan either.

Logan knew that he wanted a job in a cleaner environment than where Daniel worked and one that paid good money and did not involve teaching. Beyond that, he had few firm ideas. He made a mental note to visit with the high school counselor about his options. He would be a senior next year and was feeling a little uneasy about what to do with the rest of his life.

Like Logan, you may be trying to decide on a career path. You have probably noticed that some people really enjoy their work and others don't. Your working life occupies a substantial amount of your time, so you should strive to find a job that you enjoy. In addition, the career you choose will play a major role in your financial future because your choice will affect how much income you earn. It may dictate how much education or training you need to get—and pay for. Deciding on the best career path requires some research and careful consideration. However, keep in mind you are not locked in to a career for life. Many people change careers several times during their working years.

Prof. FIN

Here and throughout this chapter is information about major career clusters. You can use this information to help you investigate different careers.

Agriculture, Food & Natural Resources	The production, processing, marketing, distribution, financing, and development of agricultural commodities and resources, including food, fiber, wood products, natural resources, horticulture, and other plant and animal products/resources.
Architecture & Construction	Careers in designing, planning, managing, building, and maintaining the built environment.
Arts, A/V Technology & Communications	Designing, producing, exhibiting, performing, writing, and publishing multimedia content, including visual and performing arts and design, journalism, and entertainment services.

Source: www.careerclusters.org

Finance **ONLINE**

For information on the fastest growing occupations and the occupations projected to have the largest increases in employment between 2010 and 2020, see the *Occupational Outlook Handbook*—**www.bls .gov/oco/home.htm**.

DETERMINING A CAREER PATH

Perhaps the best way to start the process of determining a career path is to identify your areas of interest. Make a list of the things you enjoy doing. Logan began this process when he thought about his brother, his parents, and what he liked and disliked about his own job. Once you have listed your interests, try to identify various careers that involve those activities and interests. Later in this chapter, in the section "Sources of Career Information," you will find some sources that can help you match your interests with specific careers.

Another way to determine the types of careers you are suited for is to take a personality test. Your career counselor may be able to provide a personality test that will help you find a career that matches your personality. You may have already taken a similar test during a class on career choices.

After you identify some possible career choices, you can begin the process of screening those choices. You should consider each possible career choice in relation to the following factors: level of education or skill needed, job availability, and compensation level. Figure 5.1 shows some occupations where jobs are being created at the fastest rate for the period 2010 through 2020. As people like you and Logan begin thinking about career choices, it's a good idea to consider options where job growth is expected.

FIGURE 5.1 Fastest Growing Occupations

20 Occupations with the Highest Percent Change of Employment Between 2010–2020

Source: www.bls.gov/ooh/fastest-growing.htm

Business Management & Administration	Careers in planning, organizing, directing, and evaluating business functions essential to efficient and productive business operations.
Education & Training	Planning, managing, and providing education and training services and related learning support services, such as administration, teaching/training, administrative support, and professional support services.
Finance	Planning and related services for financial and investment planning, banking, insurance, and business financial management.
Government & Public Administration	Planning and executing government functions at the local, state, and federal levels, including governance, national security, foreign service, planning, revenue and taxation, and regulations.

Source: www.careerclusters.org

Jorn is considering getting a college degree.

Assuming he graduates in four years and tuition, books, and fees cost about $6,000 per year, how much will he spend to get his degree?

Solution: Jorn will spend at least $24,000 to get his degree (four years × $6,000 per year). However, keep in mind that he will also incur incidental expenses such as meals, gas, and other supplies that will increase his cost. If he borrows money, he will have to pay interest on the borrowed money. He will also incur opportunity costs in the form of lost wages.

Education and Skill Requirements

Some jobs that may seem interesting to you require a great deal of education and training. Are you prepared to make that kind of time and financial commitment? For example, some of you may consider a career as a medical doctor. But are you aware that becoming a physician requires seven years or more of training, much of which is very costly? Such a commitment can be worthwhile, but if this doesn't appeal to you, you may opt for a career that requires less education.

From your list of possible careers, carefully consider the education and/or skill requirements necessary. Eliminate those options that require training that exceeds what you are willing to commit to. Like all major life decisions, choosing a career requires a cost/benefit analysis. Is the ultimate benefit associated with a particular job worth the cost of acquiring the skill set? Do not focus solely on the financial costs. Be sure to consider how the extensive training will impact your quality of life.

Remember that education is generally a very good investment. Additional education may cost more now, but it is likely to pay off in a higher income for decades to come. Check out Figure 5.2 to see the general relationship between years of education and earnings. Also note that higher levels of education are associated with very low rates of unemployment. This type of job security can be critical at any time in your career but is particularly important during recessions.

Job Availability

Some people think that they would like to pursue a glamorous career, such as acting or TV broadcasting. But for most such careers, there are very few openings and the competition for them is fierce. In most areas, there is limited work for people in such professions, and the few who do succeed usually do so after many years of struggle. If you decide to pursue acting or another job with limited availability, you need to factor in job availability prior to pursuing this career option. You also need to consider what job you could do while pursuing your career—or later if the job doesn't work out. For example, if you decide to become an NFL or NBA player, what other skills could you develop as you pursue this job?

Additionally, some jobs may not be in high demand in the region where you would like to live. In that case, you may have to relocate. Moving involves substantial costs and it may take you some time to recover that

FIGURE 5.2 Comparison of Median Weekly Earnings Versus Unemployment Rate in 2011 Among Education Levels

Generally, education is costly, but it is an excellent investment that pays off in a reasonable time.

Unemployment Rate in 2011 (percent)	Education Attained	Median Weekly Earnings in 2011 (dollars)
2.5%	Doctoral degree	$1,551
2.4%	Professional degree	$1,665
3.6%	Master's degree	$1,263
4.9%	Bachelor's degree	$1,053
6.8%	Associate's degree	$768
8.7%	Some college, no degree	$719
9.4%	High school diploma	$638
14.1%	Less than a high school diploma	$451
7.6%	All workers	$797

Source: www.bls.gov/emp/ep_chart_001.txt

investment. While some companies pay all or at least a portion of relocation expenses for employees, not every company offers this benefit. Finding a new place to live, hiring a moving company, getting the utilities turned on, and the organizing hassles are not without cost.

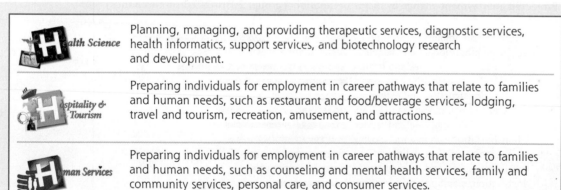

Health Science	Planning, managing, and providing therapeutic services, diagnostic services, health informatics, support services, and biotechnology research and development.
Hospitality & Tourism	Preparing individuals for employment in career pathways that relate to families and human needs, such as restaurant and food/beverage services, lodging, travel and tourism, recreation, amusement, and attractions.
Human Services	Preparing individuals for employment in career pathways that relate to families and human needs, such as counseling and mental health services, family and community services, personal care, and consumer services.

Source: www.careerclusters.org

Compensation

When considering careers, most people want to know how much money they will make—that is, what their **compensation** will be. While your list may contain a number of jobs that would be a lot of fun, many of them may not pay well. Keep in mind that you will need a minimum level of income in order to cover your expenses. You may also want to increase your net worth over time—by building up your savings, buying a home, and so on. A job that does not pay well may not allow you to cover expenses or increase your net worth. Just as Logan considered money when thinking

compensation: What a job will pay you.

Activity #1

about his future, compensation should be an important consideration of your career choice, too. Choosing a career for money alone may not be wise, but neither is ignoring how your income may affect your life.

According to the U.S. Bureau of Labor Statistics (**www.bls.gov**), during the 2010–2020 period, approximately 20.5 million jobs will be generated in the United States. The Bureau of Labor Statistics also provides information on the level of education, training, and related work experience typically needed for various occupations. The sectors that should see the largest increase in total jobs are health services as well as professional and business services.

Source: www.bls.gov/news.release/archives/ecopro_02012012.pdf

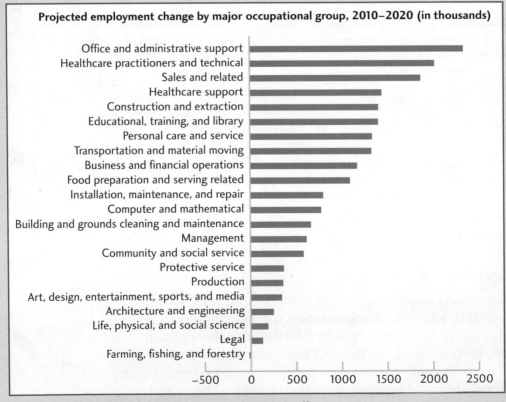

Source: www.bls.gov/news.release/archives/ecopro_02012012.pdf

If you want to know how much money certain professions pay, visit www.bls.gov/ooh/home.htm and search on a job title. You can learn the salary range of many jobs you might be interested in pursuing.

☑ CHECKPOINT

What are the steps in developing a career path?

The steps are determining interests, finding related career choices, and learning about education and skill requirements, job availability, and compensation.

SOURCES OF CAREER INFORMATION

You just read about some Web sites that list the pay of certain professions. Indeed, the Internet is an outstanding source of up-to-date career information. Web sites such as **www.careers.org** provide you with different career options, possible compensation levels for these careers, and the skill sets needed for careers in several fields, such as finance, management, construction, health, agriculture, and broadcasting. Other Web sites, such as **www .careerbuilder.com**, list the most frequently available jobs so you can evaluate those careers that are currently in high demand. Pay close attention to the number of applicants for these jobs. It is easier to get a job when the applicant pool is small. This analysis is one way to gauge the supply of qualified applicants with a particular skill set. You can also easily search for specifics on virtually every career option available to you.

Another outstanding source of information on careers is the *Occupational Outlook Handbook*. It is published by the federal government and can be found at **www.bls.gov**. Look for the link under "Publications."

The Web, of course, is only one source of information. There are many other options available that you can use to find information about interesting jobs.

Books on Careers

There are many books that will help you identify career options and the necessary skills required to pursue those careers successfully. It may be useful to study a book that simply provides a broad overview of jobs so

MATH for Personal Finance

Latrell is comparing two job opportunities. One job will pay $12 an hour and he will work 40 hours a week. The other one pays an annual salary of $22,000 and he will work 45 hours a week.

Which job pays more?

Solution: The first job will pay an annual amount of $12 × 40 hours a week × 52 weeks a year = $24,960. The second job pays $22,000 a year and requires Latrell to work five extra hours per week.

Prof. FIN

Information Technology	Building linkages in IT occupations for entry level, technical, and professional careers related to the design, development, support, and management of hardware, software, multimedia, and systems integration services.	
Law, Public Safety, Corrections & Security	Planning, managing, and providing legal, public safety, protective services, and homeland security, including professional and technical support services.	
Manufacturing	Planning, managing, and performing the processing of materials into intermediate or finished products and related professional and technical support activities such as production planning and control, maintenance, and manufacturing/process engineering.	

Source: www.careerclusters.org

that you can narrow your search. At that point, you may want to locate a book with much greater detail and focus on a specific job—for example, mechanical engineering, carpentry, or nursing.

Keep in mind that the job market changes quickly. Books that are only a few years old may be useless—or actually misleading. Make sure the information you get from a book—or from any source—is up-to-date.

Field Trips and Speakers

During your high school years, many of you will have opportunities to take field trips that will help you identify careers of interest. Your school may also have visiting speakers who will provide valuable information on what they do for a living. Make use of these opportunities to investigate various career options.

Job Experience

Think about Logan's experience unloading trucks. You may also have worked part-time jobs that allowed you to learn something about working for a living. As a result of these experiences, some of you may have eliminated certain career options, and others may have identified possible job choices. At the very least, you may have learned some broad lessons about what you do and do not like about a job. For example, you may have found that you prefer moving around to sitting at a desk or working at a workstation. You may enjoy dealing with the public—or prefer not to. These insights can be valuable.

Internships

One way to gain additional information about a particular career or job is through an **internship**—a temporary, short-term position designed to provide exposure to and training in a particular job. Often, companies will hire interns to perform various office tasks such as making copies or delivering documents. While this type of work may seem mundane, it's a good way to gain knowledge about certain types of careers. Even an unpaid internship can provide you with valuable experience and enough information to know whether a particular career interests you.

Contacts

Make use of your network of friends. Perhaps some of them have a relative who works in a career you are considering. Logan learned quite a bit about his career likes and dislikes by observing his brother and his parents. You may be able to visit with someone's parents or grandparents to learn firsthand what they do for a living. Most people will be happy to answer any questions you might have about their jobs.

A part-time job while you're in high school can help you learn about what you might like—and not like—in a job.

internship: A temporary, short-term position designed to provide exposure to and training on a particular job.

Possible answers include online sources, books, and information from personal contacts.

 CHECKPOINT

What are two ways to get career information?

GETTING THE SKILLS YOU NEED

Once you narrow your search on the types of careers that truly interest you, you should spend some time investigating the training and education you will need to be able to land that dream job. Figure 5.3 contains a list of various high-demand career choices and the education needed to get these jobs.

Training Programs

For some careers, you must obtain specific, specialized training before entering the field. Training requirements vary widely by profession. For some jobs, you may need to earn a certificate or receive a license. In some cases, you may be able to receive formal training while you are working.

FIGURE 5.3 The Future Job Market

Here are a few more jobs that are expected to grow quickly in the years ahead, along with information about median income you can expect to earn.

Job	Anticipated Percent Increase in Employment by 2020	Median Annual Wages (2010)
Healthcare support occupations	34.5	24,760
Personal care and service occupations	26.8	20,640
Healthcare practitioners and technical occupations	25.9	58,490
Community and social service occupations	24.2	39,280
Construction and extraction occupations	22.2	39,080
Computer and mathematical occupations	22.0	73,720
Business and financial operations occupations	17.3	60,670
Life, physical, and social science occupations	15.5	58,530
Education, training, and library occupations	15.3	45,690
Transportation and material moving occupations	14.8	28,400
Installation, maintenance, and repair occupations	14.7	40,120
Arts, design, entertainment, sports, and media occupations	12.6	42,870
Sales and related occupations	12.5	24,370
Building and grounds cleaning and maintenance occupations	12.1	22,490
Protective service occupations	11.0	36,660
Legal occupations	10.8	74,580
Architecture and engineering occupations	10.4	70,610
Office and administrative support occupations	10.3	30,710
Food preparation and serving related occupations	9.8	18,770
Management occupations	7.0	91,440
Production occupations	4.2	30,330
Farming, fishing, and forestry occupations	− 2.0	19,630

Sources: Employment data—Employment Projections Program, U.S. Bureau of Labor Statistics; Wage data—Occupational Employment Survey, U.S. Bureau of Labor Statistics

apprenticeships: On-the-job training programs where you acquire a skill while you are working.

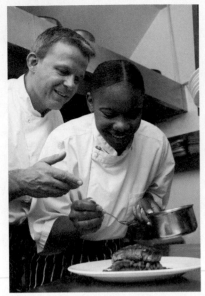

In some trades, people train on the job as apprentices.

certification: Official document or record stating that a person has met some standard for training or knowledge.

Such on-the-job training programs are sometimes called **apprenticeships**. In other cases, you may not be allowed to work in your chosen career until you have completed training. Apprenticeships are common for skilled trades such as plumbing, electrical contracting, heating and air-conditioning, and welding. Many of these skilled workers go into business for themselves after serving lengthy apprenticeships.

Additional information on the amount and type of training needed for various jobs is available on Web sites such as CareerOneStop (**www.acinet.org**) and the Bureau of Labor Statistics (**www.bls.gov**). Don't forget to utilize the *Occupational Outlook Handbook* published by the Bureau of Labor Statistics.

Be careful about training recommendations and information provided elsewhere on the Internet. Some Web sites sell training or try to get you to use their educational materials. At the extreme end, there are companies that promise to provide acting or modeling coaching as well as contacts within the industry. Most of these companies are preying on individuals who have big dreams. Some of them actually can deliver what they promise, but most cannot.

You should also be cautious about training that promises certifications. **Certification** is an official document or record stating that a person has met some standard for training or knowledge. Some certifications offered online are recognized as meaningful in the field. Others are merely the product of a good color laser printer and are worth less than the paper they are printed on. Make sure that any training you pursue is in a field with job demand and provides valid, real-world certifications if any are offered.

Education

Colleges and universities provide training in the form of education leading to a degree. Web sites such as **www.collegeboard.org** can provide you with career profiles by college major. This type of information can be useful in trying to determine whether to get a degree in something as specific as accounting or geology, or whether to pursue a broader liberal arts degree. You will find that many companies hire successful college graduates of any major since completion of the degree signals a person's ability to stick to a task and continue to learn. Many employers find these qualities as important as any particular skills, at least for entry-level jobs.

Prof. FIN

Marketing	Planning, managing, and performing marketing activities to reach organizational objectives, such as brand management, professional sales, merchandising, marketing communications, and market research.
Science, Technology, Engineering & Mathematics	Planning, managing, and providing scientific research and professional and technical services (e.g., physical science, social science, engineering) including laboratory and testing services, and research and development services.
Transportation, Distribution & Logistics	Planning, management, and movement of people, materials, and goods by road, pipeline, air, rail, and water and related professional and technical support services such as transportation infrastructure planning and management, logistics services, mobile equipment, and facility maintenance.

Source: www.careerclusters.org

University reputations vary significantly, and some may have a better reputation for certain degrees. Some jobs will require that your degree is from an accredited or certified program. **Accreditation** is an official recognition that a school or program meets a certain standard. Make sure you investigate the various types of accreditations that a university has and match those with the job market or career field you are interested in pursuing. That is, is the program accredited by the organizations that future employers will require? These accreditations are especially important in the field of nursing, some technical areas such as automotive or mechanical, and trade areas.

Learn as much as you can about the colleges you are interested in attending. What are their graduation rates? How many years does it take to graduate? What percentage of recent graduates passed their certifications, if applicable? Do firms visit the campus to recruit employees? It is always useful to learn as much as you can about the schools you are considering.

Expanding Your Education

Graduate degrees, such as a master's degree, law degree, or doctoral degree, provide you with the additional specialized knowledge and skills that should qualify you for a better job. However, there are costs associated with pursuing a graduate degree.

To begin, it can cost a lot of money to get a graduate degree. For that reason, you need to weigh these costs against the benefits to determine whether a graduate degree is right for you. Tuition, fees, books, room and board, and the opportunity cost can add up to a substantial amount of money. (Recall that opportunity cost is the cost of what you give up when you take a particular action.) For a full-time graduate program, the opportunity cost is the loss of income from a full-time job and the potential loss of social and recreational time for the time it takes you to complete the program. Is it worth it? In many cases, it will be. Only you can make that decision.

In most cases, an advanced or graduate degree enhances your employability. Many positions require a graduate degree as the minimum qualification to apply. Sometimes it is useful to get your graduate degree in a different field from your undergraduate degree. For example, engineers often find it useful to get a graduate business degree as they move into management positions within their engineering firms.

Some of you may opt to pursue a doctoral degree. You should evaluate the university carefully, since doctoral program reputations vary substantially. If you hope to teach at the college level, for example, where you get your Ph.D. may be significant. Some programs may have a local or regional reputation, others may be known nationally, and still others may have a solid international reputation. Pick the program that most closely aligns with your goals.

☑ CHECKPOINT

What are some ways people get training for different careers?

accreditation: Official recognition that a school or program meets a certain standard.

Jill is thinking about getting an MBA. She will give up making $38,000 a year for the two years it takes to complete the MBA. She will also pay $35,000 in total costs to get the degree. Assume she will make $75,000 a year after she gets her MBA.

How long will it take her to recover her investment?

Solution: Jill will be investing a total of $38,000 in lost annual wages × two years = $76,000 plus the $35,000 cost for a total of $111,000. However, she will earn $37,000 more per year after getting her MBA ($75,000 − $38,000 = $37,000). Therefore, it will take her three years to recover her investment, or $111,000 / $37,000 per year increase in salary = three years.

Activity #2

Many people get training from an apprentice program, from a college or university, or even from an online program.

JOB APPLICATION PROCESS

Most jobs require you to fill out a job application such as the one shown in Figure 5.4. Job applications provide your prospective employer with

FIGURE 5.4 Sample Job Application

For many jobs, filling out an application is the first step in the job-seeking process.

Sample Job Application

Fill out this sample application using your personal information. Include all applicable information and addresses.

PLEASE NOTE: Complete all parts of the application. If your application is incomplete, or does not clearly show the experience and/or training required, your application may not be accepted. If you have no information to enter in a section, please write N/A.

Name and Address	
Name (First, MI, Last)	Social Security Number
Mailing Address	
City, State, and Zip Code	
Home Phone	Message Phone
E-mail Address	May we use e-mail to contact you? Yes ☐ No ☐

Additional Information	
Have you been an employee of this organization in the past? Yes ☐ No ☐	
I certify that I am in compliance with the provisions of the Selective Service Act (Draft Registration). ** Yes ☐ No ☐	
I certify that I am a U.S. citizen, permanent resident, or a foreign national with authorization to work in the United States. ** Yes ☐ No ☐	
Have you ever been convicted of, or entered a plea of guilty, no contest, or had a withheld judgment to a felony? ** Yes ☐ No ☐ If Yes, please explain:	
** These questions must be answered in order to be considered for employment	

Education			
(Schools attended or special training received)			
School	From	To	Did you graduate?
Location		Type of degree or diploma	
School	From	To	Did you graduate?
Location		Type of degree or diploma	

relevant information about your previous work history that helps when he's making a decision about whether to hire you. Keep that in mind as you work during the summer. Your next employer may contact your previous employer and ask him or her how punctual you were and if you were a good worker.

FIGURE 5.4 Sample Job Application (continued)

Work History				
Job Title	From	To	Hrs/Week	Employer
Address	Phone	Supervisor		May we contact this employer? Yes ☐ No ☐
Reason for leaving?				

Work History				
Job Title	From	To	Hrs/Week	Employer
Address	Phone	Supervisor		May we contact this employer? Yes ☐ No ☐
Reason for leaving?				

Work History				
Job Title	From	To	Hrs/Week	Employer
Address	Phone	Supervisor		May we contact this employer? Yes ☐ No ☐
Reason for leaving?				

How did you find out about this position?				
Current Employee ☐	Career Fair ☐	State website ☐	Company Newsletter ☐	Job Service ☐
Monster.com ☐	Newspaper Ad ☐	Other Internet Source ☐	Prof. Organization website ☐	Radio/TV Ad ☐
	Recruiter ☐	University/College ☐	None of the above ☐	

Job Type/Shift				
Full Time ☐	Part Time ☐	Permanent ☐	Temporary ☐	6 Month ☐
9 Month ☐	Seasonal ☐	Limited Service ☐	Shift ☐	Night ☐

Signature	Date
I certify that all answers and statements on this application are true and complete to the best of my knowledge. I understand that should an investigation disclose untruthful or misleading answers, my application may be rejected, my name removed from consideration, or my employment with this company terminated.	

Résumé

résumé: A snapshot of your qualifications that includes personal background information such as education and previous work history.

Many jobs will require you to provide a **résumé**, which gives prospective employers a snapshot of your qualifications. Typically, your résumé will include your personal background information, including education and previous work history. Additionally, you should provide a list of your skills, such as computer training or language ability. Check out Logan's résumé in Figure 5.5.

FIGURE 5.5 Sample Résumé for Logan

There are a variety of ways to format a résumé. This résumé is a functional résumé that focuses on Logan's skills rather than his employment history, which might be short at this point in his life.

Logan Bolin   (555)123-4567
987 East Street, MainTown, CA 90210   lgmaintown@speeddial.com

OBJECTIVE	To obtain a position in sales using my experience working with people and handling my own business.
SALES SKILLS	Successfully serviced 30 lawn care customers yearly, handling all yard work needed Prepared brochure to advertise lawn care business Built business to current client list in one year
COMMUNICATION AND COMPUTER SKILLS	Earned top honors in Business Communication class Developed Word, Excel, PowerPoint, and Internet skills Received award for Outstanding Computer Student of the Year
ORGANIZATIONAL SKILLS	Developed work schedule for lawn care of 30 customers Scheduled FBLA Week for local chapter Organized time for homework, extracurricular activities, and lawn care business
EDUCATION	MainTown High School, MainTown, CA Business Academy Graduation, 2012
EMPLOYMENT	2010–present, Bolin Lawn Care Summer, 2009, March of Dimes Headquarters volunteer, MainTown, CA

Personal References Provided Upon Request

Example of Personal References Page for Logan

Logan Bolin
REFERENCES

Mr. Kevin Carsey	Ms. Shirley Rogers	Ms. Tena Crews
1143 Linoper Drive	Work Supervisor	NW Division Director
MainTown, CA 90210	MainTown High School	March of Dimes
(123)555-1111	1 Champion Drive	987 Bumble Bee Circle
	MainTown, CA 90210	MainTown, CA 90210

You can choose from different styles of résumés, depending on the strength of your background. For example, résumés that emphasize skills rather than work experience may be a good choice for someone with a limited work history. The Internet is a good source of information about how to structure an effective résumé that best highlights your skills.

Activity #3

Cover Letter

Generally, the more education and training you have, the more information is required during a job application. For example, many professional jobs require a cover letter, a résumé, and multiple interviews. The length of some interviews can be several days and require you to travel out of state to a specific site. Figure 5.6 contains a sample cover letter that Logan could use to apply for a job.

Activity #4

Internet Job Searches and Applications

Many companies have moved to electronic applications or pick applicants from employment sites such as MonsterCollege. Check out **college.monster.com** to learn what jobs are in demand. Learn the process of posting your own contact information.

FIGURE 5.6 Sample Cover Letter for Logan

The cover letter is Logan's introduction to the potential employer. It's his chance to highlight his strengths and to persuade the would-be employer that he should be called for an interview. Such letters should be prepared carefully.

June 6, 2013
Ms. Janie Baney
WWW Landscaping Company
53 July Road
MainTown, CA 90210

Dear Ms. Baney,

Your advertisement for a sales position, which appeared May 28 in Section C of the *MainTown Chronicle*, caught my attention because my education and training fits your needs. The advertisement states that the job involves outside landscaping sales for individual homes and businesses.

As a small business owner for the past five years, I have dealt with a variety of landscaping tasks for individual homeowners. I have also worked with other small businesses in designing and maintaining their landscapes. Budgeting, planning, and organizing are skills that are needed for the job you advertise. I can bring these skills to your company.

I would like to discuss my qualifications with you and answer any questions you have about my enclosed résumé. The best way to reach me is to call my cell phone at (555)123-4567 during business hours. I look forward to putting my skills to work for WWW Landscaping Company.

Sincerely,

Logan Bolin

Prof. FIN

The following are some keywords and phrases to use in your job application or résumé. They reflect the kinds of qualities employers are looking for. Many more lists can be found on the Internet to help you be more successful in your job search.

ability to plan	leadership
ability to train	multitasking
accurate	open-minded
adaptable	oral communication
aggressive worker	organizational skills
competitive	problem solving
creative	results oriented
customer oriented	safety conscious
ethical	self-accountable
follow instructions	self-managing
follow through	setting priorities
high energy	takes initiative
industrious	team player
innovative	

Source: *Business Communication*, page 555, Mary Ellen Guffey

Become comfortable with the job application process. Young people like you and Logan may ultimately change jobs 10 or 20 times during your lifetime and could likely change careers several times.

 CHECKPOINT

You can use paper applications and résumés or online services.

What are two ways to apply for a job?

CHAPTER REVIEW

SUMMARY

- Your career path is a choice you make. It can change throughout your life until you retire. Each time you look at a new career, you will need to review the education/skills needed, its availability, and the compensation expected.

- There are multiple ways to research jobs and careers. You may have opportunities to take field trips or listen to speakers to gather information about a career, or you may gather information by networking with family, friends, and others. Job experience will also help you make decisions about your career choice. The Internet provides many sources to help you in your career decision-making process. You can go online to find out about various careers or you can take a personality test or interest inventory to help you make your decision.

- Remember that additional training or education may be required for your career choice or when changing to a different career. As you expand your education and training, benefits will increase, but there could also be additional costs to you. You need to weigh the costs and the benefits; this will allow you to see if a change is worth your effort.

- Applying for a job may involve filling out applications, writing and posting a résumé, writing cover letters, and using online services. It is a process that most young people will go through many times in their lives.

Key Terms and Concepts

1. What is meant by **compensation** when looking at a job?

2. What is the difference between an **apprenticeship** and an **internship**?

3. Why is a program's **accreditation** important in some jobs or careers?

What Do You Know?   MyFinLitLab

1. (a) How does your choice of career affect your financial future?

   (b) What else, besides the financial impact of your choice, should you consider when choosing a career?

2. (a) Why is it important to know the educational or training requirements when deciding upon a career?

   (b) Where can one find information about education or training requirements for a job?

Answers:
Key Terms and Concepts

1. Compensation is the amount of pay you expect to receive.

2. An apprenticeship is a longer term formalized program that provides on-the-job training in a certain occupation or skill. An internship is a temporary position designed to provide a person with exposure to and limited training for a certain job.

3. In some jobs you cannot be hired or licensed by the state unless you graduate from an accredited program.

Answers:
What Do You Know?

1. (a) **Comprehension** Different careers have different compensation levels that will impact the amounts available to save and invest. (b) **Analysis** You should consider your personal likes and dislikes, the demand for jobs in that field, and where you may want to live.

2. (a) **Comprehension** You need to be prepared to invest the time and money necessary to gain the required skills. (b) **Application** Information can be found on the Internet, and in the *Occupational Outlook Handbook*, books, and other sources.

3. (a) **Comprehension** Before you invest time and money, you must know if you will be satisfied with the compensation and able to live on that amount of money. (b) **Application** The Web site www.bls.gov/ooh/ is one good source of salary data.

4. (a) **Comprehension** Investment in education often generates substantial returns in the form of higher pay over your lifetime. (b) **Analysis** One reason is lack of available jobs in some professions.

5. (a) **Comprehension** Skilled trades such as those in plumbing and electricity typically require apprenticeships. (b) **Analysis** It enables you to obtain and practice the skills required to do the job.

6. (a) **Knowledge** Certification is an official document or record stating that a person has met some standard for training or knowledge. (b) **Analysis** If employers do not recognize the certification, it will not have any monetary value nor will it help you find a job.

7. (a) **Knowledge** Colleges provide degrees. (b) **Analysis** Yes. A degree tells an employer that you have the ability to learn and also to start and complete a task.

8. (a) **Comprehension** A résumé provides prospective employers with a snapshot of your qualifications. (b) **Application** Your background, skills, and the type of job you are pursuing might influence the type of résumé you select.

9. (a) **Comprehension** You may need a cover letter, résumé, application, and list of references. (b) **Analysis** You will likely change jobs many times during your lifetime.

Answers:
What Are Your Finance Math Skills?

1. Out-of-pocket costs will be $8,000 \times 5 = $40,000.

2. Job 1 pays $31,000 + $7,000 = $38,000. Job 2 pays $20 \times 40 \times 52$ weeks = $41,600. Even when you consider the value of the vehicle furnished in the first job it makes more sense for Doug to take the second job. The pay is high enough for him to furnish a vehicle and gas and still come out ahead.

3. She will invest $6,000 \times 3 = $18,000 / $4,000 a year raise = 4.5 years to recover her cash investment.

---

3. (a) Why is it critical to know the compensation for a job?

   (b) What sources can you use to find information about compensation for different careers?

4. (a) What does it mean to say that education is a good investment?

   (b) What would be a good reason to avoid a career that requires a lot of education?

5. (a) What kinds of occupations typically require apprenticeships?

   (b) What do you think is the purpose behind this kind of training program?

6. (a) What is a certification?

   (b) Why is it important that possible employers recognize the value of any certification you might seek?

7. (a) What kinds of credentials do colleges provide?

   (b) Is it worthwhile to seek a college degree if the degree is not in a specific field or part of a specific training program?

8. (a) What is the purpose of a résumé?

   (b) What factors might influence the type of résumé you select?

9. (a) What are three items that may be needed in the application process?

   (b) Why is it especially important for younger people to get familiar with the job-seeking process?

What Are Your Finance Math Skills?   MyFinLitLab

The first three questions correlate to *Math for Personal Finance* features located throughout the chapter.

1. Asa wants to get his degree in engineering. He estimates it will take him five years to complete the degree and that he will spend about $8,000 a year for tuition, fees, books, and room and board. How much will it cost Asa to get his degree?

2. Doug has been offered two different jobs. One company has offered him $31,000 a year and will furnish a vehicle with a company gas card. The other job will pay him $20 an hour and he will work 40 hours a week. However if he takes this job he will have to furnish his own vehicle and buy his own gas. Doug believes the vehicle allowance will save him about $7,000 a year that he would otherwise have to spend on transportation. Which job pays more? Which job should Doug take?

3. Ms. McClure is thinking about getting her master's degree in education. She estimates that she will spend about $6,000 a year for three years to get her degree. Her plans are to take evening classes so she

can keep her current teaching job. When she finishes her degree, she will get a $4,000 a year raise. How long will it take her to recover her investment?

4. Tiffany makes $8 an hour and works 15 hours a week. Tosha makes $9.50 an hour and works 50 hours per month. Who will make more money this year?

5. Anton is seeking an advanced degree that requires an investment of $70,000 and a three-year commitment during which he will lose $20,000 a year in income. Without considering the interest lost on the investment, how long will it take him to recover his out-of-pocket investment and lost earnings if he makes $10,000 more per year after completing the degree?

6. If Josh spends $4,000 a year on tuition and fees, $1,200 a year on books, and foregoes earning $10,000 a year, how much will his four-year degree cost?

7. If you study an extra 10 hours a week for a year (52 weeks) and you earn a four-year scholarship valued at $50,000, what is your hourly return on your investment in study time?

8. Assume you spend $3,500 a year for the first two years attending a junior college and then you spend $6,000 a year for the remaining two years at the local college. Your friend spends $5,000 a year for four years at another local school. Compare the costs of both options.

4. Tiffany: $8 × 15 × 52 = $6,240; Tosha: ($9.50 × 50 × 12 = $5,700).

5. ($70,000 + (3 × $20,000)) = $130,000 total investment / $10,000 raise = 13 years

6. ($4,000 + $1,200 + $10,000) × 4 = $60,800

7. $50,000 / 52 × 10 = 520 study hours = $96.15 an hour

8. You: ($3,500 × 2) + ($6,000 × 2) = $19,000; your friend: $5,000 × 4 = $20,000.

What Would You Do?

Maurice is looking for a job as a salesman. As he prepares his résumé, he is discouraged by his lack of experience and education. He is confident of his abilities and is certain that he has the ability to sell. But he is concerned that no employer will give him a chance if they look at his background.

It occurs to him that if he exaggerates just a little about some of his accomplishments, he has a better chance of getting called to an interview. Then he can let his personality and charm take over.

Maurice has asked you to serve as a reference in his job search. You agree that he would make an excellent salesman, but you are not in favor of vouching for his background if you are called about it.

1. Is Maurice doing the right thing?

2. Who is hurt if Maurice gets a job based on false information?

3. How might your involvement with Maurice's plan hurt you?

What Are the Connections? Language Arts and History

Conduct a survey of four adults to find out about their careers, training, career switches, and work experiences. Put this information in a table. Put this table in a research paper explaining what you were researching, how you conducted your survey, your findings, and the conclusions you draw from this data. In your conclusions you might compare what the adults told you about their careers with what you hope for in your future career.

Teamwork

In teams, choose one of the career clusters (the 16 clusters given by Professor Fin throughout this chapter). Research all the information you can find about the cluster. Find out what course work you might need for a job in this cluster, what jobs might be considered in this cluster, salary ranges in this cluster, what education or training is necessary for this cluster, and any other interesting facts.

Create a newsletter to be placed in the counselor's office about the cluster you have researched. Make the newsletter interesting, with graphics, pictures, and facts so that your fellow students will want to learn more.

ESSENTIAL QUESTION ACTIVITIES

Complete these activities to answer this chapter's Essential Question: *What is involved in choosing a career and applying for a job in that career path?*

1. *On your own:* This chapter has provided you with information about different career paths and how to research different careers. You have also learned what needs to be done to find a job. Either on paper or using word processing software such as Microsoft Word, develop a checklist for you to use when you begin your career search and job search.

2. *As a class:* Brainstorm what is involved in finding a career and getting that job. Develop a checklist to be used as each of you begin your career search.

TEST PREP QUESTIONS

1. Which of the following is a true statement about the U.S. job market?   1. b
   a. Farming and forestry jobs are expected to increase over the next few years.
   b. Jobs in health care occupations are expected to grow more than most over the next several years.
   c. Service-related industries are not expected to produce new jobs for at least another 10 years.
   d. The job market basically remains the same from year to year.

2. A career that requires a college degree and is expected to grow in employment in the coming years is   2. b
   a. personal and home care aides.
   b. registered nurses.
   c. construction trades.
   d. social scientist.

3. If a college or university offers a nationally accredited nursing program, it most likely means that   3. c
   a. anyone who graduates from the program will get a job as a nurse.
   b. anyone in the United States who wants to be a nurse can go to that college or university.
   c. the program has been cited by a nationally recognized nursing professional organization as meeting certain standards.
   d. the program will award graduates with a nationally recognized nursing license.

4. Which of the following is a true statement?   4. a
   a. A certification is recognition that a person has acquired a certain level of knowledge or training in a particular area of study.
   b. Certification programs are regulated by the United States Department of Education.
   c. Certification programs award their certificates to everyone who enrolls in and completes their programs.
   d. A certification is a license that permits a person to practice a certain profession such as accounting or physical therapy in one or more states.

5. As a first step in selecting a career path, a person should   5. b
   a. find out which careers pay the highest salaries.
   b. determine which career areas interest him or her.
   c. look online for inexpensive certification programs.
   d. find out what majors are offered at the local college in the person's geographic area.

6. The *Occupational Outlook Handbook* is a good source for finding information about   6. c
   a. colleges that offer specific career programs.
   b. the availability of jobs in different cities.
   c. the areas that will need more employees in the coming years.
   d. the amount of money a person can expect to earn over a lifetime.

7. c

7. A person finds out that with a bachelor's degree he can expect to earn $55,000 a year as a financial researcher. If he spends two years (full-time) getting an MBA, it will cost him $25,000 a year for his education; however, he can then expect to earn a minimum of $90,000 a year as a financial analyst. If he decides to take the additional education route, to make up for the financial cost of postponing his career it will take him
   a. less than two years.
   b. slightly more than two years.
   c. almost five years.
   d. more than ten years.

8. a

8. In deciding whether to pursue additional education and training for a job, a person decides to do a cost/benefit analysis. This is a good idea because it will help her to
   a. decide whether the benefits she believes she will have in a certain job and career are worth the financial and quality of life costs associated with gaining the necessary skills and education.
   b. determine how many years it will take before she can enjoy the benefits of retirement.
   c. compare the costs of different educational programs and different colleges to the benefit of beginning a career without any additional education.
   d. determine whether the benefits package a company offers will cover the cost of the education required for the job.

9. c

9. A person's résumé should *not* include
   a. knowledge of various computer programs.
   b. career objectives.
   c. current salary.
   d. prior work experience.

10. b

10. Why do many employers say that a cover letter is as important as the résumé that it accompanies?
   a. The cover letter can be much longer than the résumé and provide details that do not belong in the résumé.
   b. The cover letter gives the writer a chance to explain why she believes that her skills and knowledge make her the ideal person for the position.
   c. Once a good cover letter is written, it can be copied in large quantities and easily sent with the résumé.
   d. A handwritten cover letter is a chance to show a potential employer a person's best handwriting.

CHAPTER 6

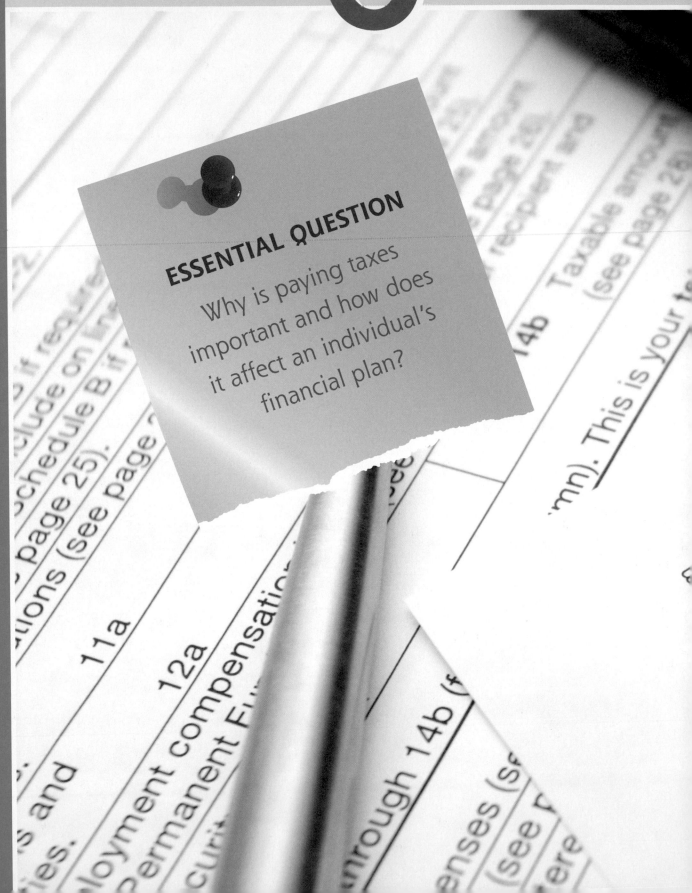

ESSENTIAL QUESTION

Why is paying taxes important and how does it affect an individual's financial plan?

PAYING TAXES

LEARNING OBJECTIVES

- Describe the basic principles of taxation and the major categories of taxes

- Explain payroll taxes

- Discuss the purpose and process of filing tax returns

- Understand how taxes affect your financial plan

KEY TERMS

adjusted gross income

capital gains

gross income

itemized deduction

payroll taxes

standard deduction

tax

tax return

Ryan's boss handed him his check and thanked him for a good work week. "You have picked up everything really fast, Ryan. I appreciate your hard work." Ryan nodded, grateful for the praise. "Thank you, sir. I've enjoyed it so far." This was Ryan's first "real" job. He'd made some money cutting lawns and raking leaves, but this was his first actual paycheck. He resisted the urge to tear open the envelope and look at his check.

Ryan was home before he finally allowed himself to look at the paycheck. Disappointment covered his face. The check was too small! He glanced at the total amount again. It read $147.76, but he knew he had worked 20 hours and was supposed to be making $8 an hour. He had been counting on getting $160—in fact he needed $150 by Monday to pay the deposit for the upcoming senior class trip. What had happened? It had to be a mistake. Then, Ryan looked at the pay stub attached to the check. He saw $160 in a box labeled "gross pay." What was gross pay? And what were FICA, net pay, and all the other little boxes on his pay stub? When would he get the rest of his money?

Ryan is learning a valuable lesson—one that virtually all working people in this country have learned: There is a difference between what workers earn and what they actually get to keep and use—that is, their **take-home pay**. The total amount of money Ryan actually earned (his hourly wage multiplied by the hours he worked) is called his **gross pay**. The amount he actually takes home is called his **net pay**. The reason for the difference between the two is taxes. Learning about the taxes the government imposes on your income, how those taxes are paid, and what you can do to plan for them, is a key step in your financial education and in building your financial plan.

TAX BASICS

tax: Money collected by a government from its citizens for the purpose of operating the government.

Ryan's take-home or net pay was $147.76 and his gross pay was $160.00. Assume the combined Social Security and Medicare (FICA) withholdings are 7.65%.

How much did Ryan pay in FICA from this check?

Solution: Ryan paid 7.65% of the $160 or $12.24 in FICA from this check.

A **tax** is money collected by a government from its citizens for the purpose of operating the government. Businesses also pay taxes. The government levies taxes on many different things. For example, most Americans pay a tax on the income they earn and on the property they own. They also pay a tax when they buy certain things—gas, tobacco, and in some states, other consumer items. Why do people pay these taxes? Tax revenue is the government's income. The government uses the taxes it collects to fund governmental services and programs. Tax revenue pays for our national defense, fire and police protection, road construction and maintenance, and schools. It pays the Social Security payments many of our parents and grandparents rely on. It helps provide medical care for the elderly and the poor. Virtually any public program you can think of is funded by tax receipts.

Sales Taxes

People pay taxes in different ways and on a variety of different things. For example, many of us pay **sales taxes** when we make a purchase at a store. That is, some of the price we pay for the item we buy is, in fact, a tax. The merchant collects this money and then sends it to the government.

The federal government does not impose a sales tax, but many state governments do. In some cases, local governments, such as city governments, may be able to charge sales taxes.

Real Estate Taxes

Sometimes, the government sends us a bill for the taxes we owe. Taxes on real estate are often handled this way. Governments calculate real estate taxes based on the value of the property. For example, property owners may pay a certain amount in property tax for each $1,000 worth of property they own. The government sends the property owner a bill for this tax.

Real estate taxes are primarily used to fund local schools. Many of you have probably heard discussions about increases on property tax rates to help provide better school facilities.

Real estate taxes vary significantly from state to state and county to county. Always check the local tax rates before moving to a new location. That new job with a big raise might not generate a higher standard of living if you have to pay much of it in taxes.

Some aircraft carriers cost several billion dollars to build and hundreds of millions of dollars to operate each year. The money for this and other government projects comes from tax revenue.

Payroll Taxes

Many people pay taxes each and every time they get paid. Like Ryan, a portion of what they earn is withheld from their paycheck by their employer. The employer then sends this money to the government. The taxes that are collected in this way are known as **payroll taxes**, which include federal and any state income taxes as well as Social Security (or FICA) withholdings. You will read more about these shortly. Refer to Figure 6.1 for a look at Ryan's pay stub. As you can see, his employer only withheld FICA taxes from Ryan's check.

Note that many workers are self-employed or earn significant income from investments. Such people do not get a regular paycheck for this

payroll taxes: Federal and state taxes withheld from a person's paycheck and sent to the government by his employer.

The four Rs of taxes are: Revenue, Redistribution, Repricing, and Representation. They help explain the purpose of taxation. The first R is the main purpose of taxes: to raise the revenue the government uses for roads, schools, hospitals, and other services the government provides. The second R refers to the taking of wealth from one part of society—the wealthy—and redistributing it to another part. The third R refers to the way taxes can sometimes be used to make some items more expensive and thus discourage their use. Taxes on cigarettes illustrate this point. The fourth R harkens to the saying "no taxation without representation," and it reflects the principle that people expect government to serve their needs in return for their financial support.

The Boston Tea Party is a famous example of people protesting taxation without representation.

FIGURE 6.1 Pay Stub

Ryan's pay stub includes information about what he has earned, what he is taking home, and why. Some stubs provide summary information for the entire year.

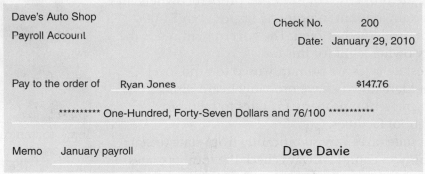

Dave's Auto Shop
Payroll Account

Check No.   200
Date: January 29, 2010

Pay to the order of   Ryan Jones $147.76

********** One-Hundred, Forty-Seven Dollars and 76/100 **********

Memo   January payroll   Dave Davie

Detach below before depositing, and save for your records:

Employee:	Jones, R.	Gross Earnings		$160.00
Pay Period:	01/29/10	Deductions:		
		Federal Income Tax	$0	
		State Income Tax	0	
		Social Security	9.92	
		Medicare	2.32	
		Insurance	0	
		Retirement Savings Plan	0	
		Charity	0	
		Health/Child Care Flex Plan	0	
		Total Deductions		12.24
		Net Pay		**$147.76**

Ryan's net pay is his gross pay of $160 minus the $12.24 of FICA taxes withheld, for a total of $147.76.

Ryan's paycheck is too small for withholding federal, state, or local taxes, but FICA taxes of $12.24 have been withheld.

income and do not have taxes withheld from it. Instead, they must make regular estimated tax payments to the federal and state governments. It is possible (though somewhat unlikely) that a young person such as Ryan should pay estimated taxes for income earned cutting lawns and doing other odd jobs. Failure to pay estimated taxes can lead to a penalty. If you earn income from such sources, you should visit **www.irs.gov** and your state's department of revenue to see if you need to file estimated taxes. Your state's department of revenue can give you information about requirements in your state.

YOU DO IT

Activity #1

The Internal Revenue Service

While the tax rules for state and local governments vary widely, all of us are subject to federal tax laws. We shall focus on those.

The **Internal Revenue Service (IRS)**, a branch of the U.S. Treasury Department, is the government body that carries out the federal tax system. The U.S. Congress makes our tax laws, but the IRS enforces the laws and collects the taxes.

Each year in which you earn an income over a certain amount, you are required to file a federal tax return with the IRS. (The minimum amount of earnings required before a person must file a return varies based on several factors. Check the IRS Web site—**www.irs.gov**—to learn if you must file a return.) Generally, a tax return consists of a form called 1040 or 1040EZ, plus any supporting documents. Figure 6.2 shows a sample of the two-page Form 1040EZ.

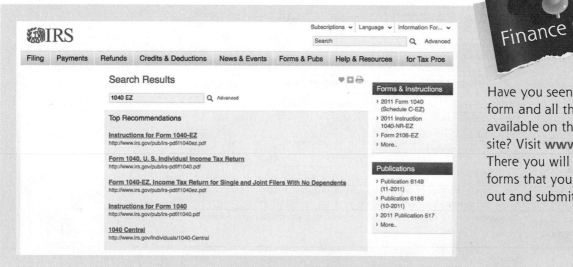

The purpose of a **tax return** is to report to the IRS all the information relative to your income taxes. This includes how much you earned from all income sources and how much you paid to the IRS through withholding and estimated payments. As part of your tax return, you must figure exactly what tax you should have paid for the tax year. If your withholding or estimated payments were greater than this amount, you will receive a refund from the government. If your withholding or estimated payments were too low, you must pay the difference to the IRS.

tax return: A formal report to the IRS that contains all the information relative to a person's income taxes for a specific year.

FIGURE 6.2 Form 1040EZ

The easiest way to file a tax return is with the form 1040EZ, although taxpayers who choose this form cannot itemize deductions.

Department of the Treasury—Internal Revenue Service

Form
1040EZ

Income Tax Return for Single and Joint Filers With No Dependents (99)

2011

OMB No. 1545-0074

Your first name and initial	Last name		Your social security number
Ryan	Jones		

If a joint return, spouse's first name and initial	Last name		Spouse's social security number

Home address (number and street). If you have a P.O. box, see instructions.
111 Doodle St.

Apt. no.

▲ Make sure the SSN(s) above are correct.

City, town or post office, state, and ZIP code. If you have a foreign address, also complete spaces below (see instructions).
Anytown, USA 11121

Presidential Election Campaign
Check here if you, or your spouse if filing jointly, want $3 to go to this fund. Checking a box below will not change your tax or refund. [X] You [ ] Spouse

Foreign country name	Foreign province/county	Foreign postal code

Income

Attach Form(s) W-2 here.

Enclose, but do not attach, any payment.

1	Wages, salaries, and tips. This should be shown in box 1 of your Form(s) W-2. Attach your Form(s) W-2.	**1**	6400 00
2	Taxable interest. If the total is over $1,500, you cannot use Form 1040EZ.	**2**	
3	Unemployment compensation and Alaska Permanent Fund dividends (see instructions).	**3**	
4	Add lines 1, 2, and 3. This is your **adjusted gross income.**	**4**	6400 00
5	If someone can claim you (or your spouse if a joint return) as a dependent, check the applicable box(es) below and enter the amount from the worksheet on back. [X] **You** [ ] **Spouse** If no one can claim you (or your spouse if a joint return), enter $9,500 if **single;** $19,000 if **married filing jointly.** See back for explanation.	**5**	5800 00
6	Subtract line 5 from line 4. If line 5 is larger than line 4, enter -0-. This is your **taxable income.** ▶	**6**	600 00

Payments, Credits, and Tax

7	Federal income tax withheld from Form(s) W-2 and 1099.	**7**	0
8a	**Earned income credit (EIC)** (see instructions).	**8a**	0
b	Nontaxable combat pay election.	8b	
9	Add lines 7 and 8a. These are your **total payments and credits.** ▶	**9**	0
10	**Tax.** Use the amount on **line 6 above** to find your tax in the tax table in the instructions. Then, enter the tax from the table on this line.	**10**	59 00

Refund

Have it directly deposited! See instructions and fill in 11b, 11c, and 11d or Form 8888.

11a	If line 9 is larger than line 10, subtract line 10 from line 9. This is your **refund.** If Form 8888 is attached, check here ▶ [ ]	**11a**	
▶ b	Routing number	▶ c Type: [ ] Checking [ ] Savings	
▶ d	Account number		

Amount You Owe

12	If line 10 is larger than line 9, subtract line 9 from line 10. This is the **amount you owe.** For details on how to pay, see instructions. ▶	**12**	59 00

Third Party Designee

Do you want to allow another person to discuss this return with the IRS (see instructions)? [ ] **Yes.** Complete below. [ ] **No**

Designee's name ▶ Phone no. ▶ Personal identification number (PIN) ▶

Sign Here

Under penalties of perjury, I declare that I have examined this return and, to the best of my knowledge and belief, it is true, correct, and accurately lists all amounts and sources of income I received during the tax year. Declaration of preparer (other than the taxpayer) is based on all information of which the preparer has any knowledge.

Joint return? See instructions.

Keep a copy for your records.

Your signature	Date	Your occupation	Daytime phone number
Spouse's signature. If a joint return, **both** must sign.	Date	Spouse's occupation	If the IRS sent you an Identity Protection PIN, enter it here (see inst.)

Paid Preparer Use Only

Print/Type preparer's name	Preparer's signature	Date	Check [ ] if self-employed	PTIN
Firm's name ▶			Firm's EIN ▶	
Firm's address ▶			Phone no.	

For Disclosure, Privacy Act, and Paperwork Reduction Act Notice, see instructions.   Cat. No. 11329W   Form **1040EZ** (2011)

FIGURE 6.2 Form 1040EZ (continued)

Use this form if

• Your filing status is single or married filing jointly. If you are not sure about your filing status, see instructions.

• You (and your spouse if married filing jointly) were under age 65 and not blind at the end of 2011. If you were born on January 1, 1947, you are considered to be age 65 at the end of 2011.

• You do not claim any dependents. For information on dependents, see Pub. 501.

• Your taxable income (line 6) is less than $100,000.

• You do not claim any adjustments to income. For information on adjustments to income, use TeleTax topics 451–453 and 455–458 (see instructions).

• The only tax credit you can claim is the earned income credit (EIC). The credit may give you a refund even if you do not owe any tax. You do not need a qualifying child to claim the EIC. For information on credits, use TeleTax topics 601, 602, 607, 608, 610, 611, and 612 (see instructions).

• You had only wages, salaries, tips, taxable scholarship or fellowship grants, unemployment compensation, or Alaska Permanent Fund dividends, and your taxable interest was not over $1,500. But if you earned tips, including allocated tips, that are not included in box 5 and box 7 of your Form W-2, you may not be able to use Form 1040EZ (see instructions). If you are planning to use Form 1040EZ for a child who received Alaska Permanent Fund dividends, see instructions.

Filling in your return

If you received a scholarship or fellowship grant or tax-exempt interest income, such as on municipal bonds, see the instructions before filling in the form. Also, see the instructions if you received a Form 1099-INT showing federal income tax withheld or if federal income tax was withheld from your unemployment compensation or Alaska Permanent Fund dividends.

For tips on how to avoid common mistakes, see instructions.

Remember, you must report all wages, salaries, and tips even if you do not get a Form W-2 from your employer. You must also report all your taxable interest, including interest from banks, savings and loans, credit unions, etc., even if you do not get a Form 1099-INT.

Worksheet for Line 5 — Dependents Who Checked One or Both Boxes

Use this worksheet to figure the amount to enter on line 5 if someone can claim you (or your spouse if married filing jointly) as a dependent, even if that person chooses not to do so. To find out if someone can claim you as a dependent, see Pub. 501.

A. Amount, if any, from line 1 on front 6400.00
   + 300.00 Enter total ▶ **A .** _6700.00_
B. Minimum standard deduction . . . . **B .** _950.00_
C. Enter the **larger** of line A or line B here . . . . **C .** _6700.00_
D. Maximum standard deduction. If **single,** enter $5,800; if **married filing jointly,** enter $11,600 . **D .** _5800.00_
E. Enter the **smaller** of line C or line D here. This is your standard deduction . . . . **E .** _5800.00_
F. Exemption amount.
   • If single, enter -0-.
   • If married filing jointly and —   } **F .** _0_
     —both you and your spouse can be claimed as dependents, enter -0-.
     —only one of you can be claimed as a dependent, enter $3,700.
G. Add lines E and F. Enter the total here and on line 5 on the front . . . . **G .** _5800.00_

(keep a copy for your records)

If you did not check any boxes on line 5, enter on line 5 the amount shown below that applies to you.

• Single, enter $9,500. This is the total of your standard deduction ($5,800) and your exemption ($3,700).

• Married filing jointly, enter $19,000. This is the total of your standard deduction ($11,600), your exemption ($3,700), and your spouse's exemption ($3,700).

Mailing Return

Mail your return by **April 17, 2012.** Mail it to the address shown on the last page of the instructions.

Form **1040EZ** (2011)

Taxes are figured based on your earnings in the calendar year—January to December. When the year is over, you have until April 15th to file your return. For example, you will be required to file your tax return for your income in the calendar year 2012 by April 15, 2013. If April 15th falls on a weekend or holiday the deadline is extended to the next business day.

Over the years, the U.S. tax code has become very complex. Tax laws provide taxpayers a variety of ways to lower their tax bills. You will read about some of these ways shortly. In fact, there are many careers that involve helping individuals and corporations to take advantage of tax laws to pay the lowest possible tax. Many attorneys and accountants make good incomes by becoming tax experts and helping people with tax issues. In this chapter we will only cover some very simple tax concepts.

 CHECKPOINT

Taxes pay the cost of government.

What is the major purpose of taxes?

UNDERSTANDING PAYROLL TAXES

As mentioned earlier, payroll taxes include Social Security and Medicare taxes as well as personal income taxes (federal and state if applicable). Medicare and Social Security taxes are also known as FICA, which is short for Federal Insurance Contributions Act. (Note that in some cases, FICA may be listed as OASDI (Old-Age, Survivors, and Disability Insurance.) **Personal income taxes** include federal income taxes and, in those states that have them, state income taxes. We will discuss each one of these in turn.

Social Security and Medicare

Take a look at Ryan's pay stub in Figure 6.1. What types of taxes did his employer withhold from his check? For most Americans, earned income, which includes wages and salary, is subject to FICA taxes. Your employer withholds FICA taxes from your paychecks and sends this amount to the government. Some of this money funds **Social Security**, which provides payments to eligible retirees and disabled people. The rest goes to **Medicare**, which provides health care coverage to mostly older Americans and some younger disabled people.

If you work for an employer, your portion of the Social Security tax is typically equal to 6.20% of your salary—up to a specific income level. However, for the years 2011 and 2012 this amount has been reduced to 4.20% of your salary. For example, in 2012, taxpayers paid the 4.20% tax only on the first $110,100 of earned income. This amount is linked to inflation and increases slightly every year. For any income you earn above the maximum, you will not have to pay the Social Security tax.

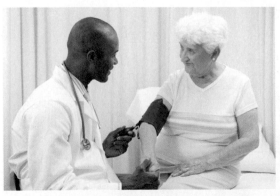

Millions of older Americans rely on Medicare for much of their health care coverage. This program is paid for in part by payroll taxes.

As just mentioned, for the years 2011 and 2012 the employee contribution portion of the Social Security tax was reduced to 4.20%. The purpose of this reduction was to help aid economic recovery from the severe recession lasting from December 2008—through June 2009. The government believed that allowing people to keep more of their income would result in increased consumer spending and help get the economy growing again. This particular provison of reducing the employee Social Security contributions will expire December 31, 2012, if Congress does not renew it. At that time the employee contribution will revert back to 6.20%.

Medicare is a government health insurance program that covers people who are age 65 and older and some people who are disabled and less than 65 years old. As you can see on Ryan's pay stub in Figure 6.1, $2.32— 1.45% of Ryan's gross earnings—went to Medicare. There is no cap on the amount of earnings subject to this tax.

For both Social Security and Medicare, your employer matches your contributions and sends the total amount to the government. Note: Self-employed people do not enjoy this employer match. In fact, they must pay both halves of the FICA tax themselves. This amounts to an extra tax on the income of those who are self-employed.

Personal Income Taxes

In addition to the FICA and Medicare taxes, your income is also subject to personal income taxes, or taxes imposed on the income you earn. It is this income that you report on your tax return. Refer to Figure 6.3 for the IRS table of individual tax rates.

As mentioned earlier, the tax code is extremely complex, and as your income increases and you begin to invest and plan for retirement, you may find it necessary to use the services of a tax professional. For simple returns, many people use tax preparation software. These programs guide you through preparing your tax returns and include all the necessary forms.

In addition to federal income taxes, many of you will pay a state income tax. The amount can be a significant factor when deciding where to live. Refer to Figure 6.4 for a listing of the states and their tax rates.

Also, some cities collect income taxes. Pay careful attention to where you live. Taxes and cost of living are factors that need to be considered in the overall equation.

MATH for Personal Finance

Brogan's grandfather made $112,000 in 2011, and the Social Security cap in 2011 was $106,800.

How much Social Security was withheld from his pay and how much Medicare was withheld from his pay?

Solution: Brogan's grandfather had 4.2% withheld from his pay for Social Security on the first $106,800 he made during 2011 for a total of $4,485.60 (.042 × $106,800). However, Medicare was withheld on the entire amount, so his Medicare withholdings were $112,000 × .0145 = $1,624.

FIGURE 6.3 2011 Individual Income Tax Rate Schedule

Two key factors affect what federal income taxes you must pay: your filing status and your total income. Generally, the more you make, the higher tax rate you pay.

Tax Rate	Single	Married/Joint*	Married/Separate	Head of Household
10%	$0–8,500	$0–17,000	$0–8,500	$0–12,150
15%	$8,501–34,500	$17,001–69,000	$8,501–34,500	$12,150–46,250
25%	$34,501–83,600	$69,001–139,350	$34,501–69,675	$46,251–19,400
28%	$83,601–174,400	$139,351–212,300	$69,676–106,150	$119,401–193,350
33%	$174,401–379,150	$212,301–379,150	$106,151–189,575	$193,351–379,150
35%	$379,151 and higher	$379,151 and higher	$189,576 and higher	$379,151 and higher

*This column must also be used by a qualifying widow(er)

FIGURE 6.4 2012 Tax Rates by State

Tax rates vary greatly from one state to the other, and this can be a significant factor in your financial planning.

	Tax Rate Range (in percents)		Number of Brackets	Income Brackets		Personal Exemptions			Federal Income Tax Deductible
	Low	High		Lowest	Highest	Single	Married	Dependents	
ALABAMA	2.0 -	5.0	3	500 (b) -	3,001 (b)	1,500	3,000	500 (e)	Yes
ALASKA	No State Income Tax								
ARIZONA	2.59 -	4.54	5	10,000 (b) -	150,001 (b)	2,100	4,200	2,100	
ARKANSAS (a)	1.0 -	7.0	6	3,899 -	32,700	23 (c)	46 (c)	23 (c)	
CALIFORNIA (a)	1.0 -	9.3 (f)	6	7,316 (b) -	48,029 (b)	102 (c)	204 (c)	315 (c)	
COLORADO	4.63		1	-----Flat rate-----		3,700 (d)	7,400 (d)	3,700 (d)	
CONNECTICUT	3.0 -	6.7	6	10,000 (b) -	250,000 (b)	13,000 (g)	24,000 (g)	0	
DELAWARE	2.2 -	6.75	6	5,000 -	60,001	110 (c)	220 (c)	110 (c)	
FLORIDA	No State Income Tax								
GEORGIA	1.0 -	6.0	6	750 (h) -	7,001 (h)	2,700	5,400	3,000	
HAWAII	1.4 -	11.00	12	2,400 (b) -	200,001 (b)	1,040	2,080	1,040	
IDAHO (a)	1.6 -	7.8	8	1,338 (b) -	26,760 (b)	3,700 (d)	7,400 (d)	3,700 (d)	
ILLINOIS	5.0		1	-----Flat rate-----		2,000	4,000	2,000	
INDIANA	3.4		1	-----Flat rate-----		1,000	2,000	2,500 (i)	
IOWA (a)	0.36 -	8.98	9	1,469 -	66,105	40 (c)	80 (c)	40 (c)	Yes
KANSAS	3.5 -	6.45	3	15,000 (b) -	30,001 (b)	2,250	4,500	2,250	
KENTUCKY	2.0 -	6.0	6	3,000 -	75,001	20 (c)	40 (c)	20 (c)	
LOUISIANA	2.0 -	6.0	3	12,500 (b) -	50,001 (b)	4,500 (j)	9,000 (j)	1,000	Yes
MAINE (a)	2.0 -	8.5	4	5,100 (b) -	20,350 (b)	2,850	5,700	2,850	
MARYLAND	2.0 -	5.5	7	1,000 -	500,001	3,200	6,400	3,200	
MASSACHUSETTS (a)	5.3		1	-----Flat rate-----		4,400	8,800	1,000	
MICHIGAN (a)	4.35		1	-----Flat rate-----		3,600	7,200	4,200 (k)	
MINNESOTA (a)	5.35 -	7.85	3	23,670 (l) -	77,731 (l)	3,700 (d)	7,400 (d)	3,700 (d)	
MISSISSIPPI	3.0 -	5.0	3	5,000 -	10,001	6,000	12,000	1,500	
MISSOURI	1.5 -	6.0	10	1,000 -	9,001	2,100	4,200	1,200	Yes (m)
MONTANA (a)	1.0 -	6.9	7	2,700 -	16,000	2,190	4,380	2,190	Yes (m)
NEBRASKA (a)	2.56 -	6.84	4	2,400 (b) -	27,001 (b)	123 (c)	246 (c)	123 (c)	
NEVADA	No State Income Tax								
NEW HAMPSHIRE	State Income Tax of 5% on Dividends and Interest Income Only								
NEW JERSEY	1.4 -	8.97	6	20,000 (n) -	500,000 (n)	1,000	2,000	1,500	
NEW MEXICO	1.7 -	4.9	4	5,500 (o) -	16,001 (o)	3,700 (d)	7,400 (d)	3,700 (d)	
NEW YORK	4.0 -	8.82	8	8,000 (b) -	1,000,000 (b)	0	0	1,000	
NORTH CAROLINA	6.0 -	7.75	3	12,750 (p) -	60,000 (p)	1,150	2,300	1,150	
NORTH DAKOTA (a)	1.51 -	3.99	5	35,350 (q) -	388,350 (q)	3,700 (d)	7,400 (d)	3,700 (d)	
OHIO (a)	0.587 -	5.925	9	5,100 -	204,200	1,650 (r)	3,300 (r)	1,650 (r)	
OKLAHOMA	0.5 -	5.25	7	1,000 (s) -	8,701 (s)	1,000	2,000	1,000	
OREGON (a)	5.0 -	9.9	4	2,000 (b) -	125,000 (b)	183 (c)	366 (c)	183 (c)	Yes (m)
PENNSYLVANIA	3.07		1	-----Flat rate-----		-----------None-----------			
RHODE ISLAND (a)	3.75 -	5.99	3	57,150 -	129,900	3,650	7,300	3,650	
SOUTH CAROLINA (a)	0.0 -	7.0	6	2,800 -	14,000	3,700 (d)	7,400 (d)	3,700 (d)	
SOUTH DAKOTA	No State Income Tax								
TENNESSEE	State Income Tax of 6% on Dividends and Interest Income Only					1,250	2,500	0	
TEXAS	No State Income Tax								
UTAH	5.0		1	-----Flat rate-----		(t)	(t)	(t)	
VERMONT (a)	3.55 -	8.95	5	35,350 (u) -	388,350 (u)	3,700 (d)	7,400 (d)	3,700 (d)	
VIRGINIA	2.0 -	5.75	4	3,000 -	17,001	930	1,860	930	
WASHINGTON	No State Income Tax								
WEST VIRGINIA	3.0 -	6.5	5	10,000 -	60,000	2,000	4,000	2,000	
WISCONSIN (a)	4.6 -	7.75	5	10,570 (v) -	232,660 (v)	700	1,400	700	
WYOMING	No State Income Tax								
DIST. OF COLUMBIA	4.0 -	8.95	4	10,000 -	350,000	1,675	3,350	1,675	

Source: www.taxadmin.org/fta/rate/ind_inc.pdf

✓ CHECKPOINT

Federal and state income taxes, Social Security, and Medicare are payroll taxes.

What are the payroll taxes?

FILING TAXES

Refer to Figure 6.2 for an example of the simplest tax return, the 1040EZ. As you can see, a tax return form allows you to record several different categories of information. These include filing status, gross income, adjusted gross income, deductions and exemptions, and refunds or payments. We will address each of these items in a little more detail. Understanding these categories will help you understand how our tax system works.

Filing Status

Taxpayers are required to specify a filing status when they submit their income tax return. They must choose one of the following options:

- Single
- Married filing jointly
- Married filing separately
- Head of household
- Qualifying widow(er) with dependent child

Generally, the tax rules and rates differ depending on which status you choose. It is important to read all of the documentation that comes with the tax forms so that you can choose the filing status that is most appropriate for you. Usually, a married couple will combine their income and file a joint return. However, in some specific cases, it may be better for a married couple to file separate returns. Usually, a single person who has a child would be better off filing as "head of household" rather than as single.

Until you reach the age of 18, most of you will be considered dependents by the IRS. As such, you can be claimed on your parent's or guardian's tax return as a dependent—someone who is dependent upon someone else for financial support. By claiming you as a dependent, your parent or guardian is able to lower what he or she owes in taxes. Note, however: Even though you may be a dependent and appear as such on someone else's tax return, you will still be required to file your own tax return if you earned enough income.

Gross Income or Total Income

The first step in calculating the federal tax you owe is to determine your gross income. **Gross income** or total income consists of the total amount of a person's income from (almost) any source. Take Ryan, for instance. The primary source of income for Ryan is the wages he earns at his job. At the end of the year, his employer will send him a document called a W-2 form that details how much money Ryan made. See Figure 6.5 for a look at Ryan's W-2 form.

Other forms of income in addition to wages and salary include interest income, dividend income, and capital gains from the sale of assets. **Capital gains** occur when you sell an asset for more than what you paid for it. For example, suppose you bought 20 shares of stock for $1,000 and later sold the shares for $2,200. The $1,200 difference is a capital gain, and it counts as gross income. Capital gains are taxed, but typically at a lower rate than other forms of income.

Gross income also includes income from tips, rental properties, and business income. Game show winnings, and any scholarship amounts that exceed the cost of tuition and books, are also considered part of gross income.

gross income: Total amount of a person's income from (almost) any source.

Activity #2

capital gains: A taxable gain that occurs when you sell an asset for more than what you paid for it.

FIGURE 6.5 W-2 Form

The W-2 form is a year-end summary of all relevant income and tax withholding information. You will receive one from your employer shortly after the end of the year.

22222	a Employee's social security number xxx-xxx-xxx	OMB No. 1545-0008		
b Employer identification number (EIN) xx-xxxxxxx			1 Wages, tips, other compensation 6400.00	2 Federal income tax withheld xxxxxxxxx
c Employer's name, address, and ZIP code Dave's Auto Shop 555 Main Street Anytown, USA 11121			3 Social security wages xxxxxxxxx	4 Social security tax withheld 268.80
			5 Medicare wages and tips xxxxxxxxx	6 Medicare tax withheld 92.80
			7 Social security tips	8 Allocated tips
d Control number xx			9	10 Dependent care benefits
e Employee's first name and initial Last name Suff. Ryan Jones 111 Doodle Street Anytown, USA 11121			11 Nonqualified plans	12a
			13 Statutory employee ☐ Retirement plan ☐ Third-party sick pay ☐	12b
			14 Other	12c
				12d
f Employee's address and ZIP code				

15 State Employer's state ID number MA	16 State wages, tips, etc. 6400.00	17 State income tax	18 Local wages, tips, etc.	19 Local income tax	20 Locality name

Form **W-2** Wage and Tax Statement   **2011**   Department of the Treasury—Internal Revenue Service

Copy 1—For State, City, or Local Tax Department

MATH for Personal Finance

Last year Colt's salary was $32,000, and he also received $1,200 in dividend income, lost $400 on the sale of one stock, and gained $650 on the sale of another stock.

What was Colt's gross income?

Solution: Colt's gross income was $32,000 + $1,200 − $400 + $650 = $33,450.

Some types of income are not included in gross income and therefore are not taxed. These include insurance reimbursements, child support payments received, moving expenses paid by an employer, and veteran's and welfare benefits.

This discussion highlights the need to keep detailed financial records. At tax time you are often required to provide a lot of information. It can be hard to remember how much you paid for a stock five years ago. Nevertheless, accuracy is important. Filing an incorrect tax return can lead to serious penalties.

Adjusted Gross Income

The next step in filling out a tax return is to figure your adjusted gross income, or AGI. **Adjusted gross income** is figured by taking the total income and subtracting certain allowable amounts. These can include contributions to certain retirement accounts, alimony payments, interest paid on student loans, and other special circumstances. Again, IRS rules detail exactly what can be subtracted from your total income to figure your AGI. For example, you may reduce your gross income by as much as $2,500 if you paid that amount in student loan interest. Your adjusted gross income will always be less than or equal to your total income.

Prof. FIN

Did you ever watch a game show and think to yourself, "Boy, would I like to win all that money or prizes"? Or maybe you think it would be great to win the lottery. As good as it sounds, all winnings, including cash and the value of any items you win, are considered as income, and you will have to pay taxes on them. These winnings are reported on Form 1099-MISC.

For example, if you have over $600 in winnings in one year, this will be taxed as income. It does not matter if these winnings are in cash or in the form of items such as cars or vacations. How much you will have to pay in taxes varies with what you have won, what your state will ask for, and how much the IRS will collect. Most say a good rule of thumb is to save 50% of what you receive as a cash prize to be paid in taxes.

Look up Richard Hatch. He won $1 million on the television reality show *Survivor* and learned the hard way what can happen if you forget to pay the taxes on your winnings. He was found guilty of tax evasion.

Expect around 50% of what you win as a cash prize to be taken up in taxes.

Deductions and Exemptions

You may be able to claim various deductions and exemptions that will reduce the amount of your AGI that is subject to income taxes. This, of course, will lower the amount of tax you pay.

The **standard deduction** is a fixed amount all people are allowed to deduct from their AGI to reduce their tax liability. The amount of the standard deduction varies according to your filing status and whether you are over the age of 65. This amount changes every year.

Many taxpayers also have the option of taking so-called itemized deductions in place of the standard deduction. **Itemized deductions** are specific expenses that, under tax law, can be deducted from income to reduce the amount of income subject to income tax. Congress has approved certain items as tax deductible in order to encourage certain behaviors. For example, Congress wants to encourage home ownership. Thus, it allows the homeowner to deduct the interest paid on a mortgage loan. Homeowners can also deduct the real estate taxes they pay. (On the other hand, in most cases, money paid on rent is not deductible.) Congress wants to encourage people to give money to charities, so it has made charitable gifts deductible. There are several other deductions that are allowed when you itemize. They include certain large medical expenses if they meet certain guidelines.

Is it smarter to take the standard deduction or to itemize deductions? This depends on the person. If the value of the itemized deductions you are entitled to is small, you will want to take the standard deduction. If the value of the itemized deductions is larger than the standard deduction, you will want to itemize. The goal, of course, is to have the smallest possible tax liability.

adjusted gross income: Income calculated by taking total income and subtracting allowable amounts that include contributions to certain retirement accounts, alimony payments, interest paid on student loans, and other expenditures that are identified by the IRS.

standard deduction: Fixed amount all people are allowed to deduct from their AGI to reduce their tax liability.

itemized deductions: Specific expenses that, under tax law, can be deducted from income to reduce the amount of income subject to income tax.

Refund or Payment

Activity #3

Accurate completion of your tax return will show you whether you need to pay additional income taxes that year, or whether you overpaid and will receive a refund. In some cases, low-income families will receive more money back in the form of an Earned Income Credit than was withheld from their paycheck. However, in most cases, you will not receive an income tax refund unless you pay taxes during that year.

Gross income is the same as total income and includes income from almost any source. The IRS allows a few sources, such as child support payments received, to be excluded from gross income.

✓ CHECKPOINT

What is included in a person's gross income?

TAXES AND YOUR FINANCIAL PLAN

As you can see, the tax system is very complex. Each person's situation is different, but all people share the same common goal: They want to take steps to lower their tax liability to the lowest possible level for their income. That way, they get to keep more of their own money rather than paying it to the government in taxes. This is just good financial sense.

Taking full advantage of the many ways to reduce your taxable income takes planning. And, the older you get and the more money you make, the more critical this planning becomes.

Still, even now you can see how you might factor in tax planning in your short-term future. For example, tax issues may influence your decision whether to buy a house or to rent an apartment. It might affect how much money you put each year into a tax-advantaged retirement account and other investments. Making these decisions will be covered in greater detail later.

As your life unfolds, you will find many other opportunities to use tax planning to your advantage. Tax planning may influence the way you save money for a college education for children you might have. It might affect when you decide to retire. Indeed, it is essential that you consider the tax implications of your financial life at all stages. Since circumstances vary widely from person to person, many people find that getting expert tax advice is an excellent investment.

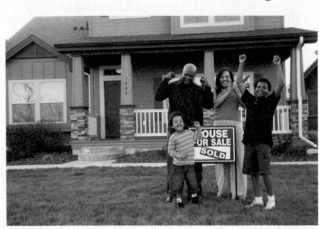

Taxes can have a big impact on major financial decisions, such as when and where to buy a home.

Think about Ryan. What are some of the things Ryan will eventually need to consider that are tax related? For starters, Ryan needs to think about where he works and lives. Remember, in some places he will pay city, state, and federal income taxes and also real estate and personal property taxes.

You must consider the tax consequences of all your financial decisions because the tax impact may make one course of action better than another.

✓ CHECKPOINT

Why are taxes an important part of your financial plan?

CHAPTER REVIEW

SUMMARY

- Taxes are monies the government collects from citizens for the purpose of operating the government. The government collects taxes in a variety of ways and forms: sales taxes, real estate taxes, and payroll taxes. The government also collects taxes from businesses. The Internal Revenue Service (IRS) is the governmental body that carries out the federal tax system.

- Payroll taxes include personal income taxes (state and federal) and Social Security and Medicare taxes. Social Security and Medicare taxes are also known as FICA. Many workers have these taxes withheld from their gross pay.

- Filing taxes involves reporting your earnings for the year on a tax return that is sent to the IRS and to any appropriate state or local tax collection agency. There are several different categories of information needed for your tax return. They include the following: filing status, gross income, adjusted gross income, deductions and exemptions, and refunds or payments.

- Tax planning is another important step in your financial plan. Taking full advantage of the many ways to reduce your taxable income takes planning. The older you get and the more money you make, the more critical this planning becomes.

Key Terms and Concepts

1. What is the purpose of the **Internal Revenue Services (IRS)**?

2. What is the difference between **Social Security** and **Medicare**?

3. What is a **capital gain**? Provide an example of a specific capital gain.

What Do You Know?   MyFinLitLab

1. (a) What is the difference between gross pay and net pay?

   (b) Why is it important to know the difference?

2. (a) Who pays taxes?

   (b) What kind of tax are you paying when you pay $1.05 for a $1 item at a convenience store?

3. (a) What agency administers the federal tax laws?

   (b) What is the purpose of a tax return?

   (c) What factors make tax rules so complicated?

Answers:
Key Terms and Concepts

1. The IRS enforces the tax laws enacted by Congress and collects the taxes.

2. **Social Security** provides payments to eligible retirees and disabled people. **Medicare** provides health care coverage to mostly older Americans and some younger disabled people.

3. **Capital gains** occur when you sell an asset for more than what you paid for it. For example, suppose you bought 20 shares of stock for $1,000 and later sold the shares for $2,200. The $1,200 difference is a capital gain.

Answers:
What Do You Know?

1. (a) **Comprehension** Net pay is equal to gross pay minus the deductions. (b) **Application** It is important because net pay is what is available to you to spend, save, and invest.

2. (a) **Comprehension** Individuals and businesses pay taxes. (b) **Analysis** This is called sales tax.

3. (a) **Knowledge** The Internal Revenue Service administers federal tax laws. (b) Comprehension You formally report your tax information to the IRS with a tax return. (c) **Analysis** The various rules designed to encourage certain behavior that have evolved over years make tax rules complicated.

4. (a) **Knowledge** Social Security, Medicare, and Medicaid are funded by FICA. (b) **Comprehension** Part of FICA withholdings are capped and not withheld above certain income levels.

5. (a) **Comprehension** In most cases, the IRS rules dictate your filing status. In some cases, you may choose the filing status that provides you with the lowest tax liability. (b) **Analysis** A married person could file a joint return with his or her spouse or file as "married filing separately."

6. (a) **Knowledge** Included in gross income are wages, salary, capital gains, interest income, dividend income, tips, rental income, and business income. (b) **Comprehension** Some types of payments not included in gross income are insurance reimbursements, child support payments, and moving expenses paid by your employer. (c) **Analysis** His FICA deductions make the difference.

7. (a) **Comprehension** Adjusted gross income is calculated by reducing gross income by certain allowable deductions. (b) **Application** Gross income will never be lower than adjusted gross income.

8. (a) **Knowledge** It is a fixed amount that all people are allowed to deduct for tax purposes. (b) **Analysis** If the standard deduction was larger than the total itemized deductions, it would result in a lower tax liability.

9. (a) **Comprehension** The federal government wants to encourage certain behaviors like charitable contributions. (b) **Analysis** The homeowner, because mortgage interest is tax deductible.

10. (a) **Comprehension** It is important because often you can grow wealth faster by using tax-sheltered investments. (b) **Analysis** Tax codes are very complex. A good tax advisor can save you money because of his or her knowledge.

4. (a) What are two programs funded by FICA?

   (b) What is one way that FICA taxes differ from the federal income tax?

5. (a) Briefly describe how your filing status is determined.

   (b) Give an example of how one person might be eligible for more than one filing status.

6. (a) List some types of income that are included in gross income.

   (b) What are some types of payments you might receive that would not be included in gross income?

   (c) In Ryan's case, what explains the difference between his gross income and his net income?

7. (a) What is the difference between gross income and adjusted gross income?

   (b) Which figure can never be lower than the other?

8. (a) What is a standard deduction?

   (b) Why would a person choose a standard deduction over itemized deductions?

9. (a) Why does the federal government allow certain itemized deductions?

   (b) Who is likely to pay lower taxes for the same level of income: A homeowner who pays $1,000 per month on a mortgage loan or a renter who pays $1,000 a month in rent?

10. (a) Why is it important to understand the tax consequences of your financial decisions?

    (b) How might hiring a tax advisor be a good investment?

Answers:
What Are Your Finance Math Skills?

1. $320 × .0765 = $24.48

2. $35,500 × .0765 = $2,715.75

3. $21,050 + $420 = $21,470

What Are Your Finance Math Skills?   MyFinLitLab

The first three questions correlate to *Math for Personal Finance* features located throughout the chapter.

1. Josh's gross pay was $320.00 this week. How much in FICA will be withheld from his check assuming the Social Security withholdings for employees is currently 6.20%? (Hint: Don't forget about the Medicare component.)

2. Amber's starting salary for her new job will be $35,500 a year. How much will she pay to the Social Security system for her first year assuming total FICA withholdings of 7.65%?

3. What is Corbin's gross income for 2012 if his salary is $21,050 and he receives $420 in interest income for the year?

4. Washburn's employer withheld $4,245 from his paycheck for federal taxes. After calculating his tax liability, he discovers he will only have to pay $3,211 this year. Will he get a tax refund and, if so, how much?

5. Cecelia bought a stock five years ago for $3,400. She sold it this year for $4,100. How much capital gain will she be required to pay taxes on?

6. Franklin made $165,000 for the tax year 2012. How much did he pay in FICA taxes?

7. Zachary has a taxable income of $70,000. How much did he pay in Medicare tax this year?

8. Joseph's standard deduction filing single is $5,800 for 2011. However, he paid $6,200 in mortgage interest and contributed $1,100 to charity. Should Joseph itemize or take his standard deduction? Explain your answer.

4. Yes—the refund will be $4,245 − $3,211 = $1,034.

5. $4,100 − $3,400 = $700

6. $(.042 \times 110,100) + (.0145 \times \$165,000)$ = $4,624.20 + $2,392.50 = $7,016.70

7. $70,000 \times .0145 = \$1,015$

8. Joseph should itemize because his itemized deductions of $6,200 + $1,100 = $7,300, which is larger than his standard deduction of $5,800.

What Would You Do?

The IRS allows for the deduction of expenses incurred in traveling to a job interview. Fritz, Erica, and their two children have used this deduction to fund their vacations for the last eight years. Each year, several months prior to their vacation, Fritz and Erica begin reviewing the online job listings for the city or cities they plan to visit. They each apply for several jobs for which they are qualified. Any applications that result in interviews are scheduled during their vacation. They are careful to deduct only those expenses allowed under the IRS Tax Code, such as mileage, meals (not the children's), and hotel and motel expenses (not the children's). This plan has resulted in between $300 and $500 in allowable tax deductions each year. Fritz and Erica have determined that in most cases, they would not accept the jobs if offered; however, if the perfect offer were to appear, they would give it serious consideration.

1. Discuss whether you think Fritz and Erica are being ethical in using the IRS Code to fund part of the expenses of their family vacation.

2. How might the behavior of Fritz and Erica affect you and other taxpayers?

3. Do you see other areas of the tax code discussed in this chapter that could be subject to abuse?

What Are the Connections? Math, Language Arts, and Technology

Research the various taxes in your area. These might include city tax, county tax, food tax, property tax, and so on. Make a chart that reflects the various taxes in your area. Be sure to include examples of each of the types of taxes, who pays them, and when they would be paid (for example, at the time of purchase or end-of-year).

Write an article for your school newspaper explaining these taxes to your fellow students and how many taxes they are already paying. Also, provide information on the types of taxes your fellow students can expect to pay when they purchase a car or other major purchases. Keep in mind that licenses and fees are types of taxes.

Teamwork Service-Learning Activity

As a team, write an informative presentation explaining the Four Rs of taxes for the children of a local elementary school (see page 97). Your presentation might be in the form of a rap, song, skit or play, or role-play. Your team might even come up with a video of their presentation that could be used with Parent Teacher Organizations in your school district.

ESSENTIAL QUESTION ACTIVITIES

Complete these activities to answer this chapter's Essential Question: *Why is paying taxes important and how does it affect an individual's financial plan?*

1. *On your own:* In this chapter, you have learned about paying taxes and the importance of taxes. Using paper or a word processing software such as Microsoft Word, write a script, newsletter, or brochure that explains why we pay taxes and how paying taxes will affect one's financial plan.

2. *As a class:* Divide into groups to develop presentations. One group can present why paying taxes is important and the other group will present how paying taxes affects an individual's financial plan.

TEST PREP QUESTIONS

1. Another name for take-home pay is
   a. gross pay.
   b. salary.
   c. net pay.
   d. income.

2. Which of the following statements about taxes is true?
   a. Only the federal government has the right to tax a person's income.
   b. Any taxes collected by the government are returned to the person when she files her income tax return.
   c. Taxes are the major source of revenue for the government.
   d. Taxes can only be taken out of a person's income when she has a full-time job.

3. From the following, select the tax that is matched with its correct explanation:
   a. Payroll tax: money deducted from a person's salary that is sent to the government by the employer.
   b. Real estate tax: money paid to the government to use for building federally subsidized housing.
   c. Sales tax: a percentage of money that the federal government deducts from the cost of new purchases.
   d. Income tax: money that an employer pays out of company profits to the federal government for each person employed.

4. If a person is self-employed and earns $70,000 annually, the person
   a. does not have to pay federal income tax because his salary is too low.
   b. must pay estimated income taxes every quarter.
   c. is only responsible for paying FICA tax to cover Social Security.
   d. will not have to pay any local or state taxes.

5. The purpose of the IRS is to
   a. pass laws to determine what will be taxed.
   b. enforce tax laws and carry out the federal tax system.
   c. prepare tax returns for businesses and individuals.
   d. cut federal taxes and distribute taxes that have been collected to local and state governments.

6. A person completes her federal 1040EZ form and sees that she paid total quarterly estimated taxes of $12,000. But the calculations show that she should have only paid $9,500 in taxes. What will happen if she sends the IRS this completed form with the necessary supporting documents?
   a. Nothing, because she completed the short form, the 1040EZ, instead of the long form, the 1040.
   b. The IRS will deduct the over payment of $2,500 from next year's taxes.
   c. She will receive a federal tax refund of $2,500.
   d. The IRS will make sure that her employer deducts the correct amount of taxes in the next year.

7. Juanita and Jessica work at the same company. Each is married and earns $75,000 per year. Juanita is paying more in taxes than Jessica. What two factors can help to explain why this is true?
   a. Juanita does not have any children and does not itemize deductions; Jessica itemizes deductions and has three children.
   b. Jessica earns an additional $15,000 from a part-time job and rents her house; Juanita owns her house and does not earn any additional income.
   c. Juanita contributes the maximum she is allowed by law to her pension plan and Jessica does not contribute more than the minimum that her employer will match to her pension plan.
   d. Jessica files her return as a single person and lets her husband claim their three children as exemptions on his taxes when he files as head of household.

8. Which of the following statements about adjusted gross income is true?
   a. It will always be higher than a person's gross income.
   b. It is the amount used to determine what a person actually has to pay in taxes.
   c. It will decrease when a person takes a deduction for real estate taxes, contributions to charities, and interest on a mortgage.
   d. It is the amount used to determine if a person gets a refund for paying Social Security taxes.

9. Which of the following statements about taxes and financial planning is true?
   a. It makes sense for everyone to use the services of a tax professional in order to avoid paying additional taxes.
   b. It is not really possible to reduce the taxes a person has to pay. Therefore, people need to save more money to pay annual taxes.
   c. Using a tax planner does not really make sense until a person is earning more than $85,000 a year.
   d. In most cases it is possible for people to reduce their tax liability by adjusting their financial plan.

10. A person looks over his pay stub and sees that in addition to paying state and federal personal income taxes, he is paying other personal taxes such as Social Security and Medicare. He is only age 20, so he is sure that his employer has made a mistake since Social Security and Medicare are for old people, and the money should be returned to him. Is he right?
   a. No. The money he is contributing to Social Security and Medicare is paying the benefits for today's older people.
   b. No. If he pays Social Security and Medicare taxes now he can start collecting benefits now.
   c. Yes. Only people within 20 years of retiring are expected to pay Social Security and Medicare taxes.
   d. Yes. He needs to let his employer know that he does not want to pay into the Social Security and Medicare benefits program in the future.

11. Which is a valid statement about a dependent?

   a. A teenager who is living at home and earns $5,500 does not have to pay taxes on that money because his parents will claim him as a dependent on their taxes.
   b. If a person is single but has two children he cannot count the children as dependents when he files his tax return.
   c. Declaring someone as a dependent on a tax return increases the taxes that have to be paid by the person filing the return.
   d. For each dependent a person has, she is able to take a deduction from the amount of taxes she owes when filing her tax return.

12. A 28-year-old earns $54,000 from his job as an illustrator. He also earned another $23,000 doing work for private clients. In May of this year he got married. His wife, also an illustrator, earned $47,000. They bought a house in June. He has always done his own taxes—filing the 1040EZ and taking the standard deductions. What advice should he follow for this year?

   a. He should file as a single person, take the standard deductions, and do his own taxes.
   b. He should file a joint return, take the standard deductions, and use an online computer program to complete the 1040EZ tax form.
   c. Because of all of the changes in his life, he should pay a tax professional to complete his taxes and figure out the most beneficial filing status and tax form for him to use.
   d. Given the changes in his life, he should do exactly what he has done in the past; however, this year he should claim his wife as a dependent.

13. A person wins $25,000 on a game show and a trip to Costa Rica worth $5,700. Does he have any tax obligation from these winnings?

   a. No. The prize is not considered earned income.
   b. Yes. However, he only has to pay taxes on the $25,000 since the trip is considered a gift.
   c. Yes. All of these winnings become part of his gross income.
   d. Yes. However, he will be able to deduct the cost of the trip next year when he returns from Costa Rica.

CHAPTER 7

ESSENTIAL QUESTION

Why is insurance an important part of a financial plan?

EM

INSURING YOUR HEALTH AND YOUR LIFE

LEARNING OBJECTIVES

- Explain why health insurance is important

- Describe different features of health insurance

- Understand the need for life insurance

- Discuss the ways people obtain insurance

KEY TERMS

co-insurance

deductible

group plan

health insurance

insurance

life insurance

preexisting condition

premium

Jontell's leg felt like it was on fire. Tears ran down her cheeks as a bystander evaluated her injury. Who knew that a pick-up game of flag football could be so dangerous? Fortunately for her, there was a medical doctor standing on the sidelines enjoying the game. The doctor gingerly probed her ankle, moving it slightly back and forth. "I can't tell if it's broken or just badly sprained, so you'll need an X-ray to find out." He smiled at her. "Either way, you'll need to stay off the leg for a while. And you won't be able to drive. Do you know if your insurance will cover an ambulance ride to the hospital?"

Jontell's leg continued to throb, but now her tears were for a different reason. She knew her parents did not have insurance and that this would be very costly for them. Why didn't she think about that before the game? She looked up at the doctor and tried to smile through her tears. "I think I'll be fine. If you could just help me to the parking lot, I'll get someone to drive me to the hospital."

insurance: A financial product that when purchased provides reimbursement paid to a person in the event of certain types of financial loss.

Unfortunately, Jontell's situation is a common one. Many people do not have insurance to protect them from loss in the event of an injury or other health problem. Yet insurance is an important component of your financial plan. A person obtains **insurance** by paying money to an insurance company, which agrees to reimburse that person in the event of certain types of financial loss. In this chapter, we will explore two essential types of insurance: health insurance and life insurance.

THE IMPORTANCE OF HEALTH INSURANCE

health insurance: A financial product that provides payment for medical services when people suffer a financial loss as a result of illness or injury.

Individuals covered by **health insurance** limit their potential liabilities when ill or injured and are ensured that they will receive adequate medical care. Remember that any time you owe someone money, you have a **liability**. Since medical care tends to be very expensive, adequate health insurance is an important component of your financial plan. People without health insurance could find their net worth quickly eliminated with one major health problem.

Sources of Health Insurance

Health insurance is available in many forms. Some people get their coverage from private companies, which make money by selling health insurance policies. Generally, this is the most expensive way to obtain insurance. Instead, many people get coverage as a company benefit. As shown in Figure 7.1, employers often pick up some or most of the cost.

Prof. FIN

To learn more about Medicare, go to www.medicare.gov. At the site, look at the choices for Medicare plans. You can also click on "Find doctors & other health professionals," enter your ZIP Code, select "Physician," and choose a specialty to find out how many specialists in your area are listed in the directory. Review the site and make a list of coverage information for Medicare.

The federal government has two health care plans, Medicare and Medicaid, which are available to some individuals. **Medicare** is a government-sponsored health insurance plan that is funded largely by taxes that most working people pay. It provides benefits to individuals who are at least age 65 and qualify for Social Security, or to individuals who are disabled. Medicare consists of two components, part A and part B. Part A is hospital insurance, which recipients receive at no cost to them. Part B covers doctor visits and other care provided outside a hospital, and recipients must pay some premium for this coverage. (In the world of insurance, **premium** means regular payments in return for insurance coverage.)

premium: Regular payments paid to an insurance company in return for insurance coverage.

Medicaid is a government-sponsored program that provides health insurance for low-income individuals. The program is administered on a state-by-state basis, so eligibility may differ for people from different states. The coverage is designed for the elderly, blind, disabled, and needy families with dependent children.

FIGURE 7.1 Employer-Provided Health Care Coverage

Employers are a major source of health care coverage, although employees must frequently pay a significant percentage of the cost of this care.

	Private Employers	State and Local Government Employers
Percentage of employers offering coverage	70%	87%
Employer share of premium (single coverage)	79%	87%
Employer share of premium (family coverage)	68%	71%

Source: www.bls.gov/news.release/pdf/ebs2.pdf

Of course, too many people, including Jontell, have no health care coverage. Her parents do not have insurance. Perhaps their employers don't offer any coverage or they cannot afford it. As a result, Jontell may have to wait until college to get health care coverage. (College students can often buy a relatively inexpensive plan that provides limited coverage.) In the meantime, Jontell's parents could face several thousands of dollars of expenses for her care.

Health Care Costs

Health insurance has received a lot of attention recently because the cost of health care has become very expensive (see Figure 7.2). Many employers are cutting back or dropping health insurance as a benefit for their employees. As the nation's population continues to age, you will hear more about health care costs and health insurance, since older people tend to have a greater need for health care. People are living longer and they require health care coverage for longer periods of time. In addition, a lot of new expensive technologies have emerged in the health care field. Fraudulent claims have also driven the cost of health insurance higher. Fraud occurs when someone submits false information in order to get a financial benefit.

Prof. FIN

Did you know that insurance fraud loss for health care is estimated to be in the billions per year?

- Under the Health Care Fraud and Abuse Control Program, convictions between 2009 and 2011 increased over 27%.

- Health Care Fraud Prevention and Enforcement Action Team (HEAT) coordinated the largest-ever federal health care fraud takedown in 2011.

- The Affordable Care Act has provided $350 million to ramp up anti-fraud efforts.

What more can you find out about health insurance fraud in the United States? Use the Internet to help you with your search.

Source: www.healthcare.gov/news/factsheets/2012/02/ medicare-fraud02142012a.html

Even though health insurance costs have increased significantly, having health insurance is a critical risk-reduction tool of your financial plan. Even minor accidents and injuries can do severe harm to your

FIGURE 7.2 Rising Health Care Costs

In ten years, health care costs for the typical American family of four have more than doubled.

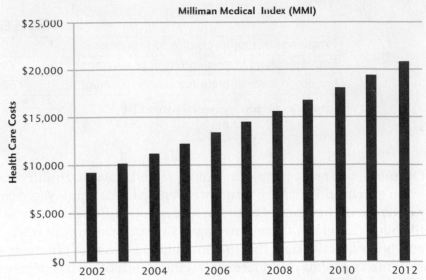

Milliman Medical Index (MMI)

Source: Figure from the "2012 Milliman Medical Index" by Lorraine Mayne, Chris Girod and Scott Weltz, from the Milliman website. Copyright © 2012 by Milliman Inc. Reprinted with permission.

Even when you're young and healthy, you may find yourself in need of costly medical care—and health insurance.

financial future. The bill for the kind of care Jontell will likely need can easily reach into the thousands. A severe injury or illness can lead to bills in the hundreds of thousands of dollars. Indeed, in 2010 health care spending by Americans averaged nearly $8,402 for each man, woman, and child. Spending is expected to rise sharply in the years ahead. One recent study found that health care costs were a factor in about half of all bankruptcies. Your decision is not whether to purchase health insurance but instead what type of plan to get and how much coverage to obtain.

In spite of the fact that health insurance is a key piece of a financial plan, many people find it too costly. A 2011 report published by the U.S. Census Bureau found that 49.9 million Americans—more than 16% of the population—didn't have any health insurance. (You can go to **www.census.gov** and click "Health Insurance" to read the latest census information.)

People without health insurance could find all of their net worth quickly eliminated with one major health problem.

 CHECKPOINT

Why is health insurance a critical part of your financial plan?

HEALTH INSURANCE FEATURES AND TERMS

Health insurance plans come in many forms and provide a range of coverage and services. However, different policies have different features, which can greatly affect the cost and the level of service you receive. When talking about health care plans, it's important that you know about the features and terms commonly used.

Indemnity Plans Versus Managed Care

Health care plans are usually classified as indemnity plans or managed care plans. Indemnity plans allow participants to seek health care from any qualified medical provider. Managed care plans limit participants to a specific list of providers. Regardless of the option available, you should be aware of the following issues.

Prof. FIN

Did you know that the high cost of health care in the United States has caused many people to look overseas for treatment? This is called "medical tourism." Simply put, many people are traveling overseas to get lower-cost medical care in foreign countries.

Although many think medical tourism is new, it actually began thousands of years ago with the Greeks. They would take pilgrimages to the small territory in the Saronic Gulf called Epidauria. Epidauria, the original medical tourism spot, was the sanctuary of the healing god, Asklepios.

In more recent times, Americans have sought healing spa treatments. One such treatment can be found in Hot Springs, Arkansas. For more than 200 years, health seekers both rich and poor have used the waters there to heal illnesses and promote relaxation. Other springs can be found

in Georgia. Can you name the American president who frequented the hot springs in Georgia? The answer is Franklin Roosevelt.

COMPARING COSTS

Approximate 2011 prices for various medical procedures in Costa Rica compared to the United States:* On average you can expect to save about 65% over treatment in the U.S.

Lasik surgery (both eyes): $1,800 versus $4,400

Spinal fusion surgery: $11,500 versus $100,000

Heart bypass surgery: $25,000 versus $144,000

Dental implant: $900 versus $2,800

Hip replacement: $12,500 versus $50,000

Airfares: Under $1,000 to more than $3,000 round-trip economy class from the United States to Costa Rica.

*Information from www.medicaltourism.com/en/compare-costs.html.

Family Coverage

The person who buys a health insurance policy or subscribes to it through an employer is known as the **policyholder**. Additionally, many health insurance plans provide coverage for immediate family members, such as a spouse and dependent children. However, children may become ineligible for coverage once they reach a certain age or status—for example, when they finish high school unless they enroll in college. The Patient Protection and Affordable Care Act (PPACA), passed in 2010, will eventually allow all young adults to remain on a parent's health insurance until they reach age 26 regardless of student status. This feature is being phased-in and may not be effective until 2014 for many policies. The PPACA, also known as the ACA, makes a number of changes to health insurance availability and coverages that may not be effective until 2014. Look at **www.healthcare.gov/ law/timeline** to see the timeline for their scheduled implementation. The safest option is to check with your insurance company about your specific policy if you have any questions.

Group Plans

group plans: Insurance plans that cover a large group of individuals, such as all the employees of a particular company or local government.

Group plans are insurance plans that cover a large group of individuals, such as all the employees of a particular company or local government. Within a group plan, an individual's high risk or loss is spread across the entire pool of group members. So, even though some group members may develop costly health problems or have much higher health risks, they have equal access to health care as those who enjoy perfect health. They also pay the same amount for coverage. By contrast, an individual or family who is not part of a group plan may pay much more for coverage if there is any history of illness or significant health risk.

Location Restrictions

Some U.S. insurance companies will cover medical care delivered inside the United States only. Others will provide coverage in foreign countries. If you travel abroad, it is a good idea to consider purchasing short-term health insurance for the duration of your trip.

Preexisting Conditions

preexisting conditions: Health conditions that existed before one's insurance policy was granted.

Insurance policies may exclude coverage for **preexisting conditions**, or health conditions that existed before your policy was granted. For example, if Jontell decides to purchase health insurance, she would probably find that her recent injury will not be covered under her new policy. However, the Affordable Care Act (ACA) mentioned earlier will prohibit insurance companies from denying coverage to individuals based on a preexisting condition. This component of the ACA will become effective in 2014. For individuals under the age of 19, this provision became effective in September 2010.

Cancellation Options

Prior to the passage of ACA, some insurance companies could cancel your health insurance policy at any time. This practice, known as rescission, is no longer legal in most cases. Many people, however, are not aware of this change in the law at this time.

Deductibles

deductible: The amount of money a policyholder pays prior to the insurance company's payment.

Some insurance policies begin paying claims only after the policyholder has paid a certain amount of money. This amount of money is known as a **deductible**. For example, your policy may have a $500 annual deductible, which means you will pay the first $500 worth of medical expenses in any given year. After you have paid that amount, your insurance company will begin to pay for some of the covered expenses. The deductible removes some of the financial burden from the insurance company. As a result, you will find that the higher the deductible, the lower your cost for insurance. Policies exist that have very high deductibles—many thousands of dollars—and comparatively low premiums. In effect, these policies trade lower insurance costs for higher risk of out-of-pocket expenses.

Coverage Limits

Many policies limit the total amount they will pay for certain procedures. Some policies may exclude some procedures completely—for example, voluntary surgeries to correct eyesight or improve appearance. Typically, experimental treatments are not covered. Many policies limit the number of days of hospital care they will pay for or the frequency of certain treatments. If you have a bill that exceeds your policy's coverage limits, you have to pay the difference.

Policies differ on coverage for prescription drugs. Some policies cover them, others do not. Some cover only certain drugs or provide only partial payment for unapproved drugs.

The Affordable Care Act prohibits plans from placing annual or lifetime limits on covered benefits. The key is to make sure you know whether the medical care or procedure you are considering is a "covered" procedure. Your best option is to study your insurance policy and ask your insurance representative prior to scheduling any nonemergency procedures.

Co-insurance

Co-insurance is the term for the share of costs for covered services that the insured person is required to pay out of his or her pocket. Co-insurance is often called a co-pay. For example, many policies have a $20 co-pay for a doctor's visit. That is, when you visit a doctor, you pay $20 and the insurance company pays the rest. Usually, co-pay amounts apply to most medical services. In many cases, you will be required to pay 20% of the cost of the treatment.

Provider Networks

Managed health care plans limit your choice of health care providers to a specific list of physicians and other medical professionals. Getting care from someone outside of this network may not be covered or may require a higher co-pay.

The two most common types of provider networks are health maintenance organizations (HMOs) and preferred provider organizations (PPOs). HMOs are based on negotiated agreements with specific doctors to provide health care. Individuals choose a primary care physician (PCP) from an approved list and must be referred for any additional specialized care. That primary care doctor may approve and arrange for care from a specialist—and set limits on the number of times the patient may visit that specialist. PPOs function similarly, but they generally provide a larger network of providers. In return for this greater flexibility, PPOs typically cost more than

MATH for Personal Finance

Michael needs laser eye surgery to correct his vision. After a visit to the ophthalmologist, he learns that the surgery will cost about $4,500 but that the procedure is not covered by his insurance.

How much will Michael be required to pay for the surgery?

Solution: Michael will be responsible for the entire cost of the surgery ($4,500) because it is not a covered procedure.

co-insurance: The share of costs for covered insurance services that the insured person is required to pay out of his or her pocket.

MATH for Personal Finance

Jontell needs surgery on her foot. Assume that she has insurance and the surgery costs $5,000 and she has a $500 deductible. She also has a 20% co-pay.

How much will Jontell have to pay for the surgery?

Solution: Jontell will have to pay the $500 deductible and then 20% of the remaining amount. Therefore, she will pay $500 + .20($5,000 − $500) = $1,400.

YOU DO IT

Activity #1

HMOs. Refer to Figure 7.3 for a comparison of the different types of private health insurance plans. Remember, some policies limit a policyholder's ability to see a specialist.

Auto Policies

Your automobile insurance will contain limited accident coverage. It may pay a portion of your medical costs associated with a vehicular accident.

 CHECKPOINT

Different features can greatly affect your costs and the level of service you receive.

Why is it important to understand the different features and terms used in health care plans?

 # LIFE INSURANCE

Life insurance helps protect a family from financial disaster in the event of a loss of income.

life insurance: An insurance plan that pays a specific person or persons when the policyholder dies.

Jontell's injury prompted her to begin thinking about insurance needs. She understood the importance of having health insurance, but she wondered about life insurance. What, exactly, was it? Did she have any? Did she need any? If so, how much should she buy?

Life insurance provides a payment to a specific person or persons when the policyholder dies. The person who receives the payment is known as a **beneficiary**. For example, a $100,000 life insurance policy in your name would pay your beneficiary $100,000 if you died. (Life insurance payments are not subject to income taxes.) Much like health insurance, people buy life insurance from a company. These policyholders pay periodic premiums. Many employers also provide fully or partially paid life insurance coverage for their employees as a benefit.

Role of Life Insurance

Life insurance is a component of your financial plan. Whether you need life insurance and how much to purchase depends on your financial goals. The most common financial goal or reason for buying life insurance is to make sure that those who depend on you have financial support in the event of

FIGURE 7.3 Comparison of Private Health Insurance Plans

The different terms and features of different managed care plans can be bewildering.

Type of Private Health Plan	Premium	Selection of Physician
Indemnity Plan	High	Flexibility to select physician or specialist
Managed care: HMOs	Relatively low	Primary care physician refers patients to specialist
Managed care: PPOs	Low, but usually higher than HMOs	There is a greater number of physicians to choose from in PPOs than in HMOs

your death. In most cases, life insurance is more critical for someone who provides income for the household. That is, it helps ensure that a bread-winner's death does not eliminate all cash coming into the household. In Jontell's case, she may not need much life insurance. Does anyone depend on her income to live?

The primary consideration for Jontell is whether she wants to provide some support for her parents in the event of her death. Sometimes, people carry a bit of life insurance to cover the costs incurred when they die. After all, "final expenses"—a funeral, cemetery plot, headstone, and so on can total several thousand dollars. Additionally, some people decide that it is wise to get a policy when they are young and healthy, because life insurance can be costly or difficult to obtain as people get older—and perhaps experience serious illness.

For these reasons, Jontell may want to think about her life insurance options. So, she will need to learn a little about the main types of life insurance.

Types of Life Insurance

Life insurance comes in several different forms. They include whole life insurance, term insurance, and universal life insurance. These forms differ in how long they provide coverage, how much they cost, and whether or not they provide any sort of benefit besides a payment at death.

Whole life insurance, sometimes referred to as permanent insurance, provides coverage for as long as the policyholder continues to pay the premium. These types of policies also build up savings for the policyholder over time. That is, part of what you pay in premiums goes into an account that grows. As this account builds a "cash value," you may be able to borrow against it or even take cash out. At some point, the cash value of the policy may be used to pay your premiums until your death. Whole life insurance policies can serve as a source of liquidity and as a kind of investment in your financial plan.

Term insurance is life insurance provided over a specific period of time. This period usually ranges between 5 and 20 years. Unlike whole life insurance, a term insurance policy builds no savings and does not serve as an investment. For these reasons, it generally has lower premiums.

Let's say a single mother with young children purchases a $100,000 benefit 20-year term life policy with her children named as beneficiaries. She would pay premiums to the insurance company. If the mother were to die during the 20-year term, the policy would pay the $100,000 benefit to her children. If she did not die during the 20-year term, the policy would simply expire. There would be no savings, and no more coverage.

Universal life insurance provides coverage for a specified term and builds savings for the policyholder. Therefore, it is a combination of term insurance and whole life insurance. Universal life allows more flexibility than other types of life insurance. You can add units of term coverage for periods of time and also alter your payments during your life. You may increase the size of your payment, and the additional amount will be invested. You may have choices about how that money is invested.

MATH for Personal Finance

The premiums for Janice's $200,000 whole life policy total $1,300 a year. A term insurance policy for $200,000 might cost Janice $400 in premiums. Janice bought the term policy and invested the difference, earning a rate of 8%.

How much money could she "make" in a year?

Solution: Janice would have $900 to invest. $900 \times .08 = $72.

Finance **ONLINE**

Web sites such as **www.insure.com** provide life insurance quotes and links to specific companies depending on the need. Go to one of these sites and get a quote for $50,000 of life insurance.

YOU DO IT

Activity #2

People buy life insurance to make sure that when they die their dependents have financial support.

 CHECKPOINT

What is the main purpose for buying life insurance?

GETTING INSURANCE

In recent times, most Americans have relied on their employers for access to health insurance. Employers often provide access to term life insurance, too. In many cases, employers pay some or even all the premiums for health or life insurance. They may also provide coverage to family members of the employee.

The availability of employer-provided coverage is significant for a number of reasons. For one thing, insurance is costly. Employer-provided benefits of this sort can represent a significant amount of money—and a large share of an employee's overall compensation.

Additionally, employer-provided plans generally provide coverage to employees and their families that they may have trouble affording on their own. While the ACA ensures access to health insurance, it can still be very expensive to buy individual health insurance. Taking advantage of your employer-provided plan can save you a substantial amount of money.

The same savings apply to life insurance if it is available through your employer. After all, insurers are not anxious to take on high risks, so purchasing individual life insurance on your own can be costly. But if you become part of an employer's group plan, you will pay no more than any other employee of that company.

There are also laws that help ensure that a person who leaves a job can continue to get access to health coverage—even if he or she has developed a serious health problem. The Health Insurance Portability and Accountability Act (**HIPAA**) ensures that workers can continue their health insurance coverage even if they switch jobs. This act prohibits insurance companies from denying new employees access to coverage based on their health or preexisting conditions. In addition, the Consolidated Omnibus Budget Reconciliation Act (**COBRA**) allows you to continue health insurance coverage for up to 18 months after your employment ends. You will, of course, be required to pay the premiums that your previous employer was paying for your coverage. COBRA and HIPAA make sure that people switching jobs have a way to maintain health insurance coverage during and after the switch. Finally, some companies even offer employees a chance to get health coverage after retirement.

Clearly, access to employer-provided health and life insurance can be a valuable benefit. But the trend in recent years is not favorable for employees of tomorrow. Health care costs are soaring in the United States. Each year, fewer and fewer employers offer health benefits to their employees. Those who offer coverage are asking employees to pay a growing share of the premiums. The availability of health benefits looms as a major challenge facing workers of tomorrow. It is certainly a factor you will need to consider when thinking about future jobs and careers.

Employers often provide a host of other insurance-related benefits. One important type is **disability insurance**, which provides regular payments to replace lost income in the event injury or illness makes it impossible to work. Other common employer-provided benefits include dental insurance, vision insurance, and other supplemental insurance policies designed to cover specific diseases such as cancer or heart disease.

There may come a time when you have to purchase health and life insurance on your own. For example, you may lose employer health coverage for a time when you switch jobs and your 18-month COBRA period has expired. Or you may decide that you want additional life insurance besides that provided by your employer. You may also decide you want to have a policy in place if you lose your job. And, if your employer does not offer it, or if you are self-employed, you may want to buy disability insurance. In many cases, unions, trade associations, and guilds may offer members the opportunity to purchase these insurance coverages at a reduced rate.

Insurance is like any other product you purchase. There are various kinds of coverage and prices. You can use the Internet to learn about the many different types of products and services. Some Web sites will help you find a company that will provide the coverage you desire for the best price. You may want to visit an insurance agent to discuss options. In any case, it is always best to shop around and compare products. Choosing insurance coverage is a major financial decision and should be made with as much information as possible about your options. Remember that health, life, and disability insurance costs also vary according to your age and health history. To receive accurate quotes, companies will ask you to fill out personal information regarding your and your family's health history. You may even need to get a physical exam before receiving coverage.

Note also that when you buy a life insurance policy, you need to be aware of the financial strength of the company. After all, you are counting on that company being able to pay a large amount of money at some unknown time in the future. There are a number of companies that rate the strength of insurers. Be sure you check the ratings of the companies you are considering, and avoid those with low ratings.

☑ CHECKPOINT

What has been the most common means of obtaining health insurance in recent years?

An employer-offered plan is the most common.

CHAPTER REVIEW

SUMMARY

- Insurance is the promise of payment to be made in the event of some kind of loss. Health insurance is a financial product that provides payment for medical services when people suffer a financial loss as a result of illness or injury. Health insurance is available in different forms: government programs, such as Medicare or Medicaid, or private companies, which make money by selling health insurance policies. Employers can offer health insurance through a group plan for their employees as a benefit.

- Insurance plans come in many forms and provide a range of coverage and services. Some issues to be aware of when considering insurance programs include the following: family coverage, location restrictions, preexisting conditions, cancellation options, deductibles, coverage limits, co-insurance, provider networks, referral limits, and prescription coverage.

- Life insurance is a component of your financial plan. The most common financial goal or reason for buying life insurance is to make sure your dependents have financial support in the event of your death. There are several options available, including term insurance, whole life insurance, and universal life insurance.

- Employers are a main source of insurance, but an individual may purchase health or life insurance through a private source. Insurance is like any other product: It is essential that you purchase it only after thoroughly investigating the options.

Answers:
Key Terms and Concepts

1. HIPAA ensures that workers can continue their health insurance coverage even if they switch jobs. This act also prohibits insurance companies from denying new employees access to coverage based on their health or preexisting conditions.

2. **Medicare** is a government-sponsored health insurance plan that provides benefits to individuals who are at least age 65 and qualify for Social Security, or to individuals who are disabled. **Medicaid** is a government-sponsored program that provides health insurance for low-income individuals. The coverage is designed for the elderly, blind, disabled, and needy families with dependent children.

3. Fraud occurs when someone submits false information in order to get a financial benefit. Preventing and detecting fraud is important to us all since fraud losses total billions of dollars per year that must be absorbed by consumers and taxpayers.

Answers:
What Do You Know?

1. (a) **Comprehension** It protects them from financial loss related to illness or injury. (b) **Analysis** The cost of health care is rising quickly and the population is aging.

2. (a) **Comprehension** Health insurance can be obtained through the private market or the government; many people get insurance through their employer. (b) **Analysis** The government feels a responsibility to help people get this critical coverage, which otherwise might be too expensive.

Key Terms and Concepts

1. What is the importance of **HIPAA?**

2. What is the difference between **Medicare** and **Medicaid?**

3. What is **fraud** and why is it important to be aware of it?

What Do You Know?   MyFinLitLab

1. (a) How do individuals benefit from having health insurance?

   (b) Why is health insurance likely to become a bigger and more complex issue in the future?

2. (a) What are the sources from which an individual can obtain health insurance?

   (b) Why do you think the government provides insurance to older and poorer Americans?

3. (a) What is a group plan?

   (b) What are the advantages of group plans?

   (c) Why do you think insurance companies are willing to offer coverage to large groups that may include people with high risks?

4. (a) What is a deductible?

   (b) What kind of person might be a good candidate for a high-deductible health insurance policy?

5. (a) What is the purpose of life insurance?

   (b) If a young person had to choose between buying health insurance and life insurance, which might he or she choose, and why?

6. (a) What is the difference between term insurance, whole life insurance, and universal life insurance?

   (b) Which might be the best choice for a young parent living on a tight budget? Explain.

7. (a) What benefit does whole life insurance provide that term insurance does not?

8. (a) What is disability insurance?

   (b) Why might younger individuals consider purchasing disability insurance?

9. (a) What are two types of supplemental health insurance policies that might be offered by an employer?

10. (a) Why might some people purchase insurance on their own?

   (b) Why is research so important when choosing insurance coverage?

What Are Your Finance Math Skills? MyFinLitLab

The first three questions correlate to the *Math for Personal Finance* features located throughout the chapter.

1. The insurance policy provided by Darrell's company has a $1,000 deductible and a 20% co-pay. How much will he have to pay for elbow surgery that will cost $9,000?

2. Gracie's insurance premiums are $131 per month. This year she also paid a $500 deductible and 20% of $3,200 for a minor accident. How much was her total health care expense this year?

3. Candice paid $2,000 for her whole life insurance policy this year. A term insurance policy with the same coverage would cost her about $700 a year. Assuming she decides to buy the term policy and invest the difference, earning a rate of 6%, how much money could she "make" in a year?

3. (a) **Knowledge** It's a plan that covers a large group of individuals. (b) **Comprehension** Insurance through group plans is often cheaper and provides better coverage. (c) **Analysis** Possible answer: The company is willing to assume the individual risk in return for selling coverage to a large number of people.

4. (a) **Knowledge** It is the amount the insured must pay before the insurance company begins providing coverage. (b) **Comprehension** Possible answer: A good candidate might be a young, healthy person who has a lower risk of serious illness or injury and who has a long time to recover from a significant expense.

5. (a) **Comprehension** Life insurance protects a person's heirs and dependents from loss associated with a person's death. (b) **Analysis** Possible answer: A young person may choose health insurance because there is a greater risk of health problems than death and because a younger person may have fewer dependents.

6. (a) **Comprehension** Term insurance provides coverage for a specified time. Whole life insurance provides insurance until the person stops paying premiums or the cash value can pay the premium. Universal insurance combines features of both—coverage for a specific time and the building of cash values. (b) **Application** Term insurance, because it is generally less costly.

7. (a) **Analysis** It builds cash value and serves as an investment that can be used as a source of cash.

8. (a) **Knowledge** It is insurance against being hurt or sick and unable to work. (b) **Analysis** Missing time from work could do great harm to a person's financial plan.

 9. (a) **Comprehension** Possible answers are cancer policies and heart health policies.

10. (a) **Comprehension** They may wish to have control of their own insurance, it may be unavailable from an employer, or they may be self-employed. (b) **Analysis** Policies, coverage, and costs vary widely.

Answers:
What Are Your Finance Math Skills?

1. $9,000 − $1,000 = $8,000 × .20 co-pay = $1,600 + $1,000 deductible = $2,600.

2. $131 × 12 = $1,572 + $500 + (.20 × $3,200) = $2,712

3. ($2,000 − $700) × .06 = $78 in interest on the savings plus she will still have the $1,300 she saved in premiums.

4. $20.

5. He is saving $200 per month so $5,000 / $200 = 25 months to save the $5,000.

6. $20 / .20 = $100 total cost so his employer pays $80 or .80 × $100.

7. $400,000 / 3 = $133,333.33 each.

8. To get the same coverage provided by the $40 a month policy she would have to pay $30 × 1.5 = $45 a month on the first policy. Therefore, the second policy is a better deal.

---

4. Jaden carried her receipt for the doctor visit to the cashier. The amount billed was $112 and she has $20 co-pay. How much will Jaden be required to pay?

5. Kevin was paying $250 a month for his health insurance coverage that had a $200 deductible. He dropped that coverage for a $50-a-month policy that had a $5,000 deductible. Assuming Kevin had no health care costs, how long would it take Kevin to save enough with his high-deductible plan to pay for a possible $5,000 out-of-pocket expense?

6. Jamarcus's employer pays 80% of his medical insurance. If the insurance costs Jamarcus $20 a week, how much is his employer paying?

7. Michelle listed her three children as equal beneficiaries on her life insurance policy. If she has a $400,000 policy, how much will each receive in the event of her death?

8. Brittany needs to buy some term life insurance. She has evaluated two 20-year policies. One policy will cost $30 a month for $100,000 in coverage. The other will cost $40 a month for $150,000 in coverage. Which policy is a better deal?

What Would You Do?

Ethan is 27 and a recent college graduate. His part-time employer through high school and college now wants him to work full time. He really enjoys the work and decides to go for it. The only problem is the job does not offer health insurance benefits. Ethan goes online to look for a health insurance company that offers benefits he can afford. Many of the companies ask the same questions. As he is filling out the information for quotes, he is uncertain how to respond to one of the questions. All the companies want to know if he smokes. Ethan does not smoke every day, but he does like to have a cigarette or two when he is out with his friends on weekends. Ethan is not sure why the insurance companies want to know this information. He thinks that smoking only one or two evenings a week is not bad. What could it hurt? Still, he is unclear what he should say when asked this question.

1. What should Ethan do? Should he tell the companies that he smokes occasionally? Explain your answer.

2. Is someone who smokes only on the weekends when out with friends a "smoker"?

3. Why do you think insurance companies want to know if a person smokes?

4. Is there an ethics issue if Ethan tells the companies he does not smoke? What does Ethan stand to lose if he tells the companies that he does not smoke?

What Are the Connections? Language Arts, Math, and Technology

Research the possible costs of health insurance. If you have access to the Internet, go to **ehealthinsurance.com**. If not, contact a local insurance agent for a quote.

1. Obtain health insurance estimates for yourself by providing your birth date and some personal information. How do the resulting plans differ? Which plan do you find most attractive? Why?

2. Now obtain dental insurance estimates by providing some personal information. Which plan do you find most attractive? Why?

3. If you have access to spreadsheet software, design a spreadsheet of the data you have obtained. If not, use paper and pencil to design the spreadsheet. Prepare a presentation of the data that helps to explain your decision for health and dental insurance.

Teamwork Service-Learning Activity

In a team, use the Internet to research health care insurance fraud. Develop a newsletter providing information about insurance fraud. Your newsletter might include information on the costs of insurance fraud to others, how insurance fraud makes health care costs rise, tips on reporting insurance fraud, and the consequences of being suspected of insurance fraud. Your newsletter could also be a Web page, multimedia presentation, or other form of getting the word out about this important subject.

ESSENTIAL QUESTION ACTIVITIES

Complete these activities to answer this chapter's Essential Question: *Why is insurance an important part of a financial plan?*

1. *On your own:* Your friends have been talking with you about putting together a financial plan as they look at the future beyond graduation. They have told you that planning for life and health insurance is not important to them because they are young and healthy. They are going to worry about that later. You want to show them why insurance should be an important part of their financial plan, so you have decided to make a brochure to show them. In your brochure, you want to be sure to include facts about the costs of not having health insurance, the benefits to their financial plan by having health insurance, and how to calculate the costs of health insurance as part of their financial plan. Assume that if they stay on their parents' health insurance plan until they are 26 years old their parents will require them to pay the additional premium.

2. *As a class:* Working in groups, brainstorm what would happen to your financial plan if life and health insurance was not a part of the plan. Present your list to the class.

1. b **1.** The reason that a person buys health or life insurance is to
   a. make sure that he will earn an income if he becomes ill or injured.
   b. limit the amount of financial loss if there is an illness, injury, or loss of life.
   c. have protection from being sued if another person is injured while visiting his home.
   d. guarantee that the person will not suffer any loss in a natural disaster such as an earthquake or hurricane.

2. a **2.** Usually the least expensive way for a person to obtain health insurance is by
   a. enrolling in an employer-provided health care plan.
   b. purchasing the insurance through a private company.
   c. using the services of the local hospital emergency room.
   d. enrolling in Medicare.

3. c **3.** A young, healthy, athletic woman receives her monthly insurance premium notice. Her premium has increased to $350 a month. She decides to drop her insurance, reasoning that she can better spend her money on a gym membership and yoga classes to relieve the stress in her back. She decides that dropping this health insurance will also enable her to start saving money in an IRA. This is a
   a. good idea because she will be getting what she needs to keep her from getting sick or injured.
   b. good idea because if she is really sick or injured, she will just go to the nearest hospital emergency room.
   c. bad idea because one bad illness or even a small injury can wipe out all of her savings.
   d. bad idea because most companies will not hire a person who does not have her own insurance.

4. d **4.** Which insurance term is *not* correctly matched with its description?
   a. Indemnity insurance plan: permits the policyholder to obtain treatment from any health care provider.
   b. Group insurance plan: covers a large number of people and reduces the premium cost to any one person by spreading risk across many people.
   c. Managed care: restricts a person to use only participating providers of health care—those who belong to the health care plan.
   d. Family coverage: the policyholder pays a lower premium in order to obtain coverage for all members of the family as long as they live at home.

5. a **5.** A person submitted his claim for reimbursement of medical expenses to his insurance company and his claim was denied. Recently he switched insurance coverage. His former insurance company always paid for the injections he received to calm down the arthritis in his knee. What is the most likely reason that the new insurance would not pay for his treatment?
   a. The injections are not a covered procedure under his new insurance policy.

b. He has not paid his co-insurance to the doctor for the services that were performed.

c. Since this is his first claim of the year, he has not met his annual deductible so the claim was rejected.

d. He has a family coverage plan and his daughter recently had to go to the doctor with a knee injury from playing soccer and her claim used up the family's coverage.

6. A person with insurance coverage ends up in the hospital with a broken wrist suffered while playing football with a group of friends. After an X-ray, MRI, doctor visit, orthopedist visit, and cast, he leaves the hospital with a bill for $9,000. He has a $2,000 annual deductible and this is his first visit to a doctor in this calendar year. He also has a 20% co-pay. The amount that he is responsible for paying is

6. a

a. $3,400.

b. nothing since he did not need to stay overnight in the hospital.

c. only the $2,000 annual deductible.

d. $1,800.

7. A person decides that she needs braces to correct her teeth. Her orthodontist agrees and tells her that it will take about 18 months to correct her teeth completely and the work will cost $7,500. Her insurance company says that this is cosmetic work and therefore it is not covered by her plan. If she goes ahead with this dental work, she will have to pay

7. b

a. $1,500, the co-insurance.

b. $7,500, the full amount.

c. $2,000, the annual deductible.

d. $2,000, the annual deductible for the first year and $1,000, half the annual deductible for the final six months.

8. Rebecca and Eduardo have medical insurance through their employers; Rebecca's coverage is through an HMO and Eduardo's is through a PPO. Which of the following is a true statement about the probable difference in coverage each will receive?

8. b

a. Rebecca's monthly premiums will probably be higher than Eduardo's.

b. Eduardo will probably have a larger provider network from which to choose doctors.

c. Eduardo will be able to go to any doctor he chooses.

d. Rebecca will be able to go to any specialist she chooses.

9. Even though preferred provider organizations (PPOs) usually charge a higher premium for insurance coverage than health maintenance organizations (HMOs), people are often willing to pay the difference because they know that the

9. c

a. HMO doctors are usually new doctors without much experience.

b. HMO only covers the first visit to a doctor; after that, the person has to pay out-of-pocket.

c. PPO usually has a greater number of doctors from which the person can select a primary care doctor and specialists.

d. PPO covers the cost of as many doctors' visits as necessary to treat a condition.

10. a   **10.** The purpose of life insurance is to
  a. provide funds to help a person's beneficiaries maintain a certain standard of living should the policyholder die.
  b. pay for large purchases such as a home or college education while the person is alive.
  c. cover the cost of nursing care and other expenses not covered by a person's health insurance.
  d. provide financial support for a policyholder's parents should they need to go into a nursing home.

11. b   **11.** Since it is true that a term life insurance policy expires at the end of the term and there are no accumulated savings, why would a single 38-year-old father of three children under the age of five decide to buy a 20-year term policy instead of a whole life policy?
  a. He will be ready to retire in 20 years and then his children can support him.
  b. Compared to whole life insurance, he can buy much more coverage for his children in case of his death for a relatively low price.
  c. Term life insurance will cover the cost of paying for college for his three children even if he is still alive.
  d. Term life insurance is designed for single people and single parents; whole life insurance is designed for married couples.

12. b   **12.** A young, healthy single person without dependents decides that she is going to buy a whole life policy that is offered where she works. Since she is engaged and is hoping to have children within five years, she thinks that buying this insurance is a good move. Is this a wise financial decision?
  a. No. She should just buy five-year term insurance now.
  b. Yes. She is young and healthy and she will get a good rate on the insurance and will have it when her family may really need it.
  c. Yes. This is a way to make sure that she will be able to pay for her children's education when they reach college age.
  d. No. She would be spending money on something she may not need for years.

13. a   **13.** A person is trying to decide between buying term life insurance and whole life insurance when someone suggests that he consider buying a universal life policy. What is an advantage of universal life that attracts many people to this financial product?
  a. It is considered the most flexible type of life insurance because it combines the ability to accumulate savings and extend the policy's term.
  b. It is less expensive than other forms of life insurance.
  c. It pays the insured person the full face value of the policy even if the person lives beyond the term of the policy.
  d. It can help a person pay off other debts by cashing in the policy for its full face value after five years.

14. A person had breast cancer while employed by a company. She was treated and has been cancer free for eight years. She has a wonderful offer for a top position at a new company but she is worried that she will not be able to get health insurance coverage. Should she worry?

a. Yes. Because she has a preexisting condition, the new company's insurance plan can refuse to cover her.

b. No. Workers are protected by law from being denied insurance if they switch jobs even if they have a preexisting condition.

c. Yes. The new company's insurance plan is only required to cover her for 18 months.

d. No. She can buy her own insurance from a private company even though it will be very expensive.

15. What is a true statement about insurance?

a. Health, life, and disability insurance premiums are the same for everyone who is less than age 65.

b. As the cost of insurance has risen, more companies are cutting back on employee coverage or requiring employees to pay a larger share of the premiums.

c. A person who is self-employed is not able to purchase disability or health insurance.

d. When a person receives information from one company on how much she will have to pay for insurance, she can anticipate that other insurance companies will charge her almost identical rates.

CHAPTER 8

ESSENTIAL QUESTION

Why is an understanding of economic conditions important to your financial plan?

THE ECONOMY AND YOU

LEARNING OBJECTIVES

- Explain how economic factors impact financial decisions

- Understand how demographic changes will impact your future

- Analyze how events in the national and global economy might affect you

KEY TERMS

business cycle
consumer price index
depression
economics
economy
global economy
gross domestic product
inflation
recession

"Do you remember this place?" Miranda's dad asked as they drove through the shabby looking town. It had been years since Miranda had driven through her grandparents' old neighborhood. The place seemed a lot different. When she was a little girl, she remembered, she loved walking downtown with her grandmother to buy an ice cream cone. Now, the ice cream parlor was gone. In fact, the main street was practically empty. There were hardly any businesses open anymore. Even the factory where grandpa had worked was boarded up.

Miranda's dad drove down her grandparents' old street. Many of the houses were run-down. "What a shame," her father muttered as he looked around the decaying neighborhood. "This used to be a very nice place. It's a good thing they sold the house when they did—before all the factories closed and people moved away. They would never be able to get that kind of money for the place today, with the recession and all."

Miranda thought about her grandparents. They seemed happy in their new condo near Miranda's family's home. They had lots of friends and were even able to do some traveling. "My dad did a great job of saving for retirement," her father said. "Now they're living a nice life and do not have to worry as much about problems in the economy."

Miranda did not really understand all of what her father was talking about. But she could tell that he was grateful that his parents had made some good decisions.

Miranda may not have understood everything her father said, but she and her family provide a great lesson in the way the economy can affect us. In this chapter, we will look at how global events can impact our financial planning.

ECONOMICS AND YOUR FINANCIAL PLAN

economics: The study of choices.

economy: The system in which individuals, businesses, governments, and the world as a whole interact.

Broad trends in the economy can have a powerful impact on the economic well-being of a particular community.

Economics is often defined as the study of choices: Economists assume that people cannot simply have everything they need and want. They must decide what they will seek, how they will seek it—and what they will do without. Economists attempt to understand ways that these decisions are made, the factors that influence them, and the impact those decisions have on others.

Each of you makes economic decisions every day. In fact, almost every decision we make could be viewed as an economic decision. How much did you spend on lunch today? What options did you pass up when you made that decision? Will you go to a movie this weekend, or will you save your money in order to buy the more costly concert tickets? Larger decisions might involve what kind of education or job training you seek, or whether to start a new business.

In economics, we study choices made by individuals. We also study the decisions of businesses and governments, and the world as a whole. The system in which all these different people and groups interact is called the **economy**.

While economics is not the main subject of this text, it is not hard to see how it might affect your financial life. As you have read, building a financial plan involves making choices. In addition, the choices or actions of others can have a big effect on you. In Miranda's grandparents' case, they made good decisions to save well for retirement and to sell their home at a time when they could get a good price for it. These good decisions helped protect them from the effects of events over which they had no control—the closing of factories and the start of an economic downturn.

We will now look at several broad economic issues and concepts that are likely to shape your economic world. Understanding or at least being aware of these issues and concepts can help you formulate your plans and make your decisions.

Note that economics is broken into two categories: macroeconomics and microeconomics. **Macroeconomics** deals with broad issues that impact the economy as a whole. **Microeconomics** focuses on the study of individual choices or decisions made by smaller units, such as a firm. While most of the issues we discuss in this chapter are macroeconomic issues, we will present them so that you can think about how they impact you on a micro level. Our goal is to provide a simple overview of economic issues; therefore, we will leave the more detailed study of supply and demand issues and the related graphic analysis to be covered in your economics course.

✓ CHECKPOINT

What does the study of economics have to do with your financial plan?

Good financial plans prepare for unexpected economic events, and some economic trends can impact financial decision making.

DEMOGRAPHIC FACTORS

Demographics is the study of human populations. Demographers look at groups of people and their unique combination of features such as race, education, gender, and age. Understanding demographics can help us predict certain needs in advance. For example, if the number of grade school age students is increasing in a certain community, we can predict that high school enrollments will increase in the near future. That community may need to plan to build more classroom space or otherwise plan to meet the need.

We can also examine demographic trends in the whole country's population. For example, two important demographic trends that will impact everyone in the United States are the "graying of America" and increased immigration. A related challenge is the future of the Social Security system.

The Graying of America

The "graying of America" refers to the fact that the number of older people in the United States is increasing at a faster rate than that of other age groups. Why is this happening? One reason is the so-called "baby boom." The **baby boom** was a period of very high birthrates after World War II that occurred between 1946 and 1964. In fact, people born during that time— baby boomers—make up about one-third of the U.S. labor force today. The leading edge of this group has started to retire. What does this mean to you?

For one thing, boomers are beginning to leave their jobs, which will open up opportunities in numerous fields. While many companies will offer options to retain some of these older workers, many boomers will opt to retire. In fact, the U.S. workforce grew by about 30% during the 1970s. In contrast, current forecasts show the U.S. workforce will increase by only 0.6% a year for the foreseeable future. This population shift will open positions and create opportunities for rapid advancement in almost every field. However, the 2008–2009 recession may cause some of the boomers to remain in the workforce longer and thus create greater competition for open jobs.

The pending retirement of the baby boomers will also have other effects. After all, older people have a unique set of needs and wants. What types of

MATH for Personal Finance

Jill needs to decide about whether to spend $10,000 on a two-year degree that will qualify her for a $28,000-a-year job or go to work now and make $18,000 a year. She will work part-time while in college and make about $8,000 a year. (For purposes of this exercise, disregard the effects of interest or inflation.)

How long will it take Jill to recover her investment if she goes to college?

Solution: Jill is giving up $10,000 a year in income for two years and spending another $10,000, so she will have a total of $30,000 invested in her education. Since the job with the degree will pay $10,000 per year more, she will need three working years to recover her investment of $30,000.

Activity #1

goods and services will this group demand? Jobs in health care and other services that serve older people will be in high demand. Historically, many retired people relocate to warmer locations. Will housing choices change for this gray population? Are there opportunities to start your own company or enter an industry that is in position to take advantage of these trends? Do you need to be concerned about how the behavior of retirees might affect housing prices where you live? Think about how these coming changes will reshape your community and create new opportunities and challenges.

Prof. FIN

Facts about the "graying of America":

- Because of healthier lifestyles, Americans have added 25 years to their life spans over the last several decades. In 2005, there were 36 million Americans over the age of 65. By 2020, this number is expected to be closer to 55 million.

- One million Americans turn age 60 every month!

Immigration

In recent decades, immigration changes have also produced some important demographic changes in the United States. Hispanic Americans are a rapidly growing share of the population. In many parts of the country, this group already forms the majority. How does this impact you? Jobs that cater to the needs of Hispanic Americans will be in high demand. If you don't already speak Spanish, you might decide to learn the language in order to create more opportunities for your career advancement.

These are just two examples of demographic trends that will reshape the United States in the years ahead. All students should consider the impact of coming shifts on career decisions.

Social Security

When you receive a paycheck from your employer, you will find that FICA taxes are deducted from your total earnings. These taxes are withheld to pay for the Social Security system. Many retirees rely on Social Security payments for at least part of their living expenses when they stop working.

Prof. FIN

Historians sometimes come up with names to describe major demographic groups or trends. Here are a few examples:

- Silent Generation—born between 1925 and 1945

- Baby Boomers—born between 1946 and 1964

- Generation X—born between 1964 and 1981

- Generation XY Cusp (MTV Generation)—born between 1975 and 1986

- Generation Y (Echo Boomers or Millennials)—born between 1981 and 2001

- Generation Z (Homelanders or Vista Generation)—born after 2001

In 1937, when the U.S. government first started collecting Social Security, there were a lot of people paying into the system and very few drawing money out. As recently as 1950, there were more than 16 workers paying FICA taxes for every one person receiving Social Security benefits. Today, that ratio is about 2.9 workers paying taxes for every one person drawing retirement. In Figure 8.1, you can see that in about 20 years, there will be just over two workers for every one person drawing Social Security.

Now remember the demographic discussion. The oldest of the seventy-six million baby boomers reached retirement age in 2008. By 2026 all of the baby boomers should reach retirement age and be eligible to retire. Who will pay for their retirement? Many of you will see that your FICA tax may increase to cover these promised benefits. You also may see benefits reduced for future retirees—you. What does that mean to your financial plan? It means that you should count on being responsible for a greater share—perhaps even all—of your own retirement.

In fact, wise people have always saved money above and beyond what they could expect from Social Security. Think again about Miranda's grandparents. They saved money during their working years, and as a result they are now enjoying a good quality of life. As a young person, time is clearly on your side. You can enjoy a comfortable retirement if you plan for it. Remember, the financial plan is a road map to achieving your goals in life. If you want to retire with plenty of money with which to do what you want, map out your path. In Figure 8.2, you can see how even a small investment can help you accumulate a large sum of money for your retirement.

MATH for Personal Finance

Assume that by 2040 there are 110 million workers in the labor force and 61 million retirees drawing Social Security.

How many workers will be paying in per retiree in 2040?

Solution: 110 / 61 = 1.8 workers per retiree.

✓ **CHECKPOINT**

What are some demographic trends that may affect your financial future?

Baby boomer retirements and immigration issues may affect your financial future.

FIGURE 8.1 Workers per Beneficiary Declining

The future of Social Security is in doubt in large part because the ratio of workers paying into the system to beneficiaries drawing out of it is shrinking.

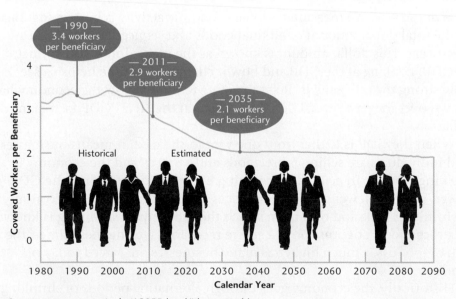

— 1990 —
3.4 workers per beneficiary

— 2011 —
2.9 workers per beneficiary

— 2035 —
2.1 workers per beneficiary

Historical   Estimated

Covered Workers per Beneficiary

1980 1990 2000 2010 2020 2030 2040 2050 2060 2070 2080 2090

Calendar Year

Source: www.ssa.gov/pubs/10055.html#demographics

Demographic Factors   **141**

FIGURE 8.2 Relationship Between the Investment Period and Your Savings at Retirement

(Assuming a $5,000 Investment and a 10% Annual Return)

Savings at Retirement

Number of Years

FACTORS IN THE LARGER ECONOMY

You have no doubt heard news commentators and politicians talk about "the economy." Indeed, all of us are part of a larger economic system, which may at one time or another be doing well—or not so well. The overall trends in the economy can have a big impact on our financial decisions. That is why it is important to have a basic understanding of how the economy generally behaves, and about significant factors that can shape its future.

Business Cycles

One of the ways we measure national economic activity is by keeping track of the total dollar amount of all final goods and services purchased in a given year. This dollar amount is known as the **gross domestic product,** or GDP. Looking at the GDP and how it changes over time helps us see how strong the economy is. Refer to Figure 8.3 to see how the economy has grown over the past several decades. Note that the "real" GDP factors in inflation.

When the GDP is higher from one year to the next, it means businesses and individuals are selling more goods and services and the economy is growing. People, in general, are earning higher incomes. When the GDP is lower, it means fewer goods and services are being sold and the economy is shrinking. A period of time in which the economy is shrinking is known as a **recession**. A **depression** is a severe recession. During these times, the risk of job loss is much higher as many businesses are forced to lay off workers.

Historically, the economy goes through alternating periods of shrinking and growth, or expansion. This pattern is known as the **business cycle**. The

MATH for Personal Finance

Factory X in the United States pays 200 workers a total of $7 million each year to produce 1.5 million widgets. Foreign factory Y employs 150 workers at a total cost of $750,000 to produce 750,000 widgets.

How do the costs per widget of the American and foreign factory compare?

Solution: The cost per widget in the United States is $7 million/1.5 million, or $4.67 per widget. The cost per widget overseas is $750,000/750,000, or $1 per widget.

FIGURE 8.3 Current-Dollar and "Real" Gross Domestic Product

	Annual GDP in billions of current dollars	Annual GDP in billions of chained 2005 dollars		Annual GDP in billions of current dollars	Annual GDP in billions of chained 2005 dollars
1975	1,637.7	4,875.4	1994	7,085.2	8,863.1
1976	1,824.6	5,136.9	1995	7,414.7	9,086.0
1977	2,030.1	5,373.1	1996	7,838.5	9,425.8
1978	2,293.8	5,672.8	1997	8,332.4	9,845.9
1979	2,562.2	5,850.1	1998	8,793.5	10,274.7
1980	2,788.1	5,834.0	1999	9,353.5	10,770.7
1981	3,126.8	5,982.1	2000	9,951.5	11,216.4
1982	3,253.2	5,865.9	2001	10,286.2	11,337.5
1983	3,534.6	6,130.9	2002	10,642.3	11,543.1
1984	3,930.9	6,571.5	2003	11,142.2	11,836.4
1985	4,217.5	6,843.4	2004	11,853.3	12,246.9
1986	4,460.1	7,080.5	2005	12,623.0	12,623.0
1987	4,736.4	7,307.0	2006	13,377.2	12,958.5
1988	5,100.4	7,607.4	2007	14,028.7	13,206.4
1989	5,482.1	7,879.2	2008	14,291.5	13,161.9
1990	5,800.5	8,027.1	2009	13,939.0	12,703.1
1991	5,992.1	8,008.3	2010	14,526.5	13,088.0
1992	6,342.3	8,280.0	2011	15,094.0	13,315.1
1993	6,667.4	8,516.2			

Source: www.bea.gov/national/xls/gdplev.xls

business cycle, shown in Figure 8.4, is one full period of economic growth followed by a period of recession. Recessions are characterized by fewer goods being sold and higher levels of unemployment.

So, how does the business cycle affect you? Think about how the recent recession lasting from December 2007 to June 2009 affected people you know. This period of time has been called "the Great Recession" because it was the worst recession since the Great Depression. Even now, unemployment rates remain high and experts predict that it will take years for the economy to put these workers back to work at the current levels of economic growth.

It is important to know that the cycle exists and that good times are always followed by bad times—which are followed again by good times. With regard to financial planning, you need to prepare during good times for the next recession. Set aside an emergency fund that will enable you to continue to pay your bills in the event of a layoff. Store up some reserves during the good economic times and live off these reserves if the economy negatively impacts your finances. Good financial planning is about making preparations that will help you weather any economic or financial storm that may arise.

Understanding the business cycle can also help you make basic life decisions. Miranda's grandparents may have had the business cycle in

gross domestic product (GDP): The total dollar amount of all final goods and services purchased within the nation's borders in a given year.

recession: A period of time in which the economy is shrinking.

depression: A severe recession.

business cycle: Alternating periods of shrinking and growth, or expansion, in the economy.

FIGURE 8.4 The Business Cycle

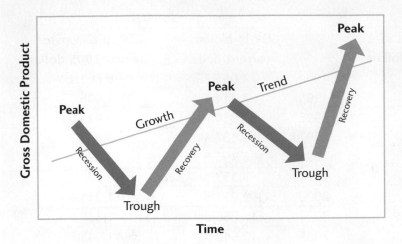

inflation: A sustained increase in the general level of prices.

consumer price index (CPI): The formal measure of inflation that tells whether things overall are more expensive now than in the past.

If you want to compare the buying power of $20 or any other amount from one year to another, visit **www.bls .gov** and click the link to the inflation calculator. It is fun and informative to see how inflation can affect your money!

mind when they sold their house during good times. And, if you were thinking of making a career change, you might consider the state of the economy. After all, it is generally much harder to find a new job during a recession than during a time of expansion. Even if you find a job, you may be first in line to be let go if the economy worsens.

Inflation and Purchasing Power

Inflation is defined as a sustained increase in the general level of prices. In other words, during a time of inflation, most things get more expensive. When inflation occurs, the purchasing power of your money goes down. Many of you may be seeing some indications of inflation. Has the price of movie tickets increased in the past few years? What about eating in a restaurant? One way of looking at inflation is to say that $20 will not buy as much today as it bought a few years ago.

The way economists measure inflation is to look up prices on a set of about 300 goods and services that most people consume during the year. Clothing, groceries, and electronic goods are all part of this "market basket" of goods. Haircuts, medical care, education, and other expenditures are also included. This price data is then used to construct the **consumer price index**, or CPI. The CPI can then be compared to previous periods to tell us if prices are going up and by how much. In other words, the CPI is the formal measure of inflation that tells us whether things overall are more expensive now than in the past.

Why do we care? We care because inflation reduces the value of our money. If we are holding some wealth in cash—for example, if we have money in a bank account—inflation causes that cash to be less valuable. Let's say we put $1,000 in the bank at a time when that money could buy 20 shopping carts full of food. Then, inflation drives up the cost of food by 5%. Now, that same $1,000 will only buy about 19 shopping carts full.

Inflation is a fairly steady presence in our economy at some level. We all feel the effects at various times. Some of you may be protected by receiving regular increases in your paychecks. Many times, employers give their employees a standard "cost of living" increase. This helps soften the impact of inflation—although it is often not enough.

Another way to protect against inflation is to hold some of your wealth in assets that tend to increase in value by more than the rate of inflation. Real estate is one example of an investment that has been regarded as good protection against inflation. But generally, such assets involve a higher degree of risk. They go up higher and fall lower than safer options. For that reason, it is not generally good practice to place all your savings and investments in such assets. As you get closer to the time when you need to rely on those investments, it may be wise to move them into less risky options.

Think again about Miranda and her grandparents. Miranda's dad was a little worried about the effect of inflation on the older couple. As retirees, the grandparents no longer enjoyed a worker's income or consistent income increases. They had to rely on their savings and Social Security to meet their needs and wants for the rest of their lives. If the costs of goods and services rose quickly—that is, if inflation were high—then the purchasing power of their savings would shrink at a faster rate.

Fortunately, Miranda's grandparents had managed to sell their old home—real estate—before its price fell. And they had invested their money wisely. As a result, they had built up enough savings to live comfortably, even though they had a reduced income and even if inflation reduced the value of their savings. Their story underlines the rewards of good planning—while also pointing out some of the risks that must be considered.

Globalization

There was a time not too long ago when the people and businesses in the United States relied very little on businesses and consumers in other countries. Miranda's grandfather, for example, worked in a factory that made goods in this country and sold them to people in this country. The factory competed only with other American factories to build the best product at the lowest price.

Today, we live in a **global economy**, in which economies of all the world's countries interact and depend on each other. You have heard it said many times, and it is true: The world is shrinking. Look at the typical products you buy. Where are they made? Check the label to see where they are manufactured. You will see places such as China, Indonesia, Turkey, and Mexico. You will find few items that are made solely in the United States. In fact, a large and growing share of what we buy and sell is imported or exported. Refer to Figure 8.5 for an eye-opener. All of this is evidence of our global economy, but how does it impact you?

global economy: The world in which economies of all countries interact and depend on each other.

Whether you go to work for a multinational corporation or the corner grocery store, the global nature of today's economy will affect you. You will deal with imported products or be involved in exporting products to other countries. You will compete for customers and jobs with people from countries around the world. You will shop for products on the Internet from all over the planet. If you have problems with your computer and call a helpline for technical support, you will likely speak to someone in a country such as India.

Miranda's grandfather's company was affected by globalization. Just as he was getting ready to retire, his company began losing sales to a company overseas that made the same product. The workers in that overseas factory earned much less money than Miranda's grandfather. In addition, the factory was not regulated by the same costly pollution controls that American factories must have. As a result, the overseas company could make and sell products for less than the American company was able to sell them. Consumers began buying more of the foreign-made goods because they cost less. Soon, other foreign companies were making the same product—also for less money than the American company. The American company could not compete. Soon after Miranda's grandfather retired, the

FIGURE 8.5 Top U.S. Trade Partners

Ranked by 2011 U.S. Total Export Value for Goods (in millions of U.S. dollars)

		Exports						Imports					
Rank	Country	2010	2011	% Change	YTD Apr. 2011	YTD Apr. 2012	% Change	2010	2011	% Change	YTD Apr. 2011	YTD Apr. 2012	% Change
1	Canada	249,105	280,890	12.8%	90,594	96,091	6.1%	277,647	315,347	13.6%	102,250	110,059	7.6%
2	Mexico	163,473	198,378	21.4%	62,219	70,396	13.1%	229,908	262,864	14.3%	83,289	92,036	10.5%
3	China	91,881	103,939	13.1%	33,965	35,419	4.3%	364,944	399,362	9.4%	115,802	127,032	9.7%
4	Japan	60,486	65,706	8.6%	21,383	22,983	7.5%	120,545	128,925	7.0%	41,088	49,634	20.8%
5	UK	48,414	55,881	15.4%	17,813	19,933	11.9%	49,775	51,236	2.9%	15,862	18,048	13.8%
6	Germany	48,161	49,156	2.1%	16,122	16,698	3.6%	82,429	98,663	19.7%	31,117	34,539	11.0%
7	Korea	38,846	43,415	11.8%	14,136	15,109	6.9%	48,875	56,661	15.9%	17,651	19,224	8.9%
8	Brazil	35,425	42,944	21.2%	13,133	13,811	5.2%	23,958	31,736	32.5%	8,740	11,823	35.3%
9	Netherlands	34,939	42,351	21.2%	13,425	13,173	−1.9%	19,055	23,451	23.1%	7,504	7,892	5.2%
10	Hong Kong	26,570	36,449	37.2%	11,337	12,979	14.5%	4,296	4,401	2.4%	1,326	1,496	12.8%

Source: www.trade.gov/mas/ian/build/groups/public/@tg_ian/documents/webcontent/tg_ian_003364.pdf

YOU DO IT

Activity #2

company closed its American factories and it opened new ones overseas. The lower-skilled factory workers lost their jobs; the higher-skilled managers kept theirs.

What does this mean to you? It means that you will need to develop the ability to adapt to a rapidly changing work force and business environment. You will need to recognize what types of skills are in demand, and you must be willing to learn new skills as the environment changes. You may change jobs based on that information, or you may make new or different investments based on that information. Some jobs, such as plumbers, electricians, and mechanics, will be difficult, if not impossible, to "outsource," or replace with a foreign source. Most health-care-related jobs will also be difficult to outsource—although the high cost of medical care is causing more and more Americans to seek care overseas.

As you create your financial plan for your life, remember that new issues will continue to emerge that will either create new opportunities or cause you to revise your plan. A number of these issues will be economic issues. Demographic trends will make some jobs in high demand and make others obsolete. The way our leaders address the Social Security problem may affect the way you save for retirement. If inflation increases to a high level, you will need to protect your wealth by holding inflation-resistant assets. The phase of the business cycle might impact you when you decide to go to graduate school. Do you see the common theme? Educate yourself on economic issues and how they might directly impact your future.

Economic growth or recession, globalization, and inflation might affect your future.

 CHECKPOINT

What are some broad economic factors that might affect your financial future?

CHAPTER REVIEW

SUMMARY

- Economics is often defined as the study of choices. Building a financial plan involves making choices. Understanding or being aware of broad economic issues and concepts can help you formulate your plans and make better financial decisions.

- Demographics is the study of human populations. It allows us to examine trends in the whole country's population. Understanding demographics can help you predict certain needs in advance and make informed career choices. Two important demographic trends that will impact everyone in the United States are the graying of America and increased immigration. Demographic trends also play an important role when looking at Social Security and planning for retirement.

- Economic activity can be measured by the gross domestic product (GDP). A period of time in which the economy is shrinking is known as a recession. A depression is a severe recession. The economy goes through alternating periods of shrinking and growth, or expansion, known as the business cycle. Knowing about and understanding the business cycle can help you make basic life decisions. You should also consider inflation and globalization when looking at your financial plan.

Key Terms and Concepts

1. How is the **consumer price index (CPI)** calculated?

2. What is the difference between **microeconomics** and **macroeconomics?**

3. How is the **gross domestic product (GDP)** calculated?

What Do You Know?   MyFinLitLab

1. (a) What is the definition of economics?

   (b) How do economic factors impact financial decisions?

2. (a) What is demographics?

   (b) What is the significance of the baby boom to young people today?

3. (a) What do demographic trends suggest about the future of Social Security?

   (b) How might a young person use this knowledge when building a financial plan?

Answers:
Key Terms and Concepts

1. The consumer price index is comprised of a market basket of about 300 goods and services a typical consumer buys. Each year the price of this market basket is calculated and compared to a base year market basket CPI in order to see how much prices have changed.

2. **Macroeconomics** deals with broad issues that impact the economy as a whole. **Microeconomics** focuses on the study of individual choices or decisions made by smaller units, such as a firm.

3. The GDP is the total dollar value of all final goods and services produced within the boundaries of a nation (produced domestically).

Answers:
What Do You Know?

1. (a) **Knowledge** It is the study of the choices people make to meet their needs and wants. (b) **Application** The condition of the larger economy can affect you and dictate certain decisions you might make, such as what kind of training to receive or what to invest in.

2. (a) **Knowledge** Demographics is the study of human populations. (b) **Analysis** The retirement of baby boomers might affect job choices and it may affect how much confidence one has in Social Security.

3. (a) **Comprehension** Demographic trends suggest that Social Security will have to undergo some significant changes in the future. (b) **Application** A good answer will include that the person might plan to rely more on personal savings for retirement.

4. (a) **Comprehension** Immigration is altering the makeup of the population and perhaps creating new job opportunities. (b) **Application** A young person may seek a career or perhaps make investments in industries that serve the changing population.

5. (a) **Comprehension** The GDP measures the total value of all final goods and services produced in the United States. (b) **Analysis** It would mean that the businesses and individuals actually produced fewer goods and services than the year before.

6. (a) **Comprehension** It has generally been up, with scattered down or slow times. The most notable down time was the The Great Recession of 2007–2009. (b) **Application** You should plan for the downturns in the business cycle by saving more during growth periods. (c) **Analysis** You should be prepared to experience occasional down times.

7. (a) **Comprehension** A depression is a severe recession.

8. (a) **Comprehension** Prices rise. (b) **Application** They will see the prices of goods they buy go up in spite of the fact that their income does not.

9. (a) **Comprehension** Our economy is integrated with those of other countries. (b) **Application** Globalization might alter and even eliminate certain industries in the United States.

Answers:
What Are Your Finance Math Skills?

1. He will forego making $14,000 × 2 = $28,000 plus he will spend $4,000 × 2 = $8,000 = $36,000. He will make $24,000 a year more ($38,000 − $14,000 = $24,000), so it will take him $36,000 / $24,000 = 1.5 years to recover his investment.

2. 102/48 = 2.125

3. $9/4.5 = $2 per shirt in the United States. $1,050,000/2,500,000 = $.42 per shirt in the foreign factory.

4. $30,000 × .03 = $900

5. $200,000 × .04 = $8,000

---

4. (a) How is immigration changing the United States today?

 (b) How might a young person use this knowledge in choosing a career?

5. (a) What does the gross domestic product measure?

 (b) What would it mean if the gross domestic product went down from one year to the next?

6. (a) How would you describe the trend of the gross domestic product in recent decades?

 (b) How does the business cycle affect your financial planning?

 (c) Based on your understanding of the business cycle, what should you be prepared for during good economic times?

7. (a) What is the difference between a recession and a depression?

8. (a) What happens to prices during inflationary times?

 (b) Why might people with a fixed income be especially concerned about inflation?

9. (a) What do we mean when we say we live in a global economy?

 (b) How might globalization affect your education or career plans?

What Are Your Finance Math Skills?   MyFinLitLab

The first three questions correlate to *Math for Personal Finance* features located throughout the chapter.

1. Jayce is thinking about going to technical school and getting a two-year degree that will qualify him for a $38,000-a-year job. He could go to work today and make $14,000 a year. How long will it take Jayce to recover his investment if he goes to college? Assume he will not work at all while in college and that he will spend $4,000 a year on tuition and books.

2. If by 2023 there are 102 million workers in the labor force and 48 million retirees drawing Social Security, how many workers will be paying in per retiree in 2023?

3. A textile factory in the United States pays 300 workers a total of $9 million each year to produce 4.5 million shirts. A foreign factory employs 225 workers at a total cost of $1,050,000 to produce 2,500,000 shirts. How do the labor costs per shirt of the American and foreign factory compare?

4. Assume that last year the consumer price index indicated that inflation was 3%. If new cars increase in price by the rate of inflation, how much will a $30,000 car increase in price?

5. If housing prices fall by 4%, how much will the value of a $200,000 home decline in price?

6. If job growth in your state is projected to be 2% and you have 11,000,000 workers, how many new jobs will be created?

7. Jordan's raise last year was 3% of her salary, but inflation numbers released yesterday indicated that inflation was 3% last year. How much did Jordan's purchasing power increase?

8. Zeke learned that he could make another $2,000 a year if he was fluent in Spanish. If he intends to learn the language and work another 10 years at that job, how much is learning Spanish worth to him?

6. $11,000,000 \times .02 = 220,000$

7. Zero. She only kept pace with inflation.

8. $\$2,000 \times 10 = \$20,000$

What Would You Do?

You are shopping for a new pair of shoes. You find a pair that you really like and that you can afford. But you notice that they are made by a company that has been in the news recently. The company shut down all of its manufacturing plants in the United States and opened new ones overseas. Also, some people have accused the company of hiring workers at very low wages and making them work in unclean surroundings.

You feel a little bad about buying shoes from that company. At the same time, you do not feel it is your responsibility to resist the trends of globalization.

1. What alternative do ordinary consumers have to buying lower-priced shoes made in other countries?

2. What alternative does the American shoemaker have to opening plants in foreign countries?

3. Do you think it is possible for a company to compete for long if its products cost more than those made elsewhere? Explain your answer.

What Are the Connections? Technology, Language Arts, and History

Research information about each of the generations: Baby boomers, Generation X, Generation Y, and the generations after these. Who are these people? What are the differences between each of these groups? What is the name of the group after "Generation Y?" How does this group differ from the previous three groups?

Develop a chart that shows your family and where each member fits into the generation groups. This can include anyone living in your house, or friends of all ages. Include the following in your chart:

1. The age of the family members or friend(s) (the year that family members or friend(s) were born).

2. The economic condition(s) that were prevalent when that generation was born.

3. Something unique about the times of that generation (music, art, books, news, and so on). This could include some fun facts you find about that time period.

4. Something that members of each generation have in common.

Teamwork

In teams, research the Great Depression. Develop a skit, poster, PowerPoint presentation, or newsletter that traces the history of the Great Depression.

You might know an older adult who lived through the Great Depression or was born near the end of it. You could interview that person to learn firsthand information about how it was living during this period. You might look up information about teenagers during the Great Depression.

ESSENTIAL QUESTION ACTIVITIES

Complete these activities to answer this chapter's Essential Question: *Why is an understanding of economic conditions important to your financial plan?*

1. *On your own:* In this chapter we focused on how the economy can impact us financially. Look through some recent popular publications, available either in print or from the Internet, and find articles about how someone was impacted financially by the economy. Provide a written summary of your findings.

2. *As a class:* Split into groups of four or five members each and develop a comprehensive presentation using the information you gleaned from your research. Show how economic conditions can impact individuals and families and explain how good financial planning can be helpful, particularly in uncertain economic conditions.

MyFinLitLab TEST PREP QUESTIONS

1. a **1.** The best definition of economics is that it is the study of
    a. unlimited wants versus limited resources.
    b. how societies govern their people.
    c. communism versus capitalism.
    d. how the stock market has developed in America.

2. b **2.** Which decision illustrates the idea that a person's financial decisions are influenced by the overall economy?
    a. A person decides to use her lunch break to work out at a gym and eat lunch at her desk rather than going out to lunch with three friends.

b. A person switches the language she is studying in college from French to Spanish after she reads a newspaper article about how the population of the United States is changing.

c. A person decides to read a book instead of going to the movies after she reads a review of the movie she was planning to see.

d. A person who buys a new M car every three years switches to a B car after comparing the features of each car.

3. The demographic trend that helps explain why there has been an increase in demand for health care workers is
    a. that Generation X is not saving for the future.
    b. declining immigration.
    c. the graying of America.
    d. the declining American birthrate.

4. National economic trends
    a. should have little or no impact on individual financial planning.
    b. should only impact individuals once they are in the workforce for more than 10 years.
    c. are the same as long-term financial goals set by individuals.
    d. should impact individual financial planning.

    4. d

5. If the real gross domestic product (GDP) is going up, it is a sign that
    a. economic trends are turning down.
    b. the economy is in a period of inflation.
    c. the economy is gaining strength.
    d. individual consumers are making more money.

    5. c

6. During a recession, it is noticeable that
    a. people are buying less and there are higher levels of unemployment.
    b. more than 20% of the United States population is living below the poverty level.
    c. the gross domestic product (GDP) is rising.
    d. businesses are expanding and people have more money to spend on leisure-time activities.

    6. a

7. As a result of globalization
    a. there are more jobs in America for unskilled workers.
    b. it is easier for American companies to compete with foreign companies for a larger share of the marketplace.
    c. more goods sold in America are produced in other parts of the world.
    d. more American goods are sold in China than Chinese goods are sold in the United States.

    7. c

8. A person is collecting his pension and is very happy that his plan has a "cost of living" increase each year. This feature helps the person from feeling the full impact of
    a. inflation.
    b. globalization.
    c. taxation.
    d. depression.

    8. a

9. How do economists measure inflation?

    a. They survey consumers and ask if they are able to buy the same number of goods today as they were a year ago.

    b. They compare the cost of today's imports from China and the Middle East to goods made in the United States.

    c. They survey employers to determine how much they are paying in salaries and for raw materials today.

    d. They compare the costs of a standard group of goods and services bought today to how much those goods cost a year ago.

10. Which of the following is a true statement about inflation?

    a. Inflation only affects senior citizens who are living on fixed incomes.

    b. Some investments are able to grow at a rate greater than the rate of inflation; these investments, however, may carry greater risk.

    c. A young person is wise to invest all of her money in real estate since it grows at a rate greater than the rate of inflation.

    d. People who are fully employed and receive annual raises are not impacted by the effects of inflation.

11. If a person earned $50,000 last year and again earns $50,000 this year, but the rate of inflation is 4%, this year's buying power when compared to last year's

    a. is $48,000.

    b. is $50,000.

    c. is $52,000.

    d. cannot be determined from the information given.

12. What is the business cycle?

    a. It is a period of economic growth followed by a period in which the economy is shrinking.

    b. It is a 20-year period during which prices for goods and services rise and then fall back to a set level.

    c. It is the annual change that takes place in the course of a business's activities from highs during holiday seasons to lows during the winter season.

    d. It is the time that it takes a business to emerge from a recession or fall back into a depression.

13. Because of globalization, an individual may have to decide whether to

    a. sell a house during a recession.

    b. take a job with an annual salary of $50,000 or a job with an annual salary of $45,000 with a guaranteed cost of living increase.

    c. invest in a company that drills for oil off the coast of Alaska.

    d. buy a pair of jeans made in America at three times the cost of jeans made in China.

UNIT
3
Spending
& Credit

CHAPTER 9

ESSENTIAL QUESTION

Why is it important to build and maintain healthy credit?

OBTAINING AND PROTECTING YOUR CREDIT

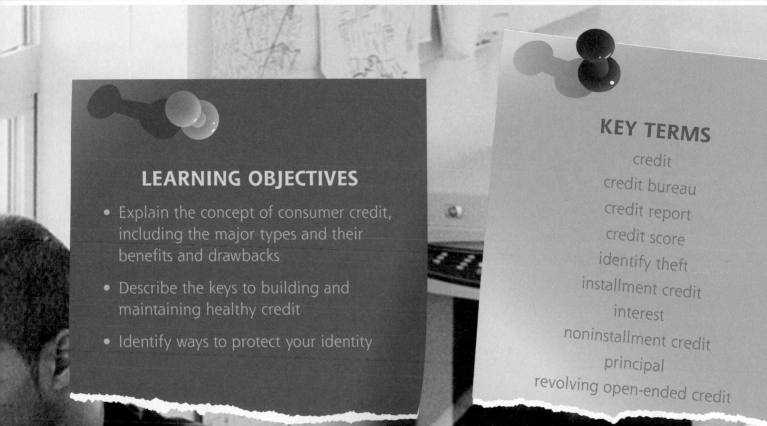

LEARNING OBJECTIVES

- Explain the concept of consumer credit, including the major types and their benefits and drawbacks

- Describe the keys to building and maintaining healthy credit

- Identify ways to protect your identity

KEY TERMS

credit

credit bureau

credit report

credit score

identify theft

installment credit

interest

noninstallment credit

principal

revolving open-ended credit

As she sat in the sales office, Nancy opened her checkbook and peered sadly again at the balance. She knew the figure was not going to change, but she wanted it to! The car she had chosen cost more than she had in her account. It was perfect, it was a very good deal, and she needed a vehicle for college. Yet in spite of the fact that she had been saving money for three years, she was still a little short.

Should she try to borrow the difference? The salesman seemed to think it was a good idea. In fact, when he told her what she might expect for a monthly payment, Nancy was thrilled. "But don't hold me to that number," he cautioned. "First, I need to check a few things with the business manager."

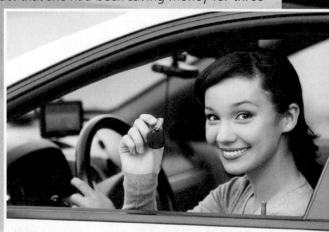

The more Nancy thought about the loan, the better the idea seemed. "It *is* a great deal, and a great car," she said to herself. "And I can manage a small monthly loan payment."

Just then the salesman returned and interrupted her thoughts. "Well, I've got good news and bad news, Nancy."

"What's the bad news?" she asked.

"With your credit history, we're not going to be able to get you a low-cost loan of the type I was thinking about. We can probably arrange a loan, but it will cost you more than the number I gave you earlier."

Nancy was puzzled. "What could be wrong with my credit history?" she wondered. "I didn't even know I had one."

credit: Money that a lender makes available to a borrower with the understanding that the borrower will repay the money in the future.

interest: Fees charged by a lender on borrowed money.

What is credit? **Credit** is money that a lender makes available to a borrower with the understanding that the borrower will repay the money in the future. Usually, borrowers also agree to pay lenders something called interest. **Interest** is the price one pays for the right to use another party's money and stated as a percentage of the amount borrowed. Think of interest as a rental fee paid for using someone else's money. Understanding how credit works—for you and against you—can help you build a strong financial plan.

THE BASICS OF CREDIT FOR CONSUMERS

Businesses offer credit to customers as a way of encouraging them to make purchases they might otherwise not be able to make at that time.

MATH for Personal Finance

Barbara borrowed $2,300 to buy some furniture and is paying 15% interest a year for the loan. The terms of the loan do not require her to pay off any of the loan balance during the first year. She only has to make interest payments.

How much interest will she pay the first year if she does not reduce the principal of the loan?

Solution: Barbara will pay $2,300 \times .15 = \$345$ in interest the first year.

Like Nancy, you will almost certainly need or want to use credit at some point in your life. One day you will want to purchase something, such as a house, a car, or a college education, for which it is difficult to save the entire amount. Used properly, credit can make it possible for you to purchase these things. Used unwisely, credit can wreak havoc in your financial life. Therefore, it is essential that you know about the major types of credit, the advantages and disadvantages of each, and about the laws that protect your right to get credit.

Types of Credit

Credit for consumers such as Nancy and you come in many forms. But all of these fall into one of three categories: noninstallment, installment, or revolving open-end credit.

Noninstallment credit is credit that is extended for a short term, such as 30 days or less. The consumer borrows the money at the time of purchase and pays off the entire amount within a short time. Noninstallment credit is typically issued by department stores, furniture stores, or other businesses selling items that cost several hundred dollars. Its purpose is to encourage immediate purchases of specific items. You may see an advertisement that says "30 days, same as cash," which describes a noninstallment credit arrangement. The ad means that the store is willing to lend you the purchase price for 30 days. If you pay it off within that time, the purchase price is the same as if you had paid cash.

This type of credit may be useful to a person who is expecting to receive money soon enough to repay the amount borrowed. An example might be a person expecting an income-tax refund. Most noninstallment credit will not incur interest charges if paid within the allotted time period.

Installment credit is also used for specific purchases but allows the borrower more time to repay the money. "Installment loans" typically require the borrower to make monthly payments. Part of each payment goes to reduce the **principal**—the total amount of money outstanding on the loan. Monthly payments also include interest charges. That is, the lender charges interest each month on the unpaid principal. So, if you have an unpaid principal of $100, the lender will charge you an agreed-upon percentage of that $100 in interest.

Installment loans may span a few years and are typically used for purchases such as lawn tractors, furniture, boats, and other big-ticket items.

FIGURE 9.1 Cash Versus Financing

Why do you think someone might choose to borrow money for 36 months rather than for a shorter period?

	Total paid	Interest paid
Cash purchase of car	$3,000.00	0
$3,000 financed for 12 months @ 12%		
12 payments of $266.55 =	$3,198.60	$198.60
$3,000 financed for 24 months @ 12%		
24 payments of $141.22 =	$3,389.29	$389.29
$3,000 financed for 36 months @ 12%		
36 payments of $99.64 =	$3,587.04	$587.04

Note that using installment credit does make the purchase of these items more costly. Refer to Figure 9.1, which shows how much interest you might pay over the life of a typical loan.

Revolving open-end credit, such as credit cards, allows consumers to borrow up to some preset maximum amount, such as $1,000 or $10,000. This **credit limit** is established based on the borrower's income level, debt level, and overall credit record. Consumers can use revolving credit to make one purchase or many. They can repay the entire amount borrowed at the end of the month or spread payments over a longer time. As they pay off money borrowed in the past, they can continue to use credit to make additional purchases as long as they do not exceed their credit limit.

Advantages of Using Credit

Should Nancy use credit to buy her car? There are obvious advantages and disadvantages. First, consider the advantages.

As you have read, credit helps you make large purchases sooner than you would if you had to save the entire purchase price in advance. Nancy has been saving for quite some time, yet she still does not have enough to buy her car outright. With credit, Nancy just may be able to purchase that car she wants and needs.

Using credit also simplifies your finances by eliminating the need to carry cash or checks. For example, you can use credit to buy your gasoline and pay for an entire month's purchases in a single monthly bill.

Using credit wisely can also help you establish a good credit history, which can make it less expensive for you to use credit in the future. This is because people with a good record of using and paying for credit—people with good **credit histories**—may be able to borrow at lower interest rates. Nancy wishes she knew this before trying to buy her car. Her lack of a credit history meant that she was not eligible for the lowest available rates.

Disadvantages of Using Credit

Credit can be costly. And, using it badly can cause serious and long-lasting damage to your financial life. Consider these points:

- *It is often easier to get credit than it is to pay it back.* If you borrow too much money, you may have difficulty making the payments, with

The longer term means lower monthly payments.

noninstallment credit: Credit that is extended for a short term, such as 30 days or less.

installment credit: Used for specific purchases but allows the borrower more time to repay the money.

principal: The total amount of money outstanding on a loan.

Activity #1

revolving open-end credit: Allows consumers to borrow up to some preset maximum amount. An example would be a credit card.

MATH for Personal Finance

Harlan used his credit card—a form of revolving open-end credit—to charge three tanks of gas this month.

If his charges were $43.12, $51.87, and $38.35, how much should he pay at the end of the month?

Solution: Harlan should pay the bill in full: $43.12 + $51.87 + $38.35 = $133.34.

MATH for Personal Finance

Sabrina charged $800 at the local sporting goods store to buy some exercise equipment. The store offers no interest for 90 days if the balance is paid in full, or 24% annually if the balance is not paid in full prior to 90 days.

How much interest will she need to pay if she lets the account go for 91 days before paying the bill?

Solution: She will pay 2%—.02—a month, since the annual rate is 24%. At 91 days, she will owe for three months—3 × .02. Therefore, her interest will be $800 × .06 = $48.

YOU DO IT

Activity #2

disastrous results. Just as a good credit history can mean lower borrowing costs, a bad credit history can make borrowing more costly—or impossible. If you borrow money to buy a house or car and fail to make payments, you could lose your possessions and all the money you have invested in them. A representative of the bank or business from which you borrowed the money can literally take away the car or remove you from the house. Then, the lender can sell the car or house—and keep the money. Finally, failure to pay off loans can lead to bankruptcy. This is a legal process in which a court takes over certain aspects of a person's financial life. It is not a good situation.

- *Credit cards pose a special danger.* They tempt us to purchase things *today* we would be wiser to save and pay for in full. In addition, credit card interest rates are usually very high, so it is extremely costly to carry a credit card balance from one month to the next. In most cases, it is wisest to use credit cards only for purchases you plan to pay off when the bill comes in—before interest charges add up. Bear in mind that if you borrow just $3,000 on a credit card that charges 21% interest annually and pay only the required minimum every month, it will take almost 23 years to pay off the balance.

What if you borrowed even more? At www.bankrate.com, there is a payment calculator where you can plug in different balances and interest rates. On the Web site, click on "Credit card payoff calculator." Are you surprised at how long it can take to pay off a credit card balance?

Credit Rights and Consumer Credit Laws

While credit can be dangerous to your financial health, it can also be invaluable. For that reason, federal law helps protect your access to credit. The **Equal Credit Opportunity Act** prohibits **creditors**—those who provide credit—from denying credit based on gender, age, race, national origin, religion, or marital status. This legislation also requires that creditors notify applicants within 30 days of whether or not they will receive credit and explain the reason for denial if credit is denied.

During the financial crisis of 2008–2009, some consumers who borrowed money were misled by financial institutions about the credit terms and financing. Consumer complaints and high default rates pushed Congress to enact two pieces of legislation that made significant changes in this industry.

The first piece of legislation was the Credit Card Accountability, Responsibility, and Disclosure Act (also called the Credit CARD Act) of 2009. This act was passed in an effort to ensure that consumers who pursue credit card services are treated fairly and have access to complete information about the fees and other provisions of the credit agreement. The Credit CARD Act also places limits on the fee amounts and types of credit card fees that can be assessed.

The second piece of legislation emerging from the financial crisis was the Financial Reform Act, also known as the Dodd-Frank Wall Street Reform and Consumer Protection Act (2010). The purpose of this law is to prevent deceptive practices in the credit granting process. The Consumer Financial Protection Bureau (CFPB) was created as part of this legislation. Its primary goal is to enforce consumer finance laws (such as those

FIGURE 9.2 Major Consumer Credit Laws

The federal government has established many laws to help ensure fair and reasonable standards for consumer credit.

THE CREDIT CARD ACCOUNTABILITY, RESPONSIBILITY, AND DISCLOSURE ACT (also called the Credit CARD Act) ensures that consumers who pursue credit card services are treated fairly and have access to complete information about the fees and other provisions of the credit agreement.

THE EQUAL CREDIT OPPORTUNITY ACT prohibits discrimination in the granting of credit on the basis of such factors as race, skin color, or sex.

THE FAIR CREDIT BILLING ACT sets up procedures requiring creditors to promptly credit your payments and correct billing mistakes and allows you to withhold payments on defective goods.

THE FAIR CREDIT REPORTING ACT sets up a procedure for correcting mistakes on your credit record.

THE FINANCIAL REFORM ACT (also known as the Dodd-Frank Wall Street Reform and Consumer Protection Act) is designed to prevent deceptive practices in the credit granting process. The Consumer Financial Protection Bureau (CFPB) was created as part of this legislation.

THE TRUTH IN LENDING ACT gives you three days to change your mind about certain credit transactions that use your home as collateral. It also limits your risk on lost or stolen credit cards.

Source: www.federalreserve.gov/pubs/consumerhdbk/

imposed by the Credit CARD Act) in order to ensure that consumers who need financial services are treated fairly and receive full disclosure of necessary information. The CFPB also attempts to prevent deceptive practices by financial institutions. In addition to credit cards, the CFPB also regulates online banking checking accounts and student loans. Figure 9.2 contains a list of some of the major consumer credit laws enacted over the past several decades.

 CHECKPOINT

What are the risks and benefits of consumer credit?

Credit is convenient and can make certain purchases possible. But credit is costly and can lead to financial problems if used unwisely.

BUILDING GOOD CREDIT

What was wrong with Nancy's credit? It's very likely that she had no credit history at all. You will sometimes read or hear about this or that person's "good credit" or "bad credit." This refers to a person's worthiness to receive credit. We all want to establish good credit. Nancy's situation helps illustrate the point. She wants to borrow money—that is, receive credit. She

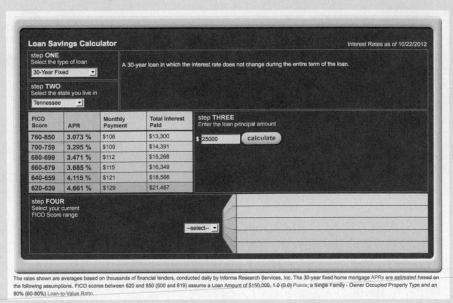

Loan Savings Calculator				Interest Rates as of 10/22/2012

step ONE Select the type of loan
30-Year Fixed — A 30-year loan in which the interest rate does not change during the entire term of the loan.

step TWO Select the state you live in
Tennessee

FICO Score	APR	Monthly Payment	Total Interest Paid
760-850	3.073 %	$106	$13,300
700-759	3.295 %	$109	$14,391
680-699	3.471 %	$112	$15,268
660-679	3.685 %	$115	$16,349
640-659	4.115 %	$121	$18,566
620-639	4.661 %	$129	$21,467

step THREE Enter the loan principal amount
$ 25000   calculate

step FOUR Select your current FICO Score range
--select--

The rates shown are averages based on thousands of financial lenders, conducted daily by Informa Research Services, Inc. The 30-year fixed home mortgage APRs are estimated based on the following assumptions. FICO scores between 620 and 850 (500 and 619) assume a Loan Amount of $150,000, 1.0 (0.0) Points, a Single Family - Owner Occupied Property Type and an 80% (60-80%) Loan-to-Value Ratio.

Source: Screenshot from the Fair Isaac Corporation website. Copyright © the Fair Isaac Corporation. Reprinted with permission.

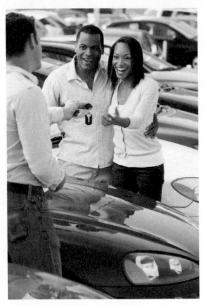

When you go to borrow money—for example, when you buy a car—the options available to you for borrowing and the interest rate you pay will depend in part on your credit history.

does not have bad credit, but she does not have good credit, either. She simply has no credit history. The result is that she may have to pay more for the credit she receives. Lenders often charge higher interest rates for people with less-than-good credit. That includes people with bad credit or people whose credit history is unproven. Therefore, it is vital that you know the process by which you build good credit and how that information is collected and reported to creditors.

Your Credit History

Each person's credit history is collected in his or her individual credit report. How many times have you borrowed money? Did you pay it back on time? Were your payments late? This information is collected about everyone who borrows money. Lenders use this information every time you apply for credit. Every time you make a credit purchase, it will further establish your credit history, good or bad.

You can help or hurt your credit history in other ways, too. Whenever you sign up and pay for utilities, such as electricity, phone, and water service, you are building your credit history. Utility companies extend credit by allowing you to use services and then billing you for them. If you fail to pay your utility bills, that information becomes part of your credit history. It can affect your ability to get credit in the future.

Credit Bureaus and Credit Scoring

Who keeps track of your credit history? Organizations known as **credit bureaus** collect credit information about individual consumers. There are three main credit bureaus: Equifax, Experian, and TransUnion. Figure 9.7, which appears later in this chapter, contains contact information for these credit bureaus.

Credit bureaus provide credit reports to potential lenders, employers, and others upon request. Your **credit report** shows every time you have applied for credit of any kind, whether or not you have paid your bills on time, if you have paid your credit cards in full every month or carried a balance, and if you have paid late fees. Any other public information about personal bankruptcies, court judgments, and inquiries by various companies or potential employers also appears in your credit report.

Everyone can access his or her credit report once every 12 months free of charge. By providing some basic personal information, you will be able to see the types of records being maintained by these credit bureaus regarding your personal credit history.

Credit Reports

Figure 9.3 shows a sample credit report. Notice that there are six categories of information contained in the report. When you apply for credit, the potential creditor will study your report and make decisions about whether or not to extend additional credit. Also, employers often use this information to make decisions about job offers, and insurance companies may use this information to determine insurance rates. A federal law called the **Fair Credit Reporting Act** limits the sharing of your financial information only to firms that have a legal purpose to evaluate this information.

It is a good idea to review your credit report now and then to make sure that it contains accurate information. Sometimes, companies make mistakes in their record keeping—mistakes that can make it into your report and hurt your financial life. Examining your report can also help you know if someone has set up a credit account in your name. This is a growing problem, as you will read.

Credit Score

Credit bureaus use your credit history to create a **credit score** that is often used to assess your creditworthiness. Individuals with higher credit scores get better interest rates on loans since they are determined to have a lower risk of defaulting. A good credit score can save you thousands of dollars in finance costs and interest charges over your lifetime.

Credit scores are calculated based on a model created by **Fair Isaac Corporation**, so they are very often called FICO scores. FICO scores will be between 300 and 850, with a higher score indicating better credit. In Figure 9.4, you can see that most people's credit scores fall in the 600–800 range.

In general, FICO scores are about 35% based on your credit history, 30% based on how much of your available credit you are using, and the rest based on other information contained in your credit report (see Figure 9.5). In 2008, FICO modified the model slightly, and some factors now weigh lighter or heavier than in the past. You should review the components used in FICO scores because it can be useful to know what aspects of your credit history are helping or hurting you the most in terms of your credit score.

credit bureaus: Organizations that collect credit information about individual consumers.

credit report: Summarizes an individual's existing and past credit history, including applications for credit of any kind, payment record for bills, whether you have paid late fees, and any other public information.

Finance ONLINE

An easy way to access your credit report is online at **www.annualcreditreport.com**. You can also phone or send mail requests for a credit report. These are processed and mailed within 15 days of receipt of your request. Go to this site and see if there is a report for you. You might be surprised!

credit score: A numeric score that uses your credit history to assess your creditworthiness.

FIGURE 9.3 What's in a Credit Report

Your credit report contains a brief record of all your past credit—and any problems that may have occurred. It's essential that your report be accurate and as free as possible of negative information.

Credit Bureau

Report Number 716-80
08/28/12

Please address all future correspondence to:

Credit Bureau
P.O. Box 0000
City, State, Zip Code
(888) 000–0000

Personal Information

Cynthia Zubicki
120 Greenmeadow Drive
Durham, NC 27704

Social Security Number: 000-00-0000

Previous Addresses:
264 Concord Road
Gilbert, AZ 85296

Last Reported Employment: Architect

401 Brownell Road
Chandler, AZ 85226

Public Record Information

Bankruptcy filed 04/09; Durham District Court; Case Number 873JM34; Liabilities: $56,987; Assets: $672

Collection Agency Account Information

North Shore Collection Agency (888) 000–0000

Collection Reported 11/08; Assigned 1/09 to North Shore Collection Agency; Client: Gilbert Medical Center; Amount: $1,267; Paid Collection Account

Credit Account Information

Company Name	Account Number	Date Opened	Individual or Joint	Months Review	Date of Last Activity	High Credit	Terms	Balance	Past Due	Status	Date Reported
Durham Savings Bank	8762096	02/08	I	6	11/08	$4,897		$2,958		Paid as Agreed	04/09
Macy's	109–82-43176	06/03	I	36	01/09	$2,000		$0		Paid as Agreed	02/09
Chester Auto Finance	873092851	03/06	I	27	02/09	$2,400	$50	$300	$200	Paid 120 days past due date	03/09

Previous Payment History: 2 times 30 days late; 2 times 60 days late

Inquiries

05/27/11 Citibank; 10/15/12 Bloomingdale's; 03/21/12 Home Depot

1. This information helps identify the report.
2. This section provides information that identifies the subject of the report.
3. Any public records related to the subject, such as bankruptcy information, appears here.
4. Unpaid accounts are turned over to so-called collection agencies. Information about such actions appear here.
5. Details about all open or closed credit accounts are listed.
6. Companies that have asked for credit information about the subject are listed here.

An alternative scoring system called VantageScore™ was created in 2006 and has been refined since the financial crisis. The VantageScore can range from 501 to 990 and is considered to be more intuitive since the scale is similar to the way a teacher might assign grades. Scores in the 900s are equivalent to "A" grades, 800s to "B" grades, and so on. Like the FICO score, the VantageScore is intended to measure the likelihood that the credit applicant will repay debt in a timely manner. VantageScore considers the same types of characteristics that are considered by FICO, such as credit utilization and credit history, but weights the factors differently. In general, both FICO and VantageScore should provide approximately the same indication of creditworthiness. However, VantageScore is not widely used at this time.

Figure 9.4 2011 Credit Score Distribution

Over half of all consumers have a credit score that is 700 or above.

Percentage of Population	Credit Score
6.2%	300–499
8.7%	500–549
9.8%	550–599
10.0%	600–649
12.1%	650–699
15.5%	700–749
19.4%	750–799
18.3%	800–850

Source: www.fico.com/en/Company/News/Pages/04-03-2012a.aspx

Here are just a few tips for improving your credit score:

- Pay your bills on time
- Keep credit cards and other "revolving credit" balances low
- Pay off debt rather than moving it around

For more tips, go to **www.myfico.com/ CreditEducation/ImproveYourScore.aspx**.

Prof. FIN

 CHECKPOINT

What are the elements of "good credit"?

Good credit means having a credit history that is generally free of credit problems, such as unpaid or late bills.

FIGURE 9.5 Credit Score Factors

What are the most important factors in figuring your credit score?

FICO® scores are calculated based on your rating in five general categories:

- Payment history—35%
- Amounts owed—30%
- Length of credit history—15%
- New credit—10%
- Types of credit used—10%

Source: Figure from MyFICO, a division of Fair Isaac. Copyright © the Fair Isaac Corporation. Reprinted with permission.

Your credit history and what you owe now.

THREATS TO YOUR CREDIT: IDENTITY THEFT

identity theft: When someone uses your personal information without your permission for personal gain.

Identity theft occurs when someone uses your personal information without your permission for personal gain. For example, someone may use your personal information to open a department store credit account and buy furniture. This account will be reported to the credit bureau under your name. And when this dishonest person does not pay the bill, your credit score will suffer. In most cases, you will not even be aware that this event has occurred until you request a copy of your credit report and find out about the account.

Some criminals use your personal information to establish totally new identities and engage in criminal activity. In severe cases, people have had their credit completely destroyed to the point where they can no longer borrow money for anything. Obviously, identity theft is illegal, but it's very difficult to detect. And, unfortunately, identity theft is increasing.

Prof. FIN

The Federal Trade Commission estimates that as many as 9 million Americans have their identities stolen each year. There is a high likelihood that you or someone you know has experienced some form of identity theft. Many of these victims report that they had out-of-pocket expenses because of identity theft. In addition, they suffered problems such as being harassed by collections agents, being denied new credit, being prevented from using their existing credit cards, having their utilities cut off, being subjected to criminal investigation or civil suit, being arrested, or having difficulties obtaining a bank account or even accessing their own bank accounts.

Using the Internet, search for more information on identity theft. Report what you find to the class.

Identity Theft Tactics

Identity thieves use a variety of tactics. For example, **shoulder surfing** occurs when someone in a public place steals your personal information by overhearing your conversation or viewing your personal information. Be cautious when someone seems to be standing too close to you when you're using a computer at a library, using a credit card at a store, and so on.

Prof. FIN

Take a quiz to assess your level of preparedness to defend against identity theft. Go to **www.privacyrights.org/itrc-quiz1.htm** and take the Identity Theft IQ Test. Print your results.

Identity thieves have been known to go through a person's trash to gather information. Credit card receipts, banking information, or even unsolicited offers for credit cards can enable someone to profit from your identity. Make sure to shred documents such as these prior to disposing of them.

Another common technique is called **skimming**. This involves simply copying your credit card or debit card numbers from your cards. Very often skimmers may be temporary employees of certain businesses. Highly advanced skimmers can even attach card reading devices to ATMs to get your bank account numbers and PIN.

Pretexting occurs when someone improperly accesses your personal information by posing as someone who needs data for one reason or another. The con artist may pose as a business or someone conducting a survey in order to get your information. When pretexting occurs online it is known as **phishing**. Common phishing techniques include e-mailing you and asking you to verify account information. **Pharming**, which is even more complex, uses e-mail viruses to redirect you from a legitimate Web site to an official-looking Web site designed to obtain your personal information.

Protecting Against and Reacting to Identity Theft

Refer to Figure 9.6 for some methods that you should employ to prevent identity theft. These steps may seem time-consuming and some may cost money, but preventing the theft of your identity is well worth the simple investment. The purchase of identity theft insurance may also be worth considering.

If you detect a sign of identity theft, act quickly. Be sure to keep copies and notes about all correspondence. Figure 9.7 provides some helpful resources that you can use to prevent and respond to identity theft.

You can see that monitoring your credit report and protecting yourself from identity theft is critical to your long-term financial health. Good credit

FIGURE 9.6 Ways to Protect Against Identity Theft

Preventing identity theft requires a little effort, but the benefits are significant.

1. Secure your wallet or purse by removing anything with your Social Security number and PIN numbers for bank or credit cards.
2. Keep a list of all credit cards and bank accounts.
3. Use a document shredder for receipts and credit card offers.
4. Don't print your Social Security number on checks.
5. Remove your name and address from local phone directories.
6. Use a locked mailbox.
7. Shop online only on secure sites.
8. Don't verify any information over the phone or by e-mail unless you initiate contact.
9. Mail all bills at the post office.
10. Monitor your bank and credit card statements.
11. Be cautious about giving credit card information over a cell phone.
12. Monitor your expected deliveries on credit card purchases.
13. Never have checks delivered to your home.
14. Install firewalls and anti-virus software on your computer.
15. Have your mail held while on vacation.

FIGURE 9.7 Useful Sources of Information to Protect Against Identity Theft

You have many allies in the fight to stop identity theft. These names and numbers can help you keep your personal information safe or limit damage if theft does occur.

How to Prevent Unsolicited Mail and Phone Calls

Stopping unwanted mail and phone calls helps block identity thieves from collecting valuable personal information. To stop unwanted credit card offers, go to www.optoutprescreen.com. You can opt out of direct mail at www.dmachoice.org.

To Opt Out of Pre-Approved Credit Card Offers

The following number can be used to notify all three major credit card bureaus that you wish to opt out of pre-approved credit card offers:

(888)5optout –or– (888)567-8688

To stop mail solicitations, write to:

DMA Mail Preference Service, P.O. Box 643, Carmel, NY 10512

To stop telephone solicitations, write to:

Telephone Preference Service, Direct Marketing Association, P.O. Box 1559, Carmel, NY 10512

Contacts if You Are Subjected to Identity Theft

Major National Credit Bureaus

Equifax, Credit Information Services, Consumer Fraud Division, P.O. Box 740241, Atlanta, GA 30374 (800)525-6285, www.credit.equifax.com

Experian, National Consumer Assistance, P.O. Box 9530, Allen, TX 75013 (888)397-3742, www.experian.com

TransUnion, Fraud Victim Assistance Department, P.O. Box 6790, Fullerton, CA 92834 (800)680-7289, www.transunion.com

Governmental Agencies

Consumer Financial Protection Bureau, (855)411-2372, www.consumerfinance.gov

Federal Trade Commission, Consumer Response Center, Room 130, 600 Pennsylvania Avenue, NW, Washington, DC 20580 (877)FTC-HELP

Social Security Administration (800)269-0271, TTY (800)325-0778, www.socialsecurity.gov

Internal Revenue Service (800)829-0433

U.S. State Department, Attn: Passport Services, 1111 19th Street, NW, Ste. 500, Washington, DC 20522 (To determine if a fraudulent passport has been issued in your name.)

U.S Postal Inspection Service (Contact your local post office)

United States Secret Service (Contact the local field office, a list of which can be found at www.secretservice.gov/field_offices.shtml)

decisions and practices pay substantial benefits over your lifetime. Poor decisions cause increased cost and limit your options for just as long.

Monitor Your Credit Report

You should check your credit report periodically. Sometimes there will be simple mistakes that could harm your credit if left alone. When you find inaccurate information, you need to contact the three main credit reporting bureaus and file a dispute related to the inaccurate information. The credit bureaus will then have to contact the creditor and verify the accuracy of the information. If the information is found to be inaccurate, the credit bureaus will make the change in your credit history. Inaccurate information is not that uncommon, so monitor your credit closely.

 CHECKPOINT

What is identity theft?

It is the improper use of someone else's personal information for financial gain.

CHAPTER REVIEW

SUMMARY

- Credit, or the ability to borrow funds that will be repaid in the future, comes in a number of different forms, including noninstallment, installment, and revolving open-end credit. Each of these has advantages and disadvantages. An advantage to credit is that it helps make large purchases easier. It also eliminates the need to carry cash or checks. A disadvantage is that credit can be costly. You can damage your financial life by borrowing more than you can afford to pay back.

- Building a good credit history is important to your financial future. Credit bureaus maintain a complete history of your credit transactions. They rate you numerically and determine your credit score and report this information to interested parties, who use this information to decide whether to extend credit and on what terms. You can obtain a free credit report from any one of the three credit bureaus to ensure that the report is accurate.

- Identity theft, which involves the use of your personal identifying information without your permission, is one of the fastest growing crimes in our country. Protecting your identity against actions such as shoulder surfing, skimming, pretexting, phishing, and pharming is vital to your good credit. Act quickly if you suspect identity theft and keep copies of all correspondence and credit transactions.

Key Terms and Concepts

1. What is the importance of the **Fair Credit Reporting Act**?

2. **Fair Isaac Corporation** created what model? How is it used today?

3. What is the Credit CARD Act?

What Do You Know? MyFinLitLab

1. (a) What are the three types of credit?

   (b) Under what conditions might a consumer find each type useful?

2. (a) What is interest?

   (b) Why might someone be willing to pay interest on a purchase rather than pay it all in cash?

3. (a) What are some advantages and disadvantages of using credit?

   (b) Of the three types of credit, which do you think poses the greatest threat to your financial future, and why?

Answers:
Key Terms and Concepts

1. The Fair Credit Reporting Act limits the sharing of your financial information only to firms that have a legal purpose to evaluate this information and therefore provides some protection against misuse of your private information.

2. The Fair Isaac Corporation created the FICO credit scoring model that assigns a numeric score to a person's credit history that provides creditors with an independent assessment of someone's creditworthiness.

3. The Credit CARD Act is the Credit Card Accountability, Responsibility, and Disclosure Act of 2009. This act was passed in an effort to ensure that consumers who pursue credit card services are treated fairly and have access to complete information about the fees and other provisions of the credit agreement. The act contains numerous other provisions designed to protect consumers.

Answers:
What Do You Know?

1. (a) **Comprehension** They are noninstallment, installment, and revolving open-end credit. (b) **Application** Noninstallment would be useful if someone is expecting to have cash soon; installment is useful for larger purchases; revolving open-end credit is useful in situations where a person wants to pay one bill rather than multiple bills—for example, for buying gas regularly.

2. (a) **Knowledge** Interest is the cost of borrowing money. (b) **Analysis** The person might want to be able to conserve cash for other purposes.

3. (a) **Comprehension** Advantages include buying things that one might not be able to buy if one had to pay for it all at once as well as cash management. Disadvantages include cost and risk to one's financial future. (b) **Analysis** Revolving open-end credit poses the greatest threat because it has the potential to get out of control without a person realizing how oppressive it has become.

4. (a) **Comprehension** Creditors cannot deny credit because of a person's gender, age, race, national origin, religion, or marital status. (b) **Analysis** By knowing why you have been denied credit, you can correct flaws and create a better application next time.

5. (a) **Knowledge** Creditors use credit history, income, and amount of current debt. (b) **Analysis** Not all lenders have the individual's best interest in mind. Ultimately, an individual is responsible for monitoring his or her financial situation.

6. (a) **Knowledge** Information may include identifying information about the report, identifying information about the applicant, public record information, information on unpaid accounts, information on all other accounts, and information about people who have inquired about the applicant's credit. (b) **Analysis** Sometimes incorrect and harmful information makes its way into your credit report.

7. (a) **Knowledge** Credit scores are calculated about 35% based on your credit history, 30% based on how much of your available credit you are using, and the rest based on other information contained in your credit report. (b) **Application** You might lower your debt, increase your income, or correct any mistake in your credit report.

8. (a) **Knowledge** Identity theft is the stealing of a person's identity in order to profit from it. (b) **Analysis** Technology has made it easier for people to access and make use of personal information.

9. (a) **Comprehension** Tactics include skimming, which is copying credit information; phishing, which is an online version of pretexting, in which an ID thief obtains your personal information on some phony pretext; and pharming, which is the use of viruses to redirect users to phony sites. (b) **Application** Possible answer: You can review your credit report regularly and take steps to secure all personal information.

Answers:
What Are Your Finance Math Skills?

1. Salinda will pay $18/12 = 1.5\%$ per month × 12 months. Therefore, she will pay $1,200 × .015 = $18 a month × 12 months = $216.

2. Hsui should pay the entire balance in order to avoid interest charges. He should pay $13.45 + $62.49 + $78.32 + $114.51 = $268.77.

3. $500 × .12 × 3/12 = $15 assuming interest is not compounded daily or monthly.

4. (a) The Equal Credit Opportunity Act prohibits creditors from denying credit for what reasons?

   (b) Why do you think it is important or helpful to know the reasons you have been denied credit?

5. (a) What three types of information do creditors use to determine a prospective borrower's creditworthiness?

   (b) Since lenders are careful who they loan to, why do you think so many people get into credit trouble?

6. (a) What are the six major areas of information that may be included on your credit report?

   (b) Why is it important to check the information on your credit report regularly?

7. (a) What factors determine your credit score?

   (b) What are some steps you might take to improve your credit score?

8. (a) What is identity theft?

   (b) How do you think technology has affected the problem of identity theft?

9. (a) Name and explain at least three tactics used by identity thieves to obtain information.

   (b) Discuss steps you can take to safeguard your personal information.

What Are Your Finance Math Skills?   MyFinLitLab

The first three questions correlate to *Math for Personal Finance* features located throughout the chapter.

1. Salinda bought a new television. The deal was attractive to her because she will be required to make monthly interest-only payments on the $1,200 purchase for the first year. How much interest will she pay each month and over the course of the first year assuming an 18% interest rate?

2. Hsui charged four items on his credit card in the past week. If his charges were $13.45, $62.49, $78.32, and $114.51 how much should he pay when his bill comes due?

3. Garvin bought skis that cost $500 at the new store opening. The store gave him 60 days of free credit. However, if he does not pay within 60 days, they will charge him a 12% annual interest rate. How much interest will Garvin pay if he lets the account go for 90 days?

4. Alan opened a $10,000 line of revolving credit at the bank. How much can he borrow if he has already borrowed $2,000 and paid back $500 of that amount?

5. Judy charged $800 worth of furniture using noninstallment credit since her tax refund is due shortly. If she intends to pay off the entire amount of her purchase, how much will she have to come up with if her refund is $535?

6. Jeremiah borrowed $1,500 from the bank to buy a home entertainment system. How much will he have to pay back in six months assuming the annual interest rate is 8% and he intends to pay the loan in full?

7. Sandy borrowed $1,600 from the bank that she will be making interest-only payments on for the first year. Assuming the annual interest rate is 12% (1% monthly), how much will she need to pay every month?

8. Rayburn's dad offered to loan him $1,000 to buy a car with an annual interest rate of 7%. Assuming he pays his dad back at the end of one year, how much will he have paid for the car?

4. $10,000 − $2,000 + $500 = $8,500 in remaining credit.

5. $800 − $535 = $265 that she will need to put with her tax refund to pay for the furniture.

6. $1,500 × .08 × 6/12 = $60 in interest plus the $1,500 = $1,560.

7. $1,600 × .01 = $16 per month in interest payment.

8. $1,000 × .07 = $70 in interest plus the original $1,000 = $1,070.

What Would You Do?

Joseph began applying for loans to go to vocational school to become an auto mechanic. He went to the bank to begin the process. While there, the loan officer saw that there were problems with Joseph's credit. It seems that the credit report showed that Joseph was behind by more than 60 days in payments on two credit cards.

The only credit that Joseph has is for his car, and he has been very good about payments. When he purchased the car, his parents said that if he ever got behind in payments they would take the car from him.

Joseph is now worried about what to do to correct what is on his credit report. Can you help him?

1. What steps should Joseph take to make corrections to his credit report?

2. What could have happened if Joseph had not found the errors in his credit report so soon?

3. What if more time had passed before he did a credit check? What would happen then?

4. What would you do to make sure your credit is good at this time?

5. Do you think it is important for people over age 16 to check their credit reports?

What Are the Connections? Language Arts

In this cartoon, Zits is concerned about his father knowing a grade on a quiz. Zits feels it is an invasion of his privacy.

Write a paper taking a stand for Zits or for his father. Defend your position. In your defense, relate the concept of "gradesnoop" to the collection of credit information about individuals by credit reporting agencies. Determine whether or not the practice is fair. Identify three ways this process can hurt or help an individual.

Teamwork

In teams, develop a public service announcement about identity theft. This could be a video to show on the school's news network or at a parent-teacher meeting. You could also put together a skit to perform for a school assembly or for your class. Or, you could publish a newsletter to tell parents what to do to protect their identity or to tell classmates what to do to begin to protect their identity.

You can go online to research different Web sites that can provide information on protecting your identity, as well as statistics about identity theft.

ESSENTIAL QUESTION ACTIVITIES

Complete these activities to answer this chapter's Essential Question: *Why is it important to build and maintain healthy credit?*

1. *On your own:* Using paper, poster board, or presentation software, provide facts for your classmates that answer the following questions:

   (a) What is included in your credit score and how is it calculated?

   (b) How do you maintain a healthy credit score?

   (c) Why is a healthy credit score important?

2. *As a group:* Looking at the three questions above, work in groups to brainstorm responses to each question. Put your answers together to make an advice checksheet that you and your classmates can use to maintain healthy credit.

TEST PREP QUESTIONS

MyFinLitLab

1. Why might a person decide to take advantage of a noninstallment credit offer?

   1. d

   a. Interest on this type of loan is much lower than interest on other types of loans.
   b. The loan can be paid back without interest charges any time within one year.
   c. The loan offered by Company A can be used to purchase items at Company B.
   d. There is no interest charged on the loan if it is paid back within a very short time.

2. A person finds the computer she needs on sale for $900. She can pay for the computer using her credit card and pay the amount borrowed over the course of many months, or she can take advantage of the store's offer for her to pay for the computer within 30 days, which will be the same as buying the computer for cash. She knows that she will receive her $1,200 salary bonus in her next paycheck. As a financially savvy consumer, she should

   2. a

   a. take advantage of the store's noninstallment credit option so she does not have to pay any interest on the loan.
   b. buy the computer using her credit card so that she can take as long as she wants to pay back the loan.
   c. buy the computer using her credit card and then deposit her bonus in her savings account so it earns interest.
   d. take advantage of the store's offer but only pay back $500 the first month and then transfer the balance owed to her credit card.

3. Under what circumstance would it make financial sense for a person to make a purchase with an installment loan?

   3. d

   a. He is currently paying off a large credit card balance and the installment loan will enable him to buy new furniture for his living room.
   b. He expects to receive a holiday bonus at the end of the year and he wants to buy a vacation package now while it is on sale.
   c. He has wanted to buy a boat for years and he does not have enough savings or revolving credit to make the purchase.
   d. He is offered a job that requires him to have a car, which he can only afford to buy with a loan.

4. If a person has a credit card with a limit of $2,000, it means that
   a. he will not be charged interest on purchases until he uses the credit card to make purchases over the $2,000 limit.
   b. he must pay the full credit card balance each month even if it is under $2,000.
   c. the credit card company is loaning him up to $2,000 to make purchases. He can pay the entire credit card balance each month or pay part of the bill and pay interest on the rest.
   d. he earns interest at the bank that issued the credit card on purchases made up to the $2,000 limit. That interest is subtracted from the balance owed each month.

5. The major purpose of the Equal Credit Opportunity Act is to
   a. make it easier for individuals to file for personal bankruptcy when they get into credit card debt.
   b. prohibit creditors from using age, religion, or race to deny credit to a person.
   c. make sure people are billed at least once a month for any outstanding debt.
   d. provide a way for people to correct mistakes that they believe have been made on their credit reports.

6. The information collected by credit bureaus such as Experian is accessible to
   a. only the person whose information has been collected.
   b. anyone who puts in a written request to the credit bureau.
   c. only banks and other financial institutions considering making a loan to the person.
   d. the person's potential employers, landlords, and lenders.

7. Everyone can obtain a free credit report once a year from each of the three main credit bureaus. It is
   a. not necessary to get a copy of the report since a person's bank reviews all depositors' credit reports for accuracy.
   b. a good idea to obtain the reports and review them for accuracy and file a written complaint if the report contains mistakes.
   c. a good idea to check your credit report each year, but nothing can be done to change the report until the information is seven years old.
   d. not necessary to review the report until a person applies for a large loan such as a mortgage or seeks employment.

8. FICO scores are based on a model created by Fair Isaac Corporation and weight five major factors to determine the score. The action that would have the greatest negative impact on changing a person's FICO score is
   a. obtaining a new credit card.
   b. having a $5,000 line of credit and using all $5,000 but paying bills on time.
   c. paying most bills on time and paying the minimum required each month.
   d. obtaining a new car loan.

9. As protection from identity theft, many people do not want to receive 9. a mail or phone calls offering preapproved credit card offers because it
    a. prevents a thief from collecting valuable personal information.
    b. reduces the amount of mail coming to a person's house.
    c. keeps a person from accepting more credit cards and getting into greater personal debt.
    d. improves a person's credit score since there are not so many financial institutions contacting the person.

10. The best way to protect against identity theft is to 10. c
    a. give out personal information such as credit card numbers only to close friends and people calling to verify personal information.
    b. print a phone number on personal checks and shop online as much as possible.
    c. check credit bureau personal credit reports regularly and keep Social Security card and PIN information in a safe place.
    d. use the same PIN number for all accounts and keep a list of credit card and bank account numbers handy.

11. "Phishing" is the identity thief technique of 11. b
    a. spreading an online computer virus using a person's credit card information.
    b. getting information from a person online by asking her to complete a survey or provide certain information to win a free vacation or product.
    c. calling a person's place of employment saying that he has been arrested and needs someone to bail him out of jail and verify that he has a job.
    d. calling a person's home and telling the person who answers that she is one of five winners of an HDTV and only has to pay $100 for shipping and taxes to receive the television.

CHAPTER 10

ESSENTIAL QUESTION

How do personal loans and purchasing decisions affect your financial plan?

PERSONAL LOANS AND PURCHASING DECISIONS

LEARNING OBJECTIVES

- Describe the key features and qualities of personal loans

- Explain the unique issues and challenges of financing a home

- Discuss the unique issues and challenges of financing an education

- Understand the unique issues and challenges of financing a car

KEY TERMS

annual percentage rate
collateral
cosigner
down payment
home equity loan
lease
mortgage
personal loan
policy rider
secured loan
unsecured loan

Kayce really wanted the dirt bike. She had recently gotten into motocross racing, and this was a sweet bike! It was probably a blur on the track. She stole a glance at her father, who was talking to the salesperson. They were deep in discussions about payment terms and interest rates. Who cared? All Kayce wanted was the bike. Of course, she needed her father for that, and he seemed concerned about something called a "teaser rate." It was beginning to look like the deal might fall through.

"Kayce, please come here," he said. Reluctantly, Kayce left the bike and walked over to her father.

"How badly do you want this bike?" Her father watched her intently.

"I think I could win some races with this one, Dad." Kayce's stomach turned flip flops. "I really want it."

"Do you want it enough to work extra at the shop to help make the payments?" asked her father.

"Sure," said Kayce. "How much will they be?"

"The bike's $5,000 and we can finance it for 48 months at 6%. That makes the monthly payment $117.42, or about 10 hours a week at the shop." He watched her expression. "Are you still in?"

Kayce looked back at the bike. "Of course I'm in."

"OK," said Kayce's father. "Let's sign the papers."

personal loans: Type of credit that is typically started at the time of purchase for a specific asset.

Kayce and her father have just agreed to obtain a personal loan to finance a dirt bike. **Personal loans** are a type of credit that is typically started at the time of purchase for a specific asset (car, boat, motorcycle, and so on).

Was it a good idea for Kayce and her father to take such a loan? We really do not have enough information to know for sure. We can say, though, that the use of personal loans is very common for the purchase of things that cost a few thousand dollars and more. You are likely to depend on personal loans for a variety of major purchases during your lifetime, and your knowledge of the process can mean the difference between smooth sailing and financial disaster.

PERSONAL LOANS

Can we reach a conclusion about the wisdom of Kayce and her father in taking a loan for the dirt bike? The details of this loan, such as the interest rate charged and the length of time over which the loan will be repaid, might tell us whether or not the loan terms were good. Our goal, therefore, is to talk about the various features of personal loans. That way, when the time comes for you to make a decision about whether or not to take a loan, you will have the information you need to make a wise choice.

Why Take a Personal Loan?

Most of us do not have the money saved to pay cash for large purchases, such as cars and boats. Or, if we do have the cash, we may consider it wiser to invest it or use it for other needs. For this reason, typically we have to take out personal loans to cover the cost of the purchase. In most cases, such purchases also require the buyer to pay a portion of the purchase price with his or her own money—a so-called **down payment**. The money from the loan then makes up the difference between the down payment and the total purchase price.

down payment: A required portion of the purchase price paid at the time of purchase.

For example, let's assume you have been saving for your first car for several years. You have set aside $2,000 for the purchase. What if you find a car you want that will cost $8,000? In this case, you might make a $2,000 down payment and take out a personal loan for the $6,000 shortfall. The lender would set up a repayment schedule that would spell out the details—called the terms of the loan. The terms include the amount of your payment, the interest rate charged, and the number of months you will need to make payments in order to repay the entire loan. At the end of that time period, assuming you have made all your payments on time, you will have paid off the loan.

Typical personal loans will have time periods of 24 to 72 months. A portion of the payment you make will pay the interest charges. The rest will be applied toward reducing the initial loan amount, which is called the principal. Your payment amount and the terms of the loan will be calculated so that you will repay the entire loan with interest with your last payment.

YOU DO IT

Activity #1

The Personal Loan Process

Banks, credit unions, and other financial institutions are usual sources for personal loans. In addition, many of the major auto companies have financing divisions that make personal loans to people who buy their cars. People who sell costly items, such as appliances and recreational equipment, may also make financing available. Like Kayce and her father, when you are ready to make a major purchase, you may be able to get a loan at the same time.

The process of taking a personal loan begins with an application. Let's check out a typical loan application, shown in Figure 10.1. Note the section of the application headed Co-Borrower/Cosigner. A **cosigner** is someone who agrees to sign the loan document and to repay the loan if the other individual stops making payments. Be careful about cosigning loans for your friends or family.

It is common to rely on credit for the purchase of expensive items, such as the boats being sold at this boat show.

cosigner: Someone other than the borrower who agrees to sign the loan document and to repay the loan if the original borrower stops making payments.

FIGURE 10.1 Example of a Loan Application

When you seek a personal loan, you will fill out a detailed form that provides you and the lender with much information.

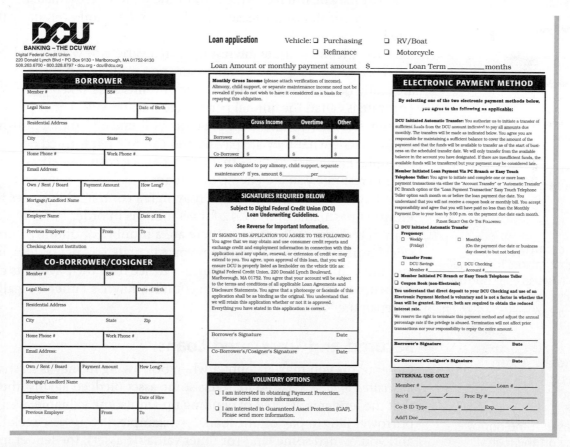

Source: From Digital Federal Credit Union website. Copyright © by the Digital Federal Credit Union. Reprinted with permission.

annual percentage rate: The rate that factors in all the financing costs so that borrowers know exactly what they are paying and can make informed decisions.

secured loan: A loan that has some asset pledged against the loan so that the lender is assured of winding up with some valuable asset if the borrower fails to pay off the loan.

Kayce's father will serve as a cosigner on her loan since she has yet to establish a credit history. As you can see, a loan application will require you to provide information so that the potential lender can make a judgment about whether or not you will be able to pay back the loan. In almost every case, you will be required to list your income. Depending on the size of the loan and on factors such as your credit history, you may be asked to provide an income statement and balance sheet. These financial statements give the lender information about your current cash inflows and outflows. It also shows whether you have any assets that you might be able to sell in order to repay the loan. In most cases, the lender will contact the credit bureaus and access your credit score. Remember, your credit report contains a snapshot of your current and previous credit history.

Loan Contract

After you apply for a loan, you may be approved or unapproved. The approval process can happen quickly in situations such as Kayce's. Many businesses are prepared to offer on-the-spot loan approval as a way of encouraging people to make purchases.

Once you are approved for a loan, you will sign a legal contract agreeing to the terms. The contract will specify the dollar amount of the loan, the interest rate to be charged, and the loan repayment schedule. This schedule includes the **maturity date**, or the date at which the loan will be completely repaid.

Recall Kayce's father's concern about a "teaser rate." This is a low interest rate that may be offered at the start of the loan to help make the loan seem like a great deal. But the teaser rate does not last, and eventually the loan's rate increases.

Indeed, lenders quote interest rates in a variety of ways. Lenders are, however, required by law to make sure you understand the interest rate you are really being charged—after all the gimmicks are taken into account. This rate is called the annual percentage rate, or APR. The **annual percentage rate** factors in all the costs of financing so that borrowers can know exactly what they are paying and can make informed decisions. For example, Figure 10.2 shows that other finance costs can effectively increase the interest rate you are paying on a loan.

In Kayce's situation, her father may sign a contract that agrees to make monthly payments of $117.42 for 48 months in order to repay a $5,000 loan that charges 6% interest. There are a number of online payment calculators available that will help you calculate payments. Plug in various amounts, interest rates, and maturities to see how the payments change. Remember, after he signs the loan contract, Kayce's father is legally liable to repay the loan.

Secured and Unsecured Loans

Other terms you may encounter when borrowing money is *secured loan* and *unsecured loan*. A **secured loan** has some asset pledged against the loan, so that the lender is assured of winding up with some valuable asset if the borrower fails to pay off the loan. For example, if you were seeking a loan and you owned some land (or other valuable asset), the lender might ask

FIGURE 10.2 Measurement of the Annual Percentage Rate

Remember, the interest rate advertised for a particular loan may be considerably different from the APR.

	Interest Expenses	Other Finance Expenses	Total Finance Expenses	Number of Years	Average Annual Finance Expenses	Annual Percentage Rate (APR)*
Bank A	$200	0	$200	1	$200	$200/$2,000 = 10%
Bank B	160	$100	260	1	260	$260/$2,000 = 13%
Bank C	120	200	320	1	320	$320/$2,000 = 16%

*The APR is calculated by dividing the average annual finance expenses by the average annual loan balance.

you to sign a document that allows them to sell your land if for some reason you did not repay the loan. This process is commonly referred to as pledging the asset. The loan, therefore, is secured by the assets pledged that may be sold to repay the loan in the event of default. We call the assets that have been pledged against loan repayment collateral.

Often, the item purchased with a loan is used as collateral. For example, Kayce's dirt bike will be used as collateral for her loan. If Kayce's father stops making payments—that is, **defaults** on the loan—the lender will repossess the dirt bike, which means that the lender will physically remove the bike from Kayce's possession. The lender will then sell the bike to someone else to recover as much as possible of the outstanding loan. Whatever Kayce and her father have paid as a down payment and monthly payments will be lost. In addition, even if the lender gets all its money back by reselling the bike, Kayce's father will still be legally liable. The lender will report his default to the credit bureaus. This will show up on his credit history and could prevent him from being able to borrow again for some time.

Unsecured loans have no collateral pledged against the loan. Sometimes these loans are called signature loans, because they are made solely on the basis of someone's good name—that is, their good credit history.

MATH for Personal Finance

Assume Kayce's loan was for $5,000 and that she will make 48 monthly payments of $117.42 to repay the loan.

How much total interest will she pay over the life of the loan?

Solution: Kayce will pay a total of $117.42 × 48 months = $5,636.16 for the bike. The price of the bike is $5,000; therefore, the interest is equal to $5,636.16 − $5,000 = $636.16.

collateral: Assets that have been pledged against loan repayment.

Personal loans make possible the purchase of large-ticket items for which most people do not have ready cash on hand.

✓ **CHECKPOINT**

What is the usual purpose of a personal loan?

FINANCING A HOME

If you're like most people, the biggest single purchase you will make in your life will be a home. Chances are also extremely good that you will finance the purchase with a loan. Knowing the unique issues surrounding the purchase of a home—and whether or not to make such a purchase—can play a big role in your financial life.

unsecured loans: Loans that have no collateral pledged against the loan.

Mortgage Loans

You have probably heard a homeowner speak of his or her mortgage. **Mortgage** is the common term for the type of loan people take to obtain a home. Technically, a mortgage is a legal instrument by which the home becomes collateral for the loan. But most people also use the word to refer to their home financing arrangement.

mortgage: Type of loan taken out to obtain a home.

For millions of Americans, purchasing a home is only possible through the use of credit.

Mortgages come in two basic forms: fixed rate and adjustable rate. With a **fixed rate mortgage**, the interest rate remains the same for the life of the loan. This means the payment will never go up or down. An **adjustable rate mortgage** (ARM) is one where the rate may go up or down over time. The rate change occurs at some preset time—for example, after a year. The amount and direction of the rate change depends on changes in economic conditions and interest rates. Because the rate goes up or down, the monthly mortgage payment will go up or down, too. Such mortgages are also called variable rate mortgages.

Why would someone choose an ARM? One reason is that the starting rate is often lower than available for fixed rate mortgages. This means lower mortgage payments—at least until the rate is reset. Remember, this reset occurs at times specified in the loan agreement. Another reason to choose an ARM is if you believe interest rates will go down in the foreseeable future. Of course, it is vital to consider the effects of an interest rate increase. On loans of $100,000 to $300,000—not uncommon for a mortgage—a change of a couple percentage points can raise monthly mortgage payments by hundreds of dollars.

Since many ARMs are fixed for the first three or five years, they also appeal to someone who frequently moves because of job transfers. If you know you will be transferred in four years and you decide that buying a home is the best option, then an adjustable rate mortgage may be a good choice. Keep in mind that ARMs shift the risk of interest rate changes to the borrower and, if interest rates go up, it can result in a significant increase in your house payment.

Many ARMs may also begin with very low teaser rates. Remember from Kayce's story: A **teaser rate** is an extremely low interest rate for a short period of time that is used as a deal sweetener. Teaser rates are designed to make your first payments as low as possible and encourage you to take out a loan. Teaser rates are used on all types of loans including vehicle and home loans.

You may have heard of something called a **subprime mortgage**. Subprime mortgages are higher interest rate mortgage loans made to people with poor credit scores. Subprimes made a lot of news in recent years due to their higher rate of mortgage default. Many mortgage companies encouraged high-risk borrowers to borrow too much money using these loans. Over time, many people found that they could not make the payments and then defaulted. These widespread defaults became known as the "subprime meltdown" or "subprime crisis." It affected not only homeowners, but also many companies that lost money when the mortgages failed. It also affected taxpayers across the country. In October 2008 the crisis spurred the passage of the Emergency Economic Stabilization Act, which committed up to $700 billion of taxpayer revenue to buy financial assets backed by these bad mortgages.

Of course, mortgages are also significant on an individual level. Often, people take mortgages for long periods of time—sometimes 30 years or more. For many, the monthly mortgage payment is the largest bill they have to pay. The consequences of defaulting on a mortgage can be huge. You could lose your home and tens of thousands of dollars or more. It is essential that you make wise and informed decisions about the benefits and drawbacks of each type of loan. That way, when it is time to purchase a home, you can make a wise decision. Make sure you don't buy a house that will demand a payment that is—or may become—more than you can afford. Remember, not all lenders have your best interest in mind.

Other Costs of Buying a Home

Home buyers also may incur certain costs when buying a home and taking out a mortgage. Common expenses include appraisal fees, home inspection fees, mortgage origination fees, loan application fees, filing fees, and title insurance to make sure that the home's title is not encumbered in some way. Some buyers may even pay "points" to buy down their interest rate. A point is equivalent to 1% of the loan amount. These costs—which are commonly referred to as "closing costs"—can total several thousands of dollars. When shopping for a mortgage, it is important to consider these fees. Some lenders waive many closing costs.

Home Equity Loans

Home equity loans and home equity lines of credit (HELOCs) have become a very popular source of personal loans for many homeowners. A **home equity loan** allows a homeowner to borrow against the equity in his or her home—that is, the difference between the home's value and the amount owed to a lender. For example, let's assume you own a home valued at $200,000 and you owe $110,000 on your mortgage. In this case, you have $90,000 equity in the home. A typical home equity loan would allow you to borrow against this equity using your home as collateral. In most cases, home equity lenders limit the total amount of a mortgage to 80% of the market value of the home. So, using the example above, you may be allowed to borrow up to another $50,000 using a home equity loan (.80 × $200,000 = $160,000, minus $110,000 already borrowed = $50,000). Be cautious about home equity loans: If you fail to pay, you could lose your home.

Many homeowners opt to establish a home equity line of credit rather than take out a loan. A **line of credit** is an agreement to allow borrowing as needed up to a certain amount of money. Let's say a homeowner is approved for a $25,000 line of credit. He or she may leave the line of credit untouched for a period of time—and so pay no interest charges. Then, one month, the homeowner may draw on the line of credit to do some home repairs. The next month, he or she may draw on the line of credit for something else. The homeowner can do this repeatedly—as long as the total amount outstanding—the principal—doesn't exceed the limit of the credit line. Each month, the homeowner pays off some of the principal, as well as the interest charged on the amount borrowed.

home equity loan: Allows a homeowner to borrow against the equity in his or her home. Equity is the difference between the home's value and the amount owed to a lender.

Home equity borrowing became very popular when home prices were rapidly increasing. People were said to draw on their growing home equity to make purchases. Home equity loans are generally a much cheaper source of personal loans, with interest rates typically tied to various market interest rates. In some cases, if the proceeds are used for home improvement, the interest paid may be tax deductible.

Of course, home equity borrowing has risks. As with a mortgage, the borrowing is secured by the home. Failure to pay can lead to the lender seizing the borrower's home—even though the amount borrowed may be a fraction of the home's full value. Also, getting home equity loans may involve closing costs.

Buying Versus Renting a Home

Buying a home is generally a good investment and one that many people aspire to. But it is not always the right decision—renting is often a good option.

The decision to buy or rent a home can be quite complicated. To begin with, the selection of homes available for rent may be entirely different from those available for purchase. In addition, when trying to decide whether to rent or buy, you must consider the following:

- How long do you plan to live in this area? In general, you should not purchase a home unless you plan to live in the area for several years. Often, there are expenses associated with a home purchase and sale that take a few years to recover. For example, you may have to pay mortgage origination fees to a lender to buy the house and then pay a sales commission to a real estate agent when you sell the house. These can total several thousands of dollars.

- Do you have money saved for a down payment? Most lenders require you to put some money down and finance the remainder. Even if you can find a lender who will make a loan with little or no down payment, you will likely have to pay more for it.

- What is the price of homes relative to the price of rent in this area? Sometimes renting is a better deal. Remember, if you rent, someone else is responsible for the property maintenance and upkeep, which can be costly. But also remember that owning a home can provide a tax deduction that can lower your taxes. And, of course, when you buy a home, remember that some of what you pay each month may be building equity and increasing your net worth. In fact, one of the primary ways that many Americans have created wealth over their lifetimes is by buying a home. All of these factors must be considered. Figure 10.3 illustrates how buying a home can create wealth—that is, increase your net worth—versus paying rent.

- Are houses increasing in value or decreasing in value in the area? Home prices often rise and fall significantly. Predicting the direction of any market is difficult, but if it seems as though housing prices are likely to fall rapidly, it might be a good idea to hold off on purchasing.

- Do you have enough knowledge of the area to buy? Sometimes you need to live in an area to find out enough information to buy a home. Where is the best shopping? How long does it take you to commute to work?

FIGURE 10.3 Effect of Homeowning and Renting on Net Worth

When deciding whether to own or rent, you must consider not only how much you can afford each month in payments, but also how those payments may affect your net worth.

	Marcos	Sonia
Housing Expense	$1,500 (Rent per month)	$1,500 (Mortgage per month)
Annual Federal Tax Benefit	$0	$350 (assuming 28% tax bracket × $1,250 in interest)
Effect on Net Worth	−$1,500	−$900 ($1,500 in payment − $250 increase in equity − $350 tax benefit)

- Rentals usually require payment of a security deposit to protect the owners from property damage done by renters who move out without paying for the damage. This is a sum of money that the property owner holds until the renter moves out. At that time, the property owner returns the deposit to the renter, minus any money used to repair damage that the renter left behind. You need to factor in the cost of the security deposit when determining whether to rent. How much are typical security deposits in the area? Do you have a pet, and will you therefore need to put up an additional pet deposit?

It is always a good idea to consult with a real estate agent who is familiar with the area to help you make these decisions. Buying a house may be the largest purchase you ever make and you should proceed with caution.

The Importance of Homeowner's and Renter's Insurance

Homeowner's insurance provides insurance protection for your house in the event of a tornado, fire, theft, or other property damage. It also provides financial protection if someone gets injured at your house and sues you. Homeowner policies vary greatly in the types of perils that are covered. Refer to Figure 10.4 for the various types. You can also add numerous additional coverages, called **policy riders**, to cover things such as jewelry or valuable heirlooms that are often not fully covered by a typical policy.

As they do when people buy a car, lenders require that homeowners purchase at least enough homeowner's insurance to cover the amount of the mortgage on the home. That way, if the house is destroyed, the homeowner will not default on the loan. But homeowner's insurance is also essential for your own protection. It should be an important component of your financial plan to protect your assets. Remember, with

MATH for Personal Finance

Brian purchased renter's insurance with a $200 deductible. Recently a fire destroyed his apartment complex and he lost all his possessions—at least $7,000 worth.

If his insurance coverage was limited to $5,000, how much will he receive from the insurance company?

Solution: The $200 deductible means he was self-insured for the first $200 in damage so he would receive $5,000 − $200 = $4,800.

policy riders: Additional insurance coverage to cover things such as jewelry or valuable heirlooms that are often not fully covered by a typical insurance policy.

FIGURE 10.4 Types of Perils Protected by Homeowner's (HO) and Renter's Insurance Policies

Homeowner's and renter's insurance can provide invaluable protection against loss. Different policies, however, cover different things.

HO-1: Protects against fire, lightning, explosions, hail, riots, vehicles, aircraft, smoke, vandalism, theft, malicious mischief, and glass breakage.

HO-2: Protects against the events identified in HO-1, along with falling objects, the weight of ice, snow, or sleet, the collapse of buildings, overflow of water or steam, power surges, and the explosion of steam or hot-water systems, frozen plumbing, heating units, air-conditioning systems, and domestic appliances.

HO-3: Protects the home and any other structures on the property against all events except those that are specifically excluded by the homeowner's policy. The events that are typically not covered by this insurance are earthquakes, floods, termites, war, and nuclear accidents. It may be possible to obtain additional insurance to protect against floods or earthquakes. This policy also protects personal assets against the events that are listed in HO-2.

HO-4: Renter's insurance. Protects personal assets from events such as theft, fire, vandalism, and smoke.

HO-5: Protects the home, other structures on the property, and personal assets against all events except those that are excluded by the specific homeowner's policy. This policy provides coverage of the home similar to that provided by HO-3, but has slightly more coverage of personal assets.

HO-6: Condominium owner's insurance. Protects personal assets from events such as theft, fire, vandalism, and smoke (review the specific policy to determine which events are covered).

HO-8: Protects the home from the same events identified in HO-1, except that it is based on repairs or cash values, not replacement costs.

each mortgage payment, you build equity in your home and add to your net worth. If you have owned a home for many years, your equity might be in the tens or even hundreds of thousands of dollars. It may represent a major share of your net worth. If the house were destroyed, you would want enough coverage not only to pay off the loan, but also to pay you back for the loss of the asset.

Many people don't realize that their possessions are not protected when they rent. For example, if you live in an apartment complex that is destroyed by fire and you lose all of your possessions, you will not be reimbursed for that loss by the building owner. Your possessions are not insured by the building's owners. However, you can purchase renter's insurance that will protect you. Renter's insurance can also cover your living expenses if the property you rent is being repaired as the result of some covered event. Renters with valuable assets should consider buying renter's insurance to protect them from loss.

 CHECKPOINT

By what means do most people finance the purchase of a home?

Most people finance their home with a mortgage.

For many people, the expense of getting an education rivals the expense of buying a home. In many cases, getting the training you need for a successful career will require borrowing money.

Student loans are another type of personal loan. Students and their families use these loans to finance the expense of going to college or trade school. Some student loans go directly to the student while others go to the student's parents. In general, student loans allow the borrower to obtain money for education bills—and to delay making payments on the borrowed money until after graduation.

Federal student loans are the largest source of student loans. Because they are guaranteed by the federal government, they also have the best terms. The government essentially acts as the cosigner on these loans and pledges to repay them if the borrower defaults. The government does this to encourage education. Remember, if you earn a degree you will likely earn much more income over your lifetime. Higher incomes mean you pay more taxes over the long run and are less likely to need other forms of government assistance. Federal Stafford loans and Federal Perkins loans are the two primary education loans made to students.

Federal Stafford Loans

Federal Stafford loans are the most common type of federal education loans. They come in two forms: subsidized and unsubsidized.

Subsidized Stafford loans are need-based. That means applicants must show a certain level of financial need in order to qualify. Subsidized Stafford loans are highly desirable because interest charges do not build up on these loans while the student is in school. So, a student can take a $5,000 loan in 2012, and at graduation in 2016, he or she will still owe just $5,000. After leaving school, subsidized Stafford loan recipients get a six-month grace period during which time interest does not accrue and payments do not have to be made. All this time, the federal government essentially pays this interest for the student. Compare this to a normal loan. Even if you could arrange not to make payments for four to five years, interest charges would build up. So, the $5,000 borrowed in 2012 might have grown to some $7,000 or more by 2016.

Unsubsidized Stafford loans are not need-based, and interest accrues on these loans while you are in school. They still offer recipients the advantage of not having to make monthly payments until leaving school. But, as you have seen, the amount of interest that can build up over four to five years is considerable. Both of these types of loans have limits on the annual and total amounts you can borrow.

Federal Perkins Loans

Federal Perkins loans are similar to Stafford loans except they are for students with "exceptional" financial need. Perkins loans carry a lower interest rate and offer a longer grace period before students have to begin

Finance ONLINE

When beginning the search for education past high school, funding may be a big consideration. The following Web site may be one place to get some help in finding funding: **studentaid.ed.gov**. This source provides information concerning federal student aid. Some other helpful sites are **www.staffordloan.com** and **www.studentloans .com**.

Research these Web sites. Develop a chart that shows the different information that can be found on each site. What would make you choose one site over the others?

Landi took out a total of $8,000 in subsidized Stafford loans for her four-year college education.

How much interest that accrued during her four years of college will she have to repay assuming a market rate of 5%?

Solution: The loan is a subsidized loan meaning the federal government waives the interest. Landi will not be liable for any interest that accrued while she was in school.

In general, they allow recipients to delay repayment of the loan until after the student graduates.

repayment. These loans go to students coming from extreme poverty who will likely not get any financial support from their parents to attend school.

The Reality of Student Loans

Keep in mind that both Perkins and Stafford loans are still loans, and you are required to repay them. Many students take out too much in student loans and have difficulty making the payments upon graduation. Remember, when you graduate you will have many more expenses that will use your income. Rent or house payments, utilities, possibly a car payment, and groceries will all chomp through your initial income very rapidly. Student loans are a useful financial aid, but students should use them with caution.

Parents also have the ability to borrow from many sources to finance a college education. All these loans have varying interest rates, repayment schedules, and maturities. They all have to be repaid. A student loan is still debt. Learn everything you can about your options, and enter into these contracts with the knowledge that you will need to repay this money at some point. You can find out more information about student loans by going to **www.salliemae.com**.

 CHECKPOINT

Why are student loans different from other kinds of personal loans?

FINANCING YOUR CAR

Another major expense for people is the car they drive. Many people finance car purchases with loans from the car dealer or from a bank or other lending institution. Car loans typically run from three to six years for new cars. Longer loan periods generally mean lower payments—but also that the borrower will pay more in interest over the life of the loan. In addition, loans of five and six years may put a car owner in the position of owing more on the car in the final months of the loan than the car is actually worth. Consider, for example, a car owner who still owes $5,000 on a loan for a now-five-year-old vehicle that has a market value of only $4,000. This could cause problems if the person wanted to sell the car, or if it were destroyed in an accident. In that situation, the owner would receive just $4,000 from the buyer or insurance company, have no car, and still owe the lender $1,000.

Used cars are a good option for many people, but often they present financing issues that a potential buyer may not face with a new car. Many sources of used car financing will only loan money on newer models that are less than five years old. In addition, the amount of the loan is typically restricted by the market value of the vehicle as determined by Kelley Blue Book or some other reputable source.

Copy of an original *Blue Book*

Consumer Edition of the *Blue Book* (1993)

Prof. FIN

When you are purchasing a car, you will often hear someone talk about its Blue Book value. The name refers to an actual book, but today you can find the Blue Book value of your car on the Kelley Blue Book Web site at **www.kbb.com**.

Did you ever wonder where the name "Kelley Blue Book" came from? It began in 1918, when young Les Kelley parked three Model T Fords in a lot and began the Kelley Kar Company. His company went on to become the largest dealership in the world.

As Les Kelley began selling one car after another, he needed more inventory, so he distributed to other dealers and banks a list of cars he wanted to buy with the prices he was willing to pay for them. As his company grew, so did the respect from others in the business. They, too, wanted to use the list Kelley had compiled. In 1926, Les Kelley published the first *Blue Book of Motor Car Values*, with an expanded list of automobile values that included new and used models. The rest is history! Go to the Kelley Blue Book site and find the value of your car, your family's car, or a friend's car.

Trademark and screenshots by Kelley Blue Book Co., Inc. Copyright © by Kelley Blue Book Co., Inc. Reprinted with permission.

Recently, the Internet has emerged as a great source for used vehicles. eBay, AutoTrader.com, and other sites sell thousands of used vehicles annually. Potential buyers can evaluate the feedback of potential sellers to determine their reputation before buying. Buyers should also use a service such as CARFAX to research a car's history prior to purchasing it to see, for example, if the car has been in an accident or in a flood. There are a number of online financing options for people with good credit, and in many cases these lenders will loan money on older vehicles based on the borrower's credit history. Don't forget that you need to factor in shipping costs or the cost of retrieving your vehicle from the seller. Many purchases may be in another state, but these long-distance vehicle purchases are becoming common since a buyer can often get a very good deal on a used car.

There are other options to buying a car with a loan. Here we will consider the benefits and drawbacks of leasing a vehicle.

Leasing Versus Buying a Car

Leasing vehicles instead of buying them has become popular in the past several years. A **lease** is essentially a long-term rental agreement. Each month, you pay a lease payment, much as you would make a payment to pay off a loan. Leasing a car offers some advantages over purchasing one. It also has some disadvantages. Therefore, the lease-versus-buy decision will not be the same for everyone.

One advantage of leasing is that it typically requires only a small down payment—or none at all. Also, lease payments for a new car are generally lower than loan payments for that same car. This is because when you lease, you pay only for use of the car for a period of time—not for the value

lease: A long-term rental agreement.

of the car itself. Finally, at the end of the lease, you return the vehicle to the dealer and do not have to worry about selling the car.

At the same time, you do not own the car, and it can never be listed as one of your assets. You cannot sell it and use the proceeds for something else. When you return it to the dealer at the end of the lease, you have nothing. Yet, while you lease the car you are responsible for keeping the car maintained in perfect condition and are liable for any damage to it.

In addition, many vehicle leases have mileage limits—12,000–15,000 miles a year is common. If you drive the vehicle more miles than specified, you may face additional charges. There are often penalties for ending the lease early. Many consumers allege that there are many hidden fees in lease agreements. Read the agreement carefully prior to signing.

The easiest way to make a lease-versus-buy decision is to compare the total cost of leasing versus buying. Refer to Figure 10.5 for an example of a simple comparison. Note that the result of this comparison could vary significantly depending on the cost of the vehicle, the length of the loan or lease, and many other factors.

YOU DO IT

Activity #2

FIGURE 10.5 Comparison of the Cost of Purchasing Versus Leasing

Leasing and purchasing a car each have their benefits and drawbacks, but you can make a good comparison of the actual costs of each option.

Cost of Purchasing the Car	Cost
1. Down payment	$1,000
2. Down payment of $1,000 results in forgone interest income:	
Forgone Interest	
Income per Year = Down Payment × Annual Interest Rate	
= $1,000 × .04 = $40	
Forgone Interest over Four Years = $40 × 4 = $160	160
3. Total monthly payments are:	
Total Monthly Payments = Monthly Payment × Number of Months	
= $412 × 48 = $19,776	19,776
Total	$20,936
Minus: Expected amount to be received when car is sold in four years	– 10,000
Total cost	$10,936

Cost of Leasing the Car for Four Years	
1. Security deposit of $800 results in forgone interest income (although you will receive your deposit back in four years):	
Forgone Interest	
Income per Year = Down Payment × Annual Interest Rate	
= $800 × .04 = $32	
Forgone Interest over Four Years = $32 × 4 = $128	$128
2. Total monthly payments are:	
Total Monthly Payments = Monthly Payment × Number of Months	
= $300 × 48 = $14,400	14,400
Total cost	$14,528

The Importance of Car Insurance

You have read about the need to insure your home against loss. It is also important to insure yourself against loss that involves your car.

Whether you lease or buy, you will be required to maintain adequate insurance on your car. Remember, insurance is a service you purchase that protects you from loss associated with unexpected events. For example, auto insurance will pay for vehicle repairs if you get in an accident. If you destroy the car in a crash, insurance will write you a check for the value of the car before its destruction.

Lenders require that you keep sufficient auto insurance to protect their investment. Think about this: If you buy a car by borrowing $15,000 from a bank, what happens if you wreck the car? You will still be required to repay the loan. And, you will have no car. What will you drive? Will you buy another car and have two car payments? Lenders know that the likelihood of loan default goes up if you can no longer drive the car. Therefore, they require insurance that will pay off the loan in the event you have a wreck. Many states also require you to maintain automobile insurance.

Auto insurance can cover you against the loss of your property—your car. It can also cover you against any damage you do to other people or their property. This is called **liability coverage**. The two primary liability components are property damage liability and bodily injury liability. Bodily injury liability covers the costs you may be responsible for if you are deemed to be at fault in a accident that injures or kills someone. Such bills can be extremely large, as you can imagine. The property damage liability will cover repairs to their vehicle if you are at fault.

Insurance can be very expensive for young drivers with limited experience. Data shows that young drivers tend to have more accidents, so their insurance is priced accordingly. Sometimes individuals find that they cannot even purchase vehicle insurance if they have too many accidents or even speeding tickets or other violations. Remember, your credit rating can also impact the amount that you pay for vehicle insurance: Poor credit translates to higher insurance rates. Be a good driver and save yourself some money.

There are a number of other factors, such as the value of your car and where you live, that impact your insurance premium. In addition, people who drive more miles every year are charged higher rates. Shop around when you buy car insurance. Premiums can vary substantially from one agency to the next.

☑ CHECKPOINT

What are two major options for paying for a new car?   You can buy or lease the vehicle.

CHAPTER REVIEW

SUMMARY

- Loans allow people to buy things and pay for them over time. People often take out personal loans for large purchases, such as cars or houses. These sorts of loans are available from a variety of sources, including banks, credit unions, and other financial institutions. They also come in many forms, including secured and unsecured loans.

- Interest rate charges on personal loans are reported as the annual percentage rate, or APR.

- When purchasing a home, you should begin by evaluating your financial situation to determine how much you can afford. Renting may be a better option. If you decide to purchase a home, you will get a loan called a mortgage. Mortgages come in two basic forms: fixed rate and adjustable rate. You will also get homeowner's insurance. Renters should purchase renter's insurance coverage on their personal belongings.

- Student loans are also common personal loans used to finance education. Federal student loans are the largest source of student loans because they are guaranteed by the federal government and have the best terms. But, like all loans, student loans must be repaid and should be taken with great care.

- While financing a car for purchase is one widely used option, some people find leasing to be an attractive alternative. Each option has benefits and drawbacks. In all cases, though, car insurance is a must.

Answers:
Key Terms and Concepts

1. A home equity loan occurs when a homeowner borrows money using the equity in their home as collateral. A home equity line of credit can be established that allows the homeowner to borrow against the equity in their home. The distinction between the two is that the home equity line of credit may never be accessed and is merely available if needed.

2. A policy rider is additional coverage added to an insurance policy. For example, you might add a policy rider to your homeowners policy that provides additional insurance coverage for jewelry or a coin collection.

3. Default occurs when you stop making payments on a loan. If the loan has an asset pledged as collateral, such as a car or house, then the asset will be repossesed. The lender will also report the default to the credit bureaus.

Answers:
What Do You Know?

1. (a) **Comprehension** Banks, credit unions, other financial institutions, and businesses that sell big-ticket items are sources of personal loans. (b) **Application** Possible answer: The person may want to use the cash for investment or some other purpose.

2. (a) **Comprehension** Lenders need to find out how likely someone is to pay back the loan. (b) **Analysis** Someone with little credit history may not be able to satisfy a lender that he or she will be able to pay off a loan.

Key Terms and Concepts

1. What is the difference between a **line of credit** and a **home equity loan**?

2. What is meant by a **policy rider**? Give two examples of what could be included in a policy rider.

3. What happens when one **defaults** on a loan?

What Do You Know?   MyFinLitLab

1. (a) List possible sources of personal loans.

   (b) Why might a person prefer to take a loan rather than spending money he or she has saved?

2. (a) Why do lenders need to collect so much personal information about people who seek loans?

   (b) Why might someone who has very little credit history have trouble obtaining a loan?

3. (a) Explain how collateral works.

(b) What would you expect to find in comparing interest rates of secured and unsecured loans?

4. (a) What are your responsibilities if you cosign a loan?

(b) What are the potential consequences of failing to live up to your responsibilities as a cosigner?

5. (a) Describe the characteristics of a fixed-rate mortgage.

(b) Why do you think some homeowners prefer a fixed rate mortgage to an adjustable rate mortgage?

6. (a) Describe some of the costs of buying a home.

(b) Why do those costs affect the decision to buy or rent?

7. (a) What kinds of loss does homeowner's insurance protect against?

(b) What would you stand to lose if you maintained a homeowner's policy that was designed only to pay off the amount you owed on a mortgage in the event of a fire or other disaster?

8. (a) Who makes possible most of the student loans in the United States?

(b) What is the government's interest in helping to make education affordable?

9. (a) What financial criteria should be considered when buying a car versus leasing?

(b) Why might you be concerned about having a too-long auto loan?

10. (a) What are the advantages and disadvantages of leasing?

(b) Give some examples of a person for whom leasing a car would not be a good idea.

What Are Your Finance Math Skills?   MyFinLitLab

The first three questions correlate to *Math for Personal Finance* features located throughout the chapter.

1. Mousa borrowed $6,000 to buy a car and he will make 36 monthly payments of $185.81 to repay the loan. How much total interest will he pay over the life of the loan?

2. Lidell bought renter's insurance with a $500 deductible to cover his possessions that he estimated to be worth approximately $10,000. A fire destroyed his apartment complex and he lost all his possessions. If his insurance coverage maxed out at $5,000, how large was the check he received from the insurance company?

3. (a) **Comprehension** Collateral is an item of value that is pledged against the loan. If a person defaults on a loan, the lender can use the collateral to recover the money. (b) **Analysis** One would expect to find secured loans to cost less because the likelihood of loss by the lender is lower.

4. (a) **Comprehension** If you cosign a loan, you agree to pay if the person borrowing the money does not. (b) **Analysis** You could have your own credit history damaged.

5. (a) **Comprehension** The rate of a fixed rate mortgage stays the same throughout the life of the loan. (b) **Analysis** They know that their costs will never change.

6. (a) **Comprehension** Costs associated with getting a mortgage—including fees for an appraisal, home inspection, mortgage origination, loan application, and title insurance. (b) **Analysis** These costs can total several thousand dollars and would be lost unless the person intends to stay in the home for a significant time.

7. (a) **Comprehension** Homeowner's insurance protects against property damage by many causes and liability in the event someone is hurt on your property. (b) **Application** You might lose all the equity you have built in your home.

8. (a) **Comprehension** The federal government administers most of the student loans. (b) **Analysis** Government has an interest in helping people get the training they need to earn good incomes and pay taxes.

9. (a) **Comprehension** Possible factors include the amount of money you have available for a down payment, how much you can afford each month, and how much you drive. (b) **Analysis** A too-long loan might leave you owing more on the car than the car is, in fact, worth.

10. (a) **Comprehension** Advantages include generally lower payments and low or no down payment. Disadvantages include the fact that leasing doesn't build any net worth. (b) **Application** Leasing might not be a good option for someone who drives a lot of miles or does not take very good care of his or her cars.

Answers:
What Are Your Finance Math Skills?

1. Mousa will make total payments of $185.81 \times 36 = \$6,689.16$. Since the car cost $6,000, he will pay $\$6,689.16 - \$6,000 = \$689.16$ in interest.

2. $\$5,000 - \$500 = \$4,500$

3. Interest accrued and was added to the loan amount because Blaine's loan is unsubsidized, so Blaine will owe $2,000 × .04 = $80 in interest, plus he will still owe the original $2,000.

4. $8,000 × .20 = $1,600

5. $8,000 − (.10 × $8,000) = $7,200; $7,200 × .8 = $5,760

6. $260,000 × .95 = $247,000

7. Any time you spread the payoff of the same amount over longer periods and charge the same interest rate, the longer term will always result in a lower payment.

8. $3,000 × .06 = $180

3. How much interest will Blaine owe when he graduates from college if he took out an unsubsidized $2,000 Stafford loan during his last year of college? The interest rate was 4% and interest was deferred during that year.

4. How much do you have to save for a down payment on a car if the price of the vehicle is $8,000 and the dealer wants a 20% down payment?

5. In the previous problem, how much will you be financing if the same terms apply but the dealer drops the price of the car by 10%?

6. If the mortgage lender requires a minimum 5% down payment on a $260,000 house, how much will you be financing?

7. Which monthly payment will be lower assuming an interest rate of 6%: a $200,000 mortgage financed for 15 years or a $200,000 mortgage financed for 30 years?

8. If you get a personal loan to attend college, how much interest will accrue in the first year on a $3,000 loan assuming market rates of interest are 6%? Assume payments are deferred until you graduate.

What Would You Do?

The agreement that Kayce had with her father was to work a few extra hours at the shop. This worked out well for Kayce at the beginning. But then the racing season got underway and Kayce was really doing great at the track. Each week it seemed that Kayce had another excuse for not being able to work the extra hours. When the next payment for the bike was due, Kayce did not have the money to pay because of all the missed hours at the shop. Kayce's father had to step in and pay for that month.

As the months progressed, it seemed that Kayce's father had to pay often for the bike because Kayce did not have the money. This extra payment was beginning to impact the family finances because Kayce's father had not planned for the bike payments in his financial budget.

1. What are Kayce's responsibilities toward the payments on the bike?

2. Is Kayce's behavior toward her father ethical?

3. What advice would you give to a parent or another person before they cosigned a personal loan?

What Are the Connections? Language Arts, Technology, and Math

Research three cars that you would like to buy. They may be new or used. Be sure to cite the source of your information. Make a chart that shows the following information for each car:

- Car's features (options available on the make, model, color, etc.)
- Year of the car

- Any down payment you will have for the purchase
- Monthly payments for the car
- Insurance for the car (you may need to gather this information from a local insurance representative)

Summarize your findings with a recommendation of which car to purchase. Be sure to defend your choice.

Teamwork

In a team, develop an advertisement for a car of your team's choice. Present all the features, consumer safety factors, incentives, and financing for the car. You may develop a colorful poster, full-page newspaper advertisement, video ad, or brochure about the car.

ESSENTIAL QUESTION ACTIVITIES

Complete these activities to answer this chapter's Essential Question: *How do personal loans and purchasing decisions affect your financial plan?*

1. *On your own:* Hopefully by now you have developed your financial plan. Refer to your plan to answer the following questions:

   (a) Where does a car loan fit into my financial plan?

   (b) When looking at my financial plan, how much of a car payment can I afford?

   (c) What other factors will influence my decision on a car loan?

2. *As a class:* Brainstorm how to decide if purchasing a car will fit into your financial plan. Think about all the factors that will influence this decision.

TEST PREP QUESTIONS

MyFinLitLab

1. Which of the following people does not have a financially sound reason for taking a personal loan?
   a. Ramon has the money to buy a car but he can invest the money and make more than he will be charged for his car loan.
   b. Carrie needs to borrow money in order to pay for her last year of college.
   c. David needs to borrow $1,000 so that he can buy season tickets to see the Yankees play.
   d. Tanya has enough money to make a 20% down payment on a new car, and she knows that she can pay the balance if she has a loan for two years.

1. c

2. Which of the following terms is *not* correctly matched with its definition?
   a. Principal: the amount borrowed.
   b. Terms of the loan: cost of the item if it is not being financed.
   c. Down payment: the amount of money the buyer gives toward the purchase.
   d. Repayment schedule: number of months needed to repay the entire loan along with the dollar amount of each payment and the interest rate.

3. Why does a lender want information about a person's current cash inflow and outflow?
   a. The information helps to determine the number of cosigners a person will need for the loan to be approved.
   b. Most lenders do not make loans to anyone whose assets are not twice his liabilities.
   c. The lender needs to know the person's credit score before making the loan.
   d. The information helps the lender make a decision on the person's ability to pay back the loan.

4. Why should a person be concerned if she has been offered a "teaser rate" on a loan?
   a. She will be forced to pay that same rate for the life of the loan.
   b. After a short time the rate will most likely go up.
   c. It is not a valid loan and the item being purchased with this loan will probably be repossessed.
   d. She will be able to get a loan at a much better interest rate in just a few months.

5. What is the purpose of a loan contract?
   a. It is an offer by the lender to sell something at a given price to another person.
   b. It is a legally binding agreement that explains the charges to be paid by the buyer and the obligations of the seller.
   c. It is a promise made to the credit bureaus that the lender will protect the buyer from bankruptcy until the loan is paid in full.
   d. It is a legally binding agreement that guarantees that the buyer will pay the lender in full and on time.

6. Why is it possible that the interest rate advertised for a loan is very different from the annual percentage rate (APR) on that loan?
   a. The APR includes fees associated with the application, credit report check, and closing costs in addition to the annual interest.
   b. The APR provides for a 10% annual discount if all loan payments are made on time.
   c. The advertised loan was not multiplied by 12 to figure out the annual percentage rate.
   d. The advertised loan is a teaser rate and the APR is the interest rate after the teaser rate is over.

7. Why should a person be very careful before agreeing to cosign a loan?   7. d
   a. The cosigner is required to deposit the amount of the loan into a special bank account until the loan is paid in full.
   b. The cosigner is agreeing to pay half of the loan.
   c. The cosigner's credit score will be changed to the score of the other borrower.
   d. If the borrower defaults on the loan, the lender will expect to receive full payment from the cosigner.

8. A person learns that the interest rate on his $2,000, one-year auto   8. c
   loan is 5%. He is about to apply for the loan when a friend says that he should first know the APR on the loan. He discovers that there is a $50 application fee, a $50 credit check fee, and a $100 charge related to other closing costs. What is the APR on this loan?
   a. The APR is 5%.
   b. The APR is 10%.
   c. The APR is 15%.
   d. The APR cannot be determined from the information given.

9. Which of the following terms is *not* correctly matched with its   9. c
   definition?
   a. Unsecured loan: no collateral is given in support of the loan.
   b. Mortgage loan: the home serves as the collateral for the loan.
   c. Secured loan: the collateral for the loan is a person's good credit history and her signature on a loan agreement.
   d. Adjustable rate mortgage: the mortgage rate can change several times over the life of the mortgage.

10. What is a sound financial reason for a person to choose an adjustable   10. a
    rate mortgage (ARM) over a fixed rate mortgage?
    a. She expects to move to another city in three or four years as her career advances.
    b. She wants to be sure that she will never have to pay more than her current mortgage amount.
    c. She believes that interest rates will be going up in the near future.
    d. She is planning to retire in this house in 30 years with the mortgage completely paid.

11. Subprime mortgages are   11. d
    a. mortgages offered at interest rates below the national average to first-time homeowners.
    b. low interest rate mortgages awarded to people with excellent credit histories.
    c. mortgages offered to people who already have at least one mortgage on their current home.
    d. high interest rate mortgages usually made to people with low credit scores.

12. How is a $50,000 home equity loan different from a $50,000 home equity line of credit?

    a. There are no interest charges on money used from the line of credit; the equity loan rate is the same as the person's mortgage interest rate.

    b. Loans require a person to complete an application and go through a credit check; lines of credit are approved if the person has an account at the bank.

    c. The person who takes the loan receives the full $50,000 at once; the person with the line of credit can borrow against the credit line for any amount up to $50,000 as money is needed.

    d. The $50,000 home equity loan must be used to improve the home; the $50,000 line of credit can be used for anything the borrower chooses.

13. When we say that a person with a home that is valued at $300,000 and who has an outstanding mortgage of $100,000 has a lot of equity in her home, we mean that she

    a. has a lot of debt.

    b. owns a large fraction of her home.

    c. will not be approved for additional loans until her mortgage is paid in full.

    d. will be considered to be at risk of defaulting on her mortgage.

14. A person's bank will only make a home equity loan if the loan and his current mortgage do not exceed 80% of the market value of the home. If he has a $200,000 mortgage and his home is appraised at $400,000, how large of a home equity loan can he hope to obtain?

    a. He can expect to obtain a loan of $80,000.

    b. He can expect to obtain a loan of $120,000.

    c. He can expect to obtain a loan of $160,000.

    d. He can expect to obtain a loan of $320,000.

15. If a person has homeowner's or renter's insurance, it will protect the person

    a. if she loses her job and cannot pay her rent.

    b. from having to file for bankruptcy.

    c. if someone falls in her house and sues her.

    d. from the bank foreclosing on her home for not making mortgage payments.

16. If a person does *not* have renter's insurance and her laptop computer is stolen from her apartment, she

    a. does not have to worry because the landlord has to pay for her loss.

    b. can still buy renter's insurance and make a claim to be reimbursed for the loss of the laptop.

    c. can file a claim for the loss through her car insurance company.

    d. will have to replace the laptop computer at her own expense.

17. A high school senior whose family is very poor wants to go to college, but the family cannot afford to pay. To help finance her education, she should try to obtain the type of loan where interest charges do not build up while she is in school and even during the first few months after graduation. This type of financing is known as a(n)

17. b

a. bank loan.
b. Federal Perkins loan.
c. subsidized Federal Stafford loan.
d. unsubsidized Federal Stafford loan.

18. A person decides to lease a $20,000 car for three years instead of buying the car and financing it with a loan. At the end of three years the car is worth $11,000. How much will he receive when he returns the car to the dealership?

18. a

a. He will only get his security deposit back if one was required minus the cost of any damages that have been done to the car.
b. He will receive $11,000, less the cost of any damages that have been done to the car.
c. He will receive whatever amount of money the dealer is able to get selling the car as a used car.
d. He will receive half of what the dealer gets from the sale of the used car.

19. A disadvantage of paying for a car with a long-term loan is that

19. c

a. the monthly loan costs are higher than the same loan taken for a shorter time.
b. the person cannot take possession of the vehicle until at least half of the loan has been paid.
c. toward the end of the loan, it is possible to owe more on the car loan than what the car is worth.
d. the loan increases in size and the interest rate on the loan goes up.

CHAPTER 11

ESSENTIAL QUESTION

How can people use a credit card correctly and to their advantage?

CREDIT CARDS AND OTHER FORMS OF CREDIT

LEARNING OBJECTIVES

- Explain how credit cards work
- Describe different credit card features
- Discuss how to use a credit card correctly
- Identify other risky credit arrangements

KEY TERMS

credit card
debt consolidation
grace period
overdraft protection
pawnbroker
payday lending

"Man, you have to find a way to come along," said Mario. "Spring break in Florida is awesome!"

Anil rolled his eyes. "You don't have to rub it in, Mario. You know I haven't got any money right now. So unless you've got the cash to lend me. . . ."

"Can't you borrow the money from your mother?" asked Mario. "Or what about that rich uncle you're always talking about?"

"No way. My mother is angry about my grades, and my uncle was just telling me about all the money he's lost in the stock market recently. I can't ask him now."

"Well . . . sorry, dude," said Mario weakly. Anil and Mario fell silent. Anil picked absent-mindedly through the stack of mail on the table. Then, he saw it.

"Hey!" said Anil. "I've got an idea!" He showed Mario the envelope. "Enjoy the freedom to pay over time," it said, and "Low introductory rate with no annual fee!" "I can get a credit card and pay for the trip that way!" said Anil.

"But Anil," asked Mario, "how are you going to pay a credit card bill if you haven't got any money?"

"Well, all I'd need to do is pay the minimum for a couple months," said Anil. "Then I'll pay the rest off when I get a job this summer."

"I don't know," said Mario. "My sister warned me about using credit cards for stuff like this. One of her good friends got into deep trouble that way."

Anil slumped back into his seat. "Who cares what happened to someone I don't even know? That would never happen to me."

The lure of easy access to credit—through credit cards and other sources—is attractive. In fact, credit cards can be a useful financial tool. But easy access to credit of the sort credit cards and certain other options offer can create serious financial difficulties. Your financial future depends on approaching this type of credit cautiously.

HOW CREDIT CARDS WORK

credit cards: Provide individuals with revolving open-end credit, which can be drawn from repeatedly up to some preset limit.

Credit cards provide people with revolving open-end credit, which they can draw from repeatedly up to some preset limit. A **credit provider**, such as a bank, agrees to make a certain amount of credit available to the cardholder. The cardholder can then use this credit as he or she wishes. Simply by presenting the card at a place of business that accepts the credit card, the cardholder can make a purchase without using any cash. He or she can continue to use the card until reaching the credit limit. Each month, the cardholder receives a bill listing all of the credit card purchases. Then, he or she pays off all or some of the borrowed money.

A credit card can be a very useful financial tool. However, it is also perhaps the easiest one to abuse. Often, people find themselves in financial trouble over the easy access to credit that credit cards afford them. Anil planned to pay for a spring break trip with a credit card—even though he had no money to pay off the debt. Does that seem wise? Let's take some time and evaluate the positive and negative of credit cards, as well as all the various features and options.

Ease of Availability and Use

Perhaps the easiest way to establish credit is to apply for a credit card. Offers abound. Many people receive credit card offers in the mail almost daily. And it isn't necessary to wait for someone to mail you an offer. You can apply for a card at banks, through Web sites, and in many other ways.

A credit card allows you to buy products and services wherever the card is honored. A wide variety of businesses honor credit cards. People typically use credit cards for lower-priced convenience purchases such as meals, gasoline, clothing, air travel, and groceries. Costly items such as houses and cars are not typical credit card purchases. As you can see in Figure 11.1, Anil used his credit card to eat at several restaurants over spring break.

Billing takes place monthly. At the end of each monthly billing cycle, you will receive a statement that identifies purchases you made during the period. The statement gives the total amount borrowed. It also gives a minimum payment you must pay. Look at Anil's statement again. You can see his minimum payment and the interest rate charged. Obviously he had fun on spring break. Note how long it will take Anil to pay off this debt if he chooses to only pay the minimum amount every month. Listing the length of time necessary to completely pay the debt when making only minimum payments is a reporting requirement mandated by the Credit CARD Act of 2009.

Credit cards offer three advantages. First, you can purchase products and services without carrying a large amount of cash or a checkbook. Second,

Today, consumers can use credit cards of all types at a wide range of businesses.

as long as you pay the balance in full at the end of each billing cycle, you do not incur any interest charges. Third, you receive a monthly statement that contains a list of your purchases for that month. This list can help you keep track of spending. Some cards provide an annual statement that aids in preparing your taxes. These statements allow you to track annual spending in various categories and help with budgeting.

Applying for a Credit Card

Credit card offers are readily available on the Internet. Before you apply for a credit card, make sure you read all the terms and fees associated with that particular card. Figure 11.2 shows a sample of typical credit card interest rates and fees. Note that after the Credit CARD Act (2009) became fully effective in 2010, credit card applicants under the age of 21 must provide proof that they have income sufficient to make payments or have an adult cosign the application.

Applying for a credit card is much like applying for a loan or other form of credit. Your potential creditor will obtain personal information from you. They will evaluate that information, such as your cash inflows or income, and current cash outflows, such as house payments or car payments. In addition, some creditors will also evaluate your assets, such as savings or other financial assets and real property.

Potential creditors will also perform a **credit check**—that is, they will access your credit report in order to examine your credit history and determine your ability to repay. Your credit report summarizes your existing lines of credit and past credit. Do you pay your bills on time or have you defaulted on any loans? This information will show up on a credit check. In general, creditors will be more likely to extend credit to people with high levels of cash inflows, low levels of cash outflows, and a good credit history. Many also evaluate potential for high cash inflows. For example, college students are often bombarded with credit card offers in spite of having low cash inflows and limited credit history. That is clearly what was happening in the case of Anil, who has no cash inflow and few assets. Potential creditors are betting on the completion of a college degree and the higher level of income that results. Some credit card companies will offer free t-shirts or other teasers to encourage people to sign up. Just remember, there is no "free lunch." You have to pay the bill every month.

Creditors may also consider economic factors. Is the economy healthy or weak? Is a recession approaching? Are people losing their jobs in unusual numbers? Creditors are more reluctant to extend credit during a weak economy.

FIGURE 11.1 Sample Credit Card Statement

Notice that Anil does not have to pay off the entire balance of his account, although he will pay a high interest rate on the balance.

1 Your First Bank	CREDIT CARD STATEMENT	SEND PAYMENT TO Box 1234 Anytown, USA

ACCOUNT NUMBER 4690-543-221	NAME Anil Doe	DATE 3/25/13	PAYMENT DUE DATE 4/15/13
CREDIT LINE $1200.00	CREDIT AVAILABLE $919.62	NEW BALANCE $280.38	MINUMUM PAYMENT DUE $20.00

REFERENCE	SOLD	POSTED	ACTIVITY	AMOUNT
568X89341	3/11	3/11	Big Stop, Jacksonville FL	64.21
7836L5696	3/11	3/12	JJ's Hotel, Daytona Beach FL	110.25
4712M2152	3/14	3/14	Q's Eats, Daytona Beach FL	33.25
1295JH128	3/16	3/17	Jim Bob's Surf Shop, Daytona Beach FL	51.28
8321GB397	3/17	3/17	The Crabby Patty, Daytona Beach FL	21.39

Minimum payment warning: If you make only the minimum payment each period, you will pay more in interest and it will take longer to pay off your balance. Consider the following example:

If you make no additional charges using this card and each month you pay...	You will pay off the balance shown on this statement in about...	And you will end up paying an estimated total of...
Only the minimum payment ($20)	1.4 years	321.38
$40	8 months	300.68

For information about credit counseling services, call 1-877-xxx-xxxx

Previous Balance	(*)		Current Amount Due	
Purchases	(*)	280.38	Amount Past Due	
Cash Advances	(*)		Amount Over Credit Line	
Payments	(*)		Minimum Payment Due	20.00
Credits	(*)			
FINANCE CHARGES	(*)			
Late Charges	(*)			
NEW BALANCE	(*)	280.38		

Finance Charge Summary	Purchases	Advances	For Customer Service Call:
Periodic Rate	1.65%	2.50%	1-800-XXX-XXXX
Annual Percentage Rate	19.80%	30.00%	For Lost or Stolen Card, call: 1-800-XXX-XXXX 24-Hour Telephone Numbers

Please make check or money order payable to Your First Bank. Include account number on front.

FIGURE 11.2 Interest and Fee Information for a Sample Credit Card

Make sure you understand the interest rate and fee information prior to applying for a credit card.

Interest Rates and Interest Charges	
Annual Percentage Rate (APR) for Purchases ①	**8.99%, 10.99%, or 12.99%** introductory APR for one year, based on your creditworthiness. After that, your APR will be **14.99%**. This APR will vary with the market based on the Prime Rate.
APR for Balance Transfers ②	**15.99%** This APR will vary with the market based on the Prime Rate.
APR for Cash Advances ③	**21.99%** This APR will vary with the market based on the Prime Rate.
Penalty APR and When It Applies ④	**28.99%** This APR may be applied to your account if you: 1. Make a late payment; 2. Go over your credit limit; 3. Make a payment that is returned; or 4. Do any of the above on another account that you have with us. **How Long Will the Penalty APR Apply?:** If your APRs are increased for any of these reasons, the Penalty APR will apply until you make six consecutive minimum payments when due.
How to Avoid Paying Interest on Purchases ⑤	Your due date is at least 25 days after the close of each billing cycle. We will not charge you any interest on purchases if you pay your entire balance by the due date each month.
Minimum Interest Charge ⑥	If you are charged interest, the charge will be no less than $1.50.
For Credit Card Tips from the Federal Reserve Board	To learn more about factors to consider when applying for or using a credit card, visit the website of the Federal Reserve Board at http://www.federalreserve.gov/creditcard.

Fees	
Set-up and Maintenance Fees ⑦	NOTICE: Some of these set-up and maintenance fees will be assessed before you begin using your card and will reduce the amount of credit you initially have available. For example, if you are assigned the minimum credit limit of $250, your initial available credit will be only about $209 (or about $204 if you choose to have an additional card).
• Annual Fee • Account Set-up Fee • Participation Fee • Additional Card Fee	$20 $20 (one-time fee) $12 annually ($1 per month) $5 annually (if applicable)
Transaction Fees ⑧ • Balance Transfer • Cash Advance • Foreign Transaction	Either $5 or 3% of the amount of each transfer, whichever is greater (maximum fee: $100). Either $5 or 3% of the amount of each cash advance, whichever is greater. 2% of each transaction in U.S. dollars.
Penalty Fees ⑨ • Late Payment • Over-the-Credit Limit • Returned Payment ⑩	$29 if balance is less than or equal to $1,000; $35 if balance is more than $1,000 $29, or the amount of the purchase if less than $29. $35

⑪

How We Will Calculate Your Balance: We use a method called "average daily balance (including new purchases)."

⑫

Loss of Introductory APR: We may end your introductory APR and apply the Penalty APR if you become more than 60 days late in paying your bill.

CALLOUT DESCRIPTIONS:

1) **APR for purchases** The interest rate you pay, on an annual basis, if you carry over balances on purchases from one billing cycle to the next. If the card has an introductory rate, you will also see the rate that applies after the introductory rate ends. Multiple interest rates may be listed here. Your rate will depend on your creditworthiness, which is based on your debt, income, credit score, and other factors, such as your history of paying bills on time.

2) **APR for balance transfers** The interest rate you pay, on an annual basis, if you transfer a balance from another card. Balance transfer fees may apply, even if the balance transfer APR is 0%. If there is an introductory rate, pay attention to when that rate ends and what the new rate will be.

3) **APR for cash advances** The interest rate you pay if you withdraw a cash advance from your credit card account. Cash advance fees may also apply. Most credit card companies charge interest immediately, starting from the date you get the cash advance.

4) **Penalty APR and when it applies** Your credit card company may increase your interest rate for several reasons. For example, if you:
   - pay your bill late,
   - go over your credit limit,
   - make a payment that is returned, or
   - do any of these on another account that you have with the same company.

   Be sure to read the terms and conditions of your card to know what can cause your interest rate to go up. If you trigger the penalty rate, your credit card company must tell you that they will be raising your rate 45 days in advance of the increase.

   How long will the penalty APR apply?
   Credit card companies must tell you how long the penalty rates will be in effect. You may be able to go back to regular rates if you pay your bills on time for a period of time (for example, 6 months). Companies may not automatically remove the penalty rates. You may have to ask your credit card company to lower the rates.

5) **How to avoid paying interest on purchases** You can avoid interest charges on purchases by paying your bill in full by the due date. About 40 percent of U.S. households pay in full each month; the remainder, about three out of five U.S. households, carry a balance and pay interest on their credit card accounts.

6) **Minimum interest charge** Credit card companies often have a minimum interest amount. These charges typically range from $0.50 to $2 per month. Even if you carry over a low balance, you can be charged a minimum amount of interest. If the minimum interest charge is $1 or less, the company does not need to disclose this charge here.

   Example: Your balance is $25 and your APR is 12%. Your card has a minimum interest charge of $2. Based on your balance of $25, your monthly interest would be $0.25 (as calculated by the APR), but instead you will be charged $2.

7) **Set-up and maintenance fees** Some credit cards offered to people with lower, or subprime, credit scores may charge a variety of fees. Some fees are charged before the card is used and may reduce the amount of credit initially available. These fees can include:
   - **Annual fee**—The amount you'll be charged during each 12-month period for having the card.
   - **Account set-up fee**—Usually a one-time fee for opening and setting up the account.
   - **Participation fee**—Usually a monthly fee for having the card.
   - **Additional card fee**—This can be a one-time fee or an annual fee for having a second card for the account.

   Example: You are assigned the minimum credit limit of $250, your initial available credit will be only about $209 (or about $204 if you choose to have an additional card).

8) **Transaction Fees (balance transfer, cash advance, foreign transaction)** Credit card companies may charge you a fee for transferring a balance, getting a cash advance, or making a transaction in a foreign country. These fees can be either a fixed dollar amount (for example, $5) or a percentage of the transaction amount (for example, 3%). If you are planning to transfer a balance, get a cash advance, or make foreign transactions, check your agreement for these fees.

9) **Penalty fees (late payment, over-the-limit, returned payment) Late payment**. Credit card companies may charge you a fee if you pay your bill late. Some companies may charge different fees depending on your balance—the higher your balance, the higher the late fee.

   Over-the-limit. If you have consented to extensions of credit that exceed your credit limit (opt-in to going over the limit), credit card companies may also charge you a fee if your balance goes over your credit limit. Rather than denying a transaction, your credit card company may let the transaction go through but then charge you a fee for going over your limit. However, this fee cannot exceed the amount of the purchase.

   Returned payment. If you make a payment, but you don't have enough money in your account to cover the payment, your credit card company may charge you a returned payment fee, just like a bounced check fee. This can happen whether you pay with a check or with a direct debit from your account.

10) **Other fees** Some cards require credit insurance, or debt cancellation, or debt suspension coverage. Credit card companies may call this "account protection" or something similar.

    Example: Your credit card offers debt suspension coverage for up to 90 days if you become unemployed. If you lose your job, you may be able to stop making payments on your credit card for about 3 months. But interest may still continue to be added to your balance during the debt suspension period.

11) **How we will calculate your balance** Credit card companies can use one of several methods to calculate your outstanding balance. The method they use can make a big difference in the interest charges you'll pay. Find out if the card calculates your balance:
    - using average balance or adjusted balance,
    - by including or excluding new purchases.

    Depending on the balance you carry over and the timing of your purchases and payments, you'll usually have a lower finance charge with:
    - the adjusted balance method,
    - the average daily balance method, excluding new purchases, or
    - the previous balance method.

    Descriptions of balance calculation methods:

    Adjusted balance method. The balance is the outstanding balance at the beginning of the billing cycle, minus payments and credits made during the billing cycle.

    Average daily balance method, including new purchases. The balance is the sum of the outstanding balances for every day in the billing cycle (including new purchases and deducting payments and credits) divided by the number of days in the billing cycle.

    Average daily balance method, excluding new purchases. The balance is the sum of the outstanding balances for every day in the billing cycle (excluding new purchases and deducting payments and credits) divided by the number of days in the billing cycle.

    Previous balance method. The balance is the outstanding balance at the beginning of the billing cycle.

12) **Loss of introductory APR** If your card has a special, lower rate that is called an "introductory rate," this area will list the ways that you can lose this lower rate. For the first year after opening an account, you can only lose an introductory rate if your account becomes more than 60 days past due.

Source: **www.federalreserve.gov/creditcard/flash/offer.pdf**

Jose just made a $532 credit sale in his uncle's electronics store. The customer paid with a Visa card. Assume Jose's uncle receives 98% of the sale after paying a 2% fee.

How much will he actually receive from the sale?

Solution: Jose's uncle will get .98 × $532 = $521.36.

Types of Credit Cards

The most popular brands of credit card include MasterCard, Visa, American Express, and Discover. MasterCard, Visa, and Discover allow the financing of purchases over time. That is, if you buy items worth, say, $500 during a billing cycle, you have the option of paying for them all at once or over a period of several months—with interest added, of course. In the past, American Express did not offer this option, but now they offer this payment flexibility on some cards.

Credit cards are recognized and accepted by most merchants in the United States and globally. Merchants accept these cards because it helps them sell goods. They know that some consumers might not make a purchase at their place of business if they are unable to use a credit card.

While credit cards help merchants, they also cost them money. That's because credit card companies receive a percentage of the purchase price in return for their services. This way, the credit card company makes money on your use of the card even if you pay off your balance every month and never pay a nickel in interest. Most cards receive between 2% and 4% of the purchase price. For example, if you buy $100 worth of goods from a store and pay with a credit card, that store would pay the credit card company between $2 and $4 for this transaction. Thus, the store makes less on a credit card purchase than on a comparable cash purchase. Obviously, a large retailer such as Wal-Mart will be able to negotiate a better deal with the credit card companies than a small retailer.

Many financial institutions issue MasterCard and Visa credit cards to individuals. Each financial institution makes its own arrangements with the credit card companies with regard to billing and financing for individuals who opt not to pay the balance in full every month. Some universities and charities also sponsor credit cards and negotiate various arrangements.

In addition to the primary issuers mentioned, there are also numerous retail cards available. Target Stores Inc., Sears, and other retail stores issue cards. Oil companies such as Shell and Exxon Mobil also issue credit cards to use at their retail outlets. In most cases, these types of specific cards cannot be used at other retail outlets. For example, your gasoline card will not be accepted at Wal-Mart. Visa and MasterCard credit cards can be used at almost any retail outlet.

A consumer can purchase goods and pay for them later—even over time.

✓ CHECKPOINT

What can a consumer do with a credit card?

CREDIT CARD FEATURES

As you shop for and use credit cards, you must become familiar with their different features and options available. Here are some of the more common ones.

Credit Limit

Credit card companies evaluate your creditworthiness not only to determine whether to extend credit but also to establish an individual credit limit. Recall that a credit limit is the maximum that you can borrow at any one time. In other words, the total amount of your outstanding debt to the credit card company cannot exceed the credit limit. So, if your credit limit is $5,000, you can buy up to $5,000 worth of goods or services—until you make a payment and reduce your outstanding balance to below $5,000. At that point, you can borrow the difference between that balance and $5,000.

Some low-income, high-risk individuals may begin with a credit limit as low as $300. Anil—who has little credit history but decent job prospects—has a limit of $1,200. Other individuals with good credit history and high incomes may have limits exceeding $25,000. A word of advice: Creditors monitor how much of your limit you keep charged up. If your card has a $5,000 limit and you keep it charged near the limit, it will negatively impact your credit score.

Activity #1

Overdraft Protection

Credit cards typically allow consumers to opt-in and receive **overdraft protection**, which is a feature that allows you to "overdraw," or exceed your credit limit. (Note that overdraft protection is also a feature of checking accounts, where it protects you in the event you write a check for more money than you have in your account.)

With credit cards, overdraft protection prevents you from attempting to use your credit card and having the charge denied because you are over your limit. Sounds great—but there is a catch. This feature should be used only in emergency situations, since an overdraft charge can be high. The Credit CARD Act passed in 2009 prohibits overdraft fees from exceeding the amount of the purchase. So, for example, if you purchase a $20 item that exceeds your credit limit, you cannot be charged an overdraft fee on that purchase that is greater than $20. However, if you purchase a larger item that exceeds your limit, the overdraft charge could be hefty. In addition, an overdraft often triggers higher interest rates on any balances you are carrying.

Individuals who do not opt-in and accept overdraft protection will simply have their charge refused because the purchase would cause them to exceed their credit limit. Some individuals prefer overdraft protection to avoid the embarrassment of being denied a charge. Others would prefer not to have this feature in order to prevent them from charging too much.

overdraft protection: Credit card feature that allows one to exceed their credit limit.

Annual Fee

Many credit card companies charge an **annual fee** of $20 to $70 for the privilege of using their card. In cases where people have good credit history and use their card frequently, companies often waive the fees. Other cards advertise no annual fees. Still others offer fee-free service for a period of time—for example, the first year or two. Read all offers carefully. All things being equal, it is better to avoid paying a fee.

Incentives to Use the Card

Some credit cards offer bonus incentives to encourage people to use their credit cards. Many offer cash-back bonuses, airline miles, donations to various charities, or the ability to cash-in accumulated points for gifts.

MATH for Personal Finance

Reese charged a pizza on her MasterCard. When she got her bill she was shocked. The pizza cost only $15.39, but the charge put her over her credit limit. Assume the company charges her a $15 overdraft charge.

How much did the pizza actually cost Reese?

Solution: The pizza cost Reese $15.39 + $15 = $30.39.

Such incentives can be quite valuable for people who make frequent use of their credit cards—and who can manage the risk that comes with such use.

Prestige Cards

Financial institutions often issue prestige cards. These cards, often called platinum or gold cards, provide additional benefits to cardholders, such as special warranties on purchased products or insurance on travel.

Grace Periods

grace period: A time allowed by credit card companies in which you are not charged interest on purchases.

Credit cards typically allow a **grace period** in which you are not charged interest on your purchases. Legally, grace periods must be at least 21 days from the time the statement is "closed," or your bill is calculated and mailed. So, if you receive your bill and pay it within the grace period, you will not pay any interest on the amount borrowed. This is, in effect, a short-term free line of credit.

Prof. FIN

Did you know that there are a variety of fees that your credit card company can charge you?

- *Annual fee* (sometimes billed monthly): Charged for having the card
- *Cash advance fee:* Charged when you use the card for a cash advance; may be a flat fee (for example, $3) or a percentage of the cash advance (for example, 3%)
- *Balance-transfer fee:* Charged when you transfer a balance from another card
- *Late-payment fee:* Charged if your payment is received after the due date
- *Over-the-credit-limit fee:* Charged if you go over your credit limit

- *Credit-limit-increase fee:* Charged if you ask for an increase in your credit limit
- *Set-up fee:* Charged when a new credit card account is opened
- *Return-item fee:* Charged if you pay your bill by check and the check is returned for insufficient funds
- *Other fees:* Some credit card companies charge a fee if you pay by telephone or to cover the costs of reporting to credit bureaus, reviewing your account, or providing other customer services

Be sure you understand all the costs associated with your credit card!

Cash Advances

Many credit cards allow **cash advances** at banks or automated teller machines (ATMs). That is, you can use your card to get cash rather than just purchasing a good or service. Anil had considered using this option to pay for much of his Florida adventure. Fortunately for him, he reconsidered. If his credit card was like most, he would have paid special transaction fees for this service, and he may also have had to pay a higher interest rate for cash advances. In addition, cash advances do not have grace periods. So, the cost of getting cash out of his credit card rather than using it for the individual purchases he made would certainly have been higher.

Financing or Interest Charges

As you know, many individuals make purchases with their credit card and then pay just a portion of the balance for several months or years. From a financial perspective, this is not a good decision. Most credit cards charge interest rates on carried balances that range between 15% and 22%. So, while using credit cards as a type of financing is convenient, it is also extremely expensive.

FIGURE 11.3 How Credit Card Companies Make Money

The profitability of the credit card business helps explain why it is relatively easy to obtain a credit card—even for someone with little sound credit history.

In addition, cardholders who make payments late may pay late fees *and* see rates increase more than 30%. Many credit card companies make more money from some consumers from late fees and other charges than they do from interest charges (see Figure 11.3).

Note also that card companies will sometimes offer low teaser rates for a three- to six-month period to encourage people to make charges and carry balances. When the teaser rates expire, the cards revert to the typical high interest rates.

Credit cards typically change interest rates as market interest rates change. If interest rates increase, so do credit card rates.

All of these features—including annual fees, overdraft protection, acceptance by merchants, interest rates, and other incentives—should be evaluated when determining which card to apply for. Be cautious about accepting too many offers. Many consumers find themselves with 10 or more credit cards that they do not necessarily need or use—or, even worse, 10 cards that they keep charged to the maximum limit.

Prepaid Cash Cards

Some companies, such as Wal-Mart, allow you to purchase a card that you can "load" with cash. That is, you give money to the store—say, $100. Then, when you use the card to make a purchase, the purchase price is deducted from the $100. You can keep using the card until the $100 is gone. Other common prepaid cards are gift cards that require the recipient to use them at a specific store, such as Home Depot or Target. Note, though, that such cards are like actual cash—with the same sort of risks. Experts estimate that a significant percentage of these cards are lost or never used. In that case, the business issuing the card keeps the cash—and the consumer loses everything.

Twila used her credit card to get a $40 cash advance at a local ATM. She intended to pay the balance in full when the bill came in. Twila paid the $40 advance back and also paid $4 in fees ($2 for the ATM and $2 for the credit card company) when the credit card statement arrived 20 days later.

What is the approximate annual interest rate that Twila paid for this advance?

Solution: The $40 advance cost her $4 for 20 days. This amounts to 4/40 or 10% for 20 days use of the money. Assuming there are 18 twenty-day periods in a year, Twila would be paying $18 \times 10\% = 180\%$ a year in interest if she did this same withdrawal every 20 days.

☑ **CHECKPOINT**

Identify five key features of a credit card.

Features include the credit limit, overdraft protection, annual fee, incentives, prestige cards, grace periods, cash advances, and finance or interest charges.

TIPS ON USING CREDIT CARDS

Credit cards are popular, widely available, and risky. The Federal Reserve has a lot of information on credit cards. Go to www.federalreserve.gov and click "Consumer Information." On the left is a link to credit cards. Click this link for a consumer's guide to credit cards. In addition, the following sections describe some general rules you can follow so that you can enjoy the benefits of having a credit card without suffering the negative consequences.

CreditCards.com

What will it take to pay off my current balance?

Inputs | Results | Graphs | Tables | About

1. Current Balance: $ 3000
2. Interest Rate (APR): 17.00 %
3. Monthly Charges: $ 0
4. Enter one of the following:

a. Desired Months to Pay Off:	b. Desired Monthly Payment:
--- months	$ 50
To calculate the monthly payment necessary to pay off your balance	To calculate the number of months it will take to pay off your balance

Calculate

Exhibit from Bankrate website. Copyright © by Creditcards.com. Reprinted with permission.

Use a Credit Card Only If You Can Cover the Bill

Use a credit card only for convenience and not as a source of financing. In other words, before you charge something, be sure you will have enough cash to pay the bill in full at the end of the month. The cost of borrowing money beyond the grace period with a credit card is just too high. For example, let's look at the following. What if you charged a $2,000 item on your credit card that carried an 18% annual rate and you paid a minimum payment equal to 2% of the balance each month? Over the course of the next 12 months you would make nearly $500 in payments but reduce the balance only by $123.56. It is much more prudent to save up for major purchases and make them when you have accumulated enough cash to cover the charge.

Impose a Tight Credit Limit on Yourself

While your credit card company will establish a credit limit, you may find it necessary to impose a stricter standard on your own spending. For example, a credit card company may establish your maximum limit at $5,000. However, you may examine your cash flows and realize there is no way you could pay a $5,000 charge every month. Your self-imposed maximum should correspond to the amount you can safely repay every month in order to prevent carrying high-interest balances on your card.

Pay Credit Card Bills First

If you do find yourself carrying credit card balances, pay them off as soon as possible. Remember—credit cards generally charge between 15% and 22% interest. This is a very high interest rate. Pay credit card balances before paying off any other, less costly debt.

Indeed, it is generally a good idea to pay off credit card debt rather than putting money into savings or investments. These generally earn less interest than credit card companies charge.

Use Savings If Necessary

If your cash inflows are not sufficient to cover this month's credit card bill, pull savings out to pay the difference. You can replenish your savings later. (This, of course, is vital. You need a source of available liquid money.) Again, chances are your savings are earning just a few percentage points in interest. Credit card debt is costing you 15% to 22%. Your money is much more wisely used to reduce that debt (see Figure 11.4).

Different credit cards charge different interest rates. The following chart is an example of different interest rates for a variety of credit cards:

Card Type	Today	Last Week
Balance Transfer	10.31%	10.03%
Low Interest	11.01%	10.97%
For Bad Credit	13.02%	13.12%
Cash Back	11.47%	11.46%
Business	11.10%	10.91%
Airline	12.75%	12.69%

These rates can change daily and can change if your credit rating goes down. It is your responsibility to keep track of the interest rate you are paying on credit cards. You can contact the credit card company to work toward getting a lower rate. You can do this more than once a year!

If You Experience Credit Card Debt Problems

It's good to avoid credit card debt problems if you can. But nobody is perfect. Sometimes, even money-savvy people miscalculate or find themselves in a tight spot. If you find yourself with high credit card debt, there are steps you can take to deal with the problem.

First, try to negotiate new terms. In some situations, when you find that you have overextended yourself financially, you may have the ability to negotiate better terms. Credit card companies will often lower interest rates or help work out more favorable repayment terms if you call them and request it. Credit card companies prefer this type of arrangement to bankruptcy or default where they may get little if any of their money back.

FIGURE 11.4 Why It Pays to Pay Off Credit Card Debt with Savings

Since savings accounts typically pay very low interest rates, you are certain to do better financially by using savings to pay down credit card debt.

Suppose you have $1,250 in a savings account and an existing credit card debt of $1,000. Should you use your savings to pay off the debt or let it be?

Leave savings alone:

$1,250 ⟶ 2% average annual return ⟶ Total interest earned by the end of one year: $25.00

Use $1,000 to pay off credit card debt:

$1,000 ⟶ Credit card balance at 22% interest ⟶ Money saved by the end of one year: $220

Credit counseling agencies are another source of help if you get into credit card debt. They can often help you negotiate better terms with your creditors.

As you try to lower your rates, limit your spending. Remember, to pay off debt you will have to have greater cash inflow than cash outflow. Reduce your spending to necessities. Take steps to increase cash inflow. Work more hours or take a second job. You may be able to borrow money from a family member or friend.

Debt consolidation may be an option as well. **Debt consolidation** means combining several small accounts into one larger account that you may be able to finance at a lower rate at a bank or with another lender. This option works best when you have assets you can pledge as collateral against the loan. For example, many people take a loan from a bank using the equity in their home as collateral. This is a so-called home equity loan. Such a loan may allow you to pay off your credit card debt, car loan, and other personal loans. You replace the three or four smaller loans with one larger loan. Rather than three or four monthly payments, you make one larger payment. If the larger loan is at a lower rate, this strategy can reduce the overall cost of your borrowing.

However, there are risks with debt consolidation. Too many people pay off their credit card debt with a home equity loan—and then run their credit card balances high again. And, of course, failure to pay off a home equity loan could have disastrous consequences—the loss of the home.

Personal bankruptcy is the last resort. **Bankruptcy** is a process in which the courts provide protection for a person who is unable to pay off his or her debts. The courts will help a bankrupt person propose a plan to repay at least a portion of his or her debts. Most bankruptcy debt workouts involve a three- to five-year repayment plan. Bankruptcy is reported to the credit bureau and listed on the person's credit report for seven years. In most cases, this will prevent the person from borrowing money during that period or ensure that the interest rate will be extremely high. Bankruptcy is a costly option.

 CHECKPOINT

What is the main rule for using credit cards wisely?

OTHER RISKY CREDIT ARRANGEMENTS

debt consolidation:
Combining several small accounts into one larger account that you may be able to finance at a lower rate at a bank or with another lender.

The problem facing Anil at the beginning of this chapter is a familiar one. A person wants to buy something today for which he or she does not have ready cash. Credit cards are one way people address this dilemma. But not everyone has access to a credit card or wants to use one. Such people have a number of options. However, most of them are not good ones. Among them are payday lending, tax refund loans, and pawn shops. It is important to understand the characteristics—and possible drawbacks—of these expensive and risky credit options.

Payday Lending

Recent years have seen the development of a new form of credit called payday lending. With **payday lending**, a lender provides cash advances at a high cost to customers who provide a check dated for some time in the future.

For example, let's say Anil had finally broken down and asked his mother for some money for his Florida trip. She reluctantly agreed—but told him he would not receive the money until March 15, when she received her annual work bonus. Unfortunately, Anil and Mario were leaving for Florida on March 10. It seemed as if Anil would be out of luck—until a friend told him about a local payday lender.

Anil found that he could go to the payday lender on March 10 and write a $500 check to the lender dated March 17—a week into the future. The lender would then give Anil $400—$500 minus a $100 fee. The payday lender would then hold Anil's check until March 17. If all went as planned, Anil would have by then received the money his mother had sent. That is, he would have had a payday. With the money in Anil's bank account, the lender would be able to cash his check and get the $500. This would end the transaction.

As you can see, payday lenders charge a very high fee for their service. Fees typically range between $15 and $30 for every $100 loaned. Loans are generally small—less than $1,000. They normally last for 7 to 14 days. This means that the fees amount to an interest rate that is equivalent to several hundred percent per year.

Payday lending has other dangers, too. If there is a delay in receiving the money you are counting on to cover your check, the check to the payday lender will bounce. The bounced check will result in additional fees. It may also damage your credit report.

Why do people use payday lending? In general, it is easy and fast and does not require a credit check. Still, you should never rely on payday lending as a source of financing. Even high-interest credit cards are a better option than a payday loan. Establish good credit and protect it so that you are never forced into a situation where you need the services of a payday lender.

Because payday lending takes advantage of the poor, many states have placed legal restrictions on the practice or banned it outright. The consumer Web site **www.paydayloaninfo.org** provides a wealth of information about the dangers of payday lending. Go to the page with information about each state and check the legal status of payday lending in your state.

payday lending: A lender who provides cash advances at a high cost to customers in exchange for one of their checks dated for some time in the future.

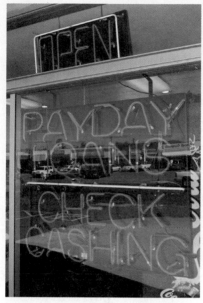

Payday lending is an extremely costly form of credit that wise consumers avoid.

Tax Refund Loans

In recent years, many people have taken short-term loans with the idea that they will use their income tax refund to repay what they have borrowed. A number of income-tax preparers offer this option during tax season. These tax anticipation loans go by many names, such as "Rapid Refund" and a variety of others.

The process is relatively simple. When people use the services of a tax professional to prepare their taxes, the preparer may offer an instant refund based on the calculated income tax refund. Remember, most employers withhold federal taxes from their employees' paychecks and send that money to the government. Often, the amount withheld is greater than what the employee will actually owe in taxes when tax returns are filed after the conclusion of the year. If, in fact, the employer withheld too much in income tax, the employee will get an income tax refund. In addition, certain provisions in the tax code also allow tax "credits" to low income individuals who paid no taxes. They, too, may receive a check from the government at tax time.

The typical fees for these loans are high. In fact, in some cases, they can be equal to an annual interest rate of over 100%. Another danger is that some people find their refunds to be lower than expected. In such a situation, the borrower would have a debt that is larger than the refund he or she receives.

Consumers need to be cautious of scams linked to tax refund advance lending. In one common scam, victims receive a call offering to speed up their tax refund for a fee charged to their credit card. Armed with the victim's credit card number, the con artist then uses the card to the available credit limit. The victim is left with a serious identity theft problem. And, of course, the victim does not receive the tax refund any earlier than he or she would have.

Pawn Shops

pawnbroker: Receives and holds items in exchange for loans that run for 30 days to as much as 3 months.

Before the development of the payday lending industry, pawn shops were a popular source of short-term loans. In many regions of the country, pawn shops still service this particular niche. A **pawnbroker**, or pawn shop representative, receives and holds items in exchange for loans that run for 30 days to as much as 3 months. Commonly pawned items are firearms, jewelry, vehicles, tools, electronic equipment, and musical instruments. These items serve as collateral for the loan. The customer signs an agreement that allows the pawnbroker to sell the item if the customer does not repay the loan within a certain time.

Prof. FIN

Did you know that pawnbrokers can be found as far back as the ancient Greek and Roman empires? Their symbol is three spheres and is attributed to the Medici family of Florence, Italy. In the Italian province of Lombardy, medieval merchants hung the three spheres in front of their houses. Many think it is symbolic of three gold coins, but the spheres were more visible and therefore attracted more attention. Others attribute the

symbol to Saint Nicholas, the patron saint of pawnbrokers, because of the story of Nicholas and the three bags of gold. The three bags of gold were supposed to have been secretly given to a poor man who had three daughters. Nicholas gave the three bags of gold, one for each daughter, so the father would have a dowry for them.

Of course, customers may redeem their item if they repay the loan prior to the due date. As with payday lenders and tax refund advance loans, the cost of a pawnshop loan can be very high. For example, if you pawn an item valued at $300 in return for $150 and do not redeem the item, you have paid several hundred percent in annual interest charges depending on the length of the loan.

Pawnbrokers often specialize in certain types of items. After all, their success depends on their ability to appraise objects being pawned.

Cell Phone Leases

If credit cards are a major source of financial difficulty, cell phone plans are not far behind. You may not think of your cell phone plan as a type of debt, but it is. Landline telephone service falls into the same category as other utilities: You pay a deposit and then you are billed monthly. If you cannot pay a bill, your service may be disconnected until the bill is paid. Cell phone plans, however, are different. Most cell phone service providers require that you sign a 12-month lease. This is a binding agreement to pay for one year's service. Plans typically charge a monthly fee ranging from $39.99 to $200 or more. These plans vary based on the number of minutes you are allowed to use, the services you have available, and on calling regions. In most cases, per-minute charges apply if you use the phone more than the plan allows. Some plans charge higher rates for other features such as data delivery via text messages and Internet access. Additional charges may apply for the downloading of ringtones and other data.

When obtaining cell phone service, always compare features and buy the plan that best suits your usage pattern. Remember: When you sign the lease agreement, you are entering into a contract. If you default, the service provider will report it to the credit bureaus. A cell phone lease is credit extended to you and should be treated as such. Early termination fees typically apply if you need to void the lease, and they can be $150 or more. Paying such a fee may be irritating, but it will prevent a negative mark on your credit report that could cost you more in the long run.

Cell phone companies also use tactics similar to credit card companies when courting new subscribers. They may use free t-shirts, phones, and other items to entice you to sign a lease. Be cautious and only sign up for what you need or want. Don't let a few dollars worth of "free" items entice you into a binding contract that obligates you for service you don't need.

✓ CHECKPOINT

What are some examples of other risky types of credit?

Payday lending, pawnbroking, tax refund lending, and even cell phone plans are risky types of credit.

MY PARENTS HAVEN'T UPGRADED THEIR CELL PHONES FOR LIKE, TWO YEARS.

MY DAD'S COMPUTER MONITOR IS THE SIZE OF A DISHWASHER

AND DON'T EVEN GET ME STARTED ON THE SPEED OF OUR INTERNET CONNECTION.

JEREMY, I HAD NO IDEA!

TECHNOLOGICALLY WE'RE ALMOST AMISH.

CHAPTER REVIEW

SUMMARY

- Credit cards provide people with convenient and easy-to-use credit, and they can be a very useful financial tool. They are also easy to apply for and obtain. A disadvantage of credit is that it is easier to obtain than to repay. The major sponsors of credit cards are Visa, MasterCard, Discover, American Express, a proprietary merchant (such as JCPenney), or some other sponsor.

- Key credit card features include the credit limit, the annual fee, the interest rate charged on credit not paid by the due date, a grace period between the closing of the statement and the date when payment is due, and the availability of cash advances. Cards may offer "prestige" versions and also incentives. Some have overdraft protection.

- Credit cards should be used with discipline. You should impose your own credit limits rather than spend up to the limit granted by the card. You should attempt to avoid financing costs, either by using income to cover the amount due or by withdrawing money from savings if necessary. Deal with any problems quickly.

- There are several other examples of credit arrangements that meet a similar need to credit cards—and carry similar risks. These include payday lending, tax refund loans, and pawnbroking. Although many people don't realize it, cell phone leases can be a costly form of credit.

Key Terms and Concepts

1. What happens when a person declares **bankruptcy?**

2. What is meant by **debt consolidation**?

3. What is the difference between a **cash advance** from a payday lender and money received from a **pawnbroker**?

What Do You Know? MyFinLitLab

1. (a) What are two advantages of using a credit card?

    (b) What is a disadvantage?

    (c) How does credit from a credit card differ from a personal loan?

2. (a) What kinds of information are creditors looking for?

    (b) Do you need to have all these attributes to get credit?

3. (a) What is a credit limit?

   (b) How can you use the credit limit to determine how much credit you can safely use?

4. (a) What is the purpose of overdraft protection?

   (b) Explain how using this feature may both help and hurt you.

5. (a) What is a grace period?

   (b) How can this feature enable you to use a credit card at no direct cost to you?

6. (a) Are all credit cards the same in their use and features?

   (b) Explain which features you would find particularly useful.

7. (a) Why is paying your credit card balance in full important?

   (b) What should you do if you can't avoid credit card debt? Explain.

8. (a) What is payday lending?

   (b) If you had the option of using a standard credit card for a $500 purchase or a payday loan, which would you choose? Why?

9. (a) What is a tax refund loan?

   (b) How is it similar to and different from a payday loan?

10. (a) How does the financial obligation of consumers to cell phone plans differ from that to landline telephone service?

    (b) What, besides money, is the major threat from misuse of a cell phone plan?

What Are Your Finance Math Skills?   MyFinLitLab

The first three questions correlate to *Math for Personal Finance* features located throughout the chapter.

1. Paula's mom just sold a new prom dress in her shop for $675. However, the customer paid for the dress with a MasterCard. Assuming Paula's mom receives 97% of the sale after paying a 3% credit card fee, how much will she actually receive from the sale?

2. Reshawda used her Visa card to put $30 worth of gas in her car. However, when she got her bill she noticed the charge put her over her credit limit. Assuming the credit card company charges her a $25 over-limit charge, how much did the gas actually cost her?

3. Kari got a $50 cash advance at a local out-of-network ATM. She paid the $55 balance in full when the bill came in. Kari's bill included the $50 cash advance and $5 in fees. Approximate the annual interest rate that Kari paid for this advance. Remember that these charges represent only one month and to approximate annual rates you need to multiply by 12.

3. (a) **Knowledge** A credit limit is the maximum amount you can borrow using a credit card. (b) **Analysis** A good answer will indicate that the credit limit may have little relationship to how much debt you can handle at any one time.

4. (a) **Comprehension** Overdraft protection protects you from borrowing beyond your credit limit. (b) **Application** This feature may protect you from the consequences of having credit denied, but it might cost you money and potentially lead to debt problems.

5. (a) **Knowledge** A grace period is the time during which the credit card company does not charge you interest after having billed you. (b) **Comprehension** If you always pay within the grace period, you can avoid paying interest charges on the amount of credit you pay off.

6. (a) **Comprehension** No. Their use and features vary. (b) **Application** Students should be able to defend their answers.

7. (a) **Comprehension** Paying the bill in full helps protect you from interest charges. (b) **Application** You should seek to pay off credit card debt as quickly as possible—by stopping savings, using savings, and borrowing from others if necessary.

8. (a) **Knowledge** Payday lending is a credit scheme in which a borrower receives cash in return for a promise—the writing of a postdated check—of paying off a significantly larger amount at some point in the future. (b) **Analysis** Use of the credit card would be wiser because if you were able to pay off the debt in the near future you could reasonably hope to avoid all interest charges, and in any case, you would pay lower interest with the credit card.

9. (a) **Knowledge** A tax refund loan is a high-interest loan based on the expectation of receiving a tax refund. (b) **Analysis** It is similar to a payday loan in that it involves paying a steep price to have quick access to money. It differs in that the receipt of a tax refund may be more certain than other forms of income.

10. (a) **Comprehension** Cell phone plans typically require a year-long lease. (b) **Analysis** Breaking a cell phone lease can be reported to the credit bureaus and harm your overall credit rating.

Answers:
What Are Your Finance Math Skills?

1. $675 × .97 = $654.75

2. $30 + $25 = $55

3. $5/50 = 10% for one month × 12 months = 120% annually

4. 24%/12 = 2% per month in interest charges × $1,000 = $20.

5. $238.49 × .97 = $231.34

6. $4,000 + $9,000 + $3,600 + $11,300 = $27,900 × .85 = $23,715

7. $23,715 × .03 = $711.45

8. $40 × 3 = $120 in total fees. This equals 120/450 = 26.7% for three months. Since there are 4 three-month periods in a year, the annual rate would be approximately 26.7% × 4 = 106.7%.

4. Assume you carry a $1,000 balance on your credit card that charges a 24% annual interest rate. How much interest will you pay for this account next month?

5. If a vendor makes a credit sale of $238.49, how much will the vendor receive after it pays the customary 3% fee to the credit card company?

6. Jim has four credit cards with limits of $4,000, $9,000, $3,600, and $11,300 respectively. If he has all of his cards charged up to 85% of his credit limit, how much does he owe?

7. In the previous question, assuming Jim pays the minimum payment next month on each card and that is 3% of the outstanding balance, how much will Jim's payments be?

8. Jerry pawned his power tools valued at $800 for $450 cash. Assuming he pays the pawnbroker $40 a month for three months and then pays the balance and retrieves his tools, what was the approximate annual interest rate for this loan?

What Would You Do?

Chen recently graduated from college and accepted a job in a new city. Furnishing his apartment had proven more costly than he anticipated. To assist him with making purchases, he applied for and received a credit card with a $5,000 credit limit. Chen planned to pay off the balance over six months.

Six months later, Chen found that there were other expenses incurred in starting a new career, which restricted him to making minimum payments only. Not only that, he had borrowed on his card to the full extent of its credit limit. Upon returning from work one day, Chen found a letter from the credit card company offering to increase his limit to $10,000 because he has been a good customer and has not missed a payment.

1. Discuss the ethics of credit card companies that offer to increase credit limits to individuals who make only minimum payments and who have maxed out their card.

2. Should Chen accept the credit card company's offer? Why or why not?

What Are the Connections? Math and Technology

Look at the following chart. It shows several situations for someone who has a $2,000 credit card balance and who charges $150 or $100 each month. You can use an online calculator to determine for each scenario how long it would take to pay off the balance and how much interest you would pay in the process.

Amount owed	Monthly charges	Monthly payments	Annual interest rate	Annual fee	Total interest expense	Time to pay off debt
$2,000	$150	$350	19%	0	_____	_____
$2,000	$150	$350	7%	0	_____	_____
$2,000	$150	$450	7%	0	_____	_____
$2,000	$100	$350	7%	0	_____	_____

Go to www.creditcards.com. Under "Tools," click "Calculators," and then click "Payoff Calculator."

1. Input the information from the first row and then click "Calculate." Note the total interest expenses and time to pay off the debt.

2. Click "Inputs." Change the annual interest rate to 7% and click "Calculate." Note the total interest expenses and time to pay off the debt.

3. Click "Inputs." Change the monthly payments to $450 and click "Calculate." Note the total interest expenses and time to pay off the debt.

4. Click "Inputs." Decrease the monthly payments to $350 and reduce the monthly charges to $100. Click "Calculate." Note the total interest expenses and time to pay off the debt.

What conclusions can be drawn from the information provided in the chart? How can such information benefit you when working on your financial plan?

Answers:
What Are the Connections?

1. $195; 11 months

2. $67; 11 months

3. $46; 7 months

4. $55; 9 months

Teamwork

In teams, look up the four leading cell phone providers in your surrounding area. Make a chart that compares the costs, features, services available, call area, and any other interesting facts. Present your information on a poster that can be displayed in the halls of your school for students to help them make a decision about purchasing one cell phone plan over another.

ESSENTIAL QUESTION ACTIVITIES

Complete these activities to answer this chapter's Essential Question:
How can people use a credit card correctly and to their advantage?

1. *On your own:* A classmate has come to you with a credit card application. The excitement of having credit is too much and you are asked to help with advice. Write a short essay that explains to your friend how credit cards work and how to use them carefully so that they are an advantage, not a hindrance, to one's credit. Be sure to explain the different types of credit, different credit card features to look for, and how this needs to be a part of a financial plan.

> **2.** *In small groups:* Brainstorm all the advantages and disadvantages of credit card use. Using the Interent, research various credit card companies and identify all their features. Report back to the class your findings and make comparisons.

TEST PREP QUESTIONS

1. c **1.** A financial tool that provides people with revolving open-end access to funds that they can draw from repeatedly up to some preset limit is known as a
   a. mortgage.
   b. certificate of deposit.
   c. credit card.
   d. checking account.

2. d **2.** Which of the following is a true statement about a credit card?
   a. It must be accepted at any place of business that accepts cash.
   b. It most often is used to make large purchases such as a car.
   c. It cannot be used to make purchases under $10.
   d. It allows a person to make purchases wherever the card is accepted.

3. a **3.** The greatest advantage of using a credit card is that it provides
   a. an easy way to establish a personal credit history.
   b. an easy way to avoid going into debt.
   c. a less expensive way to pay for college.
   d. a safe way to improve a person's credit score.

4. b **4.** Which of the following is *not* an advantage of having and using a credit card?
   a. Credit card statements help a person keep track of spending.
   b. No interest is charged if a minimum payment is made on the account each month.
   c. A person who is making most purchases with credit cards can see if he is living within his budget.
   d. A cardholder does not have to carry a lot of cash when traveling.

5. a **5.** Which of the following is a true statement?
   a. Creditors require a person to complete a credit application and will conduct a credit check before issuing a credit card.
   b. Creditors are more likely to loan money when the economy is in a recession.
   c. Creditors are likely to loan money to people who have high levels of cash outflow and low levels of cash inflow.
   d. Creditors charge all cardholders the same rate of interest on outstanding balances, purchases, and cash advances.

6. d **6.** How do credit card companies benefit when cardholders pay their bills in full each month and never have to pay interest on balances?
   a. Credit card companies charge a flat monthly 8% interest even if cardholders pay their bills in full.
   b. Credit card companies get a higher credit score if cardholders pay their bills in full.

   c. Credit card companies make most of their money by charging a monthly fee to use the company's card.

   d. Credit card companies receive 2%–4% of the purchase price of every good or service that is sold to a cardholder.

7. Which of the following credit card fees is correctly matched with its description? 7. c

   a. Credit limit: the most that can be spent for a single item using a credit card.

   b. Overdraft protection: the number of purchases that can be made by a person over their credit limit.

   c. Annual fee: fee that is charged by the company for the privilege of using the company's card.

   d. Cash advance fee: fee that is charged by the company if the cardholder goes over the credit limit and has to borrow money.

8. Even though a person has overdraft protection on her credit card, she should avoid using this feature because 8. a

   a. overdraft fees can be high, although they cannot exceed the amount of the purchase that caused the overdraft.

   b. each time a person uses overdraft protection, her credit score will drop by 50 points.

   c. using overdraft protection will cause the interest a person earns on other accounts to drop.

   d. using overdraft protection will cause the person's credit limit to be increased.

9. Which of the following credit card fees is *not* correctly matched with its description? 9. d

   a. Late-payment fee: charged if a person's payment is received after the due date.

   b. Credit-limit-increase fee: charged if a person asks for an increase in his credit limit.

   c. Balance-transfer fee: charged if a person transfers a balance from one credit card to another.

   d. Over-the-credit-limit fee: charged if a person spends too much money on all his credit cards together.

10. Which of the following is a true statement about credit cards? 10. c

   a. If a person pays her total credit card bill within the grace period, interest on the account is charged at a lower rate.

   b. If a person uses his credit card to obtain cash advances, there is no interest charged.

   c. Some credit cards encourage people to use their credit by offering them cash back if they buy a certain amount of goods or services.

   d. Some credit cards, called prestige cards, do not charge interest if the cardholder makes only the minimum payment each month.

11. A person knows that she cannot afford to pay $400 for a coat that she really wants. The financially wise action for her to take is to 11. c

   a. buy the coat with a credit card and pay as much as she can each month until it is paid off.

   b. take a cash advance using her credit card and pay for the coat that way.

   c. buy a less expensive coat that she can pay for immediately.

   d. apply for a credit limit increase to cover the cost of the coat.

12. a

12. Why would a credit card company offer a person the opportunity to open a credit card account that will charge 0% interest on purchases or balance transfers for 12 months?
   a. The credit card company expects that the person will continue to make purchases and carry a balance after the introductory period when interest charges go back to normal rates.
   b. Credit card companies get tax breaks based upon the number of people who use their cards.
   c. Late fees that are charged to all the people who take advantage of this offer make up for any money lost by not charging interest on the account.
   d. Companies that make this offer receive better ratings from consumer protection groups.

13. b

13. What is the advantage to a consumer of having a prepaid cash card?
   a. Many people never use the cards and the company gets to keep the money.
   b. The person can purchase items up to the limit on the cash card without paying any interest.
   c. Cash cards earn monthly interest.
   d. There is no credit limit when using cash cards.

14. c

14. A person with $5,000 in credit card debt with an 18.5% annual interest rate (APR) receives an end-of-year bonus of $2,000. It is generally considered a financially smart move for this person to
   a. invest the bonus money until he earns $5,000 and can pay off the credit card bill.
   b. put the money into savings so that he earns an equivalent rate of interest.
   c. pay off $2,000 of the credit card debt with the bonus so that he pays less in interest.
   d. buy the next $2,000 worth of items that he wants using the bonus money instead of credit cards.

15. a

15. If a person has mounting credit card debt and cannot pay it down, the first thing she should do is
   a. contact each credit card company with which she has an account and try to negotiate new terms such as a lower interest rate.
   b. pay one of the credit card bills each month.
   c. declare personal bankruptcy and start over with a clean slate.
   d. open a new credit card account, make all purchases using that account, and pay the minimum on the old accounts.

16. a

16. A person who has a total of $17,000 in credit card debt decides to use her house as collateral for a bank loan. She then uses her $30,000 home equity loan to pay off the credit card debt. She is now paying back one larger loan at a lower interest rate. What is the danger of using this method to pay back her debt?
   a. If she cannot pay back the equity loan, she is in danger of losing her home.
   b. There is no danger; this is a guaranteed way to get rid of debt.

    c. The credit card companies will cancel her accounts once they have been paid.

    d. Debt consolidation is the same as declaring bankruptcy and her credit score will be affected in the same way.

17. Why is a payday loan considered to be an unwise way to finance a purchase?

    a. Everyone in the company can go online to see the names of people who have had to take payday loans.

    b. The person who takes a payday loan will not be eligible for a raise for a year.

    c. Payday loans carry very high fees equivalent to more than a 100% annual interest rate (APR).

    d. The person's employer will probably give the employee who takes a payday loan a poor job evaluation.

17. c

18. If someone uses a ring worth $500 as collateral for a $200 loan, she has most likely obtained a loan from a

    a. pawnbroker.

    b. credit card company.

    c. tax preparer.

    d. payday lender.

18. a

UNIT 4

Saving & Investing

CHAPTER 12

ESSENTIAL QUESTION

Why is balancing your checking account an important part of your financial plan?

BANKING PROCEDURES AND SERVICES

LEARNING OBJECTIVES

- Explain the difference between different types of financial institutions
- Learn the basics of having a checking account, including how to balance an account
- Identify other available banking services
- Describe the two major federal insurers
- Explain the function and goals of the Federal Reserve

KEY TERMS

check
checking account
credit union
debit card
Federal Deposit Insurance Corporation (FDIC)
Federal Reserve System
fiat money
monetary policy
National Credit Union Share Insurance Fund (NCUSIF)

Ariadne was leafing though the mail when she saw an envelope addressed to her. It was from the bank where she had recently opened a checking account. Inside the envelope was a yellow slip with the words *Insufficient Funds* across the top. Below that were some numbers—it was hard to understand. As best as she could tell, the note was saying that the amount of money in her account was actually less than the amount of one of the checks she had written.

Just then, her mother walked in the room. "Mom," said Ariadne, "I just got this from the bank—what does it mean?" Her mother looked at the slip, and she sighed.

"Oh, Ariadne," she said. "You've bounced a check!"

Ariadne had heard that term before. But she wasn't sure, really, what it meant. "What's going to happen?" she asked.

"Well," said Ariadne's mother, "you're fortunate you have overdraft protection. The bank is going to cover the check and pay whomever you wrote the check to. But look here—they're charging you a $25 fee."

"Oh, great!" said Ariadne. "I write a lousy $9 check for some pizza, and it costs me $34!"

"It could have been worse, Ariadne," said her mother. "If you didn't have overdraft protection, the bank would send the check back to the pizza place—unpaid. They would probably charge you a fee, too!"

Ariadne didn't exactly feel lucky. But she was glad she had opted to go with the bank that offered overdraft protection. She was also anxious to find out how she had gotten into this situation. She wanted to be sure it never happened again.

Banks and other financial institutions offer individual services such as providing personal loans and accepting deposits. In most cases, they offer accounts that allow you to draft payments. Not only are these institutions a critical component of our personal financial plan, but they are also important to the overall economy.

Ariadne is learning directly about the value of certain banking services and about the importance of using banks properly. We will now discuss some of the basics of banking and the services they offer.

BANKS AND FINANCIAL INSTITUTIONS

There are probably several banks in your community. In addition, there may be a number of other kinds of financial institutions that offer financial services. What are the differences between these institutions? To begin, you should understand that there are two major types of financial institutions: depository institutions and nondepository institutions.

Depository Institutions

Depository institutions are financial institutions that provide traditional checking and savings accounts for individuals and businesses. They also provide loans. Depository institutions take in and secure people's money, and they loan it to people and businesses in the community. Types of depository institutions include commercial banks, savings banks, and credit unions. These institutions all serve a similar function. In general, they differ in terms of the government regulations under which they operate.

Depository institutions generally pay interest on the deposits people leave with them. Then, they use the deposits to make loans, on which they charge an even higher rate of interest. In this way, they earn a profit. They also make money by charging various fees for services. One example is the one Ariadne's bank charged her for overdraft protection. Another common fee is the monthly fee many people pay for their checking account.

Prof. FIN

Did you know that the job growth for commercial loan officers in the United States is expected to be 14% between 2010 and 2020? Compare this to 1% job growth in the banking industry for tellers. Futhermore, compare the salary and entry-level education needed for each of these jobs. In 2010, the median pay for tellers was $24,100 per year compared to $56,490 per year median pay for commercial loan officers. A teller position requires only a high school diploma or equivalent, while in most cases loan officers are required to have a bachelor's degree. Look at the difference in median pay for a degree.

You can find more information about jobs in financial services and banking industry at **www.bls.gov**, and more about loan officers at **www.bls.gov/ooh/Business-and -Financial/Loan-officers.htm** and **www .bls.gov/ooh/office-and-administrative -support/tellers.htm**.

Nondepository Institutions

Nondepository institutions consist of institutions that provide certain financial services but do not accept traditional deposits. Nondepository institutions include insurance companies, finance companies, and securities firms and investment companies. For now, we will confine our discussion to depository institutions, which we will refer to generally as banks.

Choosing a Bank

Banks and other depository institutions can differ significantly on fees charged, interest rates paid on deposits, and access to **automatic teller machines (ATMs)** and branches. Keep in mind that while you can usually access most accounts via any ATM, if the ATM is not in your bank's network, there can be significant fees charged per withdrawal. While some Internet banks pay a higher deposit rate, they also provide limited access. Everyone must weigh the pros and cons of various financial institutions when choosing a bank.

Finance ONLINE

How many financial institutions are in your local community? Go online to research the services that are provided by as many of these financial institutions you can find. Make a list of each, including their services. Do any of these institutions provide apps for tablets or smartphones? Do you use an app for your smartphone or tablet to help you track your banking transactions?

CHECKPOINT

What are two types of financial institutions?

Depository and nondepository financial institutions.

BANKING BASICS: CHECKING ACCOUNTS

One of the more widely used banking services is the checking account. It is also a service that can lead to trouble if not managed carefully. Ariadne discovered that when she wrote a bad check.

How Checking Accounts Work

When you open a **checking account** at a bank, you create an account into which you deposit money and from which you gradually withdraw money by writing checks or using a debit card.

checking account: An account into which you deposit money and from which you gradually withdraw money by writing checks or using a debit card.

check: A written order from you to your bank instructing it to pay money from your account to another party.

Most communities have a number of banks and other types of depository institutions available for the safe and secure storage of wealth.

A **check** is a written order from you to your bank instructing it to pay money from your account to another party. When you write a check and someone accepts it for payment, that party eventually presents that check to your bank. That is, the party "cashes" the check. The bank takes money out of your account equivalent to the amount of the check and gives the money to the party presenting the check. Often, this process of presenting the check to the bank and receiving payment occurs electronically. See Figure 12.1 to see a sample check and an explanation of its parts.

Most of us open checking accounts because it enables us to have an accurate payment record. It also allows us to carry less cash. Checks also make it safer to send payment via the mail. Think about it like this. If you mail a cash payment to the electric company, someone could intercept that payment and pocket the cash. If you mail a check made out to the electric company, only the electric company can cash the check. If the check is lost or stolen, nobody can get your money.

NOW Accounts

Generally, you will not earn interest on money kept in ordinary checking accounts. **Negotiable order of withdrawal (NOW) accounts** function much like checking accounts except they pay a small amount of interest on money in the account. They require you to maintain some minimum balance in order to earn interest, so they are not quite as liquid as an ordinary checking account.

Debit Cards

Many banks provide debit cards to their account holders. A debit card looks like a credit card (which may also be available from your bank), but it works differently. A **debit card** enables you to withdraw cash from your account at ATMs, or to pay directly for goods or services at many stores and restaurants. There is no credit involved—the amount of money is withdrawn immediately from your account.

Debit cards are convenient. But be cautious: Debit cards make it easy to spend money. It is also easy to forget to record ATM withdrawals or debit purchases. Make sure you record debit card withdrawals and purchases in your check register or you will find yourself overdrawn. Debit cards also require you to use a **personal identification number (PIN)**. PINs are usually four-digit numbers that you need to memorize in order to be able to use your debit card. Be careful with your PIN. No one should know it but you, since inputting this number along with your debit card will grant anyone access to your account and your cash.

Using Your Checking Account

Let's say you open an account with a deposit of $500. That amount is your balance. You should record that amount in your **check register**, a small ledger the bank will provide you for keeping track of your account balance. As you write checks or use your debit card, you will record those as well. For each check, you subtract the amount of the check from your balance,

YOU DO IT

Activity #1

debit card: Enables you to withdraw cash from your account at ATMs, or to pay directly for goods or services at many stores and restaurants.

MATH for Personal Finance

Jim's checking account balance was $541.39 at the beginning of the month. He deposited a $50 check he earned from mowing a lawn and wrote a check for $28.32. His monthly service fee was $8.

What is Jim's new account balance?

Solution: $541.39 + $50 − $28.32 − $8 = $555.07.

FIGURE 12.1 Example of a Blank Check

Checks are a convenient way to allow the transfer of funds from one person to another—without the need for cash. Checks have several safeguards to prevent theft.

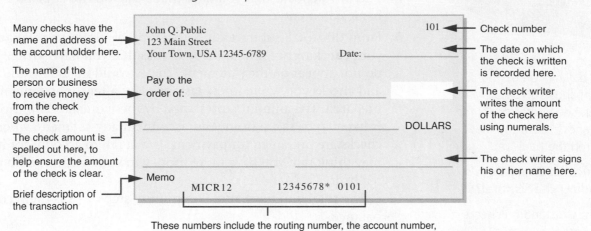

Many checks have the name and address of the account holder here.

The name of the person or business to receive money from the check goes here.

The check amount is spelled out here, to help ensure the amount of the check is clear.

Brief description of the transaction

John Q. Public
123 Main Street
Your Town, USA 12345-6789

Date: _____

Pay to the order of: _____

_____ DOLLARS

Memo _____

MICR12   12345678* 0101

Check number

The date on which the check is written is recorded here.

The check writer writes the amount of the check here using numerals.

The check writer signs his or her name here.

These numbers include the routing number, the account number, and the check numbers that enable banks to cash the checks.

---

giving you a new balance. If you make another deposit, you add that amount and update your balance.

Keeping an accurate balance is essential. If you don't know how much money is in your account, you might wind up like Ariadne. You might overdraw your account—that is, bounce a check or checks. Some checking accounts, such as Ariadne's, come with overdraft protection. This means that the bank will cash checks up to a certain amount even if you do not have money in your account. (Of course, you must pay back the bank, and pay a fee). Overdraft fees can be as small as zero for very good customers and as high as $25 or $35 for others. Some checking accounts, however, do not have overdraft protection. If you overdraw such an account, the bank will not cash any checks. In fact, they will charge you a fee for overdrawing your account. Most businesses will also charge you a fee for writing them a bad check. So, each bounced check can cost you an additional $50 to $70 depending on the fees charged. You can pay this much even if—like Ariadne—the check you wrote was for a small amount. And, if you bounce more than one check, you can pay that amount for each one.

Balancing Your Account

Even if you faithfully record deposits and checks, it is possible for errors—yours or the bank's—to occur. To discover these errors quickly, you should regularly compare your records to the bank's. Here's how you do it:

At the end of each month the bank will send you a bank statement. This lists the bank's records of all the deposits and checks written against your account. When you receive this statement you need to reconcile the bank's balance with your balance recorded in your ledger. It is helpful to use a separate sheet of paper, divided into two columns, for this exercise. One

MATH for Personal Finance

Tucker used his debit card to withdraw $40 cash from his account. However, he used an out-of-network ATM that charged him $2.50, and his own bank charged another $2 for the out-of-network withdrawal.

How much will his account be charged in total?

Solution: That was an expensive withdrawal for Tucker. His account will be reduced by $40 + $2.50 + $2 = $44.50.

YOU DO IT

Activity #2

Mary Beth's checking account balance on her bank statement shows $184.32. However, she wrote checks for $41.78 and $12.10 that have not cleared the bank yet.

How much do Mary Beth's outstanding checks total?

Solution: Outstanding checks are checks that have not cleared the bank, so the total is $41.78 + $12.10 = $53.88.

YOU DO IT

Activity #3

column represents the bank statement balance. The other represents your checkbook register balance.

1. In one column, write the balance given on the statement.

2. Add any deposits that you have made that do not appear on the bank statement.

3. From this total, subtract any ATM withdrawals you have made from your checking account and any checks that you have written that do not appear on the statement. These would include withdrawals and checks you wrote in the last few days after the statement was prepared. The amount represented by these outstanding checks is likely to be taken from your account at any moment, when the checks are presented for payment. If you fail to account for it, you may think that you have more money in your account than you really do.

   The total you have after completing steps 1–3 is the reconciled balance.

4. Now, move to the other column on your sheet. There, record the balance listed in your checkbook register.

5. To this amount, add any interest earned, and deduct any fees your bank has charged you in the last month. These amounts should be listed in your bank statement.

6. Compare the final reconciled bank balance with the reconciled balance in your register. They should be the same. If the amounts are not equal, you need to track down the mistake. It may be a math error on your part or it could be an error on the bank's part. Look at Figure 12.2 for a sample of reconciling your checking account balance.

FIGURE 12.2 Balancing a Checking Account

Reconciling what your check register says and what your bank says you have in your account is essential in preventing overdrafts. Mistakes—either by the bank or by the checking account holder—are not uncommon and can lead to confusion—and bounced checks.

Bank Statement Balance	$	Checkbook Register Balance	$
Plus Deposits in Transit *(Total of deposits that appear in your checkbook but do not appear on the bank statement)*	$	Plus Interest Earned	$
Minus Outstanding Checks ATM Withdrawals, or Debits *(Total of any checks that you have written or withdrawals you have made since the beginning of the statement period that do not appear on the bank statement)*	$	Minus Service Charges	$
Reconciled Balance	$	Reconciled Balance	$

✓ **CHECKPOINT**

Why are checking accounts useful?

They enable you to carry less cash, keep records, and mail payments securely.

OTHER BANKING SERVICES

In addition to housing and maintaining your checking account, your bank will offer a variety of different services. A few of them are discussed here.

Safety Deposit Boxes

Safety deposit boxes are usually available for rent at most banks. **Safety deposit boxes** are small containers located inside the bank vault and are used to store valuable paperwork such as wills and legal documents and small objects such as jewelry and rare coins.

Cashier's Checks, Money Orders, and Traveler's Checks

Banks are also a source of cashier's checks. A **cashier's check** is a type of check that is written to a specific payee but charged against the bank instead of your account. When you buy a cashier's check, the bank takes the money for the check out of your account immediately. Why bother paying by cashier's check? They may be accepted in situations when a personal check from your own account would not. That's because the recipient of a cashier's check does not have to worry about whether you have enough money in your account. Since it is drawn against the bank's account, the recipient can be confident he or she will get the money.

People often use cashier's checks for larger purchases and when one party does not know the other well enough to accept a personal check. Cashier's checks may also be useful if you have bounced a check and the recipient will no longer accept your personal check.

Money orders function in a similar way to cashier's checks: They are purchased for cash so that the recipient can trust that they are worth what they say they are. The United States Postal Service sells money orders for a fee. If you've bought something in an online auction, you may have used a money order to mail payment so that the seller did not have to wait for your check to clear before mailing your item.

Traveler's checks are checks written by a large financial institution with no payee specified. As with cashier's checks or money orders, people pay for them in advance. So, when a person presents a $50 traveler's check as payment, the recipient can be confident that the check can be cashed. In fact, traveler's checks are accepted around the world. Plus, travelers who lose traveler's checks can usually replace them. For this reason, when on a trip, many people carry them instead of cash.

Arrangements for Credit Payment

By now, you know that paying off borrowed money in a timely way is vital to your financial life. Bank drafts can help you perform this duty faithfully.

Bank drafts occur when you authorize someone to take money out of your bank account automatically to satisfy some financial obligation. People commonly use bank drafts to make car payments and house payments, and to pay utility bills. People also use bank drafts to make contributions to retirement accounts or other investments.

Bank drafts are an example of an electronic funds transfer. Whenever you authorize someone to access your bank account for payment or for deposit, you are making an **electronic funds transfer**.

A bank draft authorization will set a specific date on which the money is taken from your account. For example, you may set up a bank draft for your car payment that allows the finance company to withdraw $205.18 on the 21st of every month. The benefit of a bank draft is that you do not have to write a check to make the payment, and the car loan payment will be made every month on the exact date. This convenience saves time and, if you have an interest earning account, it allows you to earn interest on your money up until the due date. It also ensures you do not miss payments and suffer penalties. Bank drafts are also a good way to force you to make monthly contributions to your savings or retirement accounts.

You must be sure, of course, to account for bank drafts in your check register. Failing to do so can lead to confusion about your balance—and to bounced checks.

Other Online Services

Most banks now offer a variety of online services. You can opt to have payments drafted directly out of your account or utilize online bill payment services, transfer funds between checking and savings accounts, make loan applications, and check your bank statements. There is no doubt that in the future these online services will become more and more commonplace and more banking will be done electronically.

Services include safety deposit boxes, cashier's checks, money orders, and traveler's checks.

 CHECKPOINT

Besides checking accounts, what services are typically offered by banks?

DEPOSIT INSURANCE

One of the purposes of putting money in the bank is to keep it safe. You want to know that nobody can steal your cash. You also want to know that if the institution were to make a lot of bad loans and go bankrupt, your money would be protected. In order to offer this assurance to their customers, most financial institutions have deposit insurance on the first $250,000 you have on deposit. The major federal insurers are the **Federal Deposit Insurance Corporation (FDIC)** and the **National Credit Union Share Insurance Fund (NCUSIF)**.

Federal Deposit Insurance Corporation: Also known as the FDIC. The FDIC is a U.S. government agency that provides insurance on bank deposits.

FDIC

The federal government created the FDIC in 1933 after a rash of bank failures during the Great Depression. In many cases, depositors went to the bank to withdraw their money, only to find that the bank had gone out of business. Their savings were gone.

The bank failures shattered people's confidence in the banks generally. People began taking money out of even healthy institutions. This reaction hurt the banks and reduced the amount of money available for borrowing.

The government needed a way to restore faith in the banking system. After all, saving money is critical to economic growth. If there is no money deposited in the banks, businesses can't borrow. If they can't borrow, they won't build new factories, open new shops, and hire new workers. The entire economy will suffer.

The FDIC was meant to restore and maintain depositors' confidence in the banks by insuring people's deposits against loss. Currently, the FDIC provides deposit insurance on the first $250,000 of deposits at insured institutions. FDIC insurance covers checking accounts, savings accounts, NOW accounts, and certificates of deposit. In addition, the FDIC will insure up to $250,000 per depositor for self-directed retirement accounts. Again, each financial institution can insure up to $250,000 for an individual. So, if you had $1,000,000 in savings and wanted to make sure you were protected, you would need to place $250,000 with four different financial institutions that are not branches of the same bank.

National Credit Union Share Insurance Fund (NCUSIF): Also known as the NCUSIF. The NCUSIF is a U.S. government-backed agency that provides insurance on credit union deposits.

Many banks will display this emblem to assure customers that their money is safe. For more information on the FDIC, go to **www.fdic.gov**.

FDIC
FEDERAL DEPOSIT
INSURANCE CORPORATION

Prof. FIN

NCUSIF

The NCUSIF performs the same function for credit unions that the FDIC performs for other types of financial institutions. A **credit union** functions similarly to a bank. But, unlike a bank, a credit union has nonprofit status and is owned by its members. The National Credit Union Association (NCUA) charters and supervises credit unions and provides deposit insurance with the same limits as FDIC-insured deposits. This program is also backed by the federal government to ensure that depositors have faith in the financial system.

credit union: Functions similarly to a bank but has nonprofit status and is owned by its members.

 CHECKPOINT

Why is it important to give people confidence in the safety of their deposits?

If people lose confidence in the safety of their deposits, they may withdraw money in a panic, and that can damage even healthy banks.

THE FEDERAL RESERVE AND THE BANKING SYSTEM

The bank where you have your accounts is more than just your bank. It is part of a larger system that plays a central role in the nation's economy. At the heart of that banking system is the Federal Reserve System. The Fed, as it is known, helps regulate our banking system and, in fact, our whole economy.

Federal Reserve System: Serves as the central bank of the United States.

The Fed is the nation's bank, and it provides a variety of services that help regulate our nation's economy.

monetary policy: Primary tool to fight inflation and promote a healthy economy; involves raising or lowering of the money supply to achieve some goal.

fiat money: Money currently used in the United States; has value not because the coins and bills have some value in their own right, but because the government orders that it be accepted as payment.

Multiple Roles

The Federal Reserve Act of 1913 created the **Federal Reserve System**, which serves as the central bank of the United States. The Fed has several roles in our economy. The Fed regulates banks, making sure that they follow rules and practices designed to ensure a sound banking system. For example, the Fed ensures that banks always have cash on hand to meet the demand. Therefore, banks never have to turn away customers wishing to withdraw their money. The Fed also serves as the branch of government that clears checks.

In addition, the Fed is a major instrument for carrying out the nation's economic policies. The Fed's major economic goals are to create ongoing economic growth, encourage full employment, and promote price stability. The Fed uses monetary policy in order to achieve these goals.

Price Stability

A main goal of Fed policy is **price level stability**. In other words, the Fed focuses a lot on making sure that we don't have inflation (or deflation). **Inflation** is defined as a sustained increase in the general level of prices. When we have inflation, prices of goods and services are generally going up. Inflation is considered problematic to the government and the Fed because it harms businesses and individuals in our economy.

Inflation can especially hurt individuals on fixed incomes, such as retirees. Think about this: What if your income remained the same but prices went up by 5%? You would not be able to buy as many products after that 5% inflation. Your standard of living would decline. What if you had money in the bank earning 3%? Your money at the end of the year would now buy fewer goods and services than it would have at the beginning of the year.

Monetary Policy

The Fed uses monetary policy as its primary tool to fight inflation and promote a healthy economy. **Monetary policy** involves the raising or lowering of the money supply to achieve some goal.

Think about money for a minute. We use money to make purchases and make our payments. We use money as a way to store wealth. The money we currently use in the United States is known as fiat money. **Fiat money** has value not because the coins and bills have some value in their own right, but because the government orders that it be accepted as payment. With fiat money, a $5.00 bill is worth $5.00 because the government says it is.

Thanks to government fiat, or decree, little slips of paper and small coins have great value. For this reason, the government must carefully control how much of that paper and coin is circulating in the economy. The U.S. Treasury is in charge of printing money and minting coins, but it does so at the Fed's direction. The Fed is the agency in charge of determining how much money is in circulation.

While the physical money in circulation is the most visible part of the money supply, there is a lot of electronic money that we never see. For example, you or your parents may have their paychecks deposited electronically into their checking account. Then, they may pay bills electronically out of that account. Although they never see the money they've deposited and spent, it is still in circulation.

Recall that monetary policy involves changing the money supply. As the economy grows and more people need money to make purchases, the Fed expands the money supply. It takes steps to place more money in circulation. This includes more electronic money, paper money, and coins (see Figure 12.3).

The Fed also uses monetary policy to change interest rates and impact buying behavior. How does the Fed do this? When you borrow money, the lender charges you interest. In effect, you can think of the interest you pay as the price of money. You also know that interest rates—the price of money—go up and down. Why is that? The Fed is largely responsible. If the Fed wants to increase transactions and encourage people to spend more money, it increases the money supply. When more money is available, it drives interest rates down and encourages spending. And, when the Fed reduces the money supply, interest rates go up.

How does the money supply affect interest rates? Think about an online auction. If there are one hundred buyers for one item, the buyers will compete and the price will go up. The same thing happens in our economy. If the Fed shrinks the money supply, lots of people will compete for an item—money—that's in limited supply. The price of that money—interest rates—will go up. So, when the Fed is concerned about inflation, it will shrink the money supply. This, in turn, will drive up the price of money (that is, raise interest rates) and discourage spending. This action should slow inflation.

Understand, the procedure of increasing or decreasing the money supply is actually much more complex than simply minting or printing more money. If you want to learn more about this, check out the Federal Reserve Web site at **www.federalreserve.gov**.

FIGURE 12.3 Effects of Increased Money Supply

An increase in the money supply by the Fed has a greater impact on the economy than just the amount of the increase.

In most cases, the Fed uses the money supply to impact interest rates. However, sometimes the Fed will change the interest rate it charges to banks when it loans them money. This interest rate is known as the **discount rate**, and banks use the option of borrowing money from the Fed only on occasion. These actions—changing the money supply or changing the discount rate—are designed to slow the economy or stimulate the economy depending on what the Fed determines is needed at the time.

You can see that the Fed has to maintain a balance. It wants enough money in the economy to encourage economic growth, but not too much because that can spur inflation. And, it must understand that the actions it takes will take a while to produce the desired effect.

Pay attention to the news. You will see that the Fed is in the news a lot. Keep the Fed's overall goals in mind: stable prices, economic growth, and full employment. What is the Fed trying to do right now?

 ## ✓ CHECKPOINT

The Fed changes the money supply.

What is the main tool the Fed uses to influence the economy?

CHAPTER REVIEW

SUMMARY

- Banks and other financial institutions offer individual services such as making personal loans, accepting deposits, and providing accounts that allow you to draft payments. There are two types of institutions: depository institutions (commercial banks, savings institutions, and credit unions) and nondepository institutions (insurance companies, securities firms, and investment companies).

- One of the most widely used banking services is the checking account. Most of us open checking accounts because it allows us to have an accurate record of our payments and also to carry less cash. Many banks provide debit cards to their checking account holders. A debit card enables you to withdraw cash from your checking account at an ATM or pay directly for goods or services at stores or restaurants.

- Other services provided by banking institutions are safety deposit boxes, cashier's checks, money orders, and traveler's checks. Banks also offer services for credit payment.

- Most financial institutions have deposit insurance to protect your money up to some maximum amount. The Federal Deposit Insurance Corporation (FDIC) and the National Credit Union Share Insurance Fund (NCUSIF) are two major insurers for most financial institutions.

- The Federal Reserve, also known as the Fed, is the heart of the banking system and helps regulate banking, as well as the whole U.S. economy. The Fed regulates banks, making sure they follow rules and practices designed to ensure a sound banking system. The Fed's major economic goals are to create ongoing economic growth, encourage full employment, and promote price stability. The Fed uses monetary policy to help accomplish these goals.

Key Terms and Concepts

1. Describe **inflation**.

2. How does a **credit union** differ from a bank?

3. What is the difference between a **bank draft** and an **electronic funds transfer**?

Answers:
Key Terms and Concepts

1. Inflation is a sustained increase in the overall level of prices. Inflation erodes the purchasing power of your money and makes it cost more to buy the things you normally buy.

 2. A credit union functions similarly to a bank. But, unlike a bank, a credit union has nonprofit status and is owned by its members.

3. Bank drafts are an authorization to take money out of your bank account automatically to satisfy some financial obligation. Bank drafts are an example of an electronic funds transfer. An EFT occurs when you authorize someone to access your bank account for payment or for deposit.

Answers:
What Do You Know?

1. (a) **Comprehension** Depository institutions take in people's money into savings or checking accounts and make loans. Nondepository institutions do not accept deposits. (b) **Application** Banks and credit unions are examples of depository institutions; investment and insurance companies are examples of nondepository institutions.

2. (a) **Knowledge** Depository institutions typically offer checking and savings accounts, ATM cards, and safety deposit boxes. (b) **Analysis** The economy would suffer because there would be fewer sources of loans for businesses.

3. (a) **Comprehension** People deposit money in the account, then they write checks to draw on that money as needed. (b) **Analysis** Checking accounts allow people to carry less cash and keep records.

4. (a) **Comprehension** To balance a checking account, take the bank statement balance and add any deposits that don't appear on the statement and subtract any checks or other charges against the account. Then, take the check register balance and subtract any bank charges and add any interest earned. After these steps, the numbers should match. If not, you need to search for the source of the error. (b) **Application** If you don't notice the problem, you might lose track of the actual balance in your account and then you might bounce a check.

5. (a) **Comprehension** With a debit card, there is no credit offered, and the amounts of purchases are removed immediately from the account. (b) **Application** If you don't record your debit purchases, you could lose track of how much money you have in your account and perhaps bounce checks.

6. (a) **Comprehension** All of them are readily accepted as payment because they do not draw on an individual's account and so are certain to be easily redeemed for cash. (b) **Application** You might want to use one for a large-purchase in which the seller is not willing to accept a personal check.

7. (a) **Comprehension** The FDIC guarantees the deposits in many financial institutions up to $250,000 so that even if the bank goes out of business, the depositors' money will still be there. (b) **Comprehension** The FDIC and the NCUSIF perform the same function, but the NCUSIF covers deposits in credit unions. (c) **Analysis** A lack of confidence in the banking system could produce a panic that could destroy even healthy institutions.

What Do You Know?

MyFinLitLab

1. (a) How do depository institutions differ from nondepository institutions?

   (b) Give an example of each.

2. (a) What are some of the benefits offered by depository institutions?

   (b) How might the economy suffer if there were no banks?

3. (a) Explain how a checking account works.

   (b) What makes a checking account useful compared to an ordinary savings account?

4. (a) Describe the steps to follow when balancing your checking account.

   (b) What might happen if you do not identify a difference between your balance and the bank's balance?

5. (a) Explain how a debit card differs from a credit card.

   (b) How might use of a debit card create problems in your checking account?

6. (a) What do cashier's checks, money orders, and traveler's checks have in common?

   (b) What is a circumstance in which you might want to use one of these as opposed to a personal check?

7. (a) Explain the function(s) of the Federal Deposit Insurance Corporation (FDIC).

   (b) How does the FDIC differ from the National Credit Union Share Insurance Fund (NCUSIF)?

   (c) What might happen if people did not have confidence in the banking system?

8. (a) What role does the Fed play in banking?

   (b) Why do you think it is important for banks across the country to follow similar rules?

9. (a) What does it mean to say our money is fiat money?

   (b) How does the existence of fiat money enable the Fed to exercise control over the money supply?

What Are Your Finance Math Skills?   MyFinLitLab

The first three questions correlate to *Math for Personal Finance* features located throughout the chapter.

1. Marvin deposited $400 in his checking account but also wrote checks for $224.21 and $311.34. Assuming his original balance was $622.43, how much does he have in his account now?

2. Rashaun has $235 in his checking account but has written two checks that have not cleared for $23 and $67.50 respectively. Does he have enough money in his account to make his car payment of $202?

3. Brandy made a withdrawal of $50 cash from an ATM that was not in her network. Assuming the bank charges $2 for out-of-network withdrawals, how much will her account be charged in total?

4. Jerry has $321,000 in a bank account at his local bank. How much does he stand to lose if the bank goes out of business?

5. Ben wrote a check for $52 that was more than his account balance. The bank charges $25 for bounced checks and the local business that accepted his check charges $20 for bounced checks. How much in total would Ben have to pay for that one check?

6. Gurinda's previous checking account balance was $532.14. Since then she has written a check for $46.19 and one for $138.32. She also made a $200 deposit into her account. Assuming her monthly service charge is $6, how much is her new balance?

7. Emily logged into her checking account from her computer. She had written three checks for $34.15, $45.98, and $121.15 respectively. Only the last check was posted to her account. How much are her outstanding checks?

8. Caleb withdrew $100 from his checking account. However, he used an ATM that was not in his bank's network. Assuming his bank charges $2 for that service and the bank he used charges $3, how much will his checking account be debited?

8. (a) **Comprehension** The Fed acts as the central bank that helps regulate the operations of banks and perform tasks such as clearing checks. (b) **Analysis** It helps people have confidence in the system if all the banks operate in the same way and according to the same rules.

9. (a) **Comprehension** This means that the value of the money is determined by government fiat rather than by the inherent value of the coins and bills. (b) **Synthesize** Because the money's value is based on fiat rather than on the value of the materials from which the money is made, it is easy for the government to change the money supply.

Answers:
What Are Your Personal Finance Math Skills?

1. $622.43 + $400 − $224.21 − $311.34 = $486.88

2. $235 − $23 − $67.50 = $144.50, so he does not have enough money available to make his car payment.

3. $50 + 2 = $52

4. The first $250,000 is FDIC insured, so Jerry could lose the difference or $321,000 minus $250,000 = $71,000.

5. $52 + $25 + $20 = $97

6. $532.14 − $46.19 − $138.32 + $200 − $6 = $541.63

7. $34.15 + $45.98 = $80.13

8. $100 + $2 + $3 = $105

What Would You Do?

Susan, a recent college graduate, opened a checking account with a local bank. She asked numerous questions before deciding on this bank, including inquiring about checking account fees and annual credit card fees. When Susan returned from her first vacation in the Bahamas, she was surprised to see numerous fees on her credit card statement and her bank statement. When she called the bank, they informed her that they recently added service charges on international transactions involving their checking and credit card accounts. Susan began to protest; the bank stated that her last bank statement included a flyer detailing these changes. In looking back, Susan realized that she had, in fact, received the information, but had ignored it because it was included with considerable advertising information about purchasing CDs. The lengthy document was written in such small print that she had not bothered to read it.

a. What do you think of banks and other financial institutions' efforts to notify their customers of fee changes? Should the bank have sent a letter to customers that specifically addressed the changes to international transactions? Do you think this would have ensured that their customers would read this information and feel informed about the changes?

b. What lesson do you think Susan has learned?

c. Would you change banking institutions if this had happened to you? Why or why not?

Answer:
What Are the Connections?

The balances do not reconcile. There is a difference between the bank's and Charlene's record of the amount for check #103.

What Are the Connections? Math

Assume Charlene's checking balance and the bank's balance were reconciled last month. Using a separate sheet of paper, reconcile the following bank statement against Charlene's statement. Is there an error somewhere in Charlene's records?

Bank Statement		Charlene's Check Register	
Balance	**$1,504.00**	Charlene's Balance	$1,440.50
Interest earned	$ .07	Check #100	$60.00
Fees	$6.00	Check #101	$75.50
Check #100	$60	Check #102	$47.50
Check #101	$75.50	Check #103	$100.10
Check #103	$101.10	Check #104	$55.00
Check #104	$55.00	Check #105	$9.75
Check #105	$9.75	Check #106	$15.00

Teamwork

Work in teams to complete this activity. As a group, do the following:

1. List five important banking services to consider when deciding on a financial institution.
2. Rank them in order of importance to you.
3. Design a spreadsheet that includes the following:
   (a) Column A: Banking services in order of rankings
   (b) Columns B–D: Three financial institutions in your area
   (c) Final row: Total score

4. Use the newspaper, Internet, phone book, or other resources to find information about each of the financial institutions your group listed. Gather data about each of your banking services listed. Grade each banking service on a scale of 1–4 (1 being the least desirable and 4 being the most desirable).

5. After gathering the information, total each banking institution's column.

6. Present your information to the class in a poster, slide presentation, written report, or other format.

ESSENTIAL QUESTION ACTIVITIES

Complete these activities to answer this chapter's Essential Question: *Why is balancing your checking account an important part of your financial plan?*

1. *On your own:* Each month you will receive a bank statement for your checking account.

   (a) Describe the process for reconciling your checking account.

   (b) Why is it important to go through this process each month?

   (c) How will balancing your checking account each month affect your financial plan?

2. *As a class:* Answer the following questions:

   (a) Describe the process for reconciling your checking account.

   (b) Why is it important to go through this process each month?

   (c) How will balancing your checking account each month affect your financial plan?

TEST PREP QUESTIONS

MyFinLitLab

1. Banks do *not*
   a. take in and secure people's money.
   b. make loans to individuals and businesses.
   c. pay interest on the money on deposit with the bank.
   d. sell corporate stock to the public.

   1. d

2. Which of the following statements about banks is true?
   a. All banks in a community charge the same fees for services.
   b. When one bank raises the interest rate it gives on deposits, all other banks will match that rate of interest.
   c. ATM fees are not charged when a person uses a bank near his home.
   d. All banks must follow state and federal government regulations.

   2. d

3. b **3.** An account into which a person deposits money and then can withdraw funds by making a written order to the bank instructing it to pay money from the account to another person or a business is known as a
   a. savings account.
   b. checking account.
   c. cashier's account.
   d. credit account.

4. d **4.** Why do banks require a person to have a PIN in order to use an ATM?
   a. They want to know that a person does not have accounts at a competing bank.
   b. They want to be sure that a person has enough money in the account before writing a check.
   c. They require the information to update the customer's account.
   d. They require the number to be used along with a debit card or ATM card to help protect the person from theft.

5. a **5.** Why do many people prefer to use a debit card instead of a credit card?
   a. They can purchase items and have the money withdrawn directly from their account without having to pay interest on a credit card balance.
   b. They can earn interest on accounts equal to 5% of purchases made with the debit card.
   c. They do not have to worry about overdrawing on their checking accounts.
   d. There are no fees charged when a debit card is used to withdraw money from an out-of-network ATM.

6. b **6.** Having overdraft protection on a checking account is a good idea but it can also be an expensive feature. Why?
   a. Banks charge a monthly fee for having overdraft protection on their checking accounts.
   b. A fee, which can be as high as $25–$30, is charged when overdraft protection on the checking account is used.
   c. The bank charges 20% of the amount taken from the overdraft protection.
   d. The bank stops paying the person interest on savings accounts or CDs each time overdraft protection is used.

7. c **7.** What is the purpose of a check register?
   a. It automatically balances a person's checking account.
   b. A person who balances his own checking account does not have to pay a bank fee for the service.
   c. A person can keep track of all deposits to and withdrawals from the checking account.
   d. It protects a person from identity theft.

8. d **8.** What does it mean when a person says that she is "reconciling" her checking account?
   a. She is making sure that her checking account is not overdrawn.
   b. She is making sure that all deposits have been made to her savings account from her company's direct deposit program.

c. She is comparing her checking account balance with her savings account balance.

d. She is comparing recorded transactions in her checkbook register to the transactions that appear on the bank's monthly statement.

9. A person reconciling his checking account register with the bank's checking account statement sees that his record shows that he has $15.30 more than the bank says he has in the account. What should he do?

a. He should make out a check to his bank for $15.30.

b. He should use the balance shown on the bank's statement since it is a computer-tracked total.

c. He should contact the bank if after checking the math and recording outstanding checks, interest, and fees, he still has a different balance.

d. He should deposit $15.30 into his savings account until he is able to reconcile his account record with the bank.

9. c

10. Why do people sometimes have to use a cashier's check instead of a personal check?

a. The person is buying a large item such as a car and the dealership will only accept a check that is charged against the bank's account.

b. The person has a poor credit record and hopes to improve his credit score by using cashier's checks that are guaranteed by the bank.

c. The person does not have enough money in her checking account so she borrows money from the bank in the form of a cashier's check.

d. The person wants a safe way to transfer money from her CD that has just matured to her checking account at the bank.

10. a

11. Which of the following bank services is correctly matched with its function?

a. Money order: a check from a personal checking account that is cosigned by the bank.

b. Cashier's check: a check that the bank draws on its account with the Federal Reserve System.

c. Traveler's check: a check that a person is only able to buy in another country.

d. Bank draft: authorized withdrawal from a person's bank account to make payments such as a mortgage or car loan automatically.

11. d

12. Which of the following is *not* an advantage of having bills paid by an electronic funds transfer (EFT)?

a. The person who has an interest-earning account earns interest until the date that the money is transferred out of the account.

b. EFTs typically cost more than $1 per transaction.

c. The person who has an EFT does not have to worry about bills being paid on time.

d. An EFT saves a person from paying for stamps to mail checks to pay bills.

12. b

13. c **13.** Why did the government establish the Federal Deposit Insurance Corporation (FDIC)?
a. The government wanted to be sure that banks did not fail.
b. The government wanted to be sure that people who took bank loans would be charged a fair rate of interest.
c. The government wanted to protect people from losing their money if the banks failed.
d. The government wanted to protect the banks from being taken over by other businesses.

14. c **14.** A person has $50,000 in certificates of deposit (CDs), $25,000 in a savings account, $35,000 in a NOW account, and $12,000 in a checking account all in the same bank. If the bank fails, the amount of his money that will be protected is
a. only the $25,000 in the savings account.
b. $100,000.
c. $122,000.
d. only the $50,000 in the certificates of deposit.

15. a **15.** What is a credit union?
a. It is a nonprofit business that functions like a bank and is owned by its members.
b. It is a business that brings together a number of other businesses that offer credit to the public.
c. It is a bank that only makes loans to members of labor unions.
d. It is a business that is run by the federal government and whose job it is to make credit available to low-income people.

16. c **16.** The Federal Reserve System *cannot*
a. make sure that banks follow the rules designed to create a strong banking system.
b. adjust the amount of money in circulation in the economy.
c. prevent the economy from entering a recession.
d. require banks to keep a certain amount of money on hand to meet customers' daily need for cash.

17. d **17.** The Federal Reserve System tries to keep inflation under control by
a. lowering interest rates on the money it loans out to member banks.
b. providing more money to the federal government to spend on goods and services needed to fight a war.
c. increasing bonuses given to workers at the end of the year.
d. decreasing the supply of money that banks have available to make loans.

18. b **18.** The Federal Reserve System uses monetary policy to
a. create new businesses, close failing businesses, and loan money to consumers.
b. create ongoing economic growth, encourage full employment, and promote price stability.
c. keep the government from cutting federal jobs and increasing spending on the military.
d. keep banks from increasing interest on savings accounts and charging for checking account overdraft protection.

19. Which of the following is a true statement about the supply of money in the United States?
    a. The total money supply of the United States is coin and currency.
    b. The money supply of the United States is backed by gold.
    c. The U.S. Treasury prints more money when the Federal Reserve System directs it to take this action.
    d. The U.S. Treasury does not consider money that is transferred electronically to be part of the money supply of the United States.

20. If the Federal Reserve System is concerned about inflation increasing, what action can it take?
    a. It can increase the discount rate, which is the interest rate it charges member banks to borrow money.
    b. It can make more money available to member banks by directing the U.S. Treasury to print more money.
    c. It can lower interest rates charged for loans to consumers.
    d. It can borrow more money from the banks that are members of the Federal Reserve System.

21. Why is it said that an increase in the money supply by the Federal Reserve System has a greater impact on the economy than just the dollar amount of the increase?
    a. Inflation increases the amount of money that is in circulation.
    b. The money that banks receive is loaned out to consumers who then spend the money or deposit it in bank accounts and it is loaned out again.
    c. The money is kept in the banks so that the banks are considered to be stronger businesses and more people will deposit their own money in these banks.
    d. The increase in the supply of money will keep interest rates rising.

CHAPTER 13

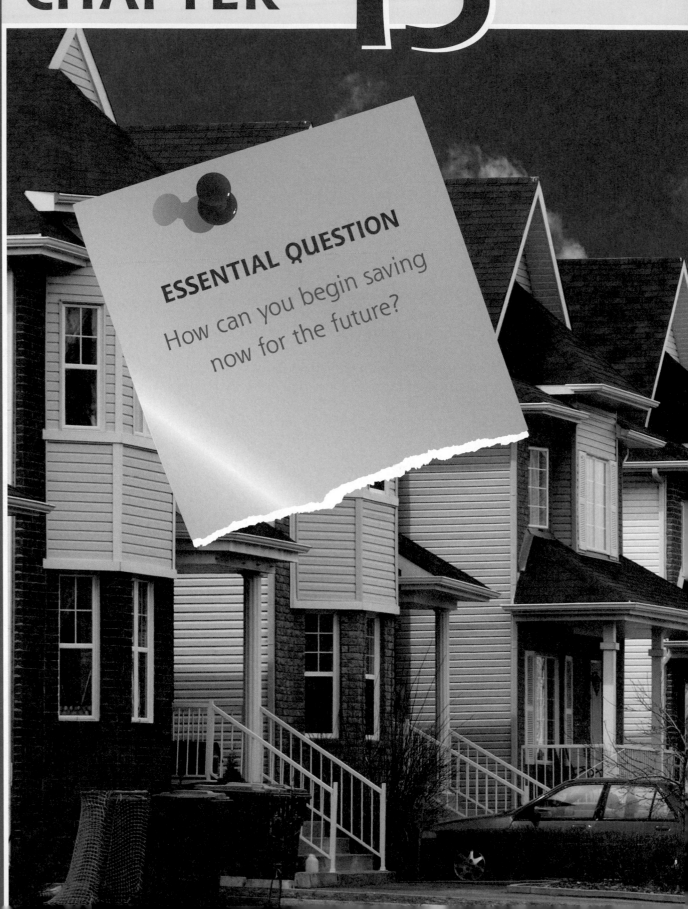

ESSENTIAL QUESTION

How can you begin saving now for the future?

METHODS OF SAVING

LEARNING OBJECTIVES

- Explore the ways in which savings can earn interest

- Examine the different types of bank accounts that can aid in saving

- Describe retirement savings options

KEY TERMS

401(k)/403(b) plans

annuity

certificate of deposit (CD)

demand deposit

Individual Retirement Account (IRA)

money market deposit account (MMDA)

pension plan

vesting

"LaTanya, I can't buy you everything you want." LaTanya's mother was irritated. "I'm not made of money."

"I know that, Mom, but I'll have to have a car someday." LaTanya stared at the car in the neighbor's driveway with a For Sale sign in the window. Their neighbor, Mr. Hawkins, was asking $2,200 for the car. "And that's a really good deal. You know Mr. Hawkins takes care of his cars."

"It doesn't matter, LaTanya. I don't have the money." Her mother sighed. "We have talked about this before. I told you a couple years ago: If you expected to have your own car, you would have to save for it yourself. I don't make enough to afford a second vehicle." With that, she walked away.

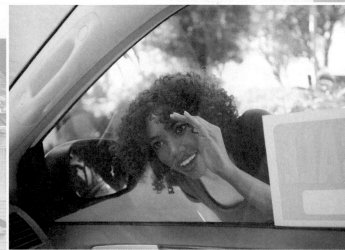

LaTanya hated to admit it, but she knew her mother was right. And, in fact, when she did all that babysitting for the Jacksons last year, she had been doing a good job of saving. She opened a bank account and deposited nearly $1,000. The babysitting had slowed down a lot since the Jacksons moved. But LaTanya began to wonder: How much interest has that account earned over the last few months? Excited, she decided to run down to the bank to find out. She knew she wouldn't have enough to buy the car. But maybe she was closer than she had thought!

While borrowing money can be a necessary and financially wise step, there is no escaping the need to save money. For much of the rest of your life, you will face the task of building up your wealth and managing your money. Placing money in various savings options will be key to your success. Here we will learn about some of the options for saving money.

INTEREST AND YOUR SAVINGS

LaTanya was wise to have opened a bank account for her savings. After all, banks are a great place to keep savings. They offer safety and security. In general, deposits up to $250,000 in bank accounts are guaranteed against loss. In addition, many types of bank accounts offer interest on deposits. So, while you are working to earn more money, your money is "working," too. It is making money and helping your savings grow. LaTanya is hopeful that this feature of her savings account has helped take her a few steps closer to buying the car she wants.

Interest Rates on Deposits

One of the ways that banks and similar financial institutions make money is by borrowing and lending money. They take in money from depositors. Then, they use that money to make loans, on which they charge interest. In other words, banks use depositors' money to make money. In fact, because depositors' money is so valuable to them, banks will often pay interest on deposits.

The amount of interest the financial institution is willing to pay depends on several factors. One factor is the length of time you are willing to commit to leaving the money on deposit. In general, the longer you are willing to leave the money, the higher the rate. In addition, deposits covered by FDIC or NCUSIF generally earn less than uninsured deposits. Other factors that determine interest rates paid on deposits include the policies of the financial institution and the market rates of interest—that is, the overall level of various interest rates charged by other banks and financial institutions doing business in the market.

MATH for Personal Finance

Candace put $1,000 in a savings account that pays 2.5% in annual interest.

How much interest will she earn during the year?

Solution: $1,000 × .025 = $25.

Market Rates of Interest

The Federal Reserve System has a significant impact on the market rates of interest. By manipulating the money supply—and therefore the price of money or interest rates—the Fed stimulates the economy or slows it down. The Fed also influences the interest rate market when it sets the discount rate, or the interest rate it charges banks for loans. The Fed does not control all interest rates, but interest rates tend to move up or down along with Fed-controlled rates.

Liquidity

Interest rates offered for deposits also differ depending on the level of liquidity the account offers. **Liquidity** refers to how quickly you can convert something to cash without significant loss of value. Accounts that offer a high degree of liquidity—that is, the ability to take money out on demand—usually offer the lowest interest rates. Why is this? Think about it from the bank's perspective. Offering people quick access to their money limits their ability to loan out that money and make money on it. Therefore, they offer these short-term depositors less. This fact will impact LaTanya, as you will see.

 CHECKPOINT

What is the relationship between liquidity and interest rates?

In general, the greater the degree of liquidity, the lower the interest rate offered.

TYPES OF BANK ACCOUNTS

Banks offer a wide range of different accounts and services. As options for saving money, each type has benefits and drawbacks. You should understand the basic features of the different types of accounts available.

Checking and NOW Accounts

Many people open basic checking accounts. These are the most liquid type of bank account, since you can access your money instantly by writing a check or using an ATM. The money put into a checking account is sometimes referred to as a **demand deposit** because it can be withdrawn at any time—on demand. The liquidity of a checking account helps explain why traditional checking accounts do not pay interest. Because they do not pay interest, they are not a very good way to save money.

There is a type of withdrawal account that functions much like a checking account and that does pay interest. This type of interest-paying demand deposit account is often referred to as a negotiable order of withdrawal (NOW) account. NOW accounts function in the same manner as checking accounts in that you can write drafts (checks) on these accounts. But most NOW accounts require you to maintain a minimum monthly balance, or they pay higher interest rates if you maintain a certain balance. This way, the bank is confident of having a certain amount of

demand deposit: Money put into a checking account that can be withdrawn at any time.

your money on hand to loan out and earn interest on. However, these accounts typically offer the lowest interest rates of any deposit account. And remember—there may be penalties if you fail to maintain a minimum balance. NOW accounts are insured.

Interest Bearing Savings Accounts

Savings accounts generally pay a little higher rate of interest on deposits than NOW accounts. These accounts are still very liquid in that you can withdraw money at any time. They do not, however, provide check-writing services. For this reason, people tend to have less transaction activity in their savings accounts and generally do not access them frequently. In LaTanya's case, this lower liquidity made it easier for her to save money. Of course, she also earned a relatively low interest rate. She will find when she checks her balance that the $1,000 she had deposited has not grown enough to make a $2,200 purchase possible.

Individuals often use a savings account to save money for specific purposes. For example, LaTanya may have had a car in mind when she opened such an account to save money from her babysitting jobs. Others use savings accounts for an emergency fund, holiday gift fund, or vacation.

Prof. FIN

Did you know that piggy banks can be traced back to the fourteenth or fifteenth centuries? Some experts think the idea came from "pygg jars," which referred to the type of clay used to make kitchen pots and jars. Money was saved in these "pygg jars," but by the eighteenth century the spelling had changed and they were known as "pig banks." It is thought that "piggy bank" caught on because pigs are so child-friendly in their shape and easy to create from clay.

A piggy bank in whatever shape is a great way to begin saving on a small scale. You may have heard stories of people who saved change until they were able to purchase something big, such as a car. One woman even saved enough change to buy a small house!

To see more about piggy banks, go to **www.piggybankpage.co.uk**.

Certificates of Deposit (CDs)

certificate of deposit (CD): A contract between an individual and the financial institution that specifies the length of time that the individual will leave a certain amount of money deposited in the account and the interest rate earned.

Certificates of deposit are a financial product offered by many financial institutions. A **certificate of deposit (CD)** is essentially a contract between an individual and the financial institution that specifies the length of time an individual will leave a certain amount of money deposited at the particular bank at a specified interest rate. CDs have a specific maturity date—that is, a future date when you can cash in the CD. For example, you might buy a $5,000 or $10,000 CD that has a one-year maturity. Common CD maturities are one month, three months, six months, one year, three years, and five years. Of course, savers can find CDs with virtually any maturity and dollar amount.

Typically, CDs offer a higher interest rate than savings accounts because the bank can count on the money being there for them to loan out. Remember, a bank makes money by loaning out money that it has on deposit. If the money is likely to be withdrawn at any time the bank cannot loan as much of it.

Again, the financial institution pays a higher interest rate for a CD because the money is locked up until maturity. You can access your money prior to maturity, but you will pay a penalty for early withdrawal. Therefore, you should consider CDs only when you know that you will not need the money until after the CD matures. Is a CD a viable option for LaTanya at this time?

Money Market Deposit Account (MMDA)

A **money market deposit account (MMDA)** has some of the features of checking accounts and some of the features of savings accounts. These accounts require you to maintain a minimum balance, have no maturity date, pay interest, and offer limited check-writing privileges. A typical MMDA might require you to keep a $2,500 minimum average monthly balance and allow you to write five checks a month. Most impose fees if your balance falls below the minimum or if you write more checks than allowed.

MMDAs differ from NOW accounts in that they provide only very limited check-writing privileges and pay a higher rate of interest. Many people use both a NOW account for their typical monthly expenditures and an MMDA to maintain a larger balance that is still liquid yet earns a slightly higher interest rate. As you can see in Figure 13.1, various money market investments have unique advantages and disadvantages.

Brooke bought a one-year $5,000 CD that pays 4% interest annually.

How much will she have at the end of the year (assuming all the interest earned is added at year's end)?

Solution: $5,000 × 1.04 = $5,200.

money market deposit accounts (MMDA): Accounts that require you to maintain a minimum balance, have no maturity date, pay interest, and offer limited check-writing privileges.

Did you ever wonder how much you would have to save to become a millionaire? Go to **www.aarp.org/money/investing/millionaire_calculator/** and use the millionaire calculator provided to determine your destiny! Put in a variety of numbers in the "Amount currently invested" and "Savings per month" boxes. How long will it take you to reach your goal?

Prof. FIN

FIGURE 13.1   Comparison of Money Market Investments

As you can see, different accounts offer different levels of liquidity, which in turn affects the account's ability to earn interest.

Money Market Investment	Advantages	Disadvantages
Checking account	Very liquid	No interest
NOW account	Very liquid	Low interest rate; minimum balance required
MMDA	Liquid	Low interest rate
Savings account	Liquid	Low interest rate
Certificate of deposit (CD)	Relatively high interest rate	Less liquid

YOU DO IT

Activity #1

By choosing options that limit liquidity—for example, NOW accounts versus checking accounts, or CDs versus savings accounts.

About Credit Unions

Credit unions differ from other depository financial institutions primarily due to their nonprofit status. A credit union does not exist to earn money for investors. Rather, it exists to serve its members—the people who deposit money in the institution. For this reason, credit unions can often pay higher interest rates on deposits than an ordinary bank can. Their expenses may be lower and any profits are redistributed to members. A credit union is a good place to check interest rates on deposits.

APY and Comparing Savings Options

Sometimes, you may find it necessary to compare savings options that have different compounding frequencies. The term compounding, or **compound interest**, refers to the way that interest added to an account earns interest. Compounding frequency, then, is how often the bank puts interest you have earned into your account—where it then can earn interest. More frequent compounding is better given the same interest rate. That's because when the interest is put in the account, it also begins to earn interest. The more frequently this happens, the more interest you earn.

When you shop for savings options, you may find the following situation: One bank advertises a 4% interest rate on a CD with annual compounding and another bank advertises a 3.95% interest rate and quarterly compounding. How do you compare those offers? Which would give you more money in the end?

Without doing some math, you can find your answer by checking the annual percentage yield. The **annual percentage yield**, or **APY**, is the interest rate that takes the compounding frequency into account. That is, it tells you what your account will really earn on an annual basis once compounding is taken into consideration. In the example above, the APY on the first offer is the same as the advertised rate—4%. The APY on the second offer is slightly higher—4.009%. That's because the interest placed in the account at the end of the first, second, and third quarters is also earning interest. Always use APY as a tool to evaluate savings options that have different compounding frequencies. Banks must make the APY available to you, although it may not be the rate advertised most prominently.

 CHECKPOINT

In general, how do people manage to achieve a higher rate of interest in their bank accounts?

RETIREMENT SAVINGS OPTIONS

Like LaTanya, you probably have some short- or intermediate-term savings goals. You might be saving for a car or simply putting money aside for a rainy day fund. For many of these goals, you would most likely use the savings options we've already discussed, such as CDs or savings accounts. But what about long-term goals? Do you know someone who has achieved

FIGURE 13.2 Relationship Between the Investment Period and Your Savings at Retirement

(Assuming a $5,000 Investment and a 10% Annual Return) Even a small investment can start to grow at a fast rate, given time.

a lifestyle you would like to have? How old are they? When did they begin thinking about financial security? Like LaTanya, your primary goal may be short-term in nature, but you don't want to neglect the future because time is your best friend when trying to accumulate wealth. If you begin early and use the large amount of time you have, even small but steady levels of saving can build to a large stockpile by retirement. Did you know that LaTanya could accumulate more than $1 million if she saved $100 a month for 40 years and averaged a 12% annual return? However, if she saves the same amount for 30 years she will have about $350,000. That extra 10 years makes a big difference, and it is because of compound interest. As your savings grow, the amount you have accumulated begins to earn far more than the amount you contribute each month. Your money begins working for you instead of you working for your money. For example, if you invest a lump sum of $5,000 today, you can accumulate a tremendous amount of wealth with time on your side. Check out Figure 13.2 to see how much difference a few years can make.

To get an even bigger shock, check out Figure 13.3. See how much you would have if you saved $5,000 every year.

Saving for retirement is a critical—but often neglected—part of a young person's financial plan. Fortunately, there are several investment and savings options designed to encourage and facilitate saving for retirement. We will briefly look at Individual Retirement Accounts (IRAs), various pension plan options, and annuities.

Finance **ONLINE**

To learn more about retirement and which plan might be best for you, you can visit **www .retirementplans.irs.gov/** and click "choose a plan." Pick one of the plans discussed on this site. What information can you share with the class about this plan? Why did you choose to review this plan?

Individual Retirement Accounts (IRAs)

Individual Retirement Accounts (IRAs) are a type of savings account created by the government to encourage people to save for retirement. To make saving in an IRA attractive, the government offers certain tax benefits that allow investors to reduce their income taxes. And, to ensure that people use IRAs only for retirement, the government put limits on when you can use IRA funds. You can withdraw IRA funds beginning at age 59½. If you withdraw

Individual Retirement Accounts (IRA): A type of savings account created by the government to encourage people to save for retirement.

Finance ONLINE

Do you want to see how your savings can grow with the power of compounding interest? There are many online calculators that can show you what can happen assuming various savings and interest rates. For example, visit **www.lfg .com**. Click "Planning Tools," then "Financial Calculators," and finally "Savings Calculators" under the heading "More Calculators." This will take you to different savings calculators. First look at the "College Tuition Planner" calculator, and then go back and use the "Cost of Waiting" calculator. Compare the results. What did you find out?

IRA funds prior to age 59½, you will pay a penalty equal to 10% of the money withdrawn, in addition to income taxes on the amount withdrawn.

All IRAs can include a range of different types of investments. For example, you can have CDs, mutual funds, or both in your IRA account.

There are two main types of IRAs: traditional IRAs and Roth IRAs. They differ in the type of tax benefit they provide.

The key features of a **traditional IRA** are that many people can make tax deductible contributions, and all earnings are tax deferred. What does this mean? **Tax deductible** means that if you are eligible and contribute, say, $3,000 in a given year, you can deduct $3,000 from your taxable income and pay no federal tax on that amount. This feature allows you to reduce your income taxes for the year you made the contribution. Some individuals may be able to receive a tax credit for contributions to an IRA. A tax credit is preferrable to a tax deduction since it reduces your tax liability by the same amount as the credit.

Traditional IRAs are also **tax deferred**, which means that the account's earnings, such as from interest, are not taxed until they are withdrawn after retirement. Tax deferral helps you in two ways: (1) a tax-deferred account will grow in value more quickly than one earning the same rate but in which earnings are taxed, and (2) when you do withdraw monies, it may be at a lower tax rate because you will be retired and most likely earning less money.

The tax-deferred benefit of traditional IRAs is available to everyone. However, certain higher-income individuals are not allowed to deduct contributions from their taxes, and there are limits on how much a person can contribute to a traditional IRA. In 2012, the contribution limits were $5,000 per person unless you are 50 or older. People over age 50 are allowed to contribute an additional $1,000 to their accounts.

The Roth IRA has the same contribution limits as the traditional IRA, but it has unique features. **Roth IRA** contributions are not tax deductible, but the earnings from an eligible account are never taxed, even after

FIGURE 13.3 Relationship Between the Number of Years You Invest Annual Savings and Your Savings at Retirement

(Assuming a $5,000 Investment and a 10% Annual Return) The effects of making regular investments are truly impressive.

withdrawal. Eligibility to contribute to a Roth IRA phases out at high levels of income. Roth IRAs also have their own rules for how the money is distributed at retirement. Eligibility to contribute to both types of IRAs phases out at high levels of income.

Which type of IRA is right for you? The answer depends on a number of factors. There are various online tools that can help you make the choice that best meets your needs. See Figure 13.4 for an example of one of these tools.

Self-employed people may be eligible for a Simplified Employee Pension IRA (**SEP-IRA**). These function much like traditional IRAs, but they have their own contribution limits.

Employer-Sponsored Retirement Plans

One of the benefits you might receive when you begin working full time is an employer-sponsored retirement plan. **Employer-sponsored retirement plans** are set up by the employer, and the employer will generally make some contributions to the plan on your behalf. These plans are designed to help you save for retirement and are often used as an incentive to attract high-quality employees. It's important to note that employers are not required to offer such plans.

Employer-sponsored plans come in two main forms: the defined-benefit plan and the defined-contribution plan. There are many variations within each category. But, in both cases, you do not pay taxes on contributions or earnings until you retire and begin making withdrawals.

Defined-benefit plans guarantee you a specific amount of income when you retire. The benefit is often based on factors such as the number of years worked and the average salary earned during your peak earning years. Such defined-benefit plans are popularly referred to as *pension plans*. Under them, the employer makes contributions to the plan on the employee's behalf. The money generally goes into a large fund and professional managers then invest and manage the fund. The employer establishes guidelines regarding the number of years a person must work before becoming eligible to withdraw money from the fund. Note that many of the restrictions and requirements of employer-sponsored retirement plans are governed by federal law.

When an eligible person retires, he or she receives the agreed-to benefit from the fund. If the retiree lives five years, he or she gets benefits for five years. If the retiree lives 25 years, he or she receives benefits for 25 years.

This process of earning eligibility for an employer benefit is known as *vesting*. For example, a worker might have to work for an employer for five years before being fully vested and eligible to withdraw full benefits.

Defined-benefit plans are less common now than in the past. This may be because people are living longer and so employers providing these plans are assuming more financial risk. In contrast, defined-contribution plans shift this risk to the retiree.

In **defined-contribution plans**, the employer contributes to the employee's retirement account but does not guarantee a specific retirement benefit. Such plans often offer the employee some control over where contributions are invested. Defined-contribution plans limit the employer's

FIGURE 13.4 Online IRA Calculator

The choice between Roth and traditional IRAs depends on a number of factors. Tools such as this can help you make the right decision.

Screenshot from www.financial.toolkit.com. Copyright © by Toolkit Media Group of Wolters Kluwer. Reprinted with permission.

Activity #2

MATH for Personal Finance

Barton's employer has a 401k plan where they match $.50 of every $1 he contributes up to $3,000.

How much will the total contributions into his 401k be this year if he contributes $3,000?

Solution: His employer will contribute an additional $3,000 × $.50 = $1,500, so his total contributions will be $3,000 + $1,500 = $4,500.

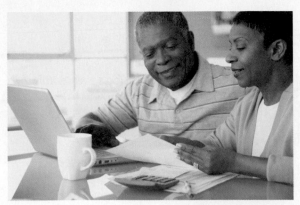

Today, more and more Americans' retirements are funded with the help of defined-contribution plans.

pension plans: A defined-benefit plan under which an employer makes contributions to the plan on the employee's behalf.

vesting: The process of earning eligibility for an employer benefit.

401(k)/403(b) plans: Allow employees to make contributions into a retirement account which may feature a range of investment options.

annuities: A type of financial product that guarantees annual payments to the owner for a fixed period of time or for a person's lifetime.

liability to the individual. The employer agrees to make regular contributions, but they are not bound to pay benefits for an unknown period of time. These plans shift more of the retirement risk to the employee, since the employee is primarily responsible for building and funding his or her own account. When an individual's funds are gone, the employer has no other obligation to that individual. The flexibility in investing and the shifting of risk to the employee has made these plans extremely popular in recent years.

401(k) and 403(b) plans are popular types of defined-contribution plans named after the sections of the IRS code that established these plans. For-profit companies can establish 401(k) plans for their employees. Nonprofit and charitable institutions can offer employees a similar type of plan, called a 403(b). **401(k)/403(b) plans** allow employees to make contributions into their own accounts, which may feature a range of investment options. The money employees contribute reduces their taxable income and therefore lowers the taxes withheld from their checks. So, for example, imagine you were contributing $500 per paycheck to a 401(k). This money would be taken from your pay before your tax was withheld. Your tax, therefore, would be lower. The taxes on this money are deferred. When you take money from your 401(k) in retirement, you pay income taxes on it then.

Many employers offer employer matching on plan contributions. So, for example, a company may offer a $.50 contribution for each $1 contributed by the employee. Most companies that elect to match employee contributions cap the amount that they are willing to match.

401(k) and other defined-contribution plans often offer you a choice about how much to contribute. Unfortunately, this decision often causes people to postpone saving for retirement. It can be hard for a young person who has many needs and wants and a relatively low salary to have the discipline to put away money for several decades down the road. But the decision not to contribute can be costly, particularly if the employer has a program where employee contributions are matched up to some level.

Annuities

Annuities are a type of financial product that guarantees annual payments to the owner for a fixed period of time or for a person's lifetime. They generally require a minimum investment—typically at least $5,000. The amount invested grows tax free and will not be taxed until disbursed to the investor/retiree.

Annuities come in two forms: fixed and variable. With a **fixed annuity**, the return and ultimate payment is a guaranteed amount. With a **variable annuity**, the return and ultimate payment depend on the performance of the investments. One word of caution: Most annuities have very high fees associated with the initial sale that goes to pay the people who sell them. Also, annuities have fees, known as surrender charges, for early withdrawal.

 CHECKPOINT

They offer retirement benefits as a way of attracting good employees.

What role do employers play in the retirement savings of many people?

CHAPTER REVIEW

SUMMARY

- Banks are a great place to keep savings. They offer safety and security and, in many cases, a chance to earn interest. Banks offer a wide range of different accounts and services. An understanding of the basic features of different types of accounts for saving money is an important part of your financial plan.

- Popular short-term saving accounts include checking accounts, NOW accounts, savings accounts, CDs, and MMDAs. Checking accounts and NOW accounts offer the most liquidity—but also the lowest rates.

- Retirement should be a key savings goal. Individual Retirement Accounts, which come in several forms, help promote retirement savings by offering some valuable tax advantages. Employers often offer retirement savings plans, normally classified as defined-benefit plans or defined-contribution plans. Today, many employers encourage employees to contribute to 401(k) or 403(b) plans. Self-employed people may be able to set up a Simplified Employee Pension IRA (SEP-IRA). Annuities are also commonly used for retirement savings.

Key Terms and Concepts

1. What is the **annual percentage yield (APY)**?

2. What is a **pension plan** and how does it differ from an **employer-sponsored retirement plan**?

3. How is **compound interest** calculated?

What Do You Know?   MyFinLitLab

1. (a) What is liquidity?

   (b) What is the relationship between the concept of liquidity and interest rates?

2. (a) What is a NOW account?

   (b) What feature of a NOW account makes it possible for a financial institution to offer interest on the account?

3. (a) Why is knowing the APY of a CD so important?

   (b) Why are rates on CDs higher than those on savings accounts?

   (c) What factor would most affect your choice of maturity date on a CD?

4. (a) **Comprehension** The key features are limited check-writing privileges and minimum balances that earn interest. (b) **Analysis** MMDAs differ from NOW accounts in that they provide only very limited check-writing privileges and pay a higher rate of interest.

5. (a) **Knowledge** An IRA is a type of retirement savings or investment account that has certain tax-advantaged features. (b) **Analysis** The government has given certain tax advantages to investors in IRAs.

6. (a) **Comprehension** *Tax deductible* means that the money invested can be deducted from income. *Tax deferred* means that taxes are not paid on earnings until some future date. (b) **Analysis** Tax deductibility allows you to reduce your income taxes for the year you make the contribution. *Tax deferred* means that the account's earnings, such as from interest, are not taxed until they are withdrawn after retirement. Tax deferral helps you in two ways: (1) a tax-deferred account will grow in value more quickly than one earning the same rate but in which earnings are taxed, and (2) when you do withdraw monies, it may be at a lower tax rate because you will be retired and most likely earning less.

7. (a) **Knowledge** Traditional and Roth IRAs are the two major types of IRAs. (b) **Application** The ability to take advantage of different features of the different types of IRA depends on one's income level.

8. (a) **Knowledge** Defined-benefit plans and defined-contribution plans are employer-sponsored retirement plans. (b) **Analysis** A defined-benefit plan is funded by the employer and sometimes with employee contributions and offers recipients a set benefit for however long the beneficiary lives. A defined-contribution plan may also be funded by the employer, often with contributions from the employee as well, but it does not guarantee a specific benefit.

9. (a) **Comprehension** 401(k) and 403(b) plans are established by employers for employees. They provide a way for pretax contributions and tax-deferred growth. (b) **Analysis** With an employee match of $.50, employees earn 50% on matched contributions—not counting the earnings or losses of invested funds.

10. (a) **Knowledge** An annuity is a type of investment that provides an annual benefit. (b) **Comprehension** A fixed annuity provides a guaranteed benefit amount. A variable annuity's benefit depends on variables such as the performance of the investment.

4. (a) What are the key features of a money market deposit account (MMDA)?

   (b) How does a money market deposit account differ from a NOW account?

5. (a) Define an Individual Retirement Account (IRA).

   (b) How has the government provided people with an incentive to use IRAs?

6. (a) What is the difference between tax deductible and tax deferred?

   (b) Compare the benefits of each.

7. (a) What are the two major types of IRAs?

   (b) How might the size of a person's income affect the decision to choose a Roth or a traditional IRA?

8. (a) What are two categories of employer-sponsored retirement plans?

   (b) Compare a defined-benefit plan to a defined-contribution plan offered by an employer.

9. (a) Discuss the general characteristics of 401(k)/403(b) plans.

   (b) If an employer is matching $.50 for each $1 you contribute, what kind of return are you earning on your initial investment to a 401(k)/403(b) plan?

10. (a) What is an annuity?

    (b) What is the difference between a fixed annuity and a variable annuity?

What Are Your Finance Math Skills?   MyFinLitLab

The first three questions correlate to *Math for Personal Finance* features located throughout the chapter.

1. How much interest will you earn on a two-year $6,000 CD that will pay annual interest of 5%? The first year's interest will remain in the CD and also earn interest during the second year.

2. If your employer matches your retirement contributions on a dollar-for-dollar basis up to $4,000, how much will be contributed to your account by the end of the first year if you take advantage of the entire match?

3. If you put $2,000 a year for three years into an IRA that earns 3% a year, how much will you have saved at the end of the third year?

4. Anita earned 2% on the $1,200 she had in savings and 3.5% on a one-year $4,000 CD. How much did she earn in interest during the year?

5. If you withdraw $10,000 from your IRA at age 35 to buy a car, how much penalty will you pay for this withdrawal?

6. How much money will Jerod earn in interest this year on a $3,000 CD that pays 5% in annual interest assuming annual compounding?

7. Assuming Brenda earns annual interest of 6% on her two-year $5,000 CD, how much will she earn in interest during the second year? Remember that her first year's interest will be added to the original principal and will earn interest during the second year.

8. If Nathaniel's employer matches 50% of the first $2,000 he contributes to his annual retirement account, how much will he have in his account assuming he takes full advantage of his employer's match?

Answers:
What Are Your Finance Math Skills?

1. $6,000 \times 1.05 = \$6,300$ at the end of the first year. $6,300 \times 1.05 = \$6,615$ at the end of the second year. Therefore, your total interest earned is $6,615 - \$6,000 = \$615$.

2. $4,000 + \$4,000 = \$8,000$

3. Assuming end-of-year contributions, you will have $2,000 earning 3% for two years, another $2,000 earning 3% for one year, and the last $2,000 goes into the account on the last day. So, $(\$2,000 \times (1.03)^2 + (\$2,000 \times 1.03) + \$2,000 = \$2,121.80 + \$2,060 + \$2,000 = \$6,181.80$.

4. $(\$1,200 \times .02) + (\$4,000 \times .035) = \$24 + \$140 = \$164$

5. The penalty is equal to 10% of the money withdrawn, so you will pay $10,000 \times .10 = \$1,000$.

6. $3,000 \times .05 = \$150$

7. $5,000 \times 1.06 = \$5,300$ at the end of the first year. She will earn $5,300 \times .06 = \$318$ in interest for the second year.

8. $2,000 + .50(\$2,000) = \$3,000$

What Would You Do?

Suzanne received holiday money from a relative. But, the relative told Suzanne that the gift came with a catch: She must save the money for college, which was three years away. After a discussion with her parents and the local banker, she decided to place the money in a money market deposit account.

Three years pass and Suzanne is making decisions about college, such as what she will need to bring, whether or not to buy a computer, how to buy books, and so forth. Fortunately for Suzanne, and as a result of her hard work, she received a number of scholarships that will go a long way toward meeting these expenses.

Then she remembers the money market account. This money was for college. She is about to go to college but would really like to have a car. She knows she doesn't need a car at college, but the idea of being on her own and having her own car is very exciting. Her parents argue that it would be more in keeping with the intention of the gift to use it to start an IRA. But they leave the decision up to her.

Suzanne has come to you for help making her decision. What would you tell her?

a. Is she bound to use the money for college needs only?

b. Is a car really a college need or just something she wants?

c. Has she earned the right to use the money as she wishes by working hard and earning scholarships to help pay for college?

What Are the Connections? Language Arts and Technology

Gather information from one banking or financial institution on the different savings options available. Collect information on rates for all kinds of savings products. Put this information in a poster for your fellow students that would help them quickly analyze the information and make a decision about the type of savings plan that is best for them.

Be sure to make a list of each type of account, how much it costs to open the account, the interest rate on the account (including the APY), and other pertinent information.

Teamwork

Bart is a college student who has never invested his funds. He has saved $1,000. Now he wants to invest this money, but he will need the $1,000 to help get an apartment when he graduates in a year.

In a group, help Bart make a decision of where to put his money so that he will get the most return on his investment.

1. Make a chart of various types of investments Bart can make with his $1,000.
2. Be sure to look at any fees or penalties he might incur when he takes the money out in a year. Will he make enough to leave some in the account or investment at the end of the year—that is, to not withdraw everything?
3. Write your group's decision on how Bart should invest his money. Use the information gathered in your chart. Be sure to give support for your group's decision.
4. Prepare a presentation for Bart about your group's decision.

ESSENTIAL QUESTION ACTIVITIES

Complete these activities to answer this chapter's Essential Question:
How can you begin saving now for the future?

1. *In small groups:* A variety of savings options have been presented in this chapter. Each group should take one of the options presented in this chapter and research more detailed information. Answer the following questions as you do your research:

   (a) What is unique about this savings option?
   (b) How do you sign up for this option?
   (c) Can you follow how the savings are growing or declining easily using the Internet?
   (d) What other information can you find about this option?
   (e) How will this savings option benefit your financial plan now and in the future?

2. *As a class:* Look at each of the savings options discussed in this chapter. Choose one option and discuss the following questions:
   (a) What is unique about this savings option?
   (b) How easy would it be to participate in this option?
   (c) How will this savings option affect your financial plan now and in the future?

TEST PREP QUESTIONS

MyFinLitLab

1. Banks use their depositors' money to make money. What is meant by this statement?
   a. The Federal Reserve System pays member banks based on the amount of money they have on deposit.
   b. Banks loan out money that they have received from depositors at a higher rate of interest than the interest they pay to their depositors.
   c. Depositors often forget how much money they have in their accounts and the banks can use that money to invest for the bank.
   d. Banks are able to print additional money based on the amount of money they have on deposit.

   1. b

2. Which of the following is an explanation for why accounts in banks pay different rates of interest at a given point in time?
   a. The Federal Reserve System is trying to stimulate the economy by lowering the discount rate.
   b. The bank gives people a higher rate of interest when the person is willing to leave money on deposit with the bank for a longer period of time.
   c. A person with a low credit score will *not* earn as high a rate of interest on a savings account as a person with a high credit score.
   d. The Federal Reserve System has directed the U.S. Treasury to make more money available.

   2. b

3. Which of the following is a true statement about liquidity?
   a. The more liquid an account, the higher the rate of interest offered by the bank.
   b. The only liquid account at a bank is a savings account.
   c. If an account has a high degree of liquidity, it means that the account owner can easily and quickly access the funds in the account.
   d. If someone needs to have money available for payment of monthly bills, the person should keep that money in an account that has low liquidity.

   3. c

4. Which of the following is *not* a true statement about checking accounts?
   a. A checking account is considered to be the most liquid type of bank account.
   b. Checking accounts are sometimes called "demand deposits" because the account owner can withdraw funds at any time from the account.

   4. d

c. Checking accounts usually do not pay interest because the banks cannot loan out money in the accounts for a long time.

d. Checking accounts are good for a young person to use when saving for a large purchase such as a car.

5. The sequence of accounts in order from the most liquid to the least liquid is

a. NOW account, CD, checking account, savings account.

b. checking account, three-month CD, savings account, NOW account.

c. checking account, NOW account, savings account, one-year CD.

d. six-month CD, checking account, savings account, NOW account.

6. A person receives gifts for her 18th birthday totaling $750. She also saved $1,500 from her summer job and keeps the money at home in a safe place. She wants to buy a car when she turns 21. She has a part-time job and plans to work full time next summer and save most of that money. She has a monthly cell phone bill and a credit card that she uses for emergencies and then pays the bill in full each month. Which of the following is the most financially wise recommendation for her when it comes to opening bank accounts at this time?

a. She should open a checking account with $1,000 and keep the rest of the money in cash at home for emergencies.

b. She should put $1,500 in a two-year CD, $600 in a checking or NOW account, and keep $150 in cash.

c. She should put $2,000 in a five-year CD and open a checking account with the $250 left.

d. She should put $750 into a savings account, $1,000 into a checking account, and keep $500 in cash at home for emergencies.

7. The difference between a money market account and other types of checking and savings accounts is that money market accounts

a. pay a higher rate of interest and require depositors to maintain a larger minimum balance than other types of checking accounts.

b. pay interest on deposits after six months and permit the account owner to write an unlimited number of checks.

c. charge a fee every time a check is written and offer higher rates of interest than CDs.

d. are the same as savings accounts with the additional feature of daily compounding.

8. How does the annual percentage yield (APY) help a person decide whether to put his money in bank A or bank B if both are offering 24-month CDs at 4.25% interest?

a. The APY will tell the person which bank has earned the highest profits in the past year.

b. The APY is able to determine whether the earnings on the CD will keep ahead of the rate of inflation.

c. If bank A has a higher credit rating than bank B, bank A will have a higher APY.

d. The APY will show the actual interest rate earned as opposed to the stated rate after the frequency of compounding is taken into effect.

9. It is said that "time is a person's best friend when it comes to planning for retirement." What does this statement mean?
   a. A person who is young has plenty of time before having to think about saving money for retirement.
   b. A young person can take advantage of the benefits of compounding by starting to invest a small amount of money regularly from an early age.
   c. By the time today's young people are ready to retire, the economy will have grown and Social Security will pay for their retirement needs.
   d. Young people tend to be healthier than old people and therefore have plenty of time before needing to spend money on health insurance.

10. Person A is age 40 and planning to retire in 25 years. Person B is age 25 and planning to retire in 40 years. Both invest $5,000 in an IRA with a guaranteed 10% annual rate of return on the investment and neither one adds to the account again. At retirement, person A has about $53,000 in his account and Person B has about $230,000 in her account. Why is there such a huge difference in the value of their IRAs?
   a. Person A's account lost money during a recession.
   b. Person B's account earned a higher rate of interest during periods of prosperity.
   c. Person A was penalized for not keeping money in the account for at least 30 years.
   d. Person B's account had longer to benefit from the compounding of interest.

11. Which of the following is a true statement about IRAs?
   a. If withdrawals are made from an IRA before the age of 59½, the person has to pay a 10% penalty plus taxes on the amount of money withdrawn.
   b. IRAs are designed to help rich people make more money and avoid paying taxes on that money while working or after retirement.
   c. An IRA account is made up of the stock from the bank where the person has the account.
   d. By encouraging people to save for retirement through IRAs, the government is saving millions of dollars in Social Security payments.

12. What is the major difference between a traditional IRA and a Roth IRA?
   a. Contributions to a Roth IRA are only tax deductible if a person earns under $50,000 a year; contributions to a traditional IRA are completely tax deductible.
   b. Earnings from a Roth IRA are never taxed whereas withdrawals from a traditional IRA are taxed.
   c. Roth IRAs do not start earning income until the person retires; traditional IRAs start earning tax-deferred income after a person reaches the age of 59½.
   d. Roth IRAs are made up of mutual funds; traditional IRAs are made up of CDs.

13. a **13.** Why are fewer employers offering defined-benefit retirement plans?
   a. As people are living longer in retirement, employers have greater financial risk as they must keep paying the retirees their pensions as long as they live.
   b. Most employees do not want to have their money kept in the same account for so many years and would rather invest their money on their own.
   c. Employers are no longer permitted to take their contribution to an employee's pension plan as a tax deduction.
   d. Employees can earn more money by investing the employer's contribution in a bank CD.

14. c **14.** How does a person who is planning to retire in 30 years benefit now from making contributions to her employer's retirement plan?
   a. Her contributions to the company's retirement plan now means that she will not have to contribute to Social Security in the future.
   b. Employers return employees' pension contributions in the form of annual bonuses.
   c. Her yearly contributions to the plan are tax deductible; therefore, they reduce the amount of income on which she has to pay taxes.
   d. The sooner she starts contributing to the plan, the sooner she can start withdrawing the money without having to pay a penalty.

15. b **15.** Why is an employer-sponsored retirement plan that includes an employer matching feature considered an important benefit offered to attract top employees?
   a. In this type of defined-contribution plan, employees are guaranteed to have enough money to live on when they retire.
   b. This benefit is like getting a raise or free money since the employer is giving the person extra money in the form of contributions to the person's retirement account.
   c. The employee benefits from the employer's financial expertise regarding the best investment products.
   d. The employer will continue to contribute to the employee's retirement plan after the employee retires to help employees keep up with cost-of-living increases.

16. a **16.** What does vesting mean?
   a. It is the amount of time that an employee has to work before he is fully eligible for an employer's benefit such as a retirement plan.
   b. It is the number of years that a person receives pension benefits after retirement.
   c. It is a guarantee of employment by the employer after a person works for the company for a certain number of years.
   d. It is the period of time that a person has to wait after retiring to collect both a pension and Social Security benefits.

17. A person earning $50,000 a year contributes 10% of her income to her retirement plan. As a result, her employer matches up to 5% of her salary as a contribution. What will be the total contribution to her retirement plan account for one year?

   a. It will be $5,000.
   b. It will be $5,250.
   c. It will be $7,500.
   d. It will be $10,500.

18. Which of the following terms is *not* correctly matched with its description?

18. d

   a. Employer-sponsored retirement plans: set up by a company to help the employees save for retirement; money is usually contributed by both the employee and the employer and the fund is managed by professional financial managers.
   b. Defined-benefit retirement plan: guarantees a person a certain amount of income when the person retires based upon the number of years worked, salary, and contributions to the plan; these plans are also known as pensions.
   c. 401(k) and 403(b) plans: defined-contribution retirement accounts that permit employees to contribute to plans that reduce their taxable income while they are working; employers often match at least part of employees' contributions.
   d. Annuities: a financial product that guarantees an employee the same income in retirement as she earned during the last three years that she worked at the company.

CHAPTER 14

ESSENTIAL QUESTION

Why would you invest and how does investing affect your financial plan?

900.00

899

899

898.00

897.50

897.00

896.00

895.00

METHODS OF INVESTING

LEARNING OBJECTIVES

- Understand the reasons for investing

- Describe the process of investing in stocks, bonds, and mutual funds

- Explore other options for investing

KEY TERMS

brokerage

commission

diversification

dividend

Securities and Exchange Commission (SEC)

shareholder

Treasury bonds

Kari stifled a sob. She had always been close to her grandfather, and the memories of the good times were still fresh even though he had passed away several years ago. It was still hard to think about his passing, but when she looked at her stock account she couldn't help it.

Gramps had given each one of his grandchildren an account that contained $10,000 worth of stock. He also gave specific instructions on what they were supposed to do with it. Kari was 18 now, and according to those instructions, she could begin to make some limited decisions with the consent of her father. Gramps had wanted his grandchildren to learn about investing, and Kari had vowed that she would.

The few years had been good to her account. Today, it was worth nearly $14,000. However, one stock had not performed well. Part of her thought she should just leave well enough alone. But she could still hear her grandfather telling her to "sell the dogs"—that is, get rid of the bad stocks. Kari was thinking about asking her father if they could sell the poorly performing stock and invest the money in another one. She had even done some research about the company she wanted to invest in. The stock price seemed low compared to the earnings, and a recent change in management offered promise for the future.

Her grandfather had insisted that Kari could not use the money until she turned 30, and she felt a responsibility to manage the fund carefully. She knew that making wise decisions would please her grandfather, and she could also see that it might pay off for her in a big way in the future.

An **investment** is something that you acquire with the goal of making money. Not everyone is as fortunate as Kari and will inherit money to invest. But if you carefully build a solid financial plan, you should find that after meeting all your obligations you may have some money available for investing. Then, you will need some knowledge about the many options available to you. Here, you will read about those options.

WHY INVEST?

As you build your financial plan, your first priority should be to save a cash reserve that is placed in liquid investments. These include the kinds of insured bank accounts such as checking accounts, certificates of deposit (CDs), and savings accounts. This is money you will use to deal with emergencies or unexpected expenses that pop up. Experts suggest building a cash reserve large enough to pay for three to six months' worth of your regular bills.

So, why not just choose these guaranteed and liquid options for all the money you set aside? Unfortunately, highly liquid, lower-risk investments generally offer very low interest rates. These kinds of accounts often barely keep pace with normal levels of inflation—or actually lag behind. Not keeping pace with inflation means that if you put $5,000 in one of these accounts and left it for several years, it would actually buy less than it did when you started. You should strive to make some investments that offer the hope of higher returns. There are certain types of investments that, historically, offer a reasonable chance of outpacing inflation *over time*. In this chapter, we will focus on such investments, including stocks, bonds, and mutual funds.

Of course, with the promise of higher returns comes higher risk. While these types of investments are more fun to watch and trade, they often do not produce steady, even results. Investments may go up and down in value unpredictably. The stock market, for example, has generally produced much higher long-term returns than more liquid investments. It also tends to have major up and down price swings. Trends in either direction may last for months, even years. Sharp increases or decreases are also possible.

Value built up over a period of months can be lost in a matter of hours. For this reason, you should consider riskier investments to be long-term investments. You should avoid—or get out of—such investments if you expect to need the money in the near future. You don't want to be in a situation where you need your money at a time when your investments are doing poorly. You want to be able to pick and choose when you sell them to your greatest advantage.

Think about Kari's case. She can't access her inheritance investments until age 30, so those funds could stay in longer-term investments. In the meantime, she needs to begin saving other monies that are more liquid.

It is also important to understand that a risk of many of these longer-term investments is the total loss of the investment. If, for instance, you buy stock or bonds in a company that goes bankrupt, you may lose all the money you invested. There is no insurance to protect you.

 CHECKPOINT

Why is it a good idea to invest money in something like stocks or bonds?

Such investments offer a reasonable potential to outpace the rate of inflation.

INVESTING IN STOCKS

Stocks are certificates that represent pieces of ownership in a company. For example, if a company has issued 100 shares of stock that represents the entire ownership of the firm, then each share of stock would be equivalent to 1% of the firm's value. In this example, each share of stock represents one share of ownership worth 1/100th of the firm's value. Most recognizable companies, such as Microsoft and Apple, have issued millions of shares, so each share represents a much smaller fraction of the firm's ownership. In general, stock ownership also carries voting rights, so each share of stock also has one vote attached to it that allows the owner to vote on the firm's board members, who in turn oversee the firm's management.

Did you know that stock certificates can be traced back to 1606? The Dutch East India Company was the first company known to issue shares of stock. See **www .stockmarketstory.com** to learn more.

Stock Exchanges

Companies issue and sell stock as a way to raise money for business operations, expansion, and other needs. However, not all companies offer shares of their stock for public sale. When a company chooses to "go public," the first sale of stock is called an **initial public offering (IPO)**. The IPO occurs in what is called the **primary market**. This initial sale is when the company receives money. That is, if the company has an IPO of a million shares that sell for $10 a share, the company receives $10,000,000 in cash—$10 × 1 million shares.

Finance ONLINE

You can learn about firms that are about to engage in an IPO and about the performance of recent IPOs by going to **www.ipohome.com**. Make a list of information that can be found on this site.

Traders on the floor of the New York Stock Exchange buy and sell stocks, creating profits—and sometimes losses—for stockholders.

Later, the shares may be bought and sold by many different investors, but those later transactions involving those same shares of stock do not provide the company with any more money.

The transactions that take place after the IPO are the ones we are more familiar with. They are the ones reported in the newspapers such as the *Wall Street Journal* or on the financial news on television. These occur in the so-called **secondary market**, which includes the organized stock exchanges such as the **New York Stock Exchange (NYSE)** or the **National Association of Securities Dealers Automatic Quotation (NASDAQ)** system. When a company begins trading on one of the organized stock exchanges, it is said to be "**publicly traded**." Many investors buy and sell stocks on these exchanges through stockbrokers such as Merrill Lynch or through Internet accounts such as E*TRADE.

You may recognize the New York Stock Exchange from the common scene on television, where someone rings the bell and everything looks like chaos, with people yelling and shouting. What's happening is actually an auction in which a lot of auctioneers are all yelling at the same time. In spite of the seeming chaos, it works remarkably well as a system for buying and selling stocks. When you place an order to buy stock in a company that is "listed"—bought and sold—on the New York Stock Exchange (NYSE), that order eventually flows through that chaotic market, and your order is carried out.

The NASDAQ is also a stock exchange, but it does not have a central location where dealers gather. Rather, it is an electronic network of dealers who buy and sell stocks.

Each day that trading occurs, the stock exchanges publish the prices at which stocks trade. Many major newspapers carry this information. It is also available online. In this way, investors can follow the value of their investments.

YOU DO IT

Activity #1

The Behavior of Investors

There are many types of investors who trade—that is, buy and sell—stocks. They include **institutional investors**, who trade large volumes of stocks on behalf of large institutions. An example of such an institution is a huge pension fund. Mutual funds, which we will discuss later in the chapter, are another good example of institutional investors. Individual investors, such as Kari and you, are also well represented in the stock market.

Prof. FIN

Stocks may be listed on one exchange and be bought and sold on several other exchanges. One type of exchange is relatively new in the United States. They are called ECNs (Electronic Communication Networks). ECNs focus on trading stocks—for example, allowing people to buy and sell after the larger main exchanges are closed—and also foreign currencies. To learn more about these ECNs, go to **www.sec.gov/answers/ecn.htm**.

Investors trade stocks to make a profit. While there are many ways to try to make money in the stock market, most investors attempt first and foremost to buy a stock at a low price with the expectation of selling it later at a higher price.

Share prices for a company tend to go up when the company succeeds at its business. For example, check out Figure 14.1 to see what factors drive stock prices up or down. So, investors are looking for good companies that seem ready to enjoy increased success in the marketplace. Skilled investors carefully research the companies and industries they want to invest in. They learn to evaluate a range of factors that can hint at future success—or failure. Kari has begun to gain these skills. With them, she has identified an investment she feels will perform better than a stock she currently owns.

Keep in mind that the stock market can go up or down. Perhaps you've heard the terms "bull market" for markets that are trending upward and "bear market" for markets that are trending down. *Bull* and *bear* are examples of some of the common jargon you hear investors use. For those of you who get more involved in the stock market, you will soon see it is akin to learning a new language.

Many companies also regularly distribute cash to **shareholders**, the people who own stock in the company. These distributions of cash are known as **dividends**. Companies pay dividends in cash, or sometimes in additional stock. Dividends are another way some stockholders make money in the stock market.

shareholders: People who own stock in a company.

dividends: Cash distributed to company shareholders.

FIGURE 14.1 Factors That May Increase or Decrease Stock Price

Nobody can tell for sure how a particular stock will perform, but these basic factors can help you make informed decisions about whether to buy or sell.

MATH for Personal Finance

Jennifer bought 900 shares of stock for $45 a share in a company's IPO.

What was her dollar return if she sold the stock two weeks later for $56 a share (excluding any commission costs)?

Solution: $900 \times \$45 = \$40,500$ that Jennifer paid for the stock. She sold the stock for $\$56 \times 900 = \$50,400$. Her return is the difference or $\$50,400 - \$40,500 = \$9,900$.

Not all companies give out dividends. For example, a company that is trying to grow rapidly may opt to use all profits to expand the business. By not paying dividends, the company may hope to be more successful in the future and reward investors then with a higher stock price. Whether a company pays dividends or seeks to maximize growth is one factor an investor should consider when purchasing a stock. Both types can be good investments, but only if they match the investor's goals for either short-term income or long-term growth.

The stock markets, unlike the banks, do not have insurance on your money. The FDIC insures your money up to $250,000 if you deposit it in a bank. The stock market has no such guarantee so it is much riskier. Check your own tolerance for the kind of risk investing in stocks involves (see Figure 14.2).

While your stock investment is not insured, there is a government agency that regulates and monitors the stock market. This agency is the **Securities and Exchange Commission (SEC)**. The word **security** is a widely used term for investments issued by corporations or governments in which the investor receives proof of ownership.

Activity #2

Securities and Exchange Commission (SEC): Government agency that regulates and monitors the stock market.

FIGURE 14.2 Risk Tolerance Quiz

Stocks are a good investment, but some people think that they involve too much risk. To determine your risk tolerance, say whether the following statements are true or false and then check the results.

Risk Tolerance	True	False
If I own stock, I will check its price at least daily if not more often.		
When driving on an interstate, and traffic and weather permit, I never drive in excess of the posted speed limit.		
If the price of my stock declines, my first reaction is to sell.		
Another stock market crash similar to 1929 could occur very unexpectedly.		
When I fly in less than perfect weather, I get nervous and concerned about my safety.		
If I sold a stock at a loss of more than 25%, it would greatly shake my confidence in my ability to invest.		
I intensely dislike blind dates.		
When I travel I write down a packing list to be sure that I don't forget anything.		
When traveling with others I prefer to do the driving.		
Before buying a bond I would want to talk to at least two other people to confirm my choice.		

Results

0 – 3 True: You have the risk tolerance to invest in individual common stocks.

4 – 6 True: You would be a nervous investor, but with more knowledge and a few successes, you could probably raise your risk tolerance to a suitable level. Mutual funds might prove a good starting point for your level of risk tolerance.

7 – 10 True: You are probably a very conservative and risk-intolerant investor who is probably better suited to a bond portfolio.

The main purpose of the SEC is to make sure that companies that offer stock for public sale provide accurate information to investors and obey established rules designed to make the stock market a "fair" game for everyone. The government needs the economy to have an active stock market. The stock market provides investors who buy the stock in the primary market with a way to sell their ownership shares at a later date. Without the liquidity that active stock markets offer, few investors would buy the initial public offerings (IPOs). This, in turn, would cut off a major source of funding that companies need to start and grow their business.

Example of a Stock Transaction

Buying or selling stocks will require you to open an account at a brokerage, a firm that provides you access to the stock markets. (Not just anyone can walk onto the floor of the New York Stock Exchange and start yelling out orders!) You can open such an account at one of many **full-service brokerage** firms that provide advice and execute your trades for you. Examples include firms such as Merrill Lynch and Edward Jones. Such firms offer a high level of service—for which you pay. Typically, firms charge customers a commission, or a fee for carrying out a transaction.

Some investors decide to go with a **discount brokerage**, which offers a reduced level of service, lower costs, and often the ability to make your trades yourself online. Examples of discount brokerages you may recognize are Scottrade and E*TRADE.

Let's go back to Kari's case. Assume she wants to sell 100 shares of XYZ Corporation at the market price. First, she might check the newspapers or online to learn the price at which the stock traded at the last session. If she's satisfied that the price is acceptable, she can submit that order to sell "at the market." Her broker, whether full-service or discount, will route the order to one of the stock exchanges. The order will be executed almost instantly at the current market price. Other investors who have submitted orders to buy that stock will purchase the shares. One word of caution: the market price at the time of execution can be different than the last price the stock traded.

Assume that when Kari sold her stock, she received $12 a share, or a total of $1,200. From that total, she must pay her broker's commission. Many discount commissions are less than $10 for this kind of transaction. A full-service broker's commission can be several times more. Kari's profit or loss on this transaction depends on what she paid for the stock and what dividends, if any, she received while she owned the stock. Figure 14.3 contains a flowchart outlining the process of how Kari sold her stock.

Let's say Kari's grandfather originally bought the stock for $11 a share. Thus, Kari would have made a return of about $1 per share. This works out to a return of 9.09%—($12 − $11)/$11.

brokerage: A firm that provides investors access to the stock markets.

commission: A fee for carrying out a transaction.

FIGURE 14.3   Selling Stock

The buying and selling of stock happens quickly and smoothly on today's stock exchanges.

Kari submits order to sell stock through online broker

↓

Online broker contacts representative at organized exchange

↓

Exchange matches Kari's "sell" order with someone else's "buy" order for same stock

↓

Exchange remits confirmation of sale back to online broker

↓

Kari receives confirmation of sale

Evelyn paid $32 a share for some stock and later received $38 a share when she sold it.

What percentage return did Evelyn make on the stock?

Solution: ($38 − $32) / 32 = .1875 or 18.75%. Keep in mind this return is not an annualized return and may be good or bad depending on how long Evelyn held the stock.

By selling shares of stock, companies raise cash they can use to build their businesses.

Since we know she held the stock for several years, and we know that the investment carried real risk, this would not be a good return. In fact, interest bearing accounts will often generate good returns and she might have gotten a better annual return investing in CDs—and enjoyed a safer investment at the same time. This example illustrates the uncertainty associated with investing in the stock market. It also explains why even a stock that increases in value may be considered a "dog." In fact, there are many stocks that actually lose value.

Of course, neither Kari nor her grandfather could have known for sure how the stock would perform. Stock investors must be prepared to evaluate their holdings regularly. They may opt to sell poor performing stocks in hopes of finding a better investment. In addition, investors are generally wise to own a number of different stocks. As risky as stocks can be, it is even riskier to depend on a single stock.

 CHECKPOINT

Why do companies sell shares of stock to investors?

INVESTING IN BONDS

Many investors place some of their money in bonds. A **bond** is basically a promissory note, or a promise to repay a certain amount of money at some point in the future. Companies, nonprofit organizations, and government agencies issue bonds as a way of basically taking a loan. Investors buy the bonds, effectively lending money to the bond issuer. In return, the investor earns interest.

How Bonds Work

Each bond has a face value (typically $1,000) and a stated rate of interest that will be paid annually to the bondholder until the bond expires. This expiration date is known as the bond's maturity, or **maturity date**. Bonds typically have maturity dates ranging from five to thirty years. The term **face value** comes from the fact that a bond's maturity value is printed on the front of the bond, also known as the bond's face. A bond's interest rate is often called its **coupon rate** because bonds originally came with booklets of prewritten coupons for the interest due on the bond. Each coupon had a date listed on which the bondholder could tear it from the booklet and take it to a bank for payment.

Consider the example of a bond issued by Company X with a face value of $1,000 at a coupon rate of 9% and a maturity date of five years. This means that every year for five years, Company X will pay each bondholder 9% of $1,000 ($90). At the end of five years, Company X will return the

Kenneth held a bond for five years that had an 8.5% coupon rate and a $1,000 face value.

How much did Kenneth receive in interest from the bond?

Solution: $1,000 × .085 − $85 per year × 5 years = $425.

$1,000 face value to the bondholder. The bondholders are loaning Company X money at that stated rate of interest. Check out Figure 14.4 for a flowchart illustrating how bonds work.

Like stocks, bonds offer investors more than one way to make money. You have just read about the regular interest payments, or **coupon payments**. In addition, bondholders can look to trade their bonds at a value higher than their face value. A bond's value moves up and down due to a number of factors, such as interest rate changes or changes in investors' beliefs in the bond issuer's ability to repay a bond. Some investors may elect to sell their bonds prior to the bond's maturity date. If the bond's sale price is more than its face value, the investor will make a profit. If the price is lower, the investor will have a loss on the sale of this bond.

Also, like stocks, most bonds carry some risk. Remember, when you purchase a bond you are basically lending the bond issuer money. If the bond issuer has financial problems, you may not get the interest you are due or your money back. Corporations can go bankrupt and leave bondholders with nothing. There are rating services that rate bonds and help investors evaluate their risk. In general, the lower the rating, the higher the interest rate the bond pays. After all, a lower-rated issuer has to find some way to attract buyers. Look at Figure 14.5 to see how bonds are rated.

Types of Bonds

Investors can choose from several types of bonds. These include Treasury bonds, federal agency bonds, municipal bonds, and corporate bonds.

The U.S. Treasury issues **Treasury bonds** to finance the debt of the United States government. Treasury bonds do not present any default risk since the federal government stands behind them. There is an active secondary market, much like the organized stock exchanges, where investors can sell Treasury bonds prior to maturity. The interest earned on Treasuries is subject to federal tax but is exempt from state and local income taxes.

The U.S. Treasury offers a variety of bond options, and maturity dates vary widely. Some options, such as certain savings bonds, do not pay regular interest but are purchased at a discount. That is, an investor buys a face value $1,000 bond for $500. At the end of the maturity date, the bond is redeemed for the full $1,000. In between, there are no coupon payments.

Federal agencies such as the Federal Housing Administration (FHA) and the Government National Mortgage Association (called Ginnie Mae) may issue bonds in order to fund projects. In these two cases, the bond proceeds are used to buy mortgages to encourage home ownership. Such bonds are known as **federal agency bonds**.

State and local governments may issue **municipal bonds** to finance large public projects, such as water and sewer systems. Investors do not pay federal taxes on the interest from municipal bonds. They may also

FIGURE 14.4 How Bonds Work

Bonds are like loans that investors make to the bond issuer.

Investor buys five-year $1,000 bond at 9% coupon rate from Company X

↓

Years 1–5 Company X gives investor $90 a year (total $450) in interest payments

↓

Year 5 Company X gives investor $1,000 back

Treasury bonds: Issued by the U.S. Treasury to finance the debt of the United States government.

Bonds are a type of investment in which the investor lends money to a bond issuer in hopes of earning interest and getting the original investment back.

FIGURE 14.5 Bond Rating Classes

Ratings help investors understand some measure of the risk they are taking, although they do not guarantee the bond's performance.

Risk Class	Standard & Poor's	Moody's
Highest quality (least risk)	AAA	Aaa
Highest quality	AA	Aa
Highest-medium quality	A	A
Medium quality	BBB	Baa
Medium-low quality	BB	Ba
Low quality	B	B
Poor quality	CCC	Caa
Very poor quality	CC	Ca
Lowest quality	DDD	C

avoid paying state and local taxes on this interest if they live in the region where the bonds originate. Municipal bonds do have a slight default risk.

Large firms may issue what are called **corporate bonds**. Corporate bonds have all degrees of risk depending on a company's strength. Companies with a solid financial position will have a low risk of default. Other companies may have a high risk of default. Bonds from companies with the highest risk are called **junk bonds**. In any case, corporate bonds have a greater likelihood of default than a U.S. government-backed bond. The top four categories of bonds shown in Figure 14.5 are considered investment-grade bonds and are reasonably safe. Anything rated below that is considered a junk bond.

Activity #3

Buying Bonds

Investors can buy and sell bonds in much the same way they trade stocks. They may use a broker, including discount brokers, to arrange transactions. Investors can also buy Treasury bonds directly from **www.treasurydirect.gov**.

The bondholder is supposed to get his or her initial investment back from the bond issuer.

 CHECKPOINT

What is supposed to happen at the end of a bond's maturity date?

MUTUAL FUNDS

Mutual funds are another investment option. **Mutual funds** sell shares to investors in order to collect a pool of money that is then used to buy various investments. A team of professional fund managers oversees these investments. The shareholders see an increase or decrease in the value of their shares based on the overall performance of the fund's investments.

Mutual funds are attractive to some investors for several reasons. Since mutual funds pool large amounts of money, the fund will typically own a wide range of investments. This process of investing in multiple investments is called **diversification**. Diversifying investments reduces risk because failure of one company (or even one industry) will not significantly impact the entire amount invested. A mutual fund will lose the amount invested in the failed company, but investments in a number of companies that are doing well should offset this loss.

diversification: The process of investing in multiple investments.

Investors who buy individual stocks and bonds can achieve diversification on their own, but it takes many purchases—and a considerable amount of money. So investors with limited funds who want to diversify may choose a mutual fund. It is possible to make a mutual fund investment with as little as $500, and this investment in a well-managed fund will be diversified.

Another advantage of mutual funds is that they are managed by experienced people. Such people *may* be better at picking good investments than a newcomer to the game of buying and selling stocks and bonds. Of course, not all mutual fund managers are successful, and some funds clearly have a better record than others.

There are thousands of mutual funds that invest in stocks and bonds, with many specializing in certain types of securities. For example, you can purchase shares in a mutual fund that only invests in Japanese companies or one that invests in gold mining stocks. Mutual fund companies and rating services categorize their funds by level of risk or whether the fund goals are producing long-term growth in share value or providing steady income for shareholders. (This is basically the same distinction as the one between stocks that pay dividends to stockholders and those that do not.) Indeed, there are several services that rate different funds based on their performance. It is relatively easy to see how funds compare with each other.

Investors can purchase mutual funds through a brokerage. They can also buy funds directly from the companies that sell them. Funds vary widely in the fees they charge. It pays to research any purchase carefully.

One type of fund that is increasing in popularity is an exchange-traded fund (ETF). ETFs provide diversification benefits similar to mutual funds, but they are typically designed to mimic a stock index like the Standard & Poor's 500 (commonly referred to as the S&P 500). In addition, ETFs typically have very low management fees. Investors can buy and sell ETFs in the same way they buy and sell stocks. This ease of buying and selling makes ETFs more accessible to small investors and has attracted billions of dollars to ETF investments in the past decade.

Remember that one of your primary reasons to invest is for retirement. For those long-term monies, you need to make sure you take advantage of the current tax laws that allow you to grow investments in a tax-sheltered retirement account such as a 401(k) or Individual Retirement Account (IRA). These accounts provide the benefit of allowing your money to grow tax free until you retire and thus accumulate a much larger sum of money as a result.

Finance **ONLINE**

One way you can learn about the wide range of mutual funds offered and the way they are evaluated is by visiting the site of one of the large mutual fund companies. For example, check out **www.vanguard .com**. (Understand that this mutual fund company—Vanguard Group—is primarily interested in selling its own funds.)

What information can you find on this Web site? How can this site be helpful to you as you think about your financial plan?

✓ **CHECKPOINT**

What is a major benefit of investing in mutual funds?

Benefits include professional management, diversification, and the possibility of investing with a small amount of money.

OTHER WAYS OF INVESTING

When you think of investments, you may first think of stocks, bonds, and mutual funds. But there are other ways to invest your money.

Real Estate

Many people have used real estate as an investment. In fact, one way millions of people invest in real estate is to buy a home. Housing values move up and down over time depending on the supply and demand for homes in an area. Think about it like this: If a factory suddenly closes in your area and a lot of people are forced to move to find work, you will see a lot of houses for sale. Sellers of those houses may lower their prices in order to sell faster. More sellers than buyers will tend to push home prices down.

The reverse is true if you have a growing region where a lot of people are moving into an area. More buyers than sellers will create a market where housing prices will be going up.

In general, home prices have increased over the very long run and created wealth for long-term homeowners. In addition, investing in real estate offers tax benefits, or the ability to take advantage of rules in the tax code that may reduce your tax liability. And, of course, you need a place to live. These factors make buying a home a good investment for most people. However, the financial crisis of 2008–2009 provided a clear illustration of the dangers of buying a house that is above your price range and how the type of financing you choose can have a tremendous impact on your budget. Thousands of homeowners lost their homes when they were unable to make the higher payments required due to interest rate resets on their adjustable rate mortgages.

Some people invest in real estate by buying rental property. You may know someone who owns apartments that he or she rents out on a monthly basis. Or you may know someone who owns and rents commercial property. Very often, real estate investors find that the rent they receive covers the payments on the loan they took to buy the property. Profits will come from the real estate increasing in value over time.

Owning a Business

Many people have a dream of owning their own business. In fact, we know from sources such as the book *The Millionaire Next Door* by Thomas Stanley and William Danko that a large number of millionaires in the United States are small business owners. Restaurants, retail stores, and services all provide opportunities for someone who works hard to generate wealth.

You may also have opportunities to invest in someone else's small business at some point. Be careful, though, since many small ventures fail. The potential rewards are very high, but the risk is very high, too.

Examples include buying real estate or starting or investing in a small business.

 CHECKPOINT

What are some investment options besides stocks, bonds, and mutual funds?

CHAPTER REVIEW

SUMMARY

- While liquid investments are important, it is important to aim for a return that will beat inflation. This generally involves making riskier investments with a longer-term goal.

- Stock is partial ownership in a company and is a good way to seek a profit. While the behavior of stocks cannot be predicted precisely, research can provide clues about which companies may be good opportunities. Brokerages, both full-service and discount, make it possible to trade stocks.

- Bonds are promissory notes from an issuer to an investor. The bond issuer generally pays interest on a regular basis, and agrees to pay back the face value at the maturity date. There are many types of bonds, including Treasury bonds, federal agency bonds, municipal bonds, and corporate bonds. The highest risk bonds are known as junk bonds. Bonds can be sold at a profit or loss before their maturity date.

- Mutual funds are another investment option. They provide diversification and professional management for a relatively low initial investment. They also allow investors to target their investments in certain industries or sectors. Investors can purchase shares in mutual funds through a brokerage or directly from the companies that sell them.

- People can also invest in real estate and in small businesses. As with any investment, there are clear risks involved, as well as the possibility for great reward.

Key Terms and Concepts

1. What should be your first priority in investing?

2. What is meant by an **initial public offering (IPO)**?

3. **Shareholders** have what purpose in a company?

What Do You Know?   MyFinLitLab

1. (a) What are stocks?

   (b) Why do investors invest in stocks?

   (c) Why are companies willing to give up a share of ownership in their enterprise?

2. (a) What is the difference between the primary and secondary stock markets?

   (b) Why do you think the price of a stock changes each day in the secondary market?

Answers:
Key Terms and Concepts

1. Your first investing priority should be to build a cash reserve equivalent to six months living expenses that you keep in liquid investments.

2. An initial public offering occurs when a company sells stock to the public for the very first time.

3. Shareholders are owners in a company that also vote on the Board of Directors, the group in charge of monitoring the company. In the IPO market shareholders provide the initial capital to the company.

Answers:
What Do You Know?

1. (a) **Knowledge** Stocks are partial ownership in a company. (b) **Comprehension** Investors hope to make money from the success of the company. (c) **Analysis** Companies want the money that stockholders are willing to pay for stock.

2. (a) **Comprehension** The primary market is where initial public offerings are sold. The secondary market is where shares are sold after the initial public offering. (b) **Analysis** The price changes because the price is set by the action of many individual buyers and sellers, which changes every day.

3. (a) **Comprehension** The NYSE is an actual place where traders buy and sell stocks. The NASDAQ is an electronic network of traders. (b) **Analysis** The NYSE has to limit the number of people who actually execute trades on the floor of the Exchange.

4. (a) **Comprehension** An individual investor is making trades on his or her own behalf. An institutional investor represents a larger group. (b) **Analysis** Possible answer: An institutional investor may take more or less risk depending on the understanding or rules of the group he or she represents.

5. (a) **Knowledge** Shareholders are people who own stock, or shares of a company. (b) **Application** Shareholders earn a return if the company pays dividends and/or if the company performs well and drives the stock price higher. In that case, the shareholder realizes a profit when he or she sells the stock.

6. (a) **Knowledge** Dividends are the periodic distribution of company revenues to a shareholder. (b) **Analysis** If an investor is seeking a company that is trying to grow, he or she may prefer that the company invests its profits rather than pay them to shareholders.

7. (a) **Comprehension** The shareholder decides to sell and issues an order to a broker. The broker communicates the order to the Exchange. A buyer then purchases the stock. (b) **Application** The brokerage is the intermediary in the transaction.

8. (a) **Knowledge** The face value of a bond is the amount that appears on the front of the bond. (b) **Application** Bondholders make money through interest payments or, potentially, if they can sell their bond at a higher price than they paid for it.

9. (a) **Knowledge** Mutual funds are large pools of money invested by many individuals for the purposes of investment and management by skilled fund managers. (b) **Analysis** Achieving diversification as an individual requires the purchase of many different investments, each of which may require a significant amount of money for an initial investment.

10. (a) **Knowledge** Purchasing real estate is the investment that homeowners have made. (b) **Application** The value of a home may go up or down significantly, and even selling a home at any price can become difficult at certain times.

3. (a) Explain the difference between the New York Stock Exchange (NYSE) and the National Association of Securities Dealers Automatic Quotation (NASDAQ) system.

   (b) Why is it necessary to use a broker to make a trade on the NYSE?

4. (a) What is the difference between an individual and an institutional investor?

   (b) Would these two types of investors likely apply similar or different standards for choosing a stock? Explain.

5. (a) Who are shareholders?

   (b) In what ways do shareholders earn returns from investing in stock?

6. (a) What are dividends?

   (b) In what circumstance might an investor prefer stocks that do not pay dividends?

7. (a) What are the basic steps of a stock transaction?

   (b) What role does the brokerage play in the process?

8. (a) What is the face value of a bond?

   (b) What are two ways bondholders can make money on bonds they own?

9. (a) What are mutual funds?

   (b) Why would it take a lot more money to achieve the diversification of a mutual fund when buying individual stocks and bonds?

10. (a) What kind of investment have millions of homeowners made?

    (b) Explain why owning a home must be considered a long-term investment.

What Are Your Finance Math Skills? MyFinLitLab

The first three questions correlate to *Math for Personal Finance* features located throughout the chapter.

1. Breanne paid $11.75 a share for stock Y last year. Today, she sold the stock for $14.25 a share. What was her percentage return, excluding the commission?

2. What is your dollar return on the sale of 250 shares of stock for $38 a share if you paid $26 a share two years ago (excluding the commission)?

3. How much interest will you receive annually on a 7% coupon rate bond with a $1,000 face value?

4. What is the total value of your stock holdings if you own 50 shares of XYZ valued at $32.50 a share, 90 shares of ABC valued at $54.25 a share, and 125 shares of DEF valued at $112.12 a share?

5. What is the total dollar amount you would make on a 9% coupon rate bond with a face value of $1,000 but for which you paid $1,035 and that you held for one year before maturity?

6. Castille sold 35 shares of stock for $47.50 a share. She bought the stock for $51 a share last year. What was her dollar return (loss), not counting the commission?

7. If you own 500 shares of stock in a company that has 100,000 shares of stock outstanding, what fraction of the firm do you own?

8. How much money did Jeremy receive in interest on a $1,000 face value bond that he held for two years and that had a 7% coupon rate?

What Would You Do?

Juanita just celebrated her 16th birthday. Her parents realized they have accumulated only half the money needed for Juanita's college education. With college only two years away, they became concerned about how they will save the remaining amount in such a short time.

June, Juanita's mother, was discussing the dilemma of financing her daughter's education with her boss, Mr. Rodriquez. Mr. Rodriquez told June of an investment his broker told him about that has doubled his money in just over one year. Mr. Rodriquez assured June that this would be a sound investment that would continue to grow and that had very little risk.

June went home to tell Juan, Juanita's father, about the information given to her by her boss. Juan thought she should ask her boss if there were any other tips he could give her from his broker to help them increase their daughter's college savings.

The next day, June asked Mr. Rodriquez if his broker had any other tips. Mr. Rodriquez told June of a small startup company that his broker believed would double within the next two years with virtually no risk. June and Juan immediately invested their daughter's college fund into the stock of this company. One year later, June and Juan received a letter from the company announcing they were out of business and closing their doors. Upon calling their broker, June found the stock was now worthless.

1. Comment on Mr. Rodriquez's ethics of assuring his employee that the investments he was recommending upon the advice of his broker could produce major rewards with virtually no risk.

2. What basic investing principle did June and Juan forget in their desire to fund their daughter's college education?

3. With less than a year to go until Juanita leaves for college, what can be done to begin saving for college?

What Are the Connections? Language Arts

Determine whether investments in stocks, bonds, or mutual funds will help you achieve some short-, intermediate-, and long-term goals. Remember that a short-term goal should be achievable within one year, an intermediate-term goal should be achievable in one to five years, and a long-term goal will take five years or more. Create a worksheet to display your goals. Have column headings as follows:

- Goals
- Yes or No
- Type of Investment
- Justification

List one or two short-, intermediate-, and long-term goals. Be sure to separate each type of goal as you are putting the information in the columns. In the Yes or No column, you will need to determine whether investing in stocks, bonds, or mutual funds is suitable for that particular goal. If the answer is no, do not complete the rest of the row for that goal. If the answer is yes, be sure to determine the type of investment you will choose, and provide a justification for that investment.

Refer to the following example when designing your worksheet:

Goals	Yes or No	Type of Investment	Justification
Short-Term			
Buying an IPod	No		
Intermediate			
Buying a car	Yes	Bonds	Short-term high-grade bonds will provide a higher return than bank accounts.
Long-Term			
Buying a house in 10 years	Yes	Diversified stock mutual funds	Mutual funds allow immediate diversification and should maximize return over a 10-year period.

After you have created your worksheet, answer the following questions:

1. Summarize your reasoning for either investing or not investing to meet your goals.

2. If you decide to invest, how much will you invest each month? How will you determine how much you will invest each month? What types of investments will you purchase? Why?

Teamwork

Each team will have an imaginary $5,000 to invest. Teams choose five stocks to watch for one week. Make a chart to collect data for each of the stocks. At the end of the week, present your stocks to the class. Provide the following information:

1. Explain why your team chose each company. Show how much stock you purchased in each company you chose.
2. Decide which stocks your team will sell and which stocks you will reinvest in. Explain your decisions to the class.

ESSENTIAL QUESTION ACTIVITIES

Complete these activities to answer this chapter's Essential Question: *Why would you invest and how does investing affect your financial plan?*

1. *On your own:* Using paper or a word processor, write a response to the following situation: Suppose your new job offers investment opportunities. Why would you choose to invest and how would you make that decision? What would investing do to your financial plan now and for the future?

2. *As a class:* Brainstorm answers to the following questions: Why would you choose to invest and how would you make that decision? What would investing do to your financial plan now and for the future?

TEST PREP QUESTIONS

MyFinLitLab

1. A person should include a cash reserve or emergency fund in his financial plan to
   a. have money available in case he wants to go on an unplanned vacation with friends.
   b. have money to pay living expenses if he loses his job or has a serious illness or injury.
   c. have money available for daily spending during retirement.
   d. have at least two months of salary in cash for current daily expenses.

   1. b

2. Financial products for a cash reserve or emergency fund—that is, money set aside for unexpected expenses—should include
   a. stocks that can make a quick profit for a person to make up for any loss in income.
   b. two-year CDs that offer higher interest rates instead of short-term CDs.
   c. government bonds that are very low risk and offer a guaranteed rate of return.
   d. liquid accounts, such as checking and savings accounts, so that money is available quickly.

   2. d

3. A person wants to use a gift of $2,000 to buy a new car when he graduates next year. He decides to purchase stock in a new, alternative energy company with the money. Is this a good idea?
   a. No, because he needs the money in a year and it may take much longer for this company to earn a profit.
   b. Yes, because alternative energy companies will guarantee investors a minimum yearly profit.
   c. Yes, because the government wants energy companies to succeed so they will protect this company from failure.
   d. No, because he would be much better off investing in the auto industry.

4. What is meant by this statement: "With the promise of higher returns comes higher risk"?
   a. When a company promises a person that investing in the company's new product will make her rich, she needs to know that it may take years for the company to produce a profit for its investors.
   b. The reason that long-term CDs provide owners with greater return on their investments is because these CDs are riskier than three-month CDs.
   c. When a person buys stock during a recession, the company has to pay the shareholder a higher dividend since the whole economy is weak.
   d. A person expects a higher return on an investment in stocks to compensate for the higher risk that a stock carries relative to a CD or savings account.

5. Which of the following is a true statement about investing in stock?
   a. A person who invests in stock can lose all of her invested money.
   b. The SEC protects a person's investments so that he always makes a minimum profit.
   c. If a stock price does not increase, the company will give the investor a share of the company's profits in the form of a dividend.
   d. If the stock is listed on one of the exchanges, it means that the company is expected to be profitable.

6. Which of the following investment products is *not* correctly paired with its description?
   a. Stock: a person has pieces of ownership in a public company.
   b. Bond: how a company or government agency takes a loan from the public.
   c. Mutual fund: a company offers the public the chance to own part of the company or to give the company a loan.
   d. Treasury bond: how the government finances federal debt.

7. Which of the following financial terms associated with the trading of stock is correctly paired with its explanation?
   a. Primary market: the place where the country's largest companies buy the securities of other large companies.
   b. Secondary market: the place where small companies access funding for expansion.

   c. Publicly traded: the method used to reach people who want to buy government securities.

   d. Institutional investment: the trading of large amounts of a security by a mutual fund or a pension fund.

8. An initial public offering (IPO) is   8. b

   a. the trading of securities of large companies on a stock exchange.

   b. the first time a company offers stock to the investing public in order to raise capital for the company.

   c. when an investor purchases a company's stock that is listed on the New York Stock Exchange.

   d. the bundling of a number of securities to create a mutual fund.

9. The sequence of actions that correctly names the steps involved in   9. b
executing a stock trade is as follows:

   a. exchange confirms sale to broker; sell order is matched with buy order; person contacts broker; person receives confirmation of sale.

   b. person submits order to buy stock to broker; broker contacts stock's representative at exchange; sell order is matched with buy order; person receives confirmation of sale.

   c. exchange confirms order with purchaser of securities; sell order is matched with buy order; person contacts broker; confirmation of trade is made with broker.

   d. person submits order to sell to broker; confirmation of trade is made with broker; sell order is matched with buy order; broker contacts stock's representative at exchange.

10. Which of the following is a true statement about the stock exchanges?   10. c

   a. A person can buy the stock of any publicly traded share on any of the exchanges.

   b. A person can only buy technology stock using an Internet account such as E*TRADE.

   c. The stock exchanges operate very much like large auctions with many people bidding on the same securities.

   d. The public needs to contact a stock broker in order to get the price on a particular security.

11. What causes the price of a share of stock to increase?   11. a

   a. More people want to buy the stock of a given company at a certain price than there are people willing to sell it at that price.

   b. The SEC agrees to insure the company issuing the new stock.

   c. The company has decided to take loans in the form of bonds to make up for the losses in sales for the year.

   d. The national rate of inflation has gone up less than the price of the products the company is making.

12. Generally, the price of a company's stock will *not* decrease because of   12. c

   a. a weak overall economy.

   b. a high interest rate.

   c. a low rate of inflation.

   d. weak sales in the industry.

13. Even if the price of Company A's stock does not go up and the person holds on to his shares, the person can make money on his investment. How is this possible?

    a. The person buys more shares of the stock of companies that are in competition with Company A.

    b. The amount of the drop in Company A's stock price can be taken as a tax deduction.

    c. Company A may declare a dividend that benefits the company's shareholders.

    d. Company A can change how the company operates, which saves the company a lot of money.

14. Why is investing in the stock market, even in very solid stocks, considered riskier than putting money in a savings account or CD?

    a. Savings accounts provide the depositor interest on his savings even when the economy is in recession.

    b. Companies may decide to put their profits into corporate growth or replace outdated equipment instead of giving dividends to their shareholders.

    c. The price of the stock may not go up but the CD will increase in value over time.

    d. The FDIC protects money in savings accounts and CDs, but money invested in the stock market is not insured by any organization.

15. What is the purpose of the Securities and Exchange Commission (SEC)?

    a. The SEC keeps the prices of stocks from falling below a certain point during a deep recession.

    b. The SEC makes sure that companies issuing stock to the public provide accurate information to investors before they purchase securities.

    c. The SEC provides advice to individual investors on which securities are appropriate to purchase at a given point in life.

    d. The SEC makes money available to companies when they initially issue shares of stock to the public.

16. Which of the following is *not* a true statement about bonds?

    a. In most cases, a bondholder will receive interest on a bond until the bond's maturity date.

    b. A bond can be issued by a nonprofit organization as well as a corporation.

    c. A bond is always a safer investment than a stock.

    d. A person can also make money on a bond by selling it before maturity if the price is higher than its purchase price.

17. Which of the following is a true statement about mutual funds?

    a. A person needs to have at least $10,000 before being able to invest in a mutual fund.

    b. The holdings of a mutual fund are determined by the Securities and Exchange Commission (SEC).

    c. Mutual funds can provide a way for a small investor to have diversified holdings in some of the country's wealthiest companies.

    d. The person who invests in a mutual fund can decide which stocks or bonds the person wants to have in the mutual fund.

CHAPTER 15

ESSENTIAL QUESTION

How does planning for retirement affect a person's financial plan?

PLANNING FOR THE FUTURE

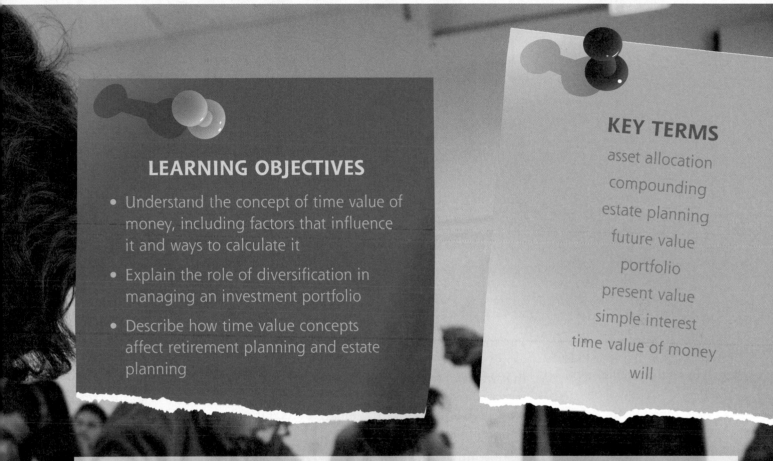

LEARNING OBJECTIVES

- Understand the concept of time value of money, including factors that influence it and ways to calculate it

- Explain the role of diversification in managing an investment portfolio

- Describe how time value concepts affect retirement planning and estate planning

KEY TERMS

asset allocation

compounding

estate planning

future value

portfolio

present value

simple interest

time value of money

will

Mark fumbled through his notes on today's lecture. He was sure he'd missed something, because the guest speaker had told them they could all be millionaires when they retired. How could that be? As far as he was aware, he'd never known a millionaire, and he wasn't going to medical school.

Mark planned on going to the career and technical school near his home to study diesel mechanics. His father worked at a trucking company and said they always needed more mechanics. From Mark's perspective, they made good money. But probably not enough, he thought, to become a millionaire.

Still, Mark was sure he heard correctly when his friend Frank told the guy that he was planning to fix air conditioners for a living, and the man assured Frank he could still become a millionaire. It was there in his notes: All Frank had to do, the lecturer said, was to live on less than what he made and begin making investments while he was very young. In fact, the man told Frank that if he would open an account at age 19 and deposit $2,000 a year in it, Frank could become a millionaire. According to the numbers he'd shown the class, if Frank invested in a mutual fund that averaged a 12% annual return, he would have over $1.5 million before he turned 60. Mark still could not be sure he had heard right, but after the lecture, he had gotten the man's card. He would call him in a few days to ask about it.

The speaker in Mark's class was right. What experts call the "time value of money" can work what seems like major miracles if you begin investing at an early age. What happens is that you begin earning a return—for example, interest—on your original investment plus any returns that you have earned in the past. Your money begins working for you instead of you working for your money. In the next few sections, we will spend some time looking at the financial math behind these miracles.

TIME VALUE OF MONEY

time value of money: The fact that money received today is worth more than money received next year or the year after.

The **time value of money** refers to the fact that money received today is worth more than money received next year or the year after. The reason is that we can put that money to work for us in various investments. This concept is so powerful that Albert Einstein stated it was one of the strongest forces on earth. And, from all accounts, Einstein was a pretty sharp guy.

Let's look at a couple of examples:

- Armin, who is 18, has pledged not to smoke. This decision could make him a millionaire by the time he retires at age 67. After all, let's assume he will save about $6.00 a day—the amount, on average, he spends on cigarettes. Each year for 49 years Armin will have available $2,190 to invest ($6.00 × 365 days). Assuming a rate of return of 8% per year, Armin would accumulate $1,161,450 by age 67!

With time on your side, even the small amount of money you save by emptying your pockets each day can be turned into a huge fortune over a period of years.

- Suppose your ancestors settled in the American colonies in 1693. At that time, one of them invested $20 at a local bank earning 5% interest annually. Also assume that this ancestor never informed his family of this transaction and that the money remained in the account accumulating interest until the year 2013, when the bank locates you and informs you of the account. Over this time, the $20 would have grown to over $120 million.

You can see that the time value of money can be put to work for you to begin saving for any number of goals, such as a new home, a vacation, or retirement. The possibilities are endless if you make the decision to postpone certain purchases now and save the money instead. Do you really need those new shoes? Couldn't you bring lunch from home rather than ordering out every day? Give some thought to your spending habits as you study the time value of money.

FIGURE 15.1 Relationship Between the Annual Return on Your Annual Savings and Your Savings at Retirement

(in 40 years, Assuming a $5,000 Annual Investment)

Earning a higher interest rate on your investments can have a huge effect on the amount of money you accumulate by retirement

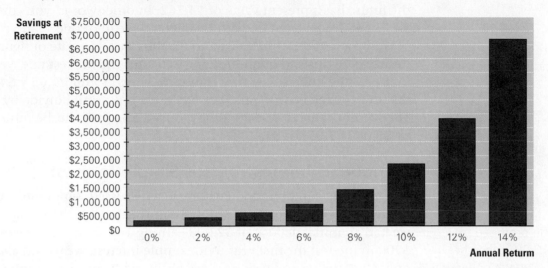

Future Value Versus Present Value

Future value is the projected value of a sum of money at some point in the future. Calculating future value, or the process of seeing how much you can accumulate by some point in the future, is perhaps the most important time value concept when focusing on wealth accumulation. You can use this time value of money tool to calculate how much you can save by the time you reach age 40 or 60 or whatever age you choose.

Let's look at an example of how your money can work for you when trying to accumulate wealth. What happens when you put $2,000 in an account that averages a 10% annual return? At the end of the first year you will have your original $2,000 plus the 10% you earned on that investment for a total of $2,200.

The next year you will have a total of $2,200 invested that you will now earn interest on. Thus, at the end of the second year you will have $2,420 ($2,200 × .10 = $220 + $2,200 = $2,420). A quick way to do this calculation is to multiply $2,200 by 1.10. This process of **compounding**, or earning interest on the principal and the interest earned in the past, will continue as long as you leave the money untouched. In fact, if you keep this original $2,000 amount invested earning 10% compounded for 40 years, you will accumulate $90,518. Imagine how much you could accumulate if you invested $2,000 every year for those 40 years! Obviously, the higher the interest rate you can earn, the more money you will accumulate for a given number of years. Figure 15.1 illustrates this point.

Present value is the value of a sum of money—for example, the million dollars you hope to have at retirement—at the present time. Present value techniques are just the opposite of future value. Instead of trying to take

MATH for Personal Finance

Assume that Jenise invested $1,000 in the stock market and earned an average annual return of 12%.

How much would she have after 50 years?

Solution: The formula solution is future value = present value × (1 + interest rate)^n, where n = number of years. Jenise will have $1,000(1.12)^{50}$ = $289,002.19.

future value: The projected value of a sum of money at some point in the future.

compounding: Earning interest on the principal and the interest earned in the past.

present value: The value of a sum of money at the present time.

simple interest: Interest earned only on the original amount or principal.

MATH for Personal Finance

Shane's uncle promised to give him $10,000 when he graduates college in one year.

What equivalent amount could Shane receive today assuming he could put the money in a CD earning 4%?

Solution: This question is asking for the present value of $10,000. So, $10,000/(1.04)^1 = $9,615.38. In other words, Shane could put $9,615.38 in a CD earning 4% and have $10,000 at the end of next year.

some amount today (present value) and seeing what it will grow to in the future (future value), you are taking some future value and bringing it back to the present.

For example, you may know that you will receive a $5,000 gift when you turn 21. How much is that amount worth today—what is its present value—assuming you are 20 years old? It depends on the interest rate you could earn, but assuming a 5% rate, the $5,000 you will receive in the future has a present value of $4,762. In other words, you could invest $4,762 at 5% and end up with $5,000 at the end of one year.

Doing a present value calculation is the exact opposite of figuring a future value. Instead of multiplying by 1 plus the interest rate, you divide by 1 plus the interest rate (see Figure 15.2). So, $5,000/1.05 = $4,762. If the future value is two years into the future you would divide by $(1.05)^2$. The present value of $5,000 to be received four years in the future would be $5,000/(1.05)^4 = $4,114.

Compound Interest Versus Simple Interest

In contrast to compound interest we just discussed, **simple interest** earns interest only on the original amount or principal. In our example in which we had an initial deposit of $2,000 earning 10% interest, we would earn $200 in interest the first year. With simple interest, we would also earn only $200 the second year because, unlike with compound interest, we would not earn interest on interest. Compounding will always create wealth faster for any given interest rate.

The Concept of an Annuity

You know that an annuity is the term used for a type of investment in which a person pays an amount of money and receives a set amount of income on a regular basis. In fact, the word *annuity* has a broader meaning. An annuity is defined as any situation in which you have equal cash flows occurring at equal intervals for a fixed period of time. Good examples of annuities are all around us. For example, a car payment is an annuity. In most cases, you make equal payments every month for some fixed number of years. House payments, or any other loan payments set up on a similar schedule, are examples of annuities.

FIGURE 15.2   Formulas for Future Value and Present Value

These formulas can help you calculate future and present values.

Formula for Calculating Future Value

Principal $\times$ (1 + Interest Rate)$^{\text{Number of Years into the Future}}$

For example:	For example:
To calculate the 2014 future value of $400 you have in 2013 assuming a 10% interest rate:	To calculate the 2013 present value of $400 you will receive in 2014 assuming a 10% interest rate:
$400 × 1.10 = $440	$400 ÷ 1.10 = $363.64
To calculate the 2017 future value of $400 you have in 2013 assuming a 10% interest rate:	To calculate the 2013 present value of $400 you will receive in 2017 assuming a 10% interest rate:
$400 × 1.10⁴ = $585.64	$400 ÷ 1.10⁴ = $273.21

Our previous example of $2,000 invested every year for 40 years earning 10% a year is also an annuity. We can also solve for the future value or present value of an annuity. This is very useful to us when we are trying to determine how much to save every year to achieve a certain goal or how much a particular payment would be for a house, car, or any asset. Review Figure 15.1 to see an example of how saving an annuity of $5,000 a year with a 10% annual return can generate a vast sum of money.

Using Financial Calculators

The concept of present and future values can seem confusing. Fortunately, you can perform both present value and future value calculations easily on a financial calculator. After you learn the appropriate keys to use, you can solve any present value or future value problem, including annuities. Online versions of these calculators are available (for example, see Figure 15.3). By following the instructions, you can figure the future value for an initial investment given a certain interest rate and period of time. You can also determine the future value of an annuity—for example, what you would wind up with if you made the same deposit each year for a period of time.

Rule of 72

One simple rule of thumb that we can often use in calculating future values is known as the **Rule of 72**. This rule allows us to see how long it would take to double our money for a given interest rate. For example, if you assume a 12% return, you can divide 72 by 12 to find out it would take roughly 6 years to double your money.

You can also use this technique to see what kind of return someone is promising you. If someone tells you that he or she can double your money in 8 years, you know that the person is expecting an annual return of about 9% since $72/8 = 9$. While its applications are limited, the Rule of 72 can be a handy tool to make quick approximations in some cases.

FIGURE 15.3   Financial Calculators

Financial calculators can perform the complicated mathematics involved in figuring future values and present values.

Input	Function
12	N
10	I
⁻5687	PV
0	PMT
?=17848.24	FV

Suppose you have $5,687 to invest in the stock market today. You like to invest for the long term and plan to choose your stocks carefully. You will invest your money for 12 years in certain stocks on which you expect a return of 10%. Although financial calculators can vary slightly in their setup, most would require inputs as shown at left.

Where:

N = number of periods

I = interest rate

PV = present value, which is the initial amount deposited

PMT = payment, which is not applicable in this problem

FV = future value of the deposit you make today, which is computed by the calculator

The PV is a negative number here, reflecting the outflow of cash to make the investment. The calculator computes the future value to be $17,848.24, which indicates that you will have $17,848.24 in your brokerage account in 12 years if you achieve a return of 10% annually on your $5,687 investment.

A fun fact about the Rule of 72: In 1494, the rule is referenced in *Summa de Arithmetica* by Fra Luca Pacioli. Pacioli brought the rule into a discussion of estimating the doubling time of an investment. Although he discusses the rule, he is not credited with its discovery. Thus, there are those who think the rule predates Pacioli.

It means that money received today has a different value than money received at some other point in time.

MATH for Personal Finance

Using future value techniques for a lump sum amount, calculate the value of a three-year annuity of $1,000 invested at 5%.

Assume you invest the first $1,000 today, the second $1,000 in one year, and the last amount in two years.

Solution: The annuity formula in a financial calculator will generate the same solution as this, but understanding the process is important. In this problem, you will simply calculate the value of each $1,000 amount and add them up. The value of the annuity equals:

$$\$1,000 \times (1.05)^3 = \$1,157.62$$
$$+ \$1,000 \times (1.05)^2 = \$1,102.50$$
$$+ \$1,000 \times (1.05)^1 = \$1,050.00$$
$$\$3,310.12$$

portfolio: An individual's investments.

✓ **CHECKPOINT**

What does the time value of money mean?

MANAGING YOUR INVESTMENTS

While many of you may opt to use a financial professional to manage your investments, you will be in charge of what strategy the professional follows. And, you should always monitor your investments—your **portfolio**—to make sure the people you have hired are following your guidelines. Every individual will have a different set of investment goals and objectives. These goals and objectives should dictate your investment guidelines or instructions you have set up with the professional for investing your money. There are two important factors to consider: (1) you should keep your portfolio diversified, and (2) you must understand that there is a risk/return trade-off in the investment arena. We will discuss both of these factors in the next sections.

Diversification

Diversification is the application of the old saying "Don't put all your eggs in one basket." That is, you should not rely on any single type of investment to achieve your financial goals. The kinds of investments you need to make in order to achieve your long-term goals, including stocks, bonds, and real estate, have a lot of uncertainty regarding their future performance. Each of these types of investments is called an **asset class**, and each carries a different level of uncertainty or risk. Each responds differently to specific events or market conditions. For these reasons, it is wise to diversify, or invest in a lot of different types of assets or asset classes. **Asset allocation** is the process of spreading your investments among asset classes—diversifying your investments. Your objective is achieving some desired return with an acceptable level of risk.

A diversified portfolio of assets will reduce your risk over time. For example, suppose you have a portion of your wealth in stocks, bonds, and real estate. When one asset class is down, you can reasonably hope that the others will offset the decline and increase in value. Different asset classes perform better during different economic periods.

Since you don't have the ability to tell in advance which assets will perform better next year, it is wise to maintain diversification. That way you should always have some assets that are doing really well to offset those that perform poorly. Make sure you are properly diversified and, for example, don't get caught with all your money in stocks in a declining stock market.

asset allocation: The process of spreading your investments among asset classes in order to diversify your investments.

Risk and Return Trade-Off

When you make an investment, you are making a trade-off between risk and return. If you want low risk, generally you must be willing to accept lower returns. Higher-risk investments will have to give a reasonable hope of higher returns to attract investors. For example, why would anyone accept the risks of investing in the stock market if the expected return were only 3%? Most of the time you could earn that return with no risk by investing in FDIC-insured bank CDs. Using the same reasoning, no one would invest in start-up companies with a high risk of failure unless the potential return were much greater than investing in established, so-called "blue-chip" companies. Every market investment carries a different level of risk and therefore should hold a reasonable hope of a different potential return. Never forget, of course, that no return is guaranteed.

The overall return you should seek for your portfolio obviously depends on your tolerance for risk. In addition, your age should also dictate to some extent the level of risk you can assume: younger people have more time to recover from a financial misstep than someone nearing retirement.

Activity #2

Too Good to Be True?

If someone promises you something that seems too good to be true, it probably is. What does this mean? Whenever you are talking about investing money, you will find that someone is out there trying to separate you from your cash. You may meet someone who promises a 20% return without any risk. Those types of promises are not reasonable, so be very cautious about jumping into an investment like that. Do you really want to trust your money to someone who is trying that hard to lure you in?

In fact, anything that is presented as a promise or as a sure thing ought to make you think twice. There are very few promises you can rely on in the financial world. You can rely on FDIC insurance. You can rely on the ability of the federal government to pay off its bonds. But beyond that, there is some risk involved in any decision you make.

There really are no get rich quick schemes. There are a number of get rich slow-but-steady schemes. Don't allow anyone to rush you into a financial commitment or trick you into thinking you can beat the system. It always pays to think about it and do some investigating on your own. Don't take anyone's word for something unless you know and trust that person 100%. It's your hard-earned money. Don't let anyone cheat you out of it.

 CHECKPOINT

Why is diversification an important part of managing your portfolio?

Different asset classes perform differently at different times and under different circumstances. Having a variety of investments in a variety of classes helps protect the investor from excessive risk.

Mark, like you, is a long way from retirement. For that reason, both of you may find it strange to be thinking about retirement planning. But there is really no better time to start the process. Why? As you can see from the time value concepts we covered in this chapter, you can accumulate wealth much more easily if you have time to put your money to work for you. You now have the ability to see how much difference it makes if you wait until you are 30 years old to begin saving for retirement. Starting at age 20 makes much more sense.

Prof. FIN

You may have heard of AARP, but do you know what they do to help with your retirement? AARP provides a wide range of services and information for people over age 50. Many times you will see discounts for AARP members at hotels, restaurants, grocery stores, and such. One day you may be interested in joining AARP not only for the discounts but also for the support this organization provides to its members. For more information, go to **www.aarp.org**.

Once you have established some financial goals, you can begin taking steps to accomplish them. For example, if you want to retire at age 55 with $2 million in the bank, you can use the time value tools to see how much you need to save every year and how much risk to take with your investments. Use a financial calculator to figure what you'd need to save to reach that or some other goal.

Think about your long-term goals. What do you want out of life? While we know that money does not buy happiness, financial worries complicate life. Financial security is not a bad thing and can be achieved with some careful planning followed by action. If all goes well, you will have income from a number of sources (but you must be careful about counting too heavily on the Social Security system to provide a significant piece of your retirement pie). You have the ability to provide your own retirement income, and if you receive any Social Security income it will be a bonus.

If you start earlier in life, you can take advantage of the power of time to achieve greater results.

 CHECKPOINT

Why is it better to begin planning for retirement at age 20 than at age 30?

ESTATE PLANNING

estate planning: The process of determining how your wealth will be allocated on or before your death.

Estate planning is even farther into the future than retirement but is something you should be aware of. **Estate planning** is the process of determining how your wealth will be allocated on or before your death. In other words, what happens to your assets when you die? Do you want them to go to the state, to a particular charity, or to your children and grandchildren? If you resolve these questions prior to your death, you are more likely to have your wishes honored. It will also make it easier on your loved ones.

Your Will

One of the most critical tasks in estate planning is the creation of a will. A **will** is a legal request for how your estate (everything you have accumulated during your life) should be distributed upon your death. If you have any surviving minor children, a will can also determine who will be their legal guardian.

In your will you can specify who will receive your estate—your **beneficiaries**, or heirs. If you die without a will (known as being **intestate**), the court will appoint an administrator who will distribute your estate according to the laws of the state. Dying intestate can result in someone getting more than you would have wanted and others getting less than you would have wanted. Figure 15.4 shows an example of a simple will.

Many people make the mistake of thinking they do not have enough assets or that they are too young to have a will. It is important to understand that you will quickly build net worth if you develop a sound financial plan, and that it is always a good idea to plan for the unexpected.

Estate Taxes

Your estate may be subject to taxes before it can be distributed to your heirs. For example, as of 2011, you can distribute up to $5 million of your estate to your children or others tax-free. However, you should be aware that these laws will change in the next 40 years. As you begin to accumulate wealth, you should review the current law on estate taxes and take the steps necessary to minimize the tax liability for your heirs.

Trusts

Estate planning often involves establishing a trust to transfer assets in a manner that avoids taxes. There are a number of types of trusts defined by law, and all are essentially legal mechanisms that help reduce tax liability as assets are transferred from one person to another. **Trusts** place assets in the custody of a third party known as a trustee. The trustee manages those assets for the designated beneficiaries. These types of arrangements can be very complex and require expert legal advice to establish properly.

✓ **CHECKPOINT**

Why is it worthwhile to engage in estate planning today?

will: A legal request for how your estate (everything you have accumulated during your life) should be distributed upon your death.

It can ensure that your wishes are followed in the future and it can relieve a burden from your loved ones.

FIGURE 15.4 A Sample Will

A will is a necessary part of estate planning for people of all ages.

WILL of James T. Smith

I, James T. Smith of the City of Denver, Colorado, declare this to be my will.

ARTICLE 1
My wife, Karen A. Smith, and I have one child, Cheryl D. Smith.

ARTICLE 2 Payment of Debt and Taxes
I direct my Executor to pay my funeral expenses, my medical expenses, the costs of administration, and my debts.

ARTICLE 3 Distribution of the Estate
I direct that my estate be distributed to my wife, Karen A. Smith. If my wife predeceases me, my estate shall be distributed to my Trustee, to be managed as explained in Article 4.

ARTICLE 4 Trust for Children
4A. Purpose. This trust provides for the support of my daughter, Cheryl D. Smith, and any other children born to me.
4B. Use of Funds. The Trustee shall use as much of the trust income and principal as necessary to care for my child (or children). When the youngest of my children reaches the age of 25, the assets of this trust shall be split equally among the children.
4C. No Survivors. If no child of mine survives until age 25, assets of the trust shall be liquidated and 100% of the proceeds shall be donated to the San Diego Humane Society.
4D. Nomination of Trustee. I appoint my brother, Edward J. Smith, to serve as Trustee. If he is unable or unwilling to serve, I appoint my sister, Marie S. Smith, to serve as Trustee.

ARTICLE 5 Executor
I appoint my wife, Karen A. Smith, to serve as Executor. If she is unable or unwilling to serve, I appoint my brother, Edward J. Smith, to serve as Executor.

ARTICLE 6 Guardian
If my spouse does not survive me, I appoint my brother, Edward J. Smith, to serve as Guardian of my children. If he is unable to serve as Guardian, I appoint my sister, Marie S. Smith, to serve as Guardian.

ARTICLE 7 Power of Executor
My Executor has the right to receive payments, reinvest payments received, pay debts owed, pay taxes owed, and liquidate assets.

ARTICLE 8 Power of Trustee
My Trustee has the right to receive income generated by the trust, reinvest income received by the trust, sell assets in the trust, and use the proceeds to invest in other assets.
IN WITNESS WHEREOF, I hereby sign and declare this document to be my Will.

James T. Smith	Date

The above-named person signed in our presence, and in our opinion is mentally competent.

Signatures of Witnesses	Addresses of Witnesses
Kenneth Tagan	44241 Lemon Street Denver, Colorado 80208
Barbara Russell	101 Courtney Street Denver, Colorado 80208

CHAPTER REVIEW

SUMMARY

- Understanding the time value of money concept can help you see vividly the importance of planning for the future. Planning for the future is easier if you know how much money you need to save and invest every month or year to achieve your goals. Seeing the power of compound interest can demonstrate how your dreams can come true. Future value calculations can help you make those determinations. Present value calculations can help you determine how much house you can afford or car payments you can handle.

- You can also use this financial math to help you evaluate different investment options and manage your portfolio. You know that a risk/return trade-off exists in which you must assume more risk to get a higher return. However, you also know that proper diversification can help you reduce risk in your investment portfolio.

- Sound investing will allow you to accumulate wealth for retirement and pass some of this wealth to your heirs.

- Estate planning and the creation of a will can help you reduce the tax liability when you pass wealth to subsequent generations.

Key Terms and Concepts

1. Why is **diversification** important in your financial portfolio?

2. What is the difference between **present value** and **future value**?

3. What does the **Rule of 72** have to do with the calculation of future values?

What Do You Know? MyFinLitLab

1. (a) What is the time value of money?

   (b) How is it related to the concept of opportunity cost?

2. (a) What is a present value?

   (b) How can present values be used in financial planning?

3. (a) Define compounding.

   (b) How is it used in financial planning?

4. (a) What is simple interest?

   (b) Compare compound interest to simple interest.

Answers:
Key Terms and Concepts

1. Diversification is the process of investing in several different asset classes in order to reduce risk of financial loss.

2. Present value is the value of something today, or at the present time. Future value is a forecast of the value of some asset at some point in the future. For example, I think that 40 acres of land will be worth $200,000 in ten years.

3. The Rule of 72 is a simple rule of thumb that you can use to determine how long it will take for something to double in value for a given percentage return.

 Answers:
What Do You Know?

1. (a) **Knowledge** The time value of money is a concept that holds that money at the present is worth something different from money at some other point in time. (b) **Synthesis** There is an opportunity cost, such as foregone interest, associated with not receiving a sum of money today.

2. (a) **Knowledge** Present value refers to the value of a sum of money today.
   (b) **Analysis** Present values can be used to figure how much money you need in the present to achieve some future goal.

3. (a) **Knowledge** Compounding is the earning of interest (or other returns) on interest (or other returns). (b) **Application** Compounding helps you save for long-term goals and overcome the effects of inflation.

4. (a) **Comprehension** Simple interest does not involve compounding.
   (b) **Application** In simple interest situations, there is no compounding—no earning of interest on interest earned in the past.

5. (a) **Knowledge** An annuity is any situation in which you have equal cash flows occurring at equal intervals. (b) **Application** Examples of annuities include car payments and mortgage payments.

6. (a) **Comprehension** Future values are the projected value of a sum of money at some point in the future. (b) **Application** You can use future values to anticipate what you will wind up with at some point in the future given a specific strategy.

7. (a) **Comprehension** A portfolio is the collection of all an individual's investments. (b) **Application** A person should invest in a variety of different asset classes.

8. (a) **Comprehension** In general, the higher the risk, the greater the potential return. (b) **Application** It is wise to sell any poorly performing asset and invest the proceeds somewhere else.

9. (a) **Knowledge** An estate is the total value of a person's investments and holdings. (b) **Knowledge** Estate planning is planning to ensure that an estate is preserved and passed on to those whom you want to receive it. (c) **Analysis** Estate planning benefits you in that you can be confident that your wishes are carried out after your death. It also benefits loved ones who survive you, since they do not have to try to interpret your wishes.

10. (a) **Knowledge** A will is a legal document that clearly states your wishes for how your estate is distributed after your death and how any surviving minors will be cared for. (b) **Comprehension** A will ensures your wishes are carried out after your death. (c) **Application** If you don't have a will, a court will decide who gets your estate and in what amounts.

Answers:
What Are Your Finance Math Skills?

1. $\$4,000(1.08)^{30} = \$40,250.63$

2. $\$6,000/(1.05)^2 = \$5,442.18$

3. $\$2,500 \times .07 \times 5 = \$875$

4. If you were using a financial calculator, you would use the following amounts and keys: $3,000 PMT (payment); 30 N (number of years); 11 I (interest rate); CPT FV (compute future value) = $597,062.63.

5. $\$2,500(1.07)^5 = \$3,506.38 - \$2,500 = \$1,006.38$

6. $\$3,000 \times (1.10)^{30} = \$52,348.21$

7. $\$4,000/1.05 = \$3,809.52$

8. $\$2,000 \times .065 \times 2 = \$260$

5. (a) What is an annuity?

   (b) Give examples of annuities.

6. (a) What are future values?

   (b) How can future values be used in financial planning?

7. (a) Explain what a portfolio is in terms of investments.

   (b) What do you need to do to achieve a diversified portfolio?

8. (a) Explain the risk and return trade-off faced by investors.

   (b) What should you do with an investment that is not achieving a return that is appropriate for the level of risk involved?

9. (a) What is an estate?

   (b) What is estate planning?

   (c) Who benefits most from estate planning?

10. (a) What is a will?

   (b) Why is a will important?

   (c) What is an example of a bad outcome from not having a will?

What Are Your Finance Math Skills?   MyFinLitLab

The first three questions correlate to *Math for Personal Finance* features located throughout the chapter.

1. How much would you accumulate if you invested $4,000 for 30 years at 8%?

2. Assuming you could earn 5% interest, what amount could you receive today that would be equal to receiving $6,000 in two years?

3. How much interest will you earn on $2,500 invested for 5 years at 7% assuming simple interest?

4. How much could you accumulate over a 30-year period if you invested $3,000 a year and earned an 11% annual return?

5. How much interest will you earn on $2,500 invested for 5 years at 7% using compound interest?

6. Niko invested $3,000 in the stock market and expects to earn 10% a year. Assuming annual compounding, how much money will Niko have in 30 years?

7. Jenny will receive $4,000 at the end of next year. Assuming she could invest the money and earn 5%, what is the present value of that gift?

8. How much will Skyler earn in simple interest on a deposit of $2,000 for two years earning 6.5% annually?

What Would You Do?

After college graduation, Amanda and George were married. They had been high school sweethearts. Both remembered a class where the teacher discussed the need to begin planning for retirement early in their lives. With this in mind, they began planning.

In their 30s, Amanda and George became once again concerned about retirement. Their family had grown and now included two children. They continued to follow the lessons learned in school about saving for retirement, but now they also needed to include saving for college educations for their two children. With other bills, saving for retirement became a lower priority for them. In a discussion with Amanda's Aunt Shea about how to handle retirement investing, Aunt Shea told them not to worry. She had provided well for them in her will. After this discussion, Amanda and George felt better about having a comfortable retirement with this inheritance to help.

Fifteen years later, Aunt Shea passed away. At the reading of her will, Amanda was surprised to learn that Aunt Shea had made the same promise to her cousins. As all four sat listening to the reading, they found that $800,000 was to be divided between them after $400,000 was donated to the university where Aunt Shea had taught for 20 years.

1. Discuss your views on the ethics of Aunt Shea's decision.

2. What do you think should be done with the inheritance for Amanda and George?

3. Looking at Amanda and George's experience, what lessons about retirement planning can be learned?

What Are the Connections? Language Arts and Mathematics

Each of you is given $1,000 in cash as graduation gifts from various relatives and family friends. You would like to invest this in a certificate of deposit (CD) so that you will have a down payment on a car when you graduate from college in five years.

1. Work in teams to find the best buy for a CD.

   (a) Look at what is being offered by three different banks.

   (b) Provide data on the interest being paid by each bank.

2. Write a recommendation for purchasing the CD that will return the most money to you at the end of the five years.

   (a) Determine how much you will have in five years to put down on a car.

   (b) Does this amount surprise you in any way?

Teamwork

As a team, develop a Public Service Announcement (PSA) about planning for the future. Your audience for this PSA is your fellow students. Think about what you have learned in this chapter about planning for the future. What would you tell them about investing, putting together a portfolio, when they need to begin planning, and retirement? You can develop your PSA as a brochure, newsletter, video, skit, or other type of announcement that is interesting, captures their attention, and teaches them the facts.

ESSENTIAL QUESTION ACTIVITIES

Complete these activities to answer this chapter's Essential Question: *How does planning for retirement affect a person's financial plan?*

1. *On your own:* Review the information in this chapter about planning for the future. Using a poster, paper, or presentation software, make a presentation that tells your audience about planning for the future and how these plans affect your financial plan. Present this to the class, your family, and your friends.

2. *As a class:* Brainstorm all the planning that needs to be done for your future after retirement and beyond. What decisions should you make? How should you put these plans together? How do these plans affect your financial plan?

MyFinLitLab **TEST PREP QUESTIONS**

1. b   **1.** Financial experts say "the time value of money" can make a person a millionaire in retirement. Which example illustrates this statement?
   a. A person deposits $50,000 into her retirement account five years before her planned retirement. The account returns an average of 10% a year.
   b. A person planning to retire at age 68 begins investing $3,000 a year into his retirement account as soon as he graduates from college and gets a job. The account's average annual return is 8%.
   c. A person planning to retire at age 70 puts $10,000 a year into a retirement account starting at age 60. The account has an annual return of 10%.
   d. A person age 50, planning to retire at age 75, deposits $100,000 into a savings account returning 2.5% annually.

2. b   **2.** Which of the following terms is *not* correctly defined?
   a. The time value of money: money received today is worth more than money received in the future because the money can be put to work earning more money.
   b. Future value: an amount of money earned in the future based on inflation.

c. Compounding: earning money on both the principal deposited in the account and interest earned on that principal in the past.

d. Present value: the value of some future sum of money in the present.

3. A person who spends $5 every day for coffee and soft drinks decides to give up this habit and invest the money instead. Every day he puts $5 in a jar and deposits the entire amount at the end of each year. Assuming the average annual rate of return on his investment is 10%, how much money will he have after five years?
   a. He will have $2,007.50.
   b. He will have $9,125.
   c. He will have $10,037.50.
   d. He will have $11,141.81

3. d

4. A person has a choice of receiving $3,000 now or $4,000 after she graduates from college in five years. She decides to take the $3,000 and invest it at an expected 10% annual rate of return. Did she make a wise decision?
   a. No, because the time value of money shows that money received in the future has more purchasing power than money received today.
   b. No, because the annual rate of inflation of 5% will cancel out any money earned on the $3,000.
   c. Yes, because $3,000 received today and invested for five years at 10% will be worth more than $4,000 received after five years.
   d. Yes, because she will have over $4,000 in her investment account after only two years of investing the money, which is three years ahead of schedule.

4. c

5. Based on the Rule of 72, the time it will take for a $5,000 investment to double in value at an annual 6% rate of interest is
   a. 7.2 years.
   b. 12 years.
   c. 36 years.
   d. impossible to know because not enough information is provided.

5. b

6. Which of the following terms is correctly matched with its definition?
   a. Diversification: the method for determining the value of a person's assets.
   b. Simple interest: the amount of money that an investment earns on a daily basis.
   c. Annuity: an insurance program such as the FDIC designed to protect a person's investments in case a company goes bankrupt.
   d. Portfolio: a complete picture of all of a person's investments and savings assets.

6. d

7. Which of the following statements about diversification is *not* accurate?
   a. Asset allocation is the process of dividing investment among several different asset classes.
   b. Having a diversified portfolio is a way to reduce risk.

7. c

c. If a person has 90% of her investments in the stock of a company that produces a variety of consumer goods, her portfolio is considered diversified.

d. The benefit of having a diversified portfolio is that if the stocks in the portfolio are falling in value, the value of the bonds or real estate in the portfolio may be going up.

8. Which of the following is a true statement about the relationship between risk and return?

a. A young person can take bigger risks in hopes of earning higher returns compared to an older person because the younger person has more time to recover in the event the risky investments decline in value.

b. A low-risk stock investment promises a guaranteed rate of return on the investment.

c. A young person with a high degree of risk tolerance should put all of her investment money in corporate bonds and U.S. Treasury bonds.

d. An older person should have riskier investments in her portfolio than a younger person because an older person needs a greater rate of return on her investments because she is close to retirement.

9. When it comes to retirement planning, it is a good idea

a. to hire a financial planner who promises that she can invest a person's money so that the person can retire at age 50.

b. for someone age 25 who wants to retire at age 55 with a $2,000,000 retirement account to figure out how much money needs to be saved and invested for the next 30 years using the time value of money and a financial calculator.

c. if people in their 20s today plan on most of their retirement income coming from Social Security.

d. not to spend the time and money to have a will prepared unless assets are above $1.5 million.

10. Estate planning is

a. naming a person to be the beneficiary of a person's assets.

b. something people should begin to work on after they retire and begin collecting retirement benefits.

c. the process of determining how a person's assets will be divided before or after a person dies.

d. the division of real estate between a person's family and the state.

11. A person should have a will to

a. guarantee that her financial portfolio remains diversified after her death.

b. protect investments in a retirement portfolio from losing value.

c. make sure that her heirs never have to pay estate taxes on the money they inherit.

d. give her the opportunity to determine how she wants her assets to be divided after her death.

Glossary

401(k)/403(b) plans Popular types of defined-contribution retirement plans. They allow employees to contribute into their accounts, which may feature a range of investment options.

accreditation An official recognition that a school or program meets a certain standard.

adjustable rate mortgage (ARM) Mortgage with a rate that may go up or down. The rate change occurs at some preset time—for example, after one year.

adjusted gross income Total income minus certain allowable amounts such as contributions to some retirement accounts, alimony payments, and interest paid on student loans.

annual fee Charged by credit card companies for the privilege of using their card.

annual percentage rate (APR) The interest rate that shows what a borrower is actually paying with all the costs of financing factored in.

annual percentage yield (APY) The interest rate that shows what an account will earn annually with compounding factored in.

annuity A situation in which there are equal cash flows occurring at equal intervals for a fixed period of time.

apprenticeship On-the-job program in which a person may receive formal training.

asset Something owned.

asset allocation The process of spreading investments among asset classes—diversifying investments.

asset classes Investments, such as stocks, bonds, and real estate, that one makes to reach long-term goals.

automatic teller machine (ATM) Provides banking customers with access to financial transactions in a public space without the need for a bank teller.

baby boom A period of very high birthrates that occurred between 1946 and 1964.

bank draft Used to authorize someone to withdraw money from a bank account automatically to satisfy some financial obligation.

bankruptcy A legal process in which a court takes over some of the finances of a person who is unable to pay his or her bills.

beneficiary A person who receives payment from a life insurance provider when the policyholder dies.

bond A promissory note to repay a certain amount of money at some future point.

brokerage A firm that provides access to the stock markets.

budget A list of planned expenses and revenues.

budgeting The process of forecasting future expenses and income.

business cycle The economic pattern of alternating periods of shrinking and expanding.

capital gain Taxable income that occurs when an asset is sold for more than it originally cost.

cash advance The ability to use a credit card to withdraw cash from a bank or ATM (rather than just purchasing a good or a service).

cash inflow Money received.

cash outflow Money spent.

cashier's check A type of check that is written to a specific payee but charged against a bank instead of an individual account.

certificate of deposit (CD) A contract between an individual and a financial institution that specifies the time that the individual will leave a certain amount of money deposited in the account and the interest rate earned.

certification An official document or record that states that a person has met some standard for training or knowledge.

check A written order from an individual to a bank that instructs the bank to pay money to another party.

check register A small ledger for keeping track of a checking account balance.

checking account An account into which a person deposits money and from which a person withdraws money by writing checks or using a debit card.

COBRA The Consolidated Omnibus Budget Reconciliation Act. It allows an individual temporarily to continue health insurance coverage at group rates.

co-insurance The share of costs for covered insurance services that an individual is required to pay out of pocket. Often called a co-pay.

collateral Assets that have been pledged against a loan repayment.

commission Fee charged by a brokerage firm for carrying out a transaction.

compensation Money earned and benefits given by employers.

compound interest Interest earned on interest added to an account.

compounding The process of earning interest on interest previously added to an account.

consumer price index (CPI) The formal measure of prices used to calculate inflation that tells us whether things overall are more expensive now than in the past.

corporate bonds Bonds issued by a large company—they have all degrees of risk depending on the strength of the corporation.

cosigner A person, other than the principal borrower, who signs for a loan and assumes equal liability for it.

coupon payment Regular interest payments on bonds.

coupon rate A bond's interest rate, so-called because originally bonds came with booklets of prewritten coupons for the interest due.

credit Money that a lender makes available to a borrower with the understanding that the borrower will repay the money.

credit bureau Organization that collects credit information about individual consumers.

credit card Provides individuals with revolving open-end credit, which they can draw from repeatedly up to some preset limit.

credit check Performed by potential creditors to access a person's credit report to examine the individual's credit history and the ability to repay.

credit history Record of credit use and payments.

credit limit A person may borrow up to this amount based on his or her income level, debt level, and overall credit record.

credit management Decision making about getting and using credit.

credit provider An entity, such as a bank, that agrees to make a certain amount of credit available to a cardholder.

credit report Summarizes an individual's existing and past lines of credit.

credit score Created by credit bureaus to assess an individual's creditworthiness.

credit union Functions similarly to a bank, but has nonprofit status and is owned by its members.

creditor Someone who provides credit.

current liability Debt that is due within one year.

debit card Enables one to withdraw cash from an ATM or to pay directly for goods or services at stores and restaurants.

debt consolidation Combining several small accounts into one larger account that may be able to be financed at a lower rate.

deductible The amount of money that a policyholder must pay before an insurance policy will begin to cover a claim.

default When a person stops making payments on a loan.

defined-benefit plan An employer-sponsored retirement plan in which an employer guarantees an employee a specific amount of income at retirement. The benefit is often based on factors such as the number of years worked and the average salary earned during peak earning years.

defined-contribution plan An employer-sponsored retirement plan in which an employer contributes to an employee's retirement account but does not guarantee a specific retirement benefit.

demand deposit Money put into a checking account that can be withdrawn at any time.

demographics The study of human populations.

depository institution A financial institution, such as a savings bank, that is legally allowed to accept monetary deposits from consumers.

depression A severe recession.

disability insurance Insures the beneficiary's earned income against the risk that sickness or injury will make working (and therefore earning) impossible.

discount brokerage Offers a reduced level of service, lower costs, and often the ability to trade online.

discount rate The interest rate the Federal Reserve System charges to banks when it loans them money.

diversification The process of investing in multiple investments.

dividend The distribution of cash to shareholders.

down payment The initial upfront portion of the total amount due on a purchase.

economics The study of the production, distribution, and consumption of goods and services. Economists seek to understand ways that individuals and businesses make decisions, the factors that influence their choices, and the impact these decisions have on others.

economy The system related to the production, distribution, exchange, and consumption of goods and services in which individuals, businesses, governments, and the world as a whole interact.

electronic funds transfer Authorization for someone to access a bank account for payment or deposit.

employer-sponsored retirement plan Set up by an employer and designed to help employees save for retirement. The employer generally contributes to the plan.

Equal Credit Opportunity Act Prohibits creditors from denying credit based on gender, age, race, national origin, religion, or marital status.

equity Ownership in something.

estate planning The process of determining how wealth will be allocated on or before a person's death.

expense Anything on which money is spent.

face value A bond's maturity value, which is printed on the front of the bond.

Fair Credit Reporting Act A federal law that limits the sharing of an individual's financial information to firms that have a legal purpose to evaluate it.

Fair Isaac Corporation Created a model on which credit scores (FICO scores) are calculated.

federal agency bonds Issued by federal agencies whose proceeds are used to buy mortgages to encourage home ownership.

Federal Deposit Insurance Corporation (FDIC) A major federal insurer that provides deposit insurance on the first $250,000 deposited in a bank account.

Federal Perkins loan Similar to a Stafford loan, but for students with "exceptional" financial need. This loan carries a lower interest rate and offers a longer grace period before repayment must begin.

Federal Reserve System The central bank of the United States.

Federal Stafford loan The most common type of federal education loan; it is available in two forms: subsidized and unsubsidized.

fiat money The money currently used in the United States. It has value because the government orders that it must be accepted as payment.

finance To pay a portion of the cost of a major purchase such as a house or a car by taking a loan.

fixed annuity A type of financial product that guarantees annual payments to the owner for a fixed period of time or for a person's lifetime. The return and ultimate payment is a guaranteed amount.

fixed expense An expense that remains the same from period to period.

fixed rate mortgage A mortgage in which the interest rate remains the same for the life of the loan.

forecast A projection about future cash flows.

forecast error The difference between the actual value and the predicted value for the corresponding period.

fraud Occurs when someone submits false information to get a financial benefit.

full-service brokerage Provides advice and executes trades for a price; for example, Merrill Lynch and Edward Jones.

future value What money is "worth" at a specified time in the future assuming a certain interest rate.

global economy The world in which economies of all countries interact and depend on each other.

grace period Time in which credit card companies do not charge interest on purchases. Typical grace periods are 20 days from the time the statement is "closed," or the bill is calculated and sent.

gross domestic product (GDP) The total dollar amount of all final goods and services purchased domestically in a given year.

gross income The total amount of a person's income.

gross pay Hourly wage multiplied by hours worked.

group plan Insurance plans that cover a large group of individuals, such as employees of a particular company or local government. Within a group plan, an individual's high risk or loss is spread across the entire pool of group members.

health insurance Provides payment to people who suffer a financial loss as a result of illness or injury.

HIPAA The Health Insurance Portability and Accounting Act ensures that workers can continue their health insurance coverage if they switch jobs. The act prohibits insurance companies from denying new employees access to coverage based on their health or preexisting conditions.

home equity loan Allows a homeowner to borrow against the equity in his or her home—that is, the difference between the home's value and the amount owed to a lender.

household asset Tangible possessions owned by a household. Furniture is one example.

identity theft When someone uses an individual's personal information without permission for personal gain.

income Money coming in through wages earned, allowance, or other sources.

individual retirement account (IRA) A type of savings account created by the government to encourage people to save for retirement.

inflation A sustained increase in the general level of prices. During a time of inflation, most things become more expensive and the purchasing power of money decreases.

initial public offering (IPO) The first sale of stock issued by a company to raise money for business operations, expansion, and other needs.

installment credit Used for specific purchases; allows the borrower more time to repay.

institutional investor One who trades large volumes of stocks on behalf of large institutions; for example, for a huge pension fund.

insurance A financial product that when purchased provides reimbursement paid to a person in the event of certain types of financial loss.

interest Fee charged by a lender on money borrowed.

intermediate-term goal A goal an individual aims to meet within the next one to five years.

Internal Revenue Service (IRS) A branch of the U.S. Treasury Department that carries out the federal tax system.

internship A temporary, short-term position designed to provide exposure to and training for a particular job.

intestate When an individual dies without having a will.

investment Something acquired with the goal of making money.

itemized deduction A specific expense that, under tax law, can be deducted from income to reduce the amount of income subject to income tax.

junk bonds Corporate bonds issued by companies with the highest risk.

lease A long-term rental agreement.

liability What is owed (debt).

liability coverage Auto insurance that covers damage to an individual's car or damage caused to other people or their property.

life insurance Provides payment to a specific person or persons when the policyholder dies.

line of credit An agreement to allow borrowing as needed up to a certain amount of money.

liquid asset Something owned that can be rapidly converted to cash without a risk of significant loss.

liquidity Available cash on hand for meeting immediate wants and needs.

long-term goal A goal that will take more than five years to accomplish.

long-term liability Liabilities that will take more than one year to pay off.

macroeconomics The study of broad economic issues that impact the economy as a whole.

market value The current quoted price at which investors buy or sell a share of common stock or a bond at a given time.

maturity date The date at which a loan will be completely repaid.

Medicaid A government-sponsored program that provides health insurance for low-income individuals.

Medicare Funded by payroll taxes. Provides health care coverage to older Americans and some younger disabled people.

microeconomics The study of individual choices or decisions made by smaller units, such as a firm.

monetary policy The raising or lowering of the money supply to achieve some goal.

money management Making decisions about how much cash or liquid assets to keep in reserve and how much to invest.

money market deposit account (MMDA) Has some features of a checking account or a savings account. These accounts require an individual to maintain a minimum balance, have no maturity date, pay interest, and offer limited check-writing privileges.

money order Functions similarly to a cashier's check. It is purchased for cash so that the recipient can trust its worth.

mortgage The common term for the type of loan people take to purchase a home.

municipal bond Issued by state and local governments to finance large public projects such as water and sewer systems.

mutual fund Sells shares to investors in order to collect a pool of money that is then used to buy various investments.

National Association of Securities Dealers Automatic Quotation (NASDAQ) system An organized stock exchange in the secondary market in which stock sales occur.

National Credit Union Share Insurance Fund (NCUSIF) A major federal insurer that provides deposit insurance on the first $250,000 deposited in a credit union account.

negotiable order of withdrawal (NOW) Functions like a checking account but pays a small amount of interest on money in the account. NOW accounts require the user to maintain a minimum balance in order to earn interest.

net pay Wages that remain after taxes are withheld (take-home pay).

net worth The difference between one's assets minus his or her liabilities.

New York Stock Exchange (NYSE) An organized stock exchange in the secondary market in which stock sales occur.

nondepository institutions Insurance companies, finance companies, securities firms, and investment companies that provide certain financial services but do not accept traditional deposits.

noninstallment credit The simplest form of consumer credit. It is usually for a very short term, such as 30 days.

opportunity cost Cost of pursuing one option instead of another expressed as the value of the activity you gave up.

overdraft protection A feature that allows a person to "overdraw," or exceed the credit limit. (Overdraft protection is also a feature of checking accounts, where it protects someone in the event that a check is written for more money than is in the account.)

pawnbroker Holds items in exchange for loans that run for 30 days to as much as three months.

payday lending A lender provides cash advances at a high cost to customers who provide a check dated for some time in the future.

payment terms Specific information about the interest rate and the time period for paying back a loan.

payroll taxes Taxes withheld from paychecks and sent to the government by employers.

pension plan A defined-benefit plan under which an employer makes contributions to the plan on the employee's behalf.

personal balance sheet Lists current assets such as cash in checking accounts and savings accounts, long-term assets such as common stock and real estate, current liabilities such as loan debt and mortgage debt due or overdue, and long-term liabilities such as mortgage and other loan debt.

personal finance Financial issues that can affect an individual.

personal financial plan Specifies financial goals and describes in detail the spending, financing, and investing plans needed to reach those goals.

personal financial planning The process of planning every aspect of personal finances.

personal identification number (PIN) Typically a four-digit number needed to access a bank account or debit card.

personal income tax A tax levied on the financial income of individuals.

personal loan A loan that is not backed by collateral. Also known as an unsecured loan, it is based solely upon the borrower's credit rating.

pharming Identity theft technique that uses e-mail viruses to redirect someone from a legitimate Web site to an official looking Web site designed to obtain personal information.

phishing Pretexting that occurs online.

policy rider Additional insurance coverage to cover things such as jewelry or valuable heirlooms that are often not fully covered by a typical insurance policy.

policyholder A person who buys a health insurance policy or subscribes to it through an employer.

portfolio An individual's investments.

preexisting condition A health condition that existed before an individual's policy was granted.

premium Regular payments paid to an insurance company in return for coverage.

present value The value of a cost or benefit computed in terms of cash today.

pretexting Occurs when someone improperly accesses an individual's personal information by posing as someone seeking data.

price level stability A goal of the Federal Reserve System to ensure that inflation or deflation does not occur.

primary market The initial sale of financial assets in which a company receives money during an IPO.

principal The total amount of money outstanding on a loan.

publicly traded When a company begins trading on one of the organized stock exchanges.

real estate Buildings and land.

recession A period of time in which the economy is shrinking.

résumé A snapshot of an individual's qualifications including background, education, and previous work history.

revolving open-end credit Allows consumers to borrow up to some preset maximum amount.

risk The possibility of a financial loss.

Roth IRA Similar to a traditional IRA, but contributions are not tax deductible. Earnings from an eligible account are never taxed, even after withdrawal.

Rule of 72 Shows how long it would take to double an amount of money for a given interest rate.

safety deposit boxes Small containers located inside a bank vault used to store valuable documents such as wills and small objects such as jewelry, rare coins, and legal documents.

sales tax Tax collected by a merchant when a purchase is made and then sent to the government.

savings account Bank account that generally pays a low rate of interest on deposits.

secondary market Transactions that take place after an IPO.

secured loan Has an asset pledged against the loan. The lender is assured of ending up with some valuable asset if the borrower fails to pay off the loan.

Securities and Exchange Commission (SEC) A government agency that regulates and monitors the stock market.

security Investment issued by a corporation or government in which the investor receives proof of ownership.

SEP-IRA An IRA for self-employed people.

shareholders People who own stock in a company.

short-term goal A goal to be accomplished within the next year.

shoulder surfing An identity theft technique that involves someone in a public place accessing personal information by listening to a conversation or viewing personal information.

simple interest Interest earned only on the original amount or principal.

skimming Identity theft technique that involves copying credit card or debit card numbers from credit or debit cards.

Social Security Funded by payroll taxes. It provides payments to eligible retirees and disabled people.

standard deduction A fixed amount individuals are allowed to deduct from their adjusted gross income to reduce their tax liability.

stock A fractional share of ownership in a company.

subprime mortgage High interest rate mortgage loan made to people with poor credit scores.

take-home pay Wages that remain after taxes are withheld (net pay).

tax Money collected by a government from its citizens and businesses in order to operate the government.

tax deductible A feature that allows people to reduce their income taxes by reducing taxable income for the year in which they make a contribution (for example, to an IRA).

tax deferred When account earnings, such as from interest, are not taxed until they are withdrawn after retirement.

tax return A report submitted to the IRS that includes all the information relative to an individual's income taxes.

teaser rate An extremely low interest rate for a short period of time that is used to entice a borrower into a deal.

term insurance Life insurance provided over a specific period of time.

time value of money Refers to the fact that money received today is worth more than money received next year or the year after.

traditional IRA An account in which people can make tax-deductible contributions and all earnings are tax deferred.

traveler's checks Checks paid for in advance and written by a large financial institution with no payee specified.

Treasury bond Issued by the U.S. Treasury Department to finance the debt of the government.

trust Legal mechanism that helps to reduce tax liability when assets are transferred from one person to another.

universal life insurance Provides coverage for a specified term and builds savings for the policyholder.

unsecured loan A loan in which there is no collateral pledged.

variable annuity A type of financial product that guarantees annual payments to the owner for a fixed time or for a lifetime. The return and ultimate payment depend on the performance of the investments.

variable expense An expense that changes from one period to the next.

vesting The process of earning eligibility for an employer benefit.

whole life insurance Provides coverage for as long as the policyholder continues to pay the premium.

will A legal request for how an individual's estate (everything accumulated during a lifetime) should be distributed upon death.

Index

Numbers

health insurance as critical part of, 120
impact of economics on, 138–139
importance and purpose of, 21–22
taxes in, 108
Financial plan components
budgeting and taxes, 23–26
communications/record-keeping, 29
decision-making process, 39–40
financing, 27–28
investing, 28–29
key terms, 21
liquidity, 26–27
overview of, 22–23
retirement, 29
review, test prep questions, 34–35
review summary, 30–33
risk management, 28
role of life insurance in, 124–125
Financial planners/advisors, 11–12
Financial Reform Act of 2010, 158–159
Financing
car, 186–189
credit cards not used for, 208
education, 185–186
financial plan decisions for, 40
financial plan for, 27–28
home, 179–184
payday lending not used for, 211
personal loans, 176–179
Fixed annuity, 256
Fixed expense, 42–43
Fixed rate mortgages, 180, 191
Four Rs of taxes, 97
Fraudulent claims, and health insurance costs, 119
Full-service brokerage firms, 273
Future value
calculating present value vs., 291–292
calculating using Rule of 72, 293–294
defined, 299
financial calculators and, 293, 300

G

GDP. *see* Gross domestic product (GDP)
Get rich quick schemes, 295
Gift cards, as prepaid cash cards, 207
Ginnie Mae (Government National Mortgage Association) bonds, 275
Global economy
adapting to, 145–146
defined, 148
Globalization
affecting career/education plans, 148
in larger economy, 145–146
Goals, personal financial
decision-making process for, 41, 44–45
evaluating options to accomplish, 43–44
planning to save for, 7
sources of information for, 11–12
statement of, 16
types of, 9–11
Google Inc., founding of, 9
Government, financing student loans, 185–186, 191
Government National Mortgage Association (Ginnie Mae) bonds, 275
Grace period, 215
Grace period, credit card, 206, 208
Graying of America, 139–140

Great Depression, FDIC created after, 233
Great Recession (2007–2009), 143, 148
Gross domestic product (GDP)
calculating, 147
current dollar and "real," 143
measuring national economic activity, 142–144, 148
trends in, 148
Gross income (total income)
exclusions from, 106
overview of, 105–106
Gross pay, 96
Group plans, health insurance, 122

H

Health care costs, 119–120
Health Care Fraud and Abuse Control Program, 119
Health Care Fraud Prevention and Enforcement Action Team (HEAT), 119
Health insurance
within auto policy, 124
cancellation options, 122
co-insurance, 123
coverage limits, 123
deductibles, 122–123
family coverage, 121–122
getting, 126–127
group plans, 122
health care costs and, 119–120
indemnity plans vs. managed care, 121
location restrictions, 122
number of Americans without, 120
preexisting conditions, 122
provider networks, 123–124
review, test prep questions, 132–135
review summary, 128–131
short-term (for travel), 122
sources of, 118–119
Health Insurance Portability and Accountability Act (HIPAA), 126
Health maintenance organizations (HMOs), 123–124
HELOCs (home equity lines of credit), 181–182
HIPAA (Health Insurance Portability and Accountability Act), 126
Hispanic Americans, demographic trends, 140
HMOs (Health maintenance organizations), 123–124
Home, as personal financial goal, 10
Home equity lines of credit (HELOCs), 181–182
Home equity loans, 181–182, 190
Homeowner's insurance, 183–184, 191
Homes, financing
buying vs. renting, 182–183
home equity, 181–182
homeowner's and renter's insurance, 183–184
mortgage loans, 179–180
other costs, 181
overview of, 179
using bank drafts to make payments on, 232
Household assets, on personal balance sheet, 58

I

Identity theft
defined, 168
overview of, 164
protecting against, 165–166, 168
tactics used, 164–165, 168
tax refund loans and, 212
Immigration, 140, 148
Incentives, credit card company, 205–206

Speakers, identifying careers of interest, 78
Specialists, finding local Medicare, 118
Standard deduction, filing taxes, 108
State income taxes
    estimated payments, 97–98
    withheld in payroll taxes, 97, 103
Statements, credit card, 201
Stock exchanges, 269–270
Stock market swings, 268–269
Stocks
    behavior of investors, 270–273
    creating personal balance sheet for, 60
    example transaction, 273–274
    factors increasing/decreasing price of, 271
    investing in, 269–270
    mutual fund investments in, 277
    overview of, 269
    as partial ownership in company, 279
Student loans, 185–186, 191
"Subprime meltdown" or "subprime crisis," 180
Subprime mortgages, 180
Subsidized Federal Stafford loans, education, 185–186

T

Take-home pay, 96
Tax deductible
    defined, 254
    Roth IRA contributions not, 254–255
    tax deferred vs., 258
Tax deferred
    benefits of traditional IRAs, 254
    tax deductible vs., 258
Tax returns, IRS
    filing taxes, 104–108
    overview of, 98–102
Taxes
    defined, 96
    estate, 297
    filing, 104–108
    gross vs. net pay and, 95–96
    Internal Revenue Service and, 98–102
    key terms, 95
    life insurance payments not subject to, 124
    payroll, 97–98, 102–104
    in personal financial planning, 5
    real estate, 97
    real estate investment benefits, 278
    review, test prep questions, 113–115
    review summary, 109–112
    sales, 96
    tax refund loans, 211–212, 215
    using tax planning, 25–26, 108

Teaser rate, loan contracts, 178
Teen spending trends, marketing to, 23–24
Term insurance, 125
Terms, negotiating credit card repayment, 209
Terms of the loan, 176
Threats, to credit, 164–165
Time periods, of typical personal loans, 176
Time value concepts, in retirement planning, 296
Time value of money
    future value vs. present value, 291–292
    retirement planning and, 290–291, 296
Total income, as gross income, 108
Traditional IRAs, 254–255
Training
    determining career path, 74
    ways to get career, 79–81
Transaction fees, credit cards, 202–203, 206
TransUnion, 160, 166
Traveler checks, 231
Treasury bonds, 275–276
Trusts, in estate planning, 297
Truth in Lending Act, 159

U

Universal life insurance, 125
Unsecured loans (signature loans), 179, 191
Unsubsidized Federal Stafford loans, education, 185–186
Used car financing, 186–187
Utilities, building credit history, 160

V

Value, future vs. present, 291–292
VantageScore™, 161
Variable annuity, 256
Variable expense, evaluating personal financial position, 42–43
Variable rate mortgages, 180
Vesting, 255
Visa credit cards, 204
Vision insurance, employer-provided, 127

W

W-2 forms, 106
Whole life (permanent) insurance, overview of, 125
Wills, estate planning and, 297–298, 300
Winnings, as gross income, 105, 107
Workforce
    adaptation to global economy, 145–146
    business cycles and, 142–144
    future of Social Security and shrinking, 141
    graying of America and, 139
    inflation, purchasing power and, 144–145